THE ECONOMICS OF CRIME AND LAW ENFORCEMENT

Edited by

LEE R. McPHETERS, Ph.D.

and

WILLIAM B. STRONGE, Ph.D.

Department of Economics
Florida Atlantic University
Boca Raton, Florida

CHARLES C THOMAS · PUBLISHER
Springfield · Illinois · U.S.A.

Published and Distributed Throughout the World by
CHARLES C THOMAS • PUBLISHER
Bannerstone House
301-327 East Lawrence Avenue, Springfield, Illinois, U.S.A.

© *1976, by* CHARLES C THOMAS • PUBLISHER
ISBN 0-398-03415-x
Library of Congress Catalog Card Number: 75-1490

Printed in the United States of America
HH-11

Library of Congress Cataloging in Publication Data

McPheters, Lee R.   comp.
  The economics of crime and law enforcement.

  Bibliography: p.
  1. Crime and criminals—Economic aspects—Addresses,
essays, lectures. 2. Law enforcement—Economic aspects
—Addresses, essays, lectures. 3. Criminal justice,
Administration of—Economic aspects—Addresses, essays,
lectures. I. Stronge, William B., joint comp. II. Title.
HV6030.M33   364   75-1490
ISBN 0-398-03415-X

CONTRIBUTORS

PROFESSOR JOHN P. ALLISON
Department of Economics
Illinois State University
Normal, Illinois

PROFESSOR KENNETH L. AVIO
Department of Economics
The University of Western Ontario
London, Ontario, Canada

PROFESSOR GARY S. BECKER
Department of Economics
The University of Chicago
Chicago, Illinois

**PROFESSOR ALFRED
BLUMSTEIN**
Urban Systems Institute
School of Urban and Public Affairs
Carnegie-Mellon University
Pittsburgh, Pennsylvania

DR. ARTHUR CAROL
Economic Advisor to Senator
William Brock
United States Senate
Washington, D. C.

PROFESSOR ROLAND CHILTON
Department of Sociology
University of Massachusetts
Amherst, Massachusetts

PROFESSOR ISAAC EHRLICH
Graduate School of Business
University of Chicago
Chicago, Illinois

**PROFESSOR BELTON M.
FLEISHER**
Department of Economics
Ohio State University
Columbus, Ohio

**PROFESSOR MICHAEL J.
GREENWOOD**
Department of Economics
Arizona State University
Tempe, Arizona

PROFESSOR JULIUS A. GYLYS
Department of Economics
The University of Toledo
Toledo, Ohio

ROBERT G. HAHN
Director
Justice Systems Group
Systems Dimensions Ltd.
Toronto, Ontario, Canada

PROFESSOR J. R. HARRIS
Department of Economics
*Massachusetts Institute of
Technology*
Cambridge, Massachusetts

DR. NELSON B. HELLER
President
*The Institute for
Public Program Analysis*
St. Louis, Missouri

**PROFESSOR E. TERRENCE
JONES**
Department of Political Science
University of Missouri
St. Louis, Missouri

PROFESSOR RICHARD C.
LARSON
*Department of Urban Studies
and Planning
Massachusetts Institute of
Technology
Cambridge, Massachusetts*

PROFESSOR ROBERT E.
MARKLAND
*Department of Management Science
University of Missouri
St. Louis, Missouri*

DAROLD MAXWELL, J.D.
San Francisco, California

PROFESSOR LLAD PHILLIPS
*Department of Economics
University of California
Santa Barbara, California*

PROFESSOR ISRAEL PRESSMAN
*City University of New York
New York, New York*

PROFESSOR MICHAEL L.
SESNOWITZ
*Department of Economics
Kent State University
Kent, Ohio*

PROFESSOR CARL S. SHOUP
*Department of Economics
Dalhousie University
Halifax, Nova Scotia, Canada*

PROFESSOR DAVID L. SJOQUIST
*Department of Economics
Georgia State University
Atlanta, Georgia*

ADELE D. SPIELBERGER
*Criminal Justice Planner
Bureau of Criminal Justice
Planning and Assistance
Florida Division of State Planning
Tallahassee, Florida*

PROFESSOR GEORGE J.
STIGLER
*Charles R. Walgreen Foundation for
the Study of American Institutions
University of Chicago
Chicago, Illinois*

PROFESSOR GORDON TULLOCK
*Center for Study of Public Choice
Virginia Polytechnic Institute and
State University
Blacksburg, Virginia*

PROFESSOR HAROLD L.
VOTEY, JR.
*Department of Economics
University of California
Santa Barbara, California*

PROFESSOR WALTER J.
WADYCKI
*Department of Quantitative Methods
University of Illinois at
Chicago Circle
Chicago, Illinois*

PROFESSOR NORMAN WALZER
*Department of Economics
Western Illinois University
Macomb, Illinois*

PROFESSOR JOHN C. WEICHER
*Department of Economics
Ohio State University
Columbus, Ohio*

FOREWORD

THIS BOOK is a collection of essays on the economics of crime and law enforcement. All of these articles have appeared previously in various professional journals. The editors have attempted to include the most important and provocative articles available. In some instances this results in contradictions from selection to selection, but such conflict is the stuff of which fruitful inquiry is formed. It is the hope of the editors that the reprinting of these works in one volume will greatly facilitate study and research by economists, criminal justice analysts, and students of crime and law enforcement.

Crime and individual criminality are not new topics for economists, nor do they represent an area of study outside the mainstream of economic investigation. Most economists would recognize the individual as the basic unit of study for economic analysis. Examination of the individual decision making process within an economic environment has been quite naturally extended beyond traditional consumption decisions to include the residential location decision, the job choice, or the decision to enter into criminal activity.

Since practically everyone has at one time or another probably broken a law punishable by fine or commitment, the relevance of the study of crime is, in fact, very general. Further, with an increasing proliferation of laws and regulations and the growing complexity and anonymity of our society, the crime choice is a decision which many people face much more frequently than other types of decisions, such as voting, which have been extensively analyzed by economists.

Jeremy Bentham, within the framework of his eighteenth century Felicific Calculus, suggested that man plans his actions to avoid pain and gain pleasure. The implication for crime control is that society should ascertain that sufficient pain is meted out to criminals to offset effectively the pleasure or gains associated with criminal acts. The modern economic approach postulates a rational decision maker, capable of calculating costs and gains associated with criminal activity in the context of his own utility function. This assumed economic man is the principal actor in many of the selections of Section I, which provides a collection of theoretical treatments of the crime choice decision and the policy implications for society.

Theory yields testable hypotheses, and a number of essential hypotheses flowing from the theoretical analyses are extended and empirically tested in Section II. The results are of importance because they confirm that economic factors and economic behavior play a significant role in the determination of variations in the incidence of criminal activity over time and space.

In Section III, the selections examine the economics of the law enforcement process with particular emphasis on the relation between police expenditures and criminal activity. If crime is to be deterred by the threat of punishment, the first link in the deterrence chain is our law enforcement agencies. These articles explore the public good aspects of police services and attempt to evaluate the effectiveness of society's police expenditures.

Finally, Section IV illustrates the diverse nature of the research tools which have been utilized in examination of the criminal justice system. A reading of these selections will undoubtedly suggest to the student further innovations in the application of modern methods of analysis.

We wish to express appreciation to Mr. Dennis Byer for helpful research assistance, Mrs. Jessica Eichrodt for her secretarial and typing support, and Mr. Larry Pitts for graphic artistry. The ultimate success of a collection of readings, of course, depends on the strength of the component selections: we are thus indebted to the many authors whose contributions have made this book possible.

Lee R. McPheters

William B. Stronge

CONTENTS

THE ECONOMICS OF CRIME AND LAW ENFORCEMENT

Section I

ECONOMIC THEORY AND CRIMINAL BEHAVIOR

Chapter 1

CRIME AND PUNISHMENT: AN ECONOMIC APPROACH

GARY S. BECKER

INTRODUCTION

SINCE THE TURN of the century, legislation in Western countries has expanded rapidly to reverse the brief dominance of laissez faire during the nineteenth century. The state no longer merely protects against violations of person and property through murder, rape, or burglary but also restricts "discrimination" against certain minorities, collusive business arrangements, "jaywalking," travel, the materials used in construction, and thousands of other activities. The activities restricted not only are numerous but also range widely, affecting persons in very different pursuits and of diverse social backgrounds, education levels, ages, races, etc. Moreover, the likelihood that an offender will be discovered and convicted and the nature and extent of punishments differ greatly from person to person and activity to activity. Yet, in spite of such diversity, some common properties are shared by practically all legislation, and these properties form the subject matter of this essay.

In the first place, obedience to law is not taken for granted, and public and private resources are generally spent in order both to prevent offenses and to apprehend offenders. In the second place, conviction is not generally considered sufficient punishment in itself; additional and sometimes severe punishments are meted out to those convicted. What determines the amount and type of resources and punishments used to enforce a piece of legislation? In particular, why does enforcement differ so greatly among different kinds of legislation?

Reprinted, with permission of the University of Chicago Press, from *Journal of Political Economy*, March/April 1968, pp. 169-217.

The main purpose of this essay is to answer normative versions of these questions, namely, how many resources and how much punishment *should* be used to enforce different kinds of legislation? Put equivalently, although more strangely, how many offenses *should* be permitted and how many offenders *should* go unpunished? The method used formulates a measure of the social loss from offenses and finds those expenditures of resources and punishments that minimize this loss. The general criterion of social loss is shown to incorporate as special cases, valid under special assumptions, the criteria of vengeance, deterrence, compensation, and rehabilitation that historically have figured so prominently in practice and criminological literature.

The optimal amount of enforcement is shown to depend on, among other things, the cost of catching and convicting offenders, the nature of punishments—for example, whether they are fines or prison terms—and the responses of offenders to changes in enforcement. The discussion, therefore, inevitably enters into issues in penology and theories of criminal behavior. A second, although because of lack of space subsidiary, aim of this essay is to see what insights into these questions are provided by our "economic" approach. It is suggested, for example, that a useful theory of criminal behavior can dispense with special theories of anomie, psychological inadequacies, or inheritance of special traits and simply extend the economist's usual analysis of choice.

BASIC ANALYSIS
The Cost of Crime

Although the word "crime" is used in the title to minimize terminological innovations, the analysis is intended to be sufficiently general to cover all violations, not just felonies—like murder, robbery, and assault, which receive so much newspaper coverage—but also tax evasion, the so-called white-collar crimes, and traffic and other violations. Looked at this broadly, "crime" is an economically important activity or "industry," notwithstanding the almost total neglect by economists.[1] Some relevant evidence

---

1. This neglect probably resulted from an attitude that illegal activity is too immoral to merit any systematic scientific attention. The influence of moral atti-

TABLE 1-I
ECONOMIC COSTS OF CRIMES

Type	Costs (Millions of Dollars)
Crimes against persons	815
Crimes against property	3,932
Illegal goods and services	8,075
Some other crimes	2,036
Total	14,858
Public expenditures on police, prosecution, and courts	3,178
Corrections	1,034
Some private costs of combatting crime	1,910
Over-all total	20,980

Source: President's Commission (1967*d*, p. 44).

recently put together by the President's Commission on Law Enforcement and Administration of Justice (the "Crime Commission") is reproduced in Table 1-I. Public expenditures in 1965 at the federal, state, and local levels on police, criminal courts and counsel, and "corrections" amounted to over $4 billion, while private outlays on burglar alarms, guards, counsel, and some other forms of protection were about $2 billion. Unquestionably, public and especially private expenditures are significantly understated, since expenditures by many public agencies in the course of enforcing particular pieces of legislation, such as state fair-employment laws,[2] are not included, and a myriad of private precautions against crime, ranging from suburban living to taxis, are also excluded.

---

tudes on a scientific analysis is seen most clearly in a discussion by Alfred Marshall. After arguing that even fair gambling is an "economic blunder" because of diminishing marginal utility, he says, "It is true that this loss of probable happiness need not be greater than the pleasure derived from the excitement of gambling, and we are then thrown back upon the induction [*sic*] that pleasures of gambling are in Bentham's phrase 'impure'; since experience shows that they are likely to engender a restless, feverish character, unsuited for steady work as well as for the higher and more solid pleasures of life" (Marshall, 1961, Note X, Mathematical Appendix).

2. Expenditures by the thirteen states with such legislation in 1959 totaled almost $2 million (see Landes, 1966).

Table 1-I also lists the Crime Commission's estimates of the direct costs of various crimes. The gross income from expenditures on various kinds of illegal consumption, including narcotics, prostitution, and mainly gambling, amounted to over $8 billion. The value of crimes against property, including fraud, vandalism, and theft, amounted to almost $4 billion,[3] while about $3 billion worth resulted from the loss of earnings due to homicide, assault, or other crimes. All the costs listed in the table total about $21 billion, which is almost 4 percent of reported national income in 1965. If the sizeable omissions were included, the percentage might be considerably higher.

Crime has probably become more important during the last forty years. The Crime Commission presents no evidence on trends in costs but does present evidence suggesting that the number of major felonies per capita has grown since the early thirties (President's Commission, 1967a). Moreover, with the large growth of tax and other legislation, tax evasion and other kinds of white-collar crime have presumably grown much more rapidly than felonies. One piece of indirect evidence on the growth of crime is the large increase in the amount of currency in circulation since 1929. For sixty years prior to that date, the ratio of currency either to all money or to consumer expenditures had declined very substantially. Since then, in spite of further urbanization and income growth and the spread of credit cards and other kinds of credit,[4] both ratios have increased sizeably.[5] This reversal

---

3. Superficially, frauds, thefts, etc., do not involve true social costs but are simply transfers, with the loss to victims being compensated by equal gains to criminals. While these are transfers, their market value is, nevertheless, a first approximation to the direct social cost. If the theft or fraud industry is "competitive," the sum of the value of the criminals' time input—including the time of "fences" and prospective time in prison—plus the value of capital input, compensation for risk, etc., would approximately equal the market value of the loss to victims. Consequently, aside from the input of intermediate products, losses can be taken as a measure of the value of the labor and capital input into these crimes, which are true social costs.

4. For an analysis of the secular decline to 1929 that stresses urbanization and the growth in incomes, see Cagan (1965, chap. iv).

5. In 1965, the ratio of currency outstanding to consumer expenditures was 0.08, compared to only 0.05 in 1929. In 1965, currency outstanding per family was a whopping $738.

can be explained by an unusual increase in illegal activity, since currency has obvious advantages over checks in illegal transactions (the opposite is true for legal transactions) because no record of a transaction remains.[6]

The Model

It is useful in determining how to combat crime in an optimal fashion to develop a model to incorporate the behavioral relations behind the costs listed in Table 1-I. These can be divided into five categories: the relations between (1) the number of crimes, called "offenses" in this essay, and the cost of offenses, (2) the number of offenses and the punishments meted out, (3) the number of offenses, arrests, and convictions and the public expenditures on police and courts, (4) the number of convictions and the costs of imprisonments or other kinds of punishments, and (5) the number of offenses and the private expenditures on protection and apprehension. The first four are discussed in turn, while the fifth is postponed until a later section.

Damages

Usually a belief that other members of society are harmed is the motivation behind outlawing or otherwise restricting an activity. The amount of harm would tend to increase with the activity level, as in the relation

$$H_i = H_i(O_i),$$

with

$$H_i' = \frac{dH_i}{dO_i} > 0,$$

(1)

where H_i is the harm from the ith activity and O_i is the activity level.[7] The concept of harm and the function relating its amount to the activity level are familiar to economists from their many discussions of activities causing external diseconomies. From this perspective, criminal activities are an important subset of

---

6. Cagan (1965, chap. iv) attributes much of the increase in currency holdings between 1929 and 1960 to increased tax evasion resulting from the increase in tax rates.

7. The ith subscript will be suppressed whenever it is to be understood that only one activity is being discussed.

the class of activities that cause diseconomies, with the level of criminal activities measured by the number of offenses.

The social value of the gain to offenders presumably also tends to increase with the number of offenses, as in

$$G = G(O),$$

with   (2)

$$G' = \frac{dG}{dO} > 0.$$

The net cost or damage to society is simply the difference between the harm and gain and can be written as

$$D(O) = H(O) - G(O). \tag{3}$$

If, as seems plausible, offenders usually eventually receive diminishing marginal gains and cause increasing marginal harm from additional offenses, $G'' < 0, H'' > 0$, and

$$D'' = H'' - G'' > 0, \tag{4}$$

which is an important condition used later in the analysis of optimality positions (see, for example, the Mathematical Appendix). Since both H' and $G' > 0$, the sign of D' depends on their relative magnitudes. It follows from (4), however, that

$$D'(O) > 0 \text{ for all } O > O_a \text{ if } D'(O_a) \geqslant 0. \tag{5}$$

Until later the discussion is restricted to the region where $D' > 0$, the region providing the strongest justification for outlawing an activity. In that section the general problem of external diseconomies is reconsidered from our viewpoint, and there $D' < 0$ is also permitted.

The top part of Table 1-I lists costs of various crimes, which have been interpreted by us as estimates of the value of resources used up in these crimes. These values are important components of, but are not identical to, the net damages to society. For example, the cost of murder is measured by the loss in earnings of victims and excludes, among other things, the value placed by society on life itself; the cost of gambling excludes both the utility to those gambling and the "external" disutility to some clergy and others; the cost of "transfers" like burglary and embezzlement excludes social attitudes toward forced wealth redistributions and also the effects on capital accumulation of the possibility of theft. Consequently, the $15 billion estimate for the cost of crime in Table 1-I may be a significant understatement of the net damages to society, not only because the costs of many white-collar crimes are omitted, but also because much of the damage is omitted even for the crimes covered.

The Cost of Apprehension and Conviction

The more that is spent on policemen, court personnel, and specialized equipment, the easier it is to discover offenses and convict offenders. One can postulate a relation between the output of police and court "activity" and various inputs of manpower, materials, and capital, as in $A = f(m,r,c)$, where f is a production function summarizing the "state of the arts." Given f and input prices, increased "activity" would be more costly, as summarized by the relation

$$C = C(A)$$

and

$$C' = \frac{dC}{dA} > 0.$$

(6)

It would be cheaper to achieve any given level of activity the cheaper were policemen,[8] judges, counsel, and juries and the more highly developed the state of the arts, as determined by technologies like fingerprinting, wiretapping, computer control, and lie-detecting.[9]

One approximation to an empirical measure of "activity" is the number of offenses cleared by conviction. It can be written as

$$A \cong pO,$$

(7)

where p, the ratio of offenses cleared by convictions to all offenses, is the over-all probability that an offense is cleared by conviction. By substituting (7) into (6) and differentiating, one has

---

8. According to the Crime Commission, 85-90 percent of all police costs consist of wages and salaries (President's Commission, 1967*a*, p. 35).

9. A task-force report by the Crime Commission deals with suggestions for greater and more efficient usage of advanced technologies (President's Commission, 1967*e*).

$$C_p = \frac{\partial C(pO)}{\partial p} = C'O > 0$$

and   (8)

$$C_o = C'p > 0$$

if $pO \neq 0$. An increase in either the probability of conviction or the number of offenses would increase total costs. If the marginal cost of increased "activity" were rising, further implications would be that

$$C_{pp} = C''O^2 > 0,$$
$$C_{oo} = C''p^2 > 0,$$ (9)

and

$$C_{po} = C_{op} = C''pO + C' > 0.$$

A more sophisticated and realistic approach drops the implication of (7) that convictions alone measure "activity," or even that p and O have identical elasticities, and introduces the more general relation

$$A = h(p, O, a). \tag{10}$$

The variable a stands for arrests and other determinants of "activity," and there is no presumption that the elasticity of h with respect to p equals that with respect to O. Substitution yields the cost function $C = C(p, O, a)$. If, as is extremely likely, h_p, h_o, and h_a are all greater than zero, then clearly C_p, C_o, and C_a are all greater than zero.

In order to insure that optimality positions do not lie at "corners," it is necessary to place some restrictions on the second derivatives of the cost function. Combined with some other assumptions, it is *sufficient* that

$$C_{pp} \gtreqqless 0,$$
$$C_{oo} \gtreqqless 0,$$ (11)

and

$$C_{po} \cong 0$$

(see the Mathematical Appendix). The first two restrictions are rather plausible, the third much less so.[10]

---

10. Differentiating the cost function yields $C_{pp} = C''(h_p)^2 + C'h_{pp}$; $C_{oo} = C''(h_o)^2 + C'h_{oo}$; $C_{po} = C''h_o h_p + C'h_{po}$. If marginal costs were rising, C_{pp} or C_{oo} could be negative only if h_{pp} or h_{oo} were sufficiently negative, which is not very likely. However, C_{po} would be approximately zero only if h_{po} were sufficiently negative, which is also unlikely. Note that if "activity" is measured by convictions alone, $h_{pp} = h_{oo} = 0$, and $h_{po} > 0$.

Table 1-I indicates that in 1965 public expenditures in the United States on police and courts totaled more than $3 billion, by no means a minor item. Separate estimates were prepared for each of seven major felonies.[11] Expenditures on them averaged about $500 per offense (reported) and about $2,000 per person arrested, with almost $1,000 being spent per murder (President's Commission, 1967a, pp. 264-65); $500 is an estimate of the average cost

$$AC = \frac{C(p, O, a)}{O}$$

of these felonies and would presumably be a larger figure if the number of either arrests or convictions were greater. Marginal costs (C_o) would be at least $500 if condition (11), $C_{oo} \geqq 0$, were assumed to hold throughout.

The Supply of Offenses

Theories about the determinants of the number of offenses differ greatly, from emphasis on skull types and biological inheritance to family upbringing and disenchantment with society. Practically all the diverse theories agree, however, that when other variables are held constant, an increase in a person's probability of conviction or punishment if convicted would generally decrease, perhaps substantially, perhaps negligibly, the number of offenses he commits. In addition, a common generalization by persons with judicial experience is that a change in the probability has a greater effect on the number of offenses than a change in the punishment, [12] although, as far as I can tell, none of the prominent theories shed any light on this relation.

The approach taken here follows the economists' usual analysis of choice and assumes that a person commits an offense if the expected utility to him exceeds the utility he could get by using his time and other resources at other activities. Some persons be-

---

11. They are wilful homicide, forcible rape, robbery, aggravated assault, burglary, larceny, and auto theft.

12. For example, Lord Shawness (1965) said, "Some judges preoccupy themselves with methods of punishment. This is their job. But in preventing crime it is of less significance than they like to think. Certainty of detection is far more important than severity of punishment." Also see the discussion of the idea of C. B. Beccaria, an insightful eighteenth-century Italian economist and criminologist, in Radzinowicz (1948, I, 282).

come "criminals," therefore, not because their basic motivation differs from that of other persons, but because their benefits and costs differ. I cannot pause to discuss the many general implications of this approach,[13] except to remark that criminal behavior becomes part of a much more general theory and does not require ad hoc concepts of differential association, anomie, and the like,[14] nor does it assume perfect knowledge, lightening-fast calculation, or any of the other caricatures of economic theory.

This approach implies that there is a function relating the number of offenses by any person to his probability of conviction, to his punishment if convicted, and to other variables, such as the income available to him in legal and other illegal activities, the frequency of nuisance arrests, and his willingness to commit an illegal act. This can be represented as

$$O_j = O_j(p_j, f_j, u_j), \tag{12}$$

where O_j is the number of offenses he would commit during a particular period, p_j his probability of conviction per offense, f_j his punishment per offense, and u_j a portmanteau variable representing all these other influences.[15]

Since only convicted offenders are punished, in effect there is "price discrimination" and uncertainty: if convicted, he pays f_j per convicted offense, while otherwise he does not. An increase in either p_j or f_j would reduce the utility expected from an offense and thus would tend to reduce the number of offenses because either the probability of "paying" the higher "price" or the "price" itself would increase.[16] That is,

$$O_{pj} = \frac{\partial O_j}{\partial p_j} < 0$$

and $\tag{13}$

$$O_{fj} = \frac{\partial O_j}{\partial f_j} < 0,$$

---

13. See, however, the discussions in Smigel (1965) and Ehrlich (1967).

14. For a discussion of these concepts, see Sutherland (1960).

15. Both p_j and f_j might be considered distributions that depend on the judge, jury, prosecutor, etc., that j happens to receive. Among other things, u_j depends on the p's and f's meted out for other competing offenses. For evidence indicating that offenders do substitute among offenses, see Smigel (1965).

16. The utility expected from committing an offense is defined as

$$EU_j = p_j U_j(Y_j - f_j) + (1 - p_j)U_j(Y_j),$$

where Y_j is his income, monetary plus psychic, from an offense; U_j is his utility

which are the generally accepted restrictions mentioned above. The effect of changes in some components of u_j could also be anticipated. For example, a rise in the income available in legal activities or an increase in law-abidingness due, say, to "education" would reduce the incentive to enter illegal activities and thus would reduce the number of offenses. Or a shift in the form of the punishment, say, from a fine to imprisonment, would tend to reduce the number of offenses, at least temporarily, because they cannot be committed while in prison.

This approach also has an interesting interpretation of the presumed greater response to a change in the probability than in the punishment. An increase in p_j "compensated" by an equal percentage reduction in f_j would not change the expected income from an offense[17] but could change the expected utility, because the amount of risk would change. It is easily shown that an increase in p_j would reduce the expected utility, and thus the number of offenses, more than an equal percentage increase in f_j[18] if j has preference for risk; the increase in f_j would have the greater effect if he has aversion to risk; and they would have the same effect if he is risk neutral.[19] The widespread generalization that

function; and f_j is to be interpreted as the monetary equivalent of the punishment. Then

$$\frac{\partial EU_j}{\partial p_j} = U_j(Y_j - f_j) - U_j(Y_j) < 0$$

and

$$\frac{\partial EU_j}{\partial f_j} = -p_j U_j'(Y_j - f_j) < 0$$

as long as the marginal utility of income is positive. One could expand the analysis by incorporating the costs and probabilities of arrests, detentions, and trials that do not result in conviction.

17. $EY_j = p_j(Y_j - f_j) + (1 - p_j)Y_j = Y_j - p_j f_j$.

18. This means than an increase in p_j "compensated" by a reduction in f_j would reduce utility and offenses.

19. From n. 16

$$\frac{-\partial EU_j}{\partial p_j} \frac{p_j}{U_j} = [U_j(Y_j) - U_j(Y_j - f_j)] \frac{p_j}{U_j} \gtrless \frac{-\partial EU_j}{\partial f_j} \frac{f_j}{U_j} = p_j U_j'(Y_j - f_j) \frac{f_j}{U_j}$$

as

$$\frac{U_j(Y_j) - U_j(Y_j - f_j)}{f_j} \gtrless U_j'(Y_j - f_j).$$

The term on the left is the average change in utility between $Y_j - f_j$ and Y_j. It would be greater than, equal to, or less than $U_j'(Y_j - f_j)$ as $U_j'' \gtrless 0$. But risk preference is defined by $U_j'' > 0$, neutrality by $U_j'' = 0$, and aversion by $U_j'' < 0$.

offenders are more deterred by the probability of conviction than by the punishment when convicted turns out to imply in the expected-utility approach that offenders are risk preferrers, at least in the relevant region of punishments.

The total number of offenses is the sum of all the O_j and would depend on the set of p_j, f_j, and u_j. Although these variables are likely to differ significantly between persons because of differences in intelligence, age, education, previous offense history, wealth, family upbringing, etc., for simplicity I now consider only their average values, p, f, and u,[20] and write the market offense function as

$$O = O(p, f, u). \tag{14}$$

This function is assumed to have the same kinds of properties as the individual functions, in particular, to be negatively related to p and f and to be more responsive to the former than the latter if, and only if, offenders on balance have risk preference. Smigel (1965) and Ehrlich (1967) estimate functions like (14) for seven felonies reported by the Federal Bureau of Investigation using state data as the basic unit of observation. They find that the relations are quite stable, as evidenced by high correlation coefficients; that there are significant negative effects on O of p and f; and that usually the effect of p exceeds that of f, indicating preference for risk in the region of observation.

A well-known result states that, in equilibrium, the real incomes of persons in risky activities are, at the margin, relatively high or low as persons are generally risk avoiders or preferrers. If offenders were risk preferrers, this implies that the real income of offenders would be lower, at the margin, than the incomes they could receive in less risky legal activities, and conversely if they were risk avoiders. Whether "crime pays" is then an implication of the attitudes offenders have toward risk and is not directly related to the efficiency of the police or the amount spent on

---

20. p can be defined as a weighted average of the p_j, as

$$p = \sum_{j=1}^{n} \frac{O_j p_j}{\sum_{i=1}^{n} O_i},$$

and similar definitions hold for f and u.

combatting crime. If, however, risk were preferred at some values of p and f and disliked at others, public policy could influence whether "crime pays" by its choice of p and f. Indeed, it is shown later that the social loss from illegal activities is usually minimized by selecting p and f in regions where risk is preferred, that is, in regions where "crime does not pay."

Punishments

Mankind has invented a variety of ingenious punishments to inflict on convicted offenders: death, torture, branding, fines, imprisonment, banishment, restrictions on movement and occupation, and loss of citizenship are just the more common ones. In the United States, less serious offenses are punished primarily by fines, supplemented occasionally by probation, petty restrictions like temporary suspension of one's driver's license, and imprisonment. The more serious offenses are punished by a combination of probation, imprisonment, parole, fines, and various restrictions on choice of occupation. A recent survey estimated for an average day in 1965 the number of persons who were either on probation, parole, or institutionalized in a jail or juvenile home (President's Commission 1967b). The total number of persons in one of these categories came to about 1,300,000, which is about 2 percent of the labor force. About one-half were on probation, one-third were institutionalized, and the remaining one-sixth were on parole.

The cost of different punishments to an offender can be made comparable by converting them into their monetary equivalent or worth, which, of course, is directly measured only for fines. For example, the cost of an imprisonment is the discounted sum of the earnings foregone and the value placed on the restrictions in consumption and freedom. Since the earnings foregone and the value placed on prison restrictions vary from person to person, the cost even of a prison sentence of given duration is not a unique quantity but is generally greater, for example, to offenders who could earn more outside of prison.[21] The cost to each offender would be

---

21. In this respect, imprisonment is a special case of "waiting time" pricing that is also exemplified by queuing (see Becker, 1965, esp. pp. 515-16, and Kleinman, 1967).

greater the longer the prison sentence, since both foregone earnings and foregone consumption are positively related to the length
of sentences.

Punishments affect not only offenders but also other members
of society. Aside from collection costs, fines paid by offenders
are received as revenue by others. Most punishments, however,
hurt other members as well as offenders: for example, imprisonment requires expenditures on guards, supervisory personnel,
buildings, food, etc. Currently about $1 billion is being spent each
year in the United States on probation, parole, and institutionalization alone, with the daily cost per case varying tremendously
from a low of $0.38 for adults on probation to a high of $11.00
for juveniles in detention institutions (President's Commission,
1967*b*).

The total social cost of punishments is the cost to offenders plus
the cost or minus the gain to others. Fines produce a gain to the
latter that equals the cost to offenders, aside from collection costs,
and so the social cost of fines is about zero, as befits a transfer
payment. The social cost of probation, imprisonment, and other
punishments, however, generally exceeds that to offenders, because others are also hurt. The derivation of optimality conditions
in the next section is made more convenient if social costs are
written in terms of offender costs as

$$f' \equiv bf, \tag{15}$$

where f' is the social cost and b is a coefficient that transforms
f into f'. The size of b varies greatly between different kinds of
punishments: $b \cong 0$ for fines, while $b > 1$ for torture, probation,
parole, imprisonment, and most other punishments. It is especially
large for juveniles in detention homes or for adults in prisons and
is rather close to unity for torture or for adults on parole.

OPTIMALITY CONDITIONS

The relevant parameters and behavioral functions have been
introduced, and the stage is set for a discussion of social policy.
If the aim simply were deterrence, the probability of conviction,
p, could be raised close to 1, and punishments, f, could be made
to exceed the gain: in this way the number of offenses, O, could

be reduced almost at will. However, an increase in p increases the social cost of offenses through its effect on the cost of combatting offenses, C, as does an increase in f if $b > 0$ through the effect on the cost of punishments, bf. At relatively modest values of p and f, these effects might outweigh the social gain from increased deterrence. Similarly, if the aim simply were to make "the punishment fit the crime," p could be set close to 1, and f could be equated to the harm imposed on the rest of society. Again, however, such a policy ignores the social cost of increases in p and f.

What is needed is a criterion that goes beyond catchy phrases and gives due weight to the damages from offenses, the costs of apprehending and convicting offenders, and the social cost of punishments. The social-welfare function of modern welfare economics is such a criterion, and one might assume that society has a function that measures the social loss from offenses. If

$$L = L(D, C, bf, O) \qquad (16)$$

is the function measuring social loss, with presumably

$$\frac{\partial L}{\partial D} > 0, \quad \frac{\partial L}{\partial C} > 0, \quad \frac{\partial L}{\partial bf} > 0, \qquad (17)$$

the aim would be to select values of f, C, and possibly b that minimize L.

It is more convenient and transparent, however, to develop the discussion at this point in terms of a less general formulation, namely, to assume that the loss function is identical with the total social loss in real income from offenses, convictions, and punishments, as in

$$L = D(O) + C(p, O) + bpfO. \qquad (18)$$

The term $bpfO$ is the total social loss from punishments, since bf is the loss per offense punished and pO is the number of offenses punished (if there are a fairly large number of independent offenses). The variables directly subject to social control are the amount spent in combatting offenses, C; the punishment per offense for those convicted, f; and the form of punishments, summarized by b. Once chosen, these variables, via the D, C, and O functions, indirectly determine p, O, D, and ultimately the loss L.

Analytical convenience suggests that p rather than C be considered a decision variable. Also, the coefficient b is assumed in this section to be a given constant greater than zero. Then p and f are the only decision variables, and their optimal values are found by differentiating L to find the two first-order optimality conditions,[22]

$$\frac{\partial L}{\partial f} = D'O_t + C'O_f + bpfO_f + bpO = 0 \qquad (19)$$

and

$$\frac{\partial L}{\partial p} = D'O_p + C'O_p + C_p + bpfO_p + bfO = 0. \qquad (20)$$

If O_f and O_p are not equal to zero, one can divide through by them, and recombine terms, to get the more interesting expressions

$$D' + C' = -bpf\left(1 - \frac{1}{\epsilon_f}\right) \qquad (21)$$

and

$$D' + C' + C_p \frac{1}{O_p} = -bpf\left(1 - \frac{1}{\epsilon_p}\right), \qquad (22)$$

where

$$\epsilon_f = -\frac{f}{O} O_f$$

and   (23)

$$\epsilon_p = -\frac{p}{O} O_p.$$

The term on the left side of each equation gives the marginal cost of increasing the number of offenses, O: in equation (21) through a reduction in f and in (22) through a reduction in p. Since $C' > 0$ and O is assumed to be in a region where $D' > 0$, the marginal cost of increasing O through f must be positive. A reduction in p partly reduces the cost of combatting offenses, and, therefore, the marginal cost of increasing O must be less when p rather than when f is reduced (Fig. 1-1); the former could even be negative if C_p were sufficiently large. Average "revenue," given by $-bpf$, is negative, but marginal revenue, given by the right-hand side of equations (21) and (22), is not necessarily negative and would be positive if the elasticities ϵ_p and ϵ_f were less than

22. The Mathematical Appendix discusses second-order conditions.

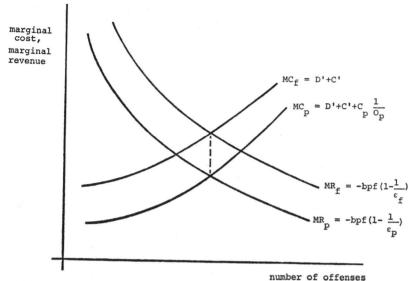

marginal
cost,
marginal
revenue

$MC_f = D' + C'$

$MC_p = D' + C' + C_p \dfrac{1}{p} O_p$

$MR_f = -bpf(1 - \dfrac{1}{\epsilon_f})$

$MR_p = -bpf(1 - \dfrac{1}{\epsilon_p})$

number of offenses

Figure 1-1

unity. Since the loss is minimized when marginal revenue equals marginal cost (Fig. 1-1), the optimal value of ϵ_f must be less than unity, and that of ϵ_p could only exceed unity if C_p were sufficiently large. This is a reversal of the usual equilibrium condition for an income-maximizing firm, which is that the elasticity of demand must exceed unity, because in the usual case average revenue is assumed to be positive.[23]

Since the marginal cost of changing O through a change in p is less than that of changing O through f, the equilibrium marginal revenue from p must also be less than that from f. But equations (21) and (22) indicate that the marginal revenue from p can be less if, and only if, $\epsilon_p > \epsilon_f$. As pointed out earlier, however, this is precisely the condition indicating that offenders have preference for risk and thus that "crime does not pay." Consequently, the loss from offenses is minimized if p and f are selected from those regions where offenders are, on balance, risk preferrers. Although only the attitudes offenders have toward

23. Thus if $b < 0$, average revenue would be positive and the optimal value of ϵ_f would be greater than 1, and that of ϵ_p could be less than 1 only if C_p were sufficiently large.

risk can directly determine whether "crime pays," rational public policy indirectly insures that "crime does not pay" through its choice of p and f.[24]

I indicated earlier that the actual p's and f's for major felonies in the United States generally seem to be in regions where the effect (measured by elasticity) of p on offenses exceeds that of f, that is, where offenders are risk preferrers and "crime does not pay" (Smigel, 1965; Ehrlich, 1967). Moreover, both elasticities are generally less than unity. In both respects, therefore, actual public policy is consistent with the implications of the optimality analysis.

If the supply of offenses depended only on pf—offenders were risk neutral—a reduction in p "compensated" by an equal percentage increase in f would leave unchanged pf, O, $D(O)$, and $bpfO$ but would reduce the loss, because the costs of apprehension and conviction would be lowered by the reduction in p. The loss would be minimized, therefore, by lowering p arbitrarily close to zero and raising f sufficiently high so that the product pf would induce the optimal number of offenses.[25] A fortiori, if offenders were risk avoiders, the loss would be minimized by setting p arbitrarily close to zero, for a "compensated" reduction in p reduces not only C but also O and thus D and $bpfO$.[26]

There was a tendency during the eighteenth and nineteenth centuries in Anglo-Saxon countries, and even today in many Communist and underdeveloped countries, to punish those convicted of criminal offenses rather severely, at the same time that the probability of capture and conviction was set at rather low

---

24. If $b < 0$, the optimality condition is that $\epsilon_p < \epsilon_f$, or that offenders are risk avoiders. Optimal social policy would then be to select p and f in regions where "crime does pay."

25. Since $\epsilon_f = \epsilon_p = \epsilon$ if O depends only on pf, and $C = 0$ if $p = 0$, the equilibrium conditions given by eqs. (21) and (22) to the single condition

$$D' = -bpf\left(1 - \frac{1}{\epsilon}\right).$$

From this condition and the relation $O = O(pf)$, the equilibrium values of O and pf could be determined.

26. If $b < 0$, the optimal solution is p about zero and f arbitrarily high if offenders are either risk neutral or risk preferrers.

values.[27] A promising explanation of this tendency is that an increased probability of conviction obviously absorbs public and private resources in the form of more policemen, judges, juries, and so forth. Consequently, a "compensated" reduction in this probability obviously reduces expenditures on combatting crime, and, since the expected punishment is unchanged, there is no "obvious" offsetting increase in either the amount of damages or the cost of punishments. The result can easily be continuous political pressure to keep police and other expenditures relatively low and to compensate by meting out strong punishments to those convicted.

Of course, if offenders are risk preferrers, the loss in income from offenses is generally minimized by selecting positive and finite values of p and f, even though there is no "obvious" offset to a compensated reduction in p. One possible offset already hinted at[27] is that judges or juries may be unwilling to convict offenders if punishments are set very high. Formally, this means that the cost of apprehension and conviction, C, would depend not only on p and O but also on f.[28] If C were more responsive to f than p, at least in some regions,[29] the loss in income could be minimized at finite values of p and f even if offenders were risk avoiders. For then a compensated reduction in p could raise, rather than lower, C and thus contribute to an increase in the loss.

Risk avoidance might also be consistent with optimal behavior if the loss function were not simply equal to the reduction in income. For example, suppose that the loss were increased by an increase in the ex post "price discrimination" between offenses that are not and those that are cleared by punishment. Then a "compensated" reduction in p would increase the "price discrimi-

---

27. For a discussion of English criminal law in the eighteenth and nineteenth centuries, see Radzinowicz (1948, Vol. I). Punishments were severe then, even though the death penalty, while legislated, was seldom implemented for less serious criminal offenses.

Recently South Vietnam executed a prominent businessman allegedly for "speculative" dealings in rice, while in recent years a number of persons in the Soviet Union have either been executed or given severe prison sentences for economic crimes.

28. I owe the emphasis on this point to Evsey Domar.

29. This is probably more likely for higher values of f and lower values of p.

nation," and the increased loss from this could more than offset the reductions in C, D, and $bpfO$.[30]

SHIFTS IN THE BEHAVIORAL RELATIONS

This section analyzes the effects of shifts in the basic behavioral relations—the damage, cost, and supply-of-offenses functions—on the optimal values of p and f. Since rigorous proofs can be found in the Mathematical Appendix, here the implications are stressed, and only intuitive proofs are given. The results are used to explain, among other things, why more damaging offenses are punished more severely and more impulsive offenders less severely.

An increase in the marginal damages from a given number of offenses, D', increases the marginal cost of changing offenses by a change in either p or f (Fig. 1-2a and b). The optimal number of offenses would necessarily decrease, because the optimal values of both p and f would increase. In this case (and, as shortly seen, in several others), the optimal values of p and f move in the same, rather than in opposite, directions.[31]

---

30. If p is the probability that an offense would be cleared with the punishment f, then $1 - p$ is the probability of no punishment. The expected punishment would be $\mu = pf$, the variance $\sigma^2 = p(1 - p)f^2$, and the coefficient of variation

$$v = \frac{\sigma}{\mu} = \sqrt{\frac{1 - p}{p}};$$

v increases monotonically from a low of zero when $p = 1$ to an infinitely high value when $p = 0$.

If the loss function equaled

$$L' = L + \psi(v), \quad \psi' > 0,$$

the optimality conditions would become

$$D' + C' = -bpf\left(1 - \frac{1}{\epsilon_f}\right) \tag{21}$$

and

$$D' + C' + C_p \frac{1}{O_p} + \psi' \frac{dv}{dp} \frac{1}{O_p} = -bpf\left(1 - \frac{1}{\epsilon_p}\right). \tag{22}$$

Since the term $\psi'(dv/dp)(1/O_p)$ is positive, it could more than offset the negative term $C_p(1/O_p)$.

31. I stress this primarily because of Bentham's famous and seemingly plausible dictum that "the more deficient in certainty a punishment is, the severer it should be" (1931, chap. ii of section entitled "Of Punishment," second rule). The dictum would be correct if p (or f) were exogenously determined and if L were minimized with respect to f (or p) alone, for then the optimal value of f (or p) would be inversely related to the given value of p (or f) (see the Mathematical Appendix). If, however, L is minimized with respect to both, then frequently they move in the same direction.

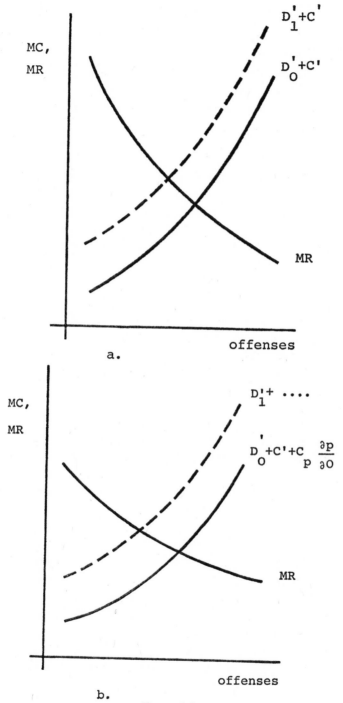

Figure 1-2

An interesting application of these conclusions is to different kinds of offenses. Although there are few objective measures of the damages done by most offenses, it does not take much imagination to conclude that offenses like murder or rape generally do more damage than petty larceny or auto theft. If the other components of the loss in income were the same, the optimal probability of apprehension and conviction and the punishment when convicted would be greater for the more serious offenses.

Table 1-II presents some evidence on the actual probabilities and punishments in the United States for seven felonies. The punishments are simply the average prison sentences served, while the probabilities are ratios of the estimated number of convictions to the estimated number of offenses and unquestionably contain a larger error (see the discussions in Smigel, 1965, and Ehrlich, 1967). If other components of the loss function are ignored, and if actual and optimal probabilities and punishments are positively related, one should find that the more serious felonies have higher probabilities and longer prison terms. And one does: in the table, which lists the felonies in decreasing order of presumed seriousness, both the actual probabilities and the prison terms are positively related to seriousness.

Since an increase in the marginal cost of apprehension and conviction for a given number of offenses, C', has identical effects as an increase in marginal damages, it must also reduce the optimal number of offenses and increase the optimal values of p and f. On the other hand, an increase in the other component of the cost of apprehension and conviction, C_p, has no direct effect on the marginal cost of changing offenses with f and *reduces* the cost of changing offenses with p (Fig. 1-3). It therefore reduces the optimal value of p and only partially compensates with an increase in f, so that the optimal number of offenses increases. Accordingly, an increase in both C' and C_p must increase the optimal f but can either increase or decrease the optimal p and optimal number of offenses, depending on the relative importance of the changes in C' and C_p.

The cost of apprehending and convicting offenders is affected by a variety of forces. An increase in the salaries of policemen in-

TABLE 1-II

PROBABILITY OF CONVICTION AND AVERAGE PRISON TERM FOR SEVERAL MAJOR FELONIES, 1960

	Murder and Non-negligent Manslaughter	Forcible Rape	Robbery	Aggravated Assault	Burglary	Larceny	Auto Theft	All These Felonies Combined
1. Average time served (months) before first release:								
a) Federal civil institutions	111.0	63.6	56.1	27.1	26.2	16.2	20.6	18.8
b) State institutions	121.4	44.8	42.4	25.0	24.6	19.8	21.3	28.4
2. Probabilities of apprehension and conviction (percent):								
a) Those found guilty of offenses known	57.9	37.7	25.1	27.3	13.0	10.7	13.7	15.1
b) Those found guilty of offenses charged	40.7	26.9	17.8	16.1	10.2	9.8	11.5	15.0
c) Those entering federal and state prisons (excludes many juveniles)	39.8	22.7	8.4	3.0	2.4	2.2	2.1	2.8

Source: 1, Bureau of Prisons (1960, Table 3); 2 (a) and (b), Federal Bureau of Investigation (1960, Table 10); 2 (c), Federal Bureau of Investigation (1961, Table 2), Bureau of Prisons (n.d., Table A1; 1961, Table 8).

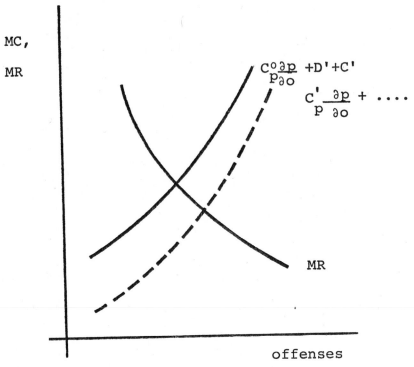

$$C^0 \frac{\partial p}{P \partial o} + D' + C'$$

$$C' \frac{\partial p}{P \partial o} + \ldots$$

MR

offenses

Figure 1-3

creases both C' and C_p, while improved police technology in the form of fingerprinting, ballistic techniques, computer control, and chemical analysis, or police and court "reform" with an emphasis on professionalism and merit, would tend to reduce both, not necessarily by the same extent. Our analysis implies, therefore, that although an improvement in technology and reform may or may not increase the optimal p and reduce the optimal number of offenses, it does reduce the optimal f and thus the need to rely on severe punishments for those convicted. Possibly this explains why the secular improvement in police technology and reform has gone hand in hand with a secular decline in punishments.

C_p, and to a lesser extent C', differ significantly between different kinds of offenses. It is easier, for example, to solve a rape or armed robbery than a burglary or auto theft, because the evidence of personal identification is often available in the former and not in the latter offenses.[32] This might tempt one to argue that the p's decline significantly as one moves across Table 1-II (left to right) primarily because the C_p's are significantly lower for the "personal" felonies listed to the left than for the "impersonal" felonies listed to the right. But this implies that the f's would increase as one moved across the table, which is patently false. Consequently, the positive correlation between p, f, and the severity of offenses observed in the table cannot be explained by a negative correlation between C_p (or C') and severity.

If $b > 0$, a reduction in the elasticity of offenses with respect to f increases the marginal revenue of changing offenses by changing f (Fig. 1-4a). The result is an increase in the optimal number of offenses and a decrease in the optimal f that is partially compensated by an increase in the optimal p. Similarly, a reduction in the elasticity of offenses with respect to p also increases the optimal number of offenses (Fig. 1-4b), decreases the optimal p, and partially compensates by an increase in f. An equal percentage reduction in both elasticities a fortiori increases the optimal number of offenses and also tends to reduce both p and f. If $b = 0$, both marginal revenue functions lie along the horizontal axis, and changes in these elasticities have no effect on the optimal values of p and f.

The income of a firm would usually be larger if it could separate, at little cost, its total market into submarkets that have substantially different elasticities of demand: higher prices would be charged in the submarkets having lower elasticities. Similarly, if the total "market" for offenses could be separated into submarkets that differ significantly in the elasticities of supply of offenses, the results above imply that if $b > 0$ the total loss would be reduced by "charging" *lower* "prices"—that is, lower p's and f's—in markets with *lower* elasticities.

---

32. "If a suspect is neither known to the victim nor arrested at the scene of the crime, the chances of ever arresting him are very slim" (President's Commission, 1967e, p. 8). This conclusion is based on a study of crimes in parts of Los Angeles during January, 1966.

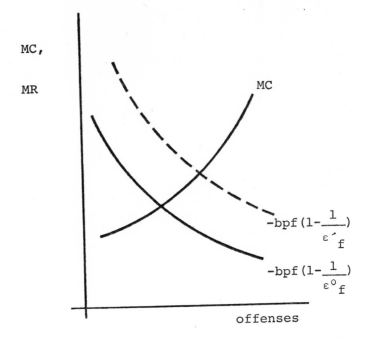

a.

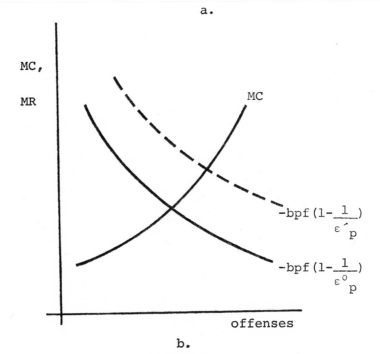

b.

Figure 1-4

Sometimes it is possible to separate persons committing the same offense into groups that have different responses to punishments. For example, unpremeditated murderers or robbers are supposed to act impulsively and, therefore, to be relatively unresponsive to the size of punishments; likewise, the insane or the young are probably less affected than other offenders by future consequences and, therefore,[33] probably less deterred by increases in the probability of conviction or in the punishment when convicted. The trend during the twentieth century toward relatively smaller prison terms and greater use of probation and therapy for such groups and, more generally, the trend away from the doctrine of "a given punishment for a given crime" is apparently at least broadly consistent with the implications of the optimality analysis.

An increase in b increases the marginal revenue from changing the number of offenses by changing p or f and thereby increases the optimal number of offenses, reduces the optimal value of f, and increases the optimal value of p. Some evidence presented earlier indicates that b is especially large for juveniles in detention homes or adults in prison and is small for fines or adults on parole. The analysis implies, therefore, that other things the same, the optimal f's would be smaller and the optimal p's larger if punishment were by one of the former rather than one of the latter methods.

FINES

Welfare Theorems and Transferable Pricing

The usual optimality conditions in welfare economics depend only on the levels and not on the slopes of marginal cost and average revenue functions, as in the well-known condition that marginal costs equal prices. The social loss from offenses was explicitly introduced as an application of the approach used in welfare economics, and yet slopes as incorporated into elasticities of supply do significantly affect the optimality conditions. Why this difference? The primary explanation would appear to be that it is

---

33. But see Becker (1962) for an analysis indicating that impulsive and other "irrational" persons may be as deterred from purchasing a commodity whose price has risen as more "rational" persons.

almost always implicitly assumed that prices paid by consumers are fully transferred to firms and governments, so that there is no social loss from payment.

If there were no social loss from punishments, as with fines, b would equal zero, and the elasticity of supply would drop out of the optimality condition given by equation (21).[34] If $b > 0$, as with imprisonment, some of the payment "by" offenders would not be received by the rest of society, and a net social loss would result. The elasticity of the supply of offenses then becomes an important determinant of the optimality conditions, because it determines the change in social costs caused by a change in punishments.

Although transferable monetary pricing is the most common kind today, the other is not unimportant, especially in underdeveloped and Communist countries. Examples in addition to imprisonment and many other punishments are the draft, payments in kind and queues and other waiting-time forms of rationing that result from legal restrictions on pricing (see Becker, 1965) and from random variations in demand and supply conditions. It is interesting, and deserves further exploration, that the optimality conditions are so significantly affected by a change in the assumptions about the transferability of pricing.

Optimality Conditions

If $b = 0$, say, because punishment was by fine, and if the cost of apprehending and convicting offenders were also zero, the two optimality conditions (21) and (22) would reduce to the same simple condition

$$D'(O) = 0. \tag{24}$$

Economists generally conclude that activities causing "external" harm, such as factories that pollute the air or lumber operations that strip the land, should be taxed or otherwise restricted in level until the marginal external harm equalled the marginal private gain, that is, until marginal net damages equalled zero, which is

---

34. It remains in eq. (22), through the slope O_p, because ordinarily prices do not affect marginal costs, while they do here through the influence of p on C.

what equation (24) says. If marginal harm always exceeded marginal gain, the optimum level would be presumed to be zero, and that would also be the implication of (24) when suitable inequality conditions were brought in. In other words, if the costs of apprehending, convicting, and punishing offenders were nil and if each offense caused more external harm than private gain, the social loss from offenses would be minimized by setting punishments high enough to eliminate all offenses. Minimizing the social loss would become identical with the criterion of minimizing crime by setting penalties sufficiently high.[35]

Equation (24) determines the optimal number of offenses, $\hat{O}$, and the fine and probability of conviction must be set at levels that induce offenders to commit just $\hat{O}$ offenses. If the economists' usual theory of choice is applied to illegal activities (see Basic Analysis), the marginal value of these penalties has to equal the marginal private gain:

$$V = G'(\hat{O}), \qquad 25)$$

where $G'(\hat{O})$ is the marginal private gain at $\hat{O}$ and V is the monetary value of the marginal penalties. Since by equations (3) and (24), $D'(\hat{O}) = H'(\hat{O}) - G'(\hat{O}) = 0$, one has by substitution in (25).

$$V = H'(\hat{O}). \qquad (26)$$

The monetary value of the penalties would equal the marginal harm caused by offenses.

Since the cost of apprehension and conviction is assumed equal to zero, the probability of apprehension and conviction could be set equal to unity without cost. The monetary value of penalties would then simply equal the fines imposed, and equation (26) would become

$$f = H'(\hat{O}). \qquad (27)$$

Since fines are paid by offenders to the rest of society, a fine determined by (27) would exactly compensate the latter for the marginal harm suffered, and the criterion of minimizing the social loss would be identical, at the margin, with the criterion of com-

---

35. "The evil of the punishment must be made to exceed the advantage of the offense" (Bentham, 1931, first rule).

pensating "victims."[36] If the harm to victims always exceeded the gain to offenders, both criteria would reduce in turn to eliminating all offenses.

If the cost of apprehension and conviction were not zero, the optimality condition would have to incorporate marginal costs as well as marginal damages and would become, if the probability of conviction were still assumed to equal unity,

$$D'(\bar{O}) + C'(\bar{O},1) = 0. \tag{28}$$

Since $C' > 0$, (28) requires that $D' < 0$ or that the marginal private gain exceed the marginal external harm, which generally means a smaller number of offenses than when $D' = 0$.[37] It is easy to show that equation (28) would be satisfied if the fine equalled the sum of marginal harm and marginal costs:

$$f = H'(\bar{O}) + C'(\bar{O}, 1).^{38} \tag{29}$$

In other words, offenders have to compensate for the cost of catching them as well as for the harm they directly do, which is a natural generalization of the usual externality analysis.

The optimality condition

$$D'(\bar{O}) + C'(\bar{O}, \hat{p}) + C_p(\bar{O}, \hat{p}) \frac{1}{O_p} = 0 \tag{30}$$

would replace equation (28) if the fine rather than the probability of conviction were fixed. Equation (30) would usually imply that $D'(\hat{O}) > 0$,[39] and thus that the number of offenses would ex-

---

36. By "victims" is meant the rest of society and not just the persons actually harmed.

37. This result can also be derived as a special case of the results in the Mathematical Appendix on the effects of increases in C'.

38. Since equilibrium requires that $f = G'(O)$, and since from (28)

$$D'(\hat{O}) = H'(\hat{O}) - G'(\hat{O}) = -C'(\hat{O},1),$$

then (29) follows directly by substitution.

39. That is, if, as seems plausible,

$$\frac{dC}{dp} = C' \frac{\partial O}{\partial p} + C_p > 0,$$

then

$$C' + C_p \frac{1}{\partial O / \partial p} < 0,$$

and

$$D'(\hat{O}) = -\left(C' + C_p \frac{1}{\partial O / \partial p}\right) > 0.$$

ceed the optimal number when costs were zero. Whether costs of apprehension and conviction increase or decrease the optimal number of offenses largely depends, therefore, on whether penalties are changed by a change in the fine or in the probability of conviction. Of course, if both are subject to control, the optimal probability of conviction would be arbitrarily close to zero, unless the social loss function differed from equation (18) (see the discussion under the heading Optimality Conditions).

The Case for Fines

Just as the probability of conviction and the severity of punishment are subject to control by society, so too is the form of punishment: legislation usually specifies whether an offense is punishable by fines, probation, institutionalization, or some combination. Is it merely an accident, or have optimality considerations determined that today, in most countries, fines are the predominant form of punishment, with institutionalization reserved for the more serious offenses? This section presents several arguments which imply that social welfare is increased if fines are used *whenever feasible*.

In the first place, probation and institutionalization use up social resources, and fines do not, since the latter are basically just transfer payments, while the former use resources in the form of guards, supervisory personnel, probation officers, and the offenders' own time.[40] Table 1-I indicates that the cost is not minor either: in the United States in 1965, about $1 billion was spent on "correction," and this estimate excludes, of course, the value of the loss in offenders' time.[41]

Moreover, the determination of the optimal number of offenses and severity of punishments is somewhat simplified by the use

---

40. Several early writers on criminology recognized this advantage of fines. For example, "Pecuniary punishments are highly economical, since all the evil felt by him who pays turns into an advantage for him who receives" (Bentham, 1931, chap. vi), and "Imprisonment would have been regarded in these old times [*ca.* tenth century] as a useless punishment; it does not satisfy revenge, it keeps the criminal idle, and do what we may, *it is costly*" (Pollock and Maitland, 1952, p. 516; my italics).

41. On the other hand, some transfer payments in the form of food, clothing, and shelter are included.

of fines. A wise use of fines requires knowledge of marginal gains and harm and of marginal apprehension and conviction costs; admittedly, such knowledge is not easily acquired. A wise use of imprisonment and other punishments must know this too, however, and, in addition, must know about the elasticities of response of offenses to changes in punishments. As the bitter controversies over the abolition of capital punishment suggest, it has been difficult to learn about these elasticities.

I suggested earlier that premeditation, sanity, and age can enter into the determination of punishments as proxies for the elasticities of response. These characteristics may not have to be considered in levying fines, because the optimal fines, as determined, say, by equation (27) or (29), do not depend on elasticities. Perhaps this partly explains why economists discussing externalities almost never mention motivation or intent, while sociologists and lawyers discussing criminal behavior invariably do. The former assume that punishment is by a monetary tax or fine, while the latter assume that non-monetary punishments are used.

Fines provide compensation to victims, and optimal fines at the margin fully compensate victims and restore the status quo ante, so that they are no worse off than if offenses were not committed.[42] Not only do other punishments fail to compensate, but they also require "victims" to spend additional resources in carrying out the punishment. It is not surprising, therefore, that the anger and fear felt toward ex-convicts who in fact have *not* "paid their debt to society" have resulted in additional punishments,[43] including legal restrictions on their political and economic opportunities[44] and informal restrictions on their social acceptance. Moreover, the absence of compensation encourages efforts to change and otherwise "rehabilitate" offenders through psychiatric coun-

---

42. Bentham recognized this and said, "To furnish an indemnity to the injured party is another useful quality in a punishment. It is a means of accomplishing two objects at once—punishing an offense and repairing it: removing the evil of the first order, and putting a stop to alarm. This is a characteristic advantage of pecuniary punishments" (1931, chap. vi).

43. In the same way, the guilt felt by society in using the draft, a forced transfer *to* society, has led to additional payments to veterans in the form of educational benefits, bonuses, hospitalization rights, etc.

44. See Sutherland (1960, pp. 267-68) for a list of some of these.

seling, therapy, and other programs. Since fines do compensate and do not create much additional cost, anger toward and fear of appropriately fined persons do not easily develop. As a result, additional punishments are not usually levied against "ex-finees," nor are strong efforts made to "rehabilitate" them.

One argument made against fines is that they are immoral because, in effect, they permit offenses to be bought for a price in the same way that bread or other goods are bought for a price.[45] A fine *can* be considered the price of an offense, but so too can any other form of punishment; for example, the "price" of stealing a car might be six months in jail. The only difference is in the units of measurement: fines are prices measured in monetary units, imprisonments are prices measured in time units, etc. If anything, monetary units are to be preferred here as they are generally preferred in pricing and accounting.

Optimal fines determined from equation (29) depend only on the marginal harm and cost and not at all on the economic positions of offenders. This has been criticized as unfair, and fines proportional to the incomes of offenders have been suggested.[46] If the goal is to minimize the social loss in income from offenses, and not to take vengeance or to inflict harm on offenders, then fines should depend on the total harm done by offenders, and not directly on their income, race, sex, etc. In the same way, the monetary value of optimal prison sentences and other punish-

---

45. The very early English law relied heavily on monetary fines, even for murder, and it has been said that "every kind of blow or wound given to every kind of person had its price, and much of the jurisprudence of the time must have consisted of a knowledge of these preappointed prices" (Pollock and Maitland, 1952, p. 451).

The same idea was put amusingly in a recent *Mutt and Jeff* cartoon which showed a police car carrying a sign that read: "Speed limit 30 M per H—$5 fine every mile over speed limit—pick out speed you can afford."

46. For example, Bentham said, "A pecuniary punishment, if the sum is fixed, is in the highest degree unequal. . . . Fines have been determined without regard to the profit of the offense, to its evil, or to the wealth of the offender. . . . Pecuniary punishments should always be regulated by the fortune of the offender. The relative amount of the fine should be fixed, not its absolute amount; for such an offense, such a part of the offender's fortune" (1931, chap. ix). Note that optimal fines, as determined by eq. (29), do depend on "the profit of the offense" and on "its evil."

ments depends on the harm, costs, and elasticities of response, but not directly on an offender's income. Indeed, if the monetary value of the punishment by, say, imprisonment were independent of income, the length of the sentence would be *inversely* related to income, because the value placed on a given sentence is positively related to income.

We might detour briefly to point out some interesting implications for the probability of conviction of the fact that the monetary value of a given fine is obviously the same for all offenders, while the monetary equivalent or "value" of a given prison sentence or probation period is generally positively related to an offender's income. It has been suggested that actual probabilities of conviction are not fixed to all offenders but usually vary with their age, sex, race, and, in particular, income. Offenders with higher earnings have an incentive to spend more on planning their offenses, on good lawyers, on legal appeals, and even on bribery to reduce the probability of apprehension and conviction for offenses punishable by, say, a given prison term, because the cost to them of conviction is relatively large compared to the cost of these expenditures. Similarly, however, poorer offenders have an incentive to use more of their time in planning their offenses, in court appearances, and the like to reduce the probability of conviction for offenses punishable by a given fine, because the cost to them of conviction is relatively large compared to the value of their time.[47] The implication is that the probability of conviction would be systematically related to the earnings of offenders: negatively for offenses punishable by imprisonment and positively for those punishable by fines. Although a negative relation for felonies and other offenses punishable by imprisonment has been frequently observed and deplored (see President's Commission, 1967c), I do not know of any studies of the relation for fines or of any recognition that the observed negative

---

47. Note that the incentive to use time to reduce the probability of a given prison sentence is unrelated to earnings, because the punishment is fixed in time, not monetary, units; likewise, the incentive to use money to reduce the probability of a given fine is also unrelated to earnings, because the punishment is fixed in monetary, not time, units.

relation may be more a consequence of the nature of the punishment than of the influence of wealth.

Another argument made against fines is that certain crimes, like murder or rape, are so heinous that no amount of money could compensate for the harm inflicted. This argument has obvious merit and is a special case of the more general principle that fines cannot be relied on exclusively whenever the harm exceeds the resources of offenders. For then victims could not be fully compensated by offenders, and fines would have to be supplemented with prison terms or other punishments in order to discourage offenses optimally. This explains why imprisonments, probation, and parole are major punishments for the more serious felonies; considerable harm is inflicted, and felonious offenders lack sufficient resources to compensate. Since fines are preferable, it also suggests the need for a flexible system of installment fines to enable offenders to pay fines more readily and thus avoid other punishments.

This analysis implies that if some offenders could pay the fine for a given offense and others could not,[48] the former should be punished solely by fine and the latter partly by other methods. In essence, therefore, these methods become a vehicle for punishing "debtors" to society. Before the cry is raised that the system is unfair, especially to poor offenders, consider the following.

Those punished would be debtors in "transactions" that were never agreed to by their "creditors," not in voluntary transactions, such as loans,[49] for which suitable precautions could be taken in advance by creditors. Moreover, punishment in any economic system based on voluntary market transactions inevitably must distinguish between such "debtors" and others. If a rich man purchases a car and a poor man steals one, the former is congratulated, while the latter is often sent to prison when apprehended. Yet the rich man's purchase is equivalent to a "theft" subsequently compensated by a "fine" equal to the price of the

---

48. In one study, about half of those convicted of misdemeanors could not pay the fines (see President's Commission, 1967c, p. 148).

49. The "debtor prisons" of earlier centuries generally housed persons who could not repay loans.

car, while the poor man, in effect, goes to prison because he cannot pay his "fine."

Whether a punishment like imprisonment in lieu of a full fine for offenders lacking sufficient resources is "fair" depends, of course, on the length of the prison term compared to the fine.[50] For example, a prison term of one week in lieu of a $10,000 fine would, if anything, be "unfair" to wealthy offenders paying the fine. Since imprisonment is a more costly punishment to society than fines, the loss from offenses would be reduced by a policy of leniency toward persons who are imprisoned because they cannot pay fines. Consequently, optimal prison terms for "debtors" would not be "unfair" to them in the sense that the monetary equivalent to them of the prison terms would be less than the value of optimal fines, which in turn would equal the harm caused or the "debt."[51]

It appears, however, that "debtors" are often imprisoned at rates

---

50. Yet without any discussion of the actual alternatives offered, the statement is made that "the money judgment assessed the punitive damages defendant hardly seems comparable in effect to the criminal sanctions of death, imprisonment, and stigmatization" ("Criminal Safeguards . . . ," 1967).

51. A formal proof is straightforward if for simplicity the probability of conviction is taken as equal to unity. For then the sole optimality condition is

$$D' + C' = -bf\left(1 - \frac{1}{\epsilon_f}\right). \tag{1'}$$

Since $D' = H' - G'$, by substitution one has

$$G' = H' + C' + bf\left(1 - \frac{1}{\epsilon_f}\right), \tag{2'}$$

and since equilibrium requires that $G' = f$,

$$f = H' + C' + bf\left(1 - \frac{1}{\epsilon_f}\right), \tag{3'}$$

or

$$f = \frac{H' + C'}{1 - b(1 - 1/\epsilon_f)}. \tag{4'}$$

If $b > 0$, $\epsilon_f < 1$, and hence by eq. (4'),

$$f < H' + C', \tag{5'}$$

where the term on the right is the full marginal harm. If p as well as f is free to vary, the analysis becomes more complicated, but the conclusion about the relative monetary values of optimal imprisonments and fines remains the same (see the Mathematical Appendix).

of exchange with fines that place a low value on time in prison. Although I have not seen systematic evidence on the different punishments actually offered convicted offenders, and the choices they made, many statutes in the United States do permit fines and imprisonment that place a low value on time in prison. For example, in New York State, Class A Misdemeanors can be punished by a prison term as long as one year or a fine no larger than $1,000 and Class B Misdemeanors, by a term as long as three months or a fine no larger than $500 (*Laws of New York*, 1965, chap. 1030, Arts. 70 and 80).[52] According to my analysis, these statutes permit excessive prison sentences relative to the fines, which may explain why imprisonment in lieu of fines is considered unfair to poor offenders, who often must "choose" the prison alternative.

Compensation and the Criminal Law

Actual criminal proceedings in the United States appear to seek a mixture of deterrence, compensation, and vengeance. I have already indicated that these goals are somewhat contradictory and cannot generally be simultaneously achieved; for example, if punishment were by fine, minimizing the social loss from offenses would be equivalent to compensating "victims" fully, and deterrence or vengeance could only be partially pursued. Therefore, if the case for fines were accepted, and punishment by optimal fines became the norm, the traditional approach to criminal law would have to be significantly modified.

First and foremost, the primary aim of all legal proceedings would become the same: not punishment or deterrence, but simply the assessment of the "harm" done by defendants. Much of traditional criminal law would become a branch of the law of torts,[53] say "social torts," in which the public would collectively sue for "public" harm. A "criminal" action would be defined fun-

---

52. "Violations," however, can only be punished by prison terms as long as fifteen days or fines no larger than $250. Since these are maximum punishments, the actual ones imposed by the courts can, and often are, considerably less. Note, too, that the courts can punish by imprisonment, by fine, or by *both* (*Laws of New York*, 1965, chap. 1030, Art. 60).

53. "The cardinal principle of damages in Anglo-American law [of torts] is that of *compensation* for the injury caused to plaintiff by defendant's breach of duty" (Harper and James, 1956, p. 1299).

damentally not by the nature of the action[54] but by the inability of a person to compensate for the "harm" that he caused. Thus an action would be "criminal" precisely because it results in uncompensated "harm" to others. Criminal law would cover all such actions, while tort law would cover all other (civil) actions.

As a practical example of the fundamental changes that would be wrought, consider the antitrust field. Inspired in part by the economist's classic demonstration that monopolies distort the allocation of resources and reduce economic welfare, the United States has outlawed conspiracies and other constraints of trade. In practice, defendants are often simply required to cease the objectionable activity, although sometimes they are also fined, become subject to damage suits, or are jailed.

If compensation were stressed, the main purpose of legal proceedings would be to levy fines equal to[55] the harm inflicted on society by constraints of trade. There would be no point to cease and desist orders, imprisonment, ridicule, or dissolution of companies. If the economist's theory about monopoly is correct, and if optimal fines were levied, firms would automatically cease any constraints of trade, because the gain to them would be less than the harm they cause and thus less than the fines expected. On the other hand, if Schumpeter and other critics are correct, and certain constraints of trade raise the level of economic welfare, fines could fully compensate society for the harm done, and yet some constraints would not cease, because the gain to participants would exceed the harm to others.[56]

---

54. Of course, many traditional criminal actions like murder or rape would still usually be criminal under this approach too.

55. Actually, fines should exceed the harm done if the probability of conviction were less than unity. The possibility of avoiding conviction is the intellectual justification for punitive, such as triple, damages against those convicted.

56. The classical view is that $D'(M)$ always is greater than zero, where M measures the different constraints of trade and D' measures the marginal damage; the critic's view is that for some M, $D'(M) < 0$. It has been shown above that if D' always is greater than zero, compensating fines would discourage all offenses, in this case constraints of trade, while if D' sometimes is less than zero, some offenses would remain (unless $C'[M]$, the marginal cost of detecting and convicting offenders, were sufficiently large relative to D').

One unexpected advantage, therefore, from stressing compensation and fines rather than punishment and deterrence is that the validity of the classical position need not be judged a priori. If valid, compensating fines would discourage all constraints of trade and would achieve the classical aims. If not, such fines would permit the socially desirable constraints to continue and, at the same time, would compensate society for the harm done.

Of course, as participants in triple-damage suits are well aware, the harm done is not easily measured, and serious mistakes would be inevitable. However, it is also extremely difficult to measure the harm in many civil suits,[57] yet these continue to function, probably reasonably well on the whole. Moreover, as experience accumulated, the margin of error would decline, and rules of thumb would develop. Finally, one must realize that difficult judgments are also required by the present antitrust policy, such as deciding that certain industries are "workably" competitive or that certain mergers reduce competition. An emphasis on fines and compensation would at least help avoid irrelevant issues by focusing attention on the information most needed for intelligent social policy.

PRIVATE EXPENDITURES AGAINST CRIME

A variety of private as well as public actions also attempt to reduce the number and incidence of crimes: guards, doormen, and accountants are employed, locks and alarms installed, insurance coverage extended, parks and neighborhoods avoided, taxis used in place of walking or subways, and so on. Table 1-I lists close to $2 billion of such expenditures in 1965, and this undoubtedly is a gross underestimate of the total. The need for private action is especially great in highly interdependent modern economies, where frequently a person must trust his resources,

---

57. Harper and James said, "Sometimes [compensation] can be accomplished with a fair degree of accuracy. But obviously it cannot be done in anything but a figurative and essentially speculative way for many of the consequences of personal injury. Yet it is the aim of the law to attain at least a rough correspondence between the amount awarded as damages and the extent of the suffering" (1956, p. 1301).

including his person, to the "care" of employees, employers, customers, or sellers.

If each person tries to minimize his expected loss in income from crimes, optimal private decisions can be easily derived from the previous discussion of optimal public ones. For each person there is a loss function similar to that given by equation (18):

$$L_j = H_j(O_j) + C_j(p_j, O_j, C, C_k) + b_j p_j f_j O_j. \qquad (31)$$

The term H_j represents the harm to j from the O_j offenses committed against j, while C_j represents his cost of achieving a probability of conviction of p_j for offenses committed against him. Note that C_j not only is positively related to O_j but also is negatively related to C, public expenditures on crime, and to C_k, the set of private expenditures by other persons.[58]

The term $b_j p_j f_j O_j$ measures the expected[59] loss to j from punishment of offenders committing any of the O_j. Whereas most punishments result in a net loss to society as a whole, they often produce a gain for the actual victims. For example, punishment by fines given to the actual victims is just a transfer payment for society but is a clear gain to victims; similarly, punishment by imprisonment is a net loss to society but is a negligible loss to victims, since they usually pay a negligible part of imprisonment costs. This is why b_j is often less than or equal to zero, at the same time that b, the coefficient of social loss, is greater than or equal to zero.

Since b_j and f_j are determined primarily by public policy on punishments, the main decision variable directly controlled by j is p_j. If he chooses a p_j that minimizes L_j, the optimality condition analogous to equation (22) is

---

58. An increase in C_k—O_j and C held constant—presumably helps solve offenses against j, because more of those against k would be solved.

59. The expected private loss, unlike the expected social loss, is apt to have considerable variance because of the small number of independent offenses committed against any single person. If j were not risk neutral, therefore, L would have to be modified to include a term that depended on the distribution of $b_j p_j f_j O_j$.

$$H'_j + C'_j + C_{jp_j} \frac{\partial p_j}{\partial O_j} = -b_j p_j f_j \left(1 - \frac{1}{\epsilon_{jp_j}}\right).^{60} \tag{32}$$

The elasticity ϵ_{jp_j} measures the effect of a change in p_j on the number of offenses committed against j. If $b_j < 0$, and if the left-hand side of equation (32), the marginal cost of changing O_j, were greater than zero, then (32) implies that $\epsilon_{jp_j} > 1$. Since offenders can substitute among victims, ϵ_{jp_j}, is probably much larger than ϵ_p, the response of the total number of offenses to a change in the average probability, p. There is no inconsistency, therefore, between a requirement from the optimality condition given by (22) that $\epsilon_p < 1$ and a requirement from (32) that $\epsilon_{jp_j} > 1$.

SOME APPLICATIONS
Optimal Benefits

Our analysis of crime is a generalization of the economist's analysis of external harm or diseconomies. Analytically, the generalization consists in introducing costs of apprehension and conviction, which make the probability of apprehension and conviction an important decision variable, and in treating punishment by imprisonment and other methods as well as by monetary payments. A crime is apparently not so different analytically from any other activity that produces external harm and when crimes are punishable by fines, the analytical differences virtually vanish.

---

60. I have assumed that

$$\frac{\partial C}{\partial p_j} = \frac{\partial C_k}{\partial p_j} = 0,$$

in other words, that j is too "unimportant" to influence other expenditures. Although usually reasonable, this does suggest a modification to the optimality conditions given by eqs. (21) and (22). Since the effects of public expenditures depend on the level of private ones, and since the public is sufficiently "important" to influence private actions, eq. (22) has to be modified to

$$D' + C' + C_p \frac{\partial p}{\partial O} + \sum_{i=1}^{n} \frac{dC}{dC_i} \frac{dC_i}{dp} \frac{\partial p}{\partial O} = -bpf \left(1 + \frac{1}{\epsilon_p}\right), \tag{22'}$$

and similarly for eq. (21). "The" probability p is, of course, a weighted average of the p_j. Eq. (22′) incorporates the presumption that an increase in public expenditures would be partially thwarted by an induced decrease in private ones.

Discussions of external economies or advantages are usually perfectly symmetrical to those of diseconomies, yet one searches in vain for analogues to the law of torts and criminality. Generally, compensation cannot be collected for the external advantages as opposed to harm caused, and no public officials comparable to policemen and district attorneys apprehend and "convict" benefactors rather than offenders. Of course, there is public interest in benefactors: medals, prizes, titles, and other privileges have been awarded to military heroes, government officials, scientists, scholars, artists, and businessmen by public and private bodies. Among the most famous are Nobel Prizes, Lenin Prizes, the Congressional Medal of Honor, knighthood, and patent rights. But these are piecemeal efforts that touch a tiny fraction of the population and lack the guidance of any body of law that codifies and analyzes different kinds of advantages.

Possibly the explanation for this lacuna is that criminal and tort law developed at the time when external harm was more common than advantages, or possibly the latter have been difficult to measure and thus considered too prone to favoritism. In any case, it is clear that the asymmetry in the law does not result from any analytical asymmetry, for a formal analysis of advantages, benefits, and benefactors can be developed that is quite symmetrical to the analysis of damages, offenses, and offenders. A function $A(B)$, for example, can give the net social advantages from B benefits in the same way that $D(O)$ gives the net damages from O offenses. Likewise, $K(B, p_1)$ can give the cost of apprehending and rewarding benefactors, where p_1 is the probability of so doing, with K' and $K_p > 0$; $B(p_1, a, v)$ can give the supply of benefits, where a is the award per benefit and v represents other determinants, with $\partial B/\partial p_1$ and $\partial B/\partial a > 0$; and b_1 can be the fraction of a that is a net loss to society. Instead of a loss function showing the decrease in social income from offenses, there can be a profit function showing the increase in income from benefits:

$$\Pi = A(B) - K(B, p_1) - b_1 p_1 a B. \qquad (33)$$

If Π is maximized by choosing appropriate values of p_1 and a, the optimality conditions analogous to equations (21) and (22) are

$$A' - K' = b_1 p_1 a \left(1 + \frac{1}{e_a}\right) \tag{34}$$

and

$$A' - K' - K_p \frac{\partial p_1}{\partial B} = b_1 p_1 a \left(1 + \frac{1}{e_p}\right), \tag{35}$$

where

$$e_a = \frac{\partial B}{\partial a} \frac{a}{B}$$

and

$$e_p = \frac{\partial B}{\partial p_1} \frac{p_1}{B}$$

are both greater than zero. The implications of these equations are related to and yet differ in some important respects from those discussed earlier for (21) and (22).

For example, if $b_1 > 0$, which means that a is not a pure transfer but costs society resources, clearly (34) and (35) imply that $e_p > e_a$, since both $K_p > 0$ and $\partial p_1 / \partial B > 0$. This is analogous to the implication of (21) and (22) that $\epsilon_p > \epsilon_f$, but, while the latter implies that, at the margin, offenders are risk *preferrers*, the former implies that, at the margin, benefactors are risk *avoiders*.[61] Thus, while the optimal values of p and f would be in a region where "crime does not pay"—in the sense that the marginal income of criminals would be less than that available to them in less risky legal activities—the optimal values of p_1 and a would be where "benefits do pay"—in the same sense that the marginal income of benefactors would exceed that available to them in less

---

61. The relation $e_p > e_a$ holds if, and only if,

$$\frac{\partial EU}{\partial p_1} \frac{p_1}{U} > \frac{\partial EU}{\partial a} \frac{a}{U}, \tag{1'}$$

where

$$EU = p_1 U(Y + a) + (1 - p_1) U(Y) \tag{2'}$$

(see the discussion on pp. 14-15). By differentiating eq. (2'), one can write (1') as

or

$$p_1 [U(Y + a) - U(Y)] > p_1 a U'(Y + a), \tag{3'}$$

$$\frac{U(Y + a) - U(Y)}{a} > U'(Y + a). \tag{4'}$$

But (4') holds if everywhere $U'' < 0$ and does not hold if everywhere $U'' \geqq 0$, which was to be proved.

risky activities. In this sense it "pays" to do "good" and does not "pay" to do "bad."

As an illustration of the analysis, consider the problem of rewarding inventors for their inventions. The function $A(B)$ gives the total social value of B inventions, and A' gives the marginal value of an additional one. The function $K(B, p_1)$ gives the cost of finding and rewarding inventors; if a patent system is used, it measures the cost of a patent office, of preparing applications, and of the lawyers, judges, and others involved in patent litigation.[62] The elasticities e_p *and* e_a measure the response of inventors to changes in the probability and magnitude of awards, while b_1 measures the social cost of the method used to award inventors. With a patent system, the cost consists in a less extensive use of an invention than would otherwise occur, and in any monopoly power so created.

Equations (34) and (35) imply that with any system having $b_1 > 0$, the smaller the elasticities of response of inventors, the smaller should be the probability and magnitude of awards. (The value of a patent can be changed, for example, by changing its life.) This shows the relevance of the controversy between those who maintain that most inventions stem from a basic desire "to know" and those who maintain that most stem from the prospects of financial awards, especially today with the emphasis on systematic investment in research and development. The former quite consistently usually advocate a weak patent system, while the latter equally consistently advocate its strengthening.

Even if A', the marginal value of an invention, were "sizeable," the optimal decision would be to abolish property rights in an invention, that is, to set $p_1 = 0$, if b_1 and K[63] were sufficiently large and/or the elasticities e_p and e_a sufficiently small. Indeed,

---

62. These costs are not entirely trivial: for example, in 1966 the U.S. Patent Office alone spent $34 million (see Bureau of the Budget, 1967), and much more was probably spent in preparing applications and in litigation.

63. Presumably one reason patents are not permitted on basic research is the difficulty (that is, cost) of discovering the ownership of new concepts and theorems.

practically all arguments to eliminate or greatly alter the patent system have been based either on its alleged costliness, large K or b_1, or lack of effectiveness, low e_p or e_a (see, for example, Plant, 1934, or Arrow, 1962).

If a patent system were replaced by a system of cash prizes, the elasticities of response would become irrelevant for the determination of optimal policies, because b_1 would then be approximately zero.[64] A system of prizes would, moreover, have many of the same other advantages that fines have in punishing offenders (see the discussion under Fines). One significant advantage of a patent system, however, is that it automatically "meters" A', that is, provides an award that is automatically positively related to A', while a system of prizes (or of fines and imprisonment) has to estimate A' (or D') independently and often somewhat arbitrarily.

The Effectiveness of Public Policy

The anticipation of conviction and punishment reduces the loss from offenses and thus increases social welfare by discouraging some offenders. What determines the increase in welfare, that is "effectiveness," of public efforts to discourage offenses? The model developed earlier in this chapter (optimality conditions) can be used to answer this question if social welfare is measured by income and if "effectiveness" is defined as a ratio of the maximum feasible increase in income to the increase if all offenses causing net damages were abolished by fiat. The maximum feasible increase is achieved by choosing optimal values of the probability of apprehension and conviction, p, and the size of punishments, f

---

64. The right side of both (34) and (35) would vanish, and the optimality conditions would be

$$A' - K' = 0 \tag{34'}$$

and

$$A' - K' - K_p \frac{\partial p_1}{\partial B} = 0. \tag{35'}$$

Since these equations are not satisfied by any finite values of p_1 and a, there is a difficulty in allocating the incentives between p_1 and a (see the similar discussion for fines under the heading, Fines).

(assuming that the coefficient of social loss from punishment, b, is given).[65]

Effectiveness so defined can vary between zero and unity and depends essentially on two behavioral relations: the cost of apprehension and conviction and the elasticities of response of offenses to changes in p and f. The smaller these costs or the greater these elasticities, the smaller the cost of achieving any given reduction in offenses and thus the greater the effectiveness. The elasticities may well differ considerably among different kinds of offenses. For example, crimes of passion, like murder or rape, or crimes of youth, like auto theft, are often said to be less responsive to changes in p and f than are more calculating crimes by adults, like embezzlement, antitrust violation, or bank robbery. The elasticities estimated by Smigel (1965) and Ehrlich (1967) for seven major felonies do differ considerably but are not clearly smaller for murder, rape, auto theft, and assault than for robbery, burglary, and larceny.[66]

Probably effectiveness differs among offenses more because of differences in the costs of apprehension and conviction than in the elasticities of response. An important determinant of these costs, and one that varies greatly, is the time between commission and detection of an offense.[67] For the earlier an offense is detected, the earlier the police can be brought in and the more likely that the victim is able personally to identify the offender. This suggests that effectiveness is greater for robbery than for a related felony like burglary, or for minimum-wage and fair-employment legisla-

---

65. In symbols, effectiveness is defined as

$$E = \frac{D(O_1) - [D(\hat{O}) + C(\hat{p}, \hat{O}) + b\hat{p}\hat{f}\hat{O}]}{D(O_1) - D(O_2)}$$

where $\hat{p}$, $\hat{f}$, and $\hat{O}$ are optimal values, O_1 offenses would occur if $p = f = 0$, and O_2 is the value of O that minimizes D.

66. A theoretical argument that also casts doubt on the assertion that less "calculating" offenders are less responsive to changes in p and f can be found in Becker (1962).

67. A study of crimes in parts of Los Angeles during January, 1966, found that "more than half the arrests were made within 8 hours of the crime, and almost two-thirds were made within the first week" (President's Commission 1967*e*, p. 8).

tion than for other white-collar legislation like antitrust and public-utility regulation.[68]

A Theory of Collusion

The theory developed in this essay can be applied to any effort to preclude certain kinds of behavior, regardless of whether the behavior is "unlawful." As an example, consider efforts by competing firms to collude in order to obtain monopoly profits. Economists lack a satisfactory theory of the determinants of price and output policies by firms in an industry, a theory that could predict under what conditions perfectly competitive, monopolistic, or various intermediate kinds of behavior would emerge. One by-product of our approach to crime and punishment is a theory of collusion that appears to fill a good part of this lacuna.[69]

The gain to firms from colluding is positively related to the elasticity of their marginal cost curves and is inversely related to the elasticity of their collective demand curve. A firm that violates a collusive arrangement by pricing below or producing more than is specified can be said to commit an "offense" against the collusion. The resulting harm to the collusion would depend on the number of violations and on the elasticities of demand and marginal cost curves, since the gain from colluding depends on these elasticities.

If violations could be eliminated without cost, the optimal solution would obviously be to eliminate all of them and to engage in pure monopoly pricing. In general, however, as with other kinds of offenses, there are two costs of eliminating violations. There is first of all the cost of discovering violations and of "apprehending" violators. This cost is greater the greater the desired probability of detection and the greater the number of violations. Other things the same, the latter is usually positively related to the number of firms in an industry, which partly explains why economists typically relate monopoly power to concentration. The cost

---

68. Evidence relating to the effectiveness of actual, which are not necessarily optimal, penalties for these white-collar crimes can be found in Stigler (1962, 1966), Landes (1966), and Johnson (1967).

69. Jacob Mincer first suggested this application to me.

of achieving a given probability of detection also depends on the number of firms, on the number of customers, on the stability of customer buying patterns, and on government policies toward collusive arrangements (see Stigler, 1964).

Second, there is the cost to the collusion of punishing violators. The most favorable situation is one in which fines could be levied against violators and collected by the collusion. If fines and other legal recourse are ruled out, methods like predatory price-cutting or violence have to be used, and they hurt the collusion as well as violators.

Firms in a collusion are assumed to choose probabilities of detection, punishments to violators, and prices and outputs that minimize their loss from violations, which would at the same time maximize their gain from colluding. Optimal prices and outputs would be closer to the competitive position the more elastic demand curves were, the greater the number of sellers and buyers, the less transferable punishments were, and the more hostile to collusion governments were. Note that misallocation of resources could not be measured simply by the deviation of actual from competitive outputs but would depend also on the cost of enforcing collusions. Note further, and more importantly, that this theory, unlike most theories of pricing, provides for continuous variation, from purely competitive through intermediate situations to purely monopolistic pricing. These situations differ primarily because of differences in the "optimal" number of violations, which in turn are related to differences in the elasticities, concentrations, legislation, etc., already mentioned.

These ideas appear to be helpful in understanding the relative success of collusions in illegal industries themselves! Just as firms in legal industries have an incentive to collude to raise prices and profits, so too do firms producing illegal products, such as narcotics, gambling, prostitution, and abortion. The "syndicate" is an example of a presumably highly successful collusion that covers several illegal products.[70] In a country like the United States that prohibits collusions, those in illegal industries would seem to have

---

70. An interpretation of the syndicate along these lines is also found in Schilling (1967).

an advantage, because force and other illegal methods could be used against violators without the latter having much legal recourse. On the other hand, in countries like prewar Germany that legalized collusions, those in legal industries would have an advantage, because violators could often be legally prosecuted. One would predict, therefore, from this consideration alone, relatively more successful collusions in illegal industries in the United States, and in legal ones in prewar Germany.

SUMMARY AND CONCLUDING REMARKS

This essay uses economic analysis to develop optimal public and private policies to combat illegal behavior. The public's decision variables are its expenditures on police, courts, etc., which help determine the probability (p) that an offense is discovered and the offender apprehended and convicted, the size of the punishment for those convicted (f), and the form of the punishment: imprisonment, probation, fine, etc. Optimal values of these variables can be chosen subject to, among other things, the constraints imposed by three behavioral relations. One shows the damages caused by a given number of illegal actions, called offenses (O), another the cost of achieving a given p, and the third the effect of changes in p and f on O.

"Optimal" decisions are interpreted to mean decisions that minimize the social loss in income from offenses. This loss is the sum of damages, costs of apprehension and conviction, and costs of carrying out the punishments imposed, and can be minimized simultaneously with respect to p, f, and the form of f unless one or more of these variables is constrained by "outside" considerations. The optimality conditions derived from the minimization have numerous interesting implications that can be illustrated by a few examples.

If carrying out the punishment were costly, as it is with probation, imprisonment, or parole, the elasticity of response of offenses with respect to a change in p would generally, in equilibrium, have to exceed its response to a change in f. This implies, if entry into illegal activities can be explained by the same model of choice that economists use to explain entry into legal activities, that offenders are (at the margin) "risk preferrers." Consequently, illegal activities "would not pay" (at the margin) in the sense that the real income received would be less than what could be received in less risky legal activities. The conclusion that "crime would not pay" is an optimality condition and not an implication about the efficiency of the police or courts; indeed, it holds for any level of efficiency, as long as optimal values of p and f appropriate to each level are chosen.

If costs were the same, the optimal values of both p and f would be greater, the greater the damage caused by an offense. Therefore, offenses like murder and rape should be solved more frequently and punished more severely than milder offenses like auto theft and petty larceny. Evidence on actual probabilities and punishments in the United States is strongly consistent with this implication of the optimality analysis.

Fines have several advantages over other punishments: for example, they conserve resources, compensate society as well as punish offenders, and simplify the determination of optimal p's and f's. Not surprisingly, fines are the most common punishment and have grown in importance over time. Offenders who cannot pay fines have to be punished in other ways, but the optimality analysis implies that the monetary value to them of these punishments should generally be less than the fines.

Vengeance, deterrence, safety, rehabilitation, and compensation are perhaps the most important of the many desiderata proposed throughout history. Next to these, minimizing the social loss in income may seem narrow, bland, and even quaint. Unquestionably, the income criterion can be usefully generalized in several directions, and a few have already been suggested in the essay. Yet one should not lose sight of the fact that it is more general and powerful than it may seem and actually includes more dramatic desiderata as special cases. For example, if punishment were by an optimal fine, minimizing the loss in income would be equivalent to compensating "victims" fully and would eliminate the "alarm" that so worried Bentham; or it would be equivalent to deterring all offenses causing great damage if the cost of apprehending, convicting, and punishing these offenders were relatively small. Since the same could also be demonstrated for vengeance or rehabilitation, the moral should be clear: minimizing the loss in income is actually very general and thus is *more useful* than these catchy and dramatic but inflexible desiderata.

This essay concentrates almost entirely on determining optimal policies to combat illegal behavior and pays little attention to actual policies. The small amount of evidence on actual policies that I have examined certainly suggests a positive correspondence with optimal policies. For example, it is found for seven major felonies in the United States that more damaging ones are penalized more severely, that the elasticity of response of offenses to changes in p exceeds the response to f, and that both are usually less than unity, all as predicted by the optimality analysis. There are, however, some discrepancies too: for example, the actual tradeoff between imprisonment and fines in different statutes is frequently less, rather than the predicted more, favorable to those imprisoned. Although many more studies of actual policies are needed, they are seriously hampered on the empirical side by grave limitations in the quantity and quality of data on offenses, convictions, costs, etc., and on the analytical side by the absence of a reliable theory of political decision-making.

Reasonable men will often differ on the amount of damages or benefits caused by different activities. To some, any wage rates set by competitive labor markets are permissible, while to others, rates below a certain minimum are violations of basic rights; to some, gambling, prostitution, and even abortion should be freely available to anyone willing to pay the market price, while to others, gambling is sinful and abortion is murder. These differences are basic to the development and implementation of public policy but have been excluded from my inquiry. I assume consensus on damages and benefits and simply try to work out rules for an optimal implementation of this consensus.

The main contribution of this essay, as I see it, is to demonstrate that optimal policies to combat illegal behavior are part of an optimal allocation of resources. Since economics has been developed to handle resource allocation, an "economic" framework becomes applicable to, and helps enrich, the analysis of illegal behavior. At the same time, certain unique aspects of the latter enrich economic analysis: some punishments, such as imprisonments, are necessarily nonmonetary and are a cost to society as well as to offenders; the degree of uncertainty is a decision variable that enters both the revenue and cost functions; etc.

Lest the reader be repelled by the apparent novelty of an "economic" framework for illegal behavior, let him recall that two important contributors to criminology during the eighteenth and nineteenth centuries, Beccaria and Bentham, explicitly applied an economic calculus. Unfortunately, such an approach has lost favor during the last hundred years, and my efforts can be viewed as a resurrection, modernization, and thereby I hope improvement on these much earlier pioneering studies.

MATHEMATICAL APPENDIX

This Appendix derives the effects of changes in various parameters on the optimal values of p and f. It is assumed throughout that $b > 0$ and that equilibrium occurs where

$$\frac{\partial D}{\partial O} + \frac{\partial C}{\partial O} + \frac{\partial C}{\partial p}\frac{\partial p}{\partial O} = D' + C' + C_p\frac{\partial p}{\partial O} > 0;$$

the analysis could easily be extended to cover negative values of b and of this marginal cost term. The conclusion in the text that $D'' + C'' > 0$ is relied on here. I take it to be a reasonable first approximation that the elasticities of O with respect to p or f are constant. At several places a sufficient condition for the conclusions reached is that

$$C_{po} = C_{Op} = \frac{\partial^2 C}{\partial p\partial O} = \frac{\partial^2 C}{\partial O\partial p}$$

is "small" relative to some other terms. This condition is utilized in the form of a strong assumption that $C_{po} = 0$, although I cannot claim any supporting intuitive or other evidence.

The social loss in income from offenses has been defined as

$$L = D(O) + C(O, p) + bpfO. \tag{A1}$$

If b and p were fixed, the value of f that minimized L would be found from the necessary condition

$$\frac{\partial L}{\partial f} = 0 = (D' + C') \frac{\partial O}{\partial f} + bpf(1 - E_f) \frac{\partial O}{\partial f}, \qquad (A2)$$

or

if

$$0 = D' + C' + bpf(1 - E_f), \qquad (A3)$$

$$\frac{\partial O}{\partial f} = O_f \neq 0,$$

where

$$E_f = \frac{-\partial_f}{\partial O} \frac{O}{f}$$

The sufficient condition would be that $\partial^2 L / \partial f^2 > 0$; using $\partial L / \partial f = 0$ and E_f is constant, this condition becomes

$$\frac{\partial^2 L}{\partial f^2} = (D'' + C'')O_f^2 + bp(1 - E_f)O_f > 0, \qquad (A4)$$

or

$$\Delta \equiv D'' + C'' + bp(1 - E_f) \frac{1}{O_f} > 0. \qquad (A5)$$

Since $D' + C' > 0$, and b is not less than zero, equation (A3) implies that $E_f > 1$. Therefore Δ would be greater than zero, since we are assuming that $D'' + C'' > 0$; and $\hat{f}$, the value of f satisfying (A3), would minimize (locally) the loss L.

Suppose that D' is positively related to an exogenous variable a. The effect of a change in a on $\hat{f}$ can be found by differentiating equation (A3):

$$D'a + (D'' + C'')O_f \frac{d\hat{f}}{da} + bp(1 - E_f) \frac{d\hat{f}}{da} = 0,$$

or

$$\frac{d\hat{f}}{da} = \frac{-D'a(1/O_f).}{\Delta} \qquad (A6)$$

Since $\Delta > 0$, $O_f < 0$, and by assumption $D'_a > 0$, then

$$\frac{d\hat{f}}{da} = \frac{+}{+} > 0. \qquad (A7)$$

In a similar way it can be shown that, if C' is positively related to an exogenous variable β,

$$\frac{d\hat{f}}{d\beta} = \frac{-C_\beta'(1/O_f)}{\Delta} = \frac{+}{+} > 0. \qquad (A8)$$

If b is positively related to γ, then

$$(D'' + C'')O_f \frac{d\hat{f}}{d\gamma} + bp(1 - E_t)\frac{d\hat{f}}{d\gamma} + pf(1 - E_f)b\gamma = 0,$$

or

$$\frac{d\hat{f}}{d\gamma} = \frac{-b_\gamma pf(1 - E_f)(1/O_f)}{\Delta}. \qquad (A9)$$

Since $1 - E_f < 0$, and by assumption $b_\gamma > O$,

$$\frac{d\hat{f}}{d\gamma} = \frac{-}{+} < 0. \qquad (A10)$$

Note that since $1/E_f < 1$,

$$\frac{d(p\hat{f}O)}{d\gamma} < 0. \qquad (A11)$$

If E_f is positively related to δ, then

$$\frac{d\hat{f}}{d\delta} = \frac{E_{f\delta}bpf(1/O_t)}{\Delta} = \frac{-}{+} < 0. \qquad (A12)$$

Since the elasticity of O with respect to f equals

$$\epsilon_f = -O_f \frac{f}{O} = \frac{1}{E_f},$$

by (A12), a reduction in ϵ_f would reduce $\hat{f}$.

Suppose that p is related to the exogeneous variable r. Then the effect of a shift in r on $\hat{f}$ can be found from

$$(D'' + C'')O_f \frac{d\hat{f}}{dr} + (D'' + C'')O_p p_r + C_{po}p_r$$
$$+ bp(1 - E_f)\frac{\partial \hat{f}}{\partial r} + bf(1 - E_f)p_r = 0,$$

or

$$\frac{d\hat{f}}{dr} = \frac{-(D'' + C'')O_p(1/O_f)p_r - bf(1 - E_f)p_r(1/O_f),}{\Delta} \qquad (A13)$$

since by assumption $C_{po} = 0$. Since $O_p < 0$, and $(D'' + C'') > 0$,

$$\frac{d\hat{f}}{dr} = \frac{(-) + (-)}{+} = \frac{-}{+} < 0. \qquad (A14)$$

If f rather than p were fixed, the value of p that minimizes L, $\hat{p}$, could be found from

$$\frac{\partial L}{\partial p} = \left[D' + C' + C_p \frac{1}{O_p} + bpf(1 - E_p) \right] O_p = 0, \qquad (A15)$$

as long as

$$\frac{\partial^2 L}{\partial p^2} = \left[(D'' + C'')O_p + C'_p + C_{pp}\frac{1}{O_p} + C_{po} + C_p \frac{\partial^2 p}{\partial O \partial p} \right.$$
$$\left. + bf(1 - E_p) \right] O_p > 0. \quad \text{(A16)}$$

Since $C'_p = C_{po} = 0$, (A16) would hold if

$$\Delta' \equiv D'' + C'' + C_{pp}\frac{1}{O_p^2} + C_p \frac{1}{O_p}\frac{\partial^2 p}{\partial O \partial p} + bf(1 - E_p)\frac{1}{O_p} > 0. \quad \text{(A17)}$$

It is suggested in the text that C_{pp} is generally greater than zero. If, as assumed,

$$D' + C' + C_p \frac{1}{O_p} > 0,$$

equation (A15) implies that $E_p > 1$ and thus that

$$bf(1 - E_p)\frac{1}{O_p} > 0.$$

If E_p were constant, $\partial^2 p / \partial O \partial p$ would be negative,[71] and, therefore, $C_p(1/O_p)(\partial^2 p/\partial O \partial p)$ would be positive. Hence, none of the terms of (A17) are negative, and a value of p satisfying equation (A15) would be a local minimum.

The effects of changes in different parameters on $\hat{p}$ are similar to those already derived for $\hat{f}$ and can be written without comment:

$$\frac{d\hat{p}}{da} = \frac{-D'_a(1/O_p)}{\Delta'} > 0, \quad \text{(A18)}$$

$$\frac{d\hat{p}}{d\beta} = \frac{-C'_\beta(1/O_p)}{\Delta'} > 0, \quad \text{(A19)}$$

and

$$\frac{d\hat{p}}{d\gamma} = \frac{-b_\gamma pf(1 - E_p)(1/O_p)}{\Delta'} < 0. \quad \text{(A20)}$$

---

71. If E_p and E_f are constants, $O = kp^{-a}f^{-b}$, where $a = 1/E_p$ and $b = 1/E_f$. Then

$$\frac{\partial p}{\partial O} = -\frac{1}{ka}p^{a+1}f^b,$$

and

$$\frac{\partial^2 p}{\partial O \partial p} = \frac{-(a+1)}{ka}p^a f^b < 0.$$

If E_p is positively related to δ',

$$\frac{d\hat{p}}{d\delta'} = \frac{E_{p\delta'}bpf(1/O_p)}{\Delta'} < 0. \qquad \text{(A21)}$$

If C_p were positively related to the parameter s, the effect of a change in s on $\hat{p}$ would equal

$$\frac{d\hat{p}}{ds} = \frac{-C_{ps}(1/O_p{}^2)}{\Delta'} < 0. \qquad \text{(A22)}$$

If f were related to the exogenous parameter t, the effect of a change in t on $\hat{p}$ would be given by

$$\frac{d\hat{p}}{dt} = \frac{-(D'' + C'')O_pf_t(1/O_p) - bf(1 - E_p)f_t(1/O_p) - C_p(\partial^2p/\partial O\,\partial f)f_t(1/O_p)}{\Delta'} < 0 \qquad \text{(A23)}$$

(with $C_{po} = 0$), since all the terms in the numerator are negative.

If both p and f were subject to control, L would be minimized by choosing optimal values of both variables simultaneously. These would be given by the solutions to the two first-order conditions, equations (A2) and (A15), assuming that certain more general second-order conditions were satisfied. The effects of changes in various parameters on these optimal values can be found by differentiating both first-order conditions and incorporating the restrictions of the second-order conditions.

The values of p and f satisfying (A2) and (A15), $\hat{p}$ and $\hat{f}$, minimize L if

$$L_{pp} > 0, \ L_{ff} > 0, \qquad \text{(A24)}$$

and

$$L_{pp}L_{ff} > L^2{}_{fp} = L^2{}_{pf} \qquad \text{(A25)}$$

But $L_{pp} = O_p{}^2\Delta'$, and $L_{ff} = O_f{}^2\Delta$, and since both Δ' and Δ have been shown to be greater than zero, (A24) is proved already, and only (A25) remains. By differentiating L_f with respect to p and utilizing the first-order condition that $L_f = 0$, one has

$$L_{fp} = O_fO_p[D'' + C'' + bf(1 - E_f)p_0] = O_fO_p\Sigma, \qquad \text{(A26)}$$

where Σ equals the term in brackets. Clearly $\Sigma > 0$.

By substitution, (A25) becomes

$$\Delta\Delta' > \Sigma^2, \qquad \text{(A27)}$$

and (A27) holds if Δ and Δ' are both greater than Σ. $\Delta > \Sigma$ means that

$$D'' + C'' + bp(1 - E_f)f_0 > D'' + C'' + bf(1 - E_f)p_0,$$

(A28)

or

$$\frac{bfp}{O}(1 - E_f)E_t < \frac{bpf}{O}(1 - E_f)E_p.$$

(A29)

Since $1 - E_f < 0$, (A29) implies that

$$E_f > E_p,$$

(A30)

which necessarily holds given the assumption that $b > 0$; prove this by combining the two first-order conditions (A2) and (A15). $\Delta' > \Sigma$ means that

$$D'' + C'' + C_{pp}p_0{}^2 + C_p p_0 p_{0p} + bf(1 - E_p)p_0 > D'' + C'' + bf(1 - E_f)p_0.$$

(A31)

Since $C_{pp}p_0{}^2 > 0$, and $p_0 < 0$, this necessarily holds if

$$C_p p p_{0p} + bpf(1 - E_p) < bpf(1 - E_f).$$

(A32)

By eliminating $D' + C'$ from the first-order conditions (A2) and (A15) and by combining terms, one has

$$C_p p_0 - bpf(E_p - E_f) = 0.$$

(A33)

By combining (A32) and (A33), one gets the condition

$$C_p p p_{0p} < C_p p_0,$$

(A34)

or

$$E_{p_0,p} = \frac{p}{p_0}\frac{\partial p_0}{\partial p} > 1.$$

(A35)

It can be shown that

$$E_{p_0,p} = 1 + \frac{1}{E_p} > 1,$$

(A36)

and, therefore, (A35) is proven.

It has now been proven that the values of p and f that satisfy the first-order conditions (A2) and (A15) do indeed minimize (locally) L. Changes in different parameters change these optimal values, and the direction and magnitude can be found from the two linear equations

$$O_f\Delta\,\frac{\partial \bar{f}}{\partial z} + O_p\Sigma\,\frac{\partial \bar{p}}{\partial z} = C_1$$

and $\hspace{6cm}$ (A37)

$$O_f \Sigma \frac{\partial \tilde{f}}{\partial z} + O_p \Delta' \frac{\partial \tilde{p}}{\partial z} = C_2.$$

By Cramer's rule,

$$\frac{\partial \tilde{f}}{\partial z} = \frac{C_1 O_p \Delta' - C_2 O_p \Sigma}{O_p O_f (\Delta \Delta' - \Sigma^2)} = \frac{O_p (C_1 \Delta' - C_2 \Sigma)}{+}, \hspace{1cm} (A38)$$

$$\frac{\partial \tilde{p}}{\partial z} = \frac{C_2 O_f \Delta - C_1 O_f \Sigma}{O_p O_f (\Delta \Delta' - \Sigma^2)} = \frac{O_f (C_2 \Delta - C_1 \Sigma)}{+}, \hspace{1cm} (A39)$$

and the signs of both derivatives are the same as the signs of the numerators.

Consider the effect of a change in D' resulting from a change in the parameter a. It is apparent that $C_1 = C_2 = -D'_a$, and by substitution

$$\frac{\partial \tilde{f}}{\partial a} = \frac{- O_p D'_a (\Delta' - \Sigma)}{+} = \frac{+}{+} > 0 \hspace{1cm} (A40)$$

and

$$\frac{\partial \tilde{p}}{\partial a} = \frac{- O_p D'_a (\Delta - \Sigma)}{+} = \frac{+}{+} > 0, \hspace{1cm} (A41)$$

since O_f and $O_p < 0$, $D'_a > 0$, and Δ and $\Delta' > \Sigma$.

Similarly, if C' is changed by a change in β, $C_1 = C_2 = -C'_\beta$,

$$\frac{\partial \tilde{f}}{\partial \beta} = \frac{-O_p C'_\beta (\Delta' - \Sigma)}{+} = \frac{+}{+} > 0, \hspace{1cm} (A42)$$

and

$$\frac{\partial \tilde{p}}{\partial \beta} = \frac{-O_f C'_\beta (\Delta - \Sigma)}{+} = \frac{+}{+} > 0. \hspace{1cm} (A43)$$

If E_f is changed by a change in δ, $C_1 = E_{f\delta} bpf$, $C_2 = 0$,

$$\frac{\partial \tilde{f}}{\partial \delta} = \frac{O_p E_f bpf \Delta'}{+} = \frac{-}{+} < 0, \hspace{1cm} (A44)$$

and

$$\frac{\partial \tilde{p}}{\partial \delta} = \frac{- O_f E_f bpf \Sigma}{+} = \frac{+}{+} > 0. \hspace{1cm} (A45)$$

Similarly, if E_p is changed by a change in δ', $C_1 = 0$, $C_2 = E_{p\delta'} bpf$,

$$\frac{\partial \tilde{f}}{\partial \delta'} = - \frac{O_p E_{p\delta'} bpf \Sigma}{+} = \frac{+}{+} > 0, \hspace{1cm} (A46)$$

and

$$\frac{\partial \tilde{p}}{\partial \delta'} = \frac{O_f E_{p\delta'} bpf \Delta}{+} = \frac{-}{+} < 0. \tag{A47}$$

If b is changed by a change in γ, $C_1 = -b_\gamma pf(1 - E_f)$, $C_2 = -b_\gamma pf(1 - E_p)$, and

$$\frac{\partial \tilde{f}}{\partial \gamma} = \frac{-O_p b_\gamma pf[(1 - E_f)\Delta' - (1 - E_p)\Sigma]}{+} = \frac{-}{+} < 0, \tag{A48}$$

since $E_f > E_p > 1$ and $\Delta' > \Sigma$; also,

$$\frac{\partial \tilde{p}}{\partial \gamma} = \frac{- O_f b_\gamma pf[(1 - E_p)\Delta - (1 - E_f)\Sigma]}{+} = \frac{+}{+} > 0, \tag{A49}$$

for it can be shown that $(1 - E_p)\Delta > (1 - E_f)\Sigma$.[72] Note that when f is held constant the optimal value of p is decreased, not increased, by an increase in γ.

If C_p is changed by a change in s, $C_2 = -p_0 C_{ps}$, $C_1 = 0$,

$$\frac{\partial \tilde{f}}{\partial s} = \frac{O_p p_0 C_{ps}\Sigma}{+} = \frac{C_{ps}\Sigma}{+} = \frac{+}{+} > 0, \tag{A50}$$

and

$$\frac{\partial \tilde{p}}{\partial s} = \frac{- O_f p_0 C_{ps}\Delta}{+} = \frac{-}{+} < 0. \tag{A51}$$

REFERENCES

Arrow, Kenneth J.: Economic welfare and allocation of resources for invention, In National Bureau Committee for Economic Research: *The Rate and Direction of Inventive Activity: Economic and Social Factors.* Princeton, Princeton U Pr (for the Natl Bureau of Econ Res), 1962.

---

72. The term $(1 - E_p)\Delta$ would be greater than $(1 - E_f)\Sigma$ if

$$(D'' + C'')(1 - E_p) + bp(1 - E_f)(1 - E_p)f_0 > (D'' + C'')(1 - E_f) + bf(1 - E_f)^2 p_0,$$

or

$$(D'' + C'')(E_f - E_p) > -\frac{bpf}{O}(1 - E_f)\left[(1 - E_p)\frac{f_0 O}{f} - (1 - E_f)\frac{p_0 O}{p}\right],$$

$$(D'' + C'')(E_f - E_p) > -\frac{bpf}{O}(1 - E_f)[(1 - E_p)(E_f) - (1 - E_f)E_p],$$

$$(D'' + C'')(E_f - E_p) > -\frac{bpf}{O}(1 - E_f)(E_f - E_p).$$

Since the left-hand side is greater than zero, and the right-hand side is less than zero, the inequality must hold.

Becker, Gary S.: Irrational behavior and economic theory. *J.P.E.*, Vol. LXX, February, 1962.
————: A theory of the allocation of time. *Econ J*, Vol. LXXV, September, 1965.
Bentham, Jeremy: *Theory of Legislation.* New York, Har Brace, 1931.
Bureau of the Budget: *The Budget of United States Government, 1968, Appendix.* Washington, U.S. Government Printing Office, 1967.
Bureau of Prisons: *Prisoners Released from State and Federal Institutions.* ("National Prisoner Statistics.") Washington, U.S. Dept. of Justice, 1960.
————: *Characteristics of State Prisoners, 1960.* ("National Prisoner Statistics.") U.S. Dept. of Justice, n.d.
————: *Federal Prisons, 1960.* Washington, U.S. Dept. of Justice, 1961.
Cagan, Phillip: *Determinants and Effects of Changes in the Stock of Money, 1875-1960.* New York, Columbia U Pr (for the Natl Bureau of Econ Res), 1965.
Criminal safeguards and the punitive damages defendant. *Univ Chicago Law Rev*, Vol. XXXIV, Winter, 1967.
Ehrlich, Isaac: The Supply of Illegitimate Activities, Unpublished manuscript, Columbia Univ., New York, 1967.
Federal Bureau of Investigation. *Uniform Crime Reports for the United States.* Washington, U.S. Dept. of Justice, 1960.
————: *Ibid.*, 1961.
Harper, F. V., and James, F.: *The Law of Torts.* Boston, Little, 1956, Vol. II.
Johnson, Thomas: The Effects of the Minimum Wage Law, Unpublished Ph.D. dissertation, Columbia Univ., New York, 1967.
Kleinman, E.: *The Choice between Two "Bads"—Some Economic Aspects of Criminal Sentencing,* Unpublished manuscript, Hebrew Univ., Jerusalem, 1967.
Landes, William: *The Effect of State Fair Employment Legislation on the Economic Position of Nonwhite Males,* Unpublished Ph.D. dissertation, Columbia Univ., New York, 1966.
Laws of New York, Vol. II, 1965.
Marshall, Alfred: *Principles of Economics,* 8th ed. New York, Macmillan, 1961.
Plant, A.: The economic theory concerning patents for inventions. *Economica*, Vol. I, February, 1934.
Pollock, F., and Maitland, F. W.: *The History of English Law,* 2d ed. Cambridge, Cambridge U. Pr, 1952, Vol. II.
President's Commission on Law Enforcement and Administration of Justice: *The Challenge of Crime in a Free Society.* Washington, U.S. Government Printing Office, 1967 (*a*).
————: *Corrections.* ("Task Force Reports.") Washington, U.S. Government Printing Office, 1967 (*b*).

————: *The Courts.* ("Task Force Reports.") Washington, U.S. Government Printing Office, 1967(c).

————: *Crime and Its Impact—an Assessment.* ("Task Force Reports.") Washington, U.S. Government Printing Office, 1967(d).

————: *Science and Technology.* ("Task Force Reports.") Washington, U.S. Government Printing Office, 1967(e).

Radzinowicz, L.: *A History of English Criminal Law and Its Administration from 1750.* London, Stevens & Sons, 1948, Vol. I.

Schilling, T. C.: Economic analysis of organized crime. In President's Commission on Law Enforcement and Administration of Justice: *Organized Crime.* ("Task Force Reports.") Washington, U.S. Government Printing Office, 1967.

Shawness, Lord: Crime *does* pay because we do not back up the police. *New York Times Magazine,* June 13. 1965.

Smigel, Arleen: *Crime and Punishment: An Economic Analysis,* Unpublished M.A. thesis, Columbia Univ., New York, 1965.

Stigler, George J.: What can regulators regulate? The case of electricity. *J Law and Econ,* Vol. V, October, 1962.

————: A theory of oligopoly. *J.P.E.,* Vol. LXXII, February, 1964.

————: The economic effects of the antitrust laws. *J Law Econ,* Vol. IX, October, 1966.

Sutherland, E. H.: *Principles of Criminology,* 6th ed. Philadelphia, Lippincott, 1960.

Chapter 2

ON THE ECONOMICS OF
LAW AND ORDER

JOHN R. HARRIS

PROFESSOR BECKER has recently demonstrated the usefulness of "conventional" economic analysis in coming to grips with what is usually considered to be a noneconomic problem—crime and punishment (Becker 1968). In the article, he derives criteria for optimal levels of expenditure on law enforcement and form of punishment subject to a given legal framework. The point of this paper is that the legal framework need not be taken as constant but is itself subject to policy choice. Therefore, I propose to extend the Becker framework to take account of this additional area of social choice and compare the implications of this model with the original, less complete version.

Among countries and over time, one can find enormous variations in "rules of the game" pertaining to standards of evidence, presumption of guilt, rights to counsel, and procedures for arrest and indictment. Rulings of the U.S. Supreme Court upholding rights of accused persons and restricting the freedom of police to obtain evidence in certain ways have become a major political issue of late.

Indeed, the Becker model as formulated would seem to agree with some proponents of "law and order" who argue that it is undesirable to tie the hands of the police with legal niceties. After all, it is quite clear that the costs of apprehending and convicting a given percentage of offenders will be lower without these con-

This paper was written while I was Visiting Research Fellow, University College, Nairobi, Kenya. Financial support from the Rockefeller Foundation is gratefully acknowledged.

Reprinted, with permission of the University of Chicago Press, from *Journal of Political Economy*, January/February 1970, pp. 165-174.

ventions than it would be with them. Note that in certain conditions, such as a state of martial law, many legal safeguards are relaxed, presumably to apprehend a maximum proportion of offenders with minimum cost. Despite Geneva Conventions, it has not been unknown for occupying armies to punish entire communities when certain offenses are thought to have been committed by some members. Military policies in Kenya during the Mau Mau Emergency and in Vietnam have smacked of this at times. Why are such apparent cost-minimizing procedures not pursued more generally? The answer must be that there are social costs of other types incurred when apprehension and conviction are made easier.

Certainly there is a loss to society if an innocent person is wrongly punished. It follows from the logic of probabilistic systems that, as the probability of a guilty person going unpunished (a Type I error) is reduced the probability of an innocent person being punished (a Type II error) is increased. The lower the cost of apprehending and punishing a given proportion of offenders at a given level of offenses, the higher will be the incidence of wrongful punishment. (It should be noted that even if convictions do not result, such procedures as "stop and search" or wiretapping impose forms of punishment on the innocent.) Obviously, the harsher the punishment, the greater is the social loss when it is imposed wrongly.[1] This can be represented as

$$R = R(p, O, a, f), \tag{1}$$

where R is the social loss from wrongful punishment, p is the probability of an offender being convicted, O is the number of offenses committed, a is a variable which reflects the degree of legal safeguards for suspects (greater safeguards are reflected in a higher value of a), and f is the punishment meted out to a convicted person.[2] In accordance with the above discussion, it

1. There is evidence (Schwartz and Skolnick, 1964) that individuals who have been brought to trial and acquitted for certain offenses bear continuing punishment from society in the form of job discrimination, in addition to the not inconsiderable punishments of pretrial incarceration and the cost of legal defense.

2. I follow Becker in suppressing the subscripts which indicate the particular offense. There would be one such loss function for each class of crime; the arguments of the function would each be crime specific.

is assumed that

$$R_p, R_0, R_f > 0,$$
$$R_a < 0,$$

(2)

where the subscripts indicate partial derivatives of R with respect to the subscripted variable. It is further assumed that

$$R_{pp}, R_{00}, R_{ff} > 0,$$
$$R_{aa} < 0,$$
$$R_{p0} = R_{0p}, \quad R_{pf} = R_{fp}, \quad R_{0f} = R_{f0} > 0,$$
$$R_{pa} = R_{ap}, \quad R_{0a} = R_{a0}, \quad R_{af} = R_{fa} < 0.$$

(3)

The supply of offenses can be indicated as

$$O = O(p, f, a, u),$$

(4)

where u is an undefined structural parameter (see Becker 1968, p. 178). It is assumed that

$$O_p, O_f < 0, O_a > 0,$$
$$O_{pp} \; O_{ff} > 0, O_{aa} < 0.$$

(5)

The term $O_a > 0$ reflects the oft-stated notion that legal protection encourages crime, while the previous two terms reflect the deterrent effects of conviction and punishment. The second derivatives reflect diminishing marginal rates of deterrence and encouragement which seem reasonable a priori.[3]

---

3. Evidence on the deterrent effects of apprehension and punishment is needed. It is likely, however, that crimes of passion are less affected than those more subject to calculation. It should also be recognized that, when punishment exceeds what are considered reasonable levels or is applied without selectivity, criminal acts may become politicized and thereby increase in frequency. This is particularly evident in military occupations where harsh administration of law has sometimes contributed to the formation of an organized resistance movement. There is some evidence that resentment of the law has recently contributed to organized defiance in U.S. cities. Even if punishment has a deterrent effect on the frequency of a particular crime, it may have unintended effects on the severity of the criminal act. An example is provided by the introduction in Uganda of a mandatory death penalty for robbery. No evidence is available to determine whether the incidence of robbery has decreased since the legislation, but it is clear that a greater proportion of robberies now end in murder of the victim since the criminal has an incentive to eliminate witnesses without incurring any additional penalty if caught.

Following Becker, I define the direct social loss from a crime as

$$D = D(O),$$
$$D' > 0, \quad D'' > 0 \tag{6}$$

and the social loss from imposing punishment as

$$bpOf, \tag{7}$$

where b is a parameter reflecting the social losses from imposing a particular punishment f.[4] Generally, b will be presumed to be positive.

The cost of apprehending and convicting offenders can be indicated as

$$C = C(p, O, a), \tag{8}$$

with

$$C_p, C_O, C_a > 0 \tag{9}$$

and

$$C_{pp}, C_{OO}, C_{aa} > 0,$$
$$C_{pO} = C_{Op} \cong 0,$$
$$C_{pa} = C_{ap} > 0, \tag{10}$$
$$C_{Oa} = C_{aO} > 0.$$

With these building blocks, the total loss to society arising from crime, crime fighting, and punishment can be written as

$$L = D(O) + C(p, O, a,) + R(p, O, a, f) + bpOf. \tag{11}$$

Given control over the values of p, f, and a, society is assumed to attempt to minimize the value of L. The first-order conditions for such minimization are

$$\frac{\partial L}{\partial P} D'O_p + C_OO_p + R_OO_p + C_p + R_p + bpfO_p + bfO = 0, \tag{12}$$

$$\frac{\partial L}{\partial f} = D'O_f + C_OO_f + R_OO_f + R_f + bpfO_f + bpO = 0, \tag{13}$$

---

4. A very different view of the rationale for declaring certain acts to be deviant is set forth by Erikson (1964). He argues that deviance is necessary for societal boundary definition and maintenance. "Thus deviance cannot be dismissed simply as behavior which *disrupts* stability in society, but may itself be, in controlled quantities, an important condition for *preserving* stability" (p. 15, italics in original).

and

$$\frac{\partial L}{\partial a} = D'O_a + C_0 O_a + R_0 O_a + C_a + R_a + bpf O_a = 0. \quad (14)$$

Providing O_p, O_f, and O_a are not equal to zero, these conditions can be rewritten as

$$D' + C_0 + R_0 + (C_p + R_p)\frac{1}{O_p} = -bpf\left(1 - \frac{1}{\epsilon_p}\right), \quad (15)$$

$$D' + C_0 + R_0 + R_f\frac{1}{O_f} = -bpf\left(1 - \frac{1}{\epsilon_f}\right), \quad (16)$$

and

$$(D' + C_0 + R_0 + bpf)\, O_a = -(C_a + R_a), \quad (17)$$

where

$$\epsilon_f = -\frac{f}{O}O_f,$$
$$\quad (18)$$
$$\epsilon_p = -\frac{p}{O}O_p.$$

Conditions (15) and (16) differ from Becker's first-order conditions by the terms $[R_0 + R_p(1/O_p)]$ and $[R_0 + R_f(1/O_f)]$, respectively. In each case the marginal cost of increasing the number of offenses (through decreasing p in [15] and f in [16]) is increased by the fact that, with more offenses, more innocent persons will be punished and is diminished by the fact that, as p declines, so will the probability of an innocent person being punished and that, as f declines, the severity of unjust punishment declines. Although it is not possible to specify the relative magnitudes of these terms with any precision in the absence of empirical specification of the R function, it seems reasonable to assume that these terms will be negative in sign—that is, social losses from unjust punishment will be more sensitive to changing p and f than to changes in the level of offenses. If that is indeed the case, and if the right-hand sides of equations (15) and (16) are held constant, it follows that the optimum levels of crime will be higher (for a given legal framework) than they would be in the absence of the R term in (11). Conversely, the optimal intensity of apprehension and the level of punishment will likely be lowered when social costs of unjust convictions are taken into account.

It is also likely that Becker's conditions ϵ_p, $\epsilon_f < 1$, and $\epsilon_p < \epsilon_f$

will continue to hold, although the addition of negative terms on the left-hand sides of both (15) and (16) relax the requirements.

Equation (17) gives the additional first-order condition arising from the fact that a is a parameter subject to policy choice. The left-hand side can be interpreted as the marginal cost of the additional crime arising from increasing the legal safeguards for suspected offenders. All of the terms on the left-hand side are positive. Therefore, the equation will hold only if the right-hand side is also positive. Since $C_a > 0$ and $R_a < 0$, it follows that the social gain from reducing the number of unjustly punished persons must exceed the social cost imposed on the law-enforcement system by such safeguards by some (perhaps considerable) margin.

It can be shown (see Appendix) that, for given levels of p and f, a shift in the R function such that R_p or R_f are increased will call for an increase in a. With a and f held constant, such a shift in the R function will call for a reduction of p. And with a and p held constant, such a shift will call for a reduction in f. The interpretation is clear; if the perceived social loss arising from unjust punishment rises, greater legal safeguards and lower levels of apprehension and punishment will be called for. Alternatively, increased loss from crimes calls for increases in apprehension and punishment and for relaxed legal safeguards. If costs of apprehension rise, harsher punishments and relaxed legal safeguards will be required. However, in these latter two cases, the increases in punishment and relaxation of legal safeguards will be less than they would be in the absence of the R function.[5]

This analysis may help shed some light on the recent public controversies over U.S. Supreme Court rulings. It is quite clear that loss from crimes and unjust punishment will be evaluated differently by different individuals. With respect to crimes against property, property owners have more to lose and will, therefore, judge potential loss to be greater than will those people with little to lose. Also, higher-income persons are more likely to feel the

5. When all three parameters—p, f, a—are free to vary simultaneously, these same findings are likely to hold, although the signs of the terms are in general ambiguous and depend on restrictions on relative magnitudes of cross-partial derivatives that are hard to justify a priori.

sting of taxes being raised to cover increasing costs of providing police and court protection.

On the other hand, one's estimate of the loss from unjust punishment is at least in part related to one's prospects of suffering such a fate. It is fairly well established that arbitrary police action is more likely to be directed against low-income, poorly dressed individuals from ethnic minorities. Furthermore, higher-income, better-educated individuals are more likely to be aware of their rights and to be able to obtain legal counsel and bail. One need have but little contact with the law to be aware that treatment varies widely among social groups.

Therefore, it is little wonder that support of measures like "stop and search" receive much greater support from the white community, which has more to lose from crime and less chance of being apprehended without cause than does the black community. It is interesting to speculate on the historical relationship between guarantees of civil liberties and rights under law and growing political power of previously disenfranchised classes. Was it not at least in part the political power of those classes that suffered most from arbitrary and unjust punishment that led to greater legal safeguards for all? Does the growing public clamor over law and order reflect growing stratification—of the movement of the United States toward "two nations, one black and one white?"

It is also interesting to note that in some recently independent African countries there has been considerable increase in harsh punishment of late as law and order has become a leading political issue. Uganda recently introduced mandatory death penalties for armed robbery, and the same has been proposed in Kenya. A rather severe vagrancy act, removing some previous safeguards against arbitrary search and arrest, was enacted in Kenya in 1969. Introduction and strengthening of detention laws have also been commonplace (Zolberg 1966, pp. 66, 78, 82-87). Former British colonies inherited English Common Law with its entire tradition of procedures and rights. Although under colonial rule administrative and extralegal punishments were often resorted to—(the Kenya emergency of 1952 to 1959 is a notable example [Rosberg and Nottingham 1966, esp. Chaps. 1 and 8]) the ideas and practices of British law were generally held in high regard by nationalist leaders and, at the time of independence, were generally considered legitimate.

It is tempting to interpret the move toward tightening of the law and increasing harshness of punishment as evidence of growing social and economic stratification within these societies. With respect to political "crimes," it is obvious that a political class feels great potential loss from acts of political opposition which it suppresses through law. But these political classes have also become property-owning classes (Sklar 1963, 1964; Bretton 1966). More stringent laws aimed at crimes against property may reflect the fact that this class has more to lose from such crimes and at the same time is itself relatively immune from arbitrary police action and unwarranted punishment.

This extended framework provides an approach to the problem of law and order. It takes into account the legal framework which, along with intensity of police activity and levels of punishment, is subject to policy choice. While we may well admire the relative power of economic analysis to illuminate such a problem, the latter discussion of an optimal legal framework should also serve to make clear the limitations of such an approach. Optimal levels of the policy variables depend on how various losses are perceived. It is clear that these losses will be perceived differently among social and economic groups within any society. The political process will determine how the interests of various groups will be reconciled or which groups will be able to impose their will on the rest of the society. Unfortunately, the economic approach is rather powerless to shed light on resolution of group conflict.

APPENDIX

The social loss from offenses, apprehension, unjust punishment, and punishment has been defined as

$$L = D(O) + C(p, O, f, a) + R(p, O, f, a) + bpfO. \quad (A1)$$

If p and f were fixed, the value of a that minimizes $L(\hat{a})$ can be found from

$$L_a = \frac{\partial L}{\partial_a} = \left[D' + C_0 + R_0 + (C_a + R_a) \frac{1}{O_a} + bpf \right] O_a = 0,$$

$$(A2)$$

providing

$$L_{aa} = \frac{\partial^2 L}{\partial_a{}^2} = \left[D'' + C_{oo} + R_{oo} + 2(C_{oa} + R_{oa}) \frac{1}{O_a} \right.$$

$$\left. + (C_{aa} + R_{aa}) \frac{1}{O_a{}^2} + (C_a + R_a)\left(\frac{-O_{aa}}{O_a{}^3}\right) \right] O_a{}^2 > 0. \quad (A3)$$

All of the terms in (A3) are positive except for R_{oa}, R_{aa}, and R_a. Thus, the magnitude of these variables will have to be restricted if (A3) is to hold. There is no a priori reason to believe that (A3) will not in general be satisfied.

Suppose that D' is positively related to an exogenous variable β. The effect of a change in β on $\hat{a}$ can be found by differentiating (A2):

$$D'_\beta + L_{aa} \frac{d\hat{a}}{d\beta} = 0. \quad (A4)$$

Since O_a, $L_{aa} > 0$, and by assumption $D'_\beta > 0$,

$$\frac{d\hat{a}}{d\beta} = \frac{-D'_\beta O_a}{L_{aa}} = \frac{-}{+} < 0. \quad (A5)$$

Similarly, if C_o, C_p, *and* C_a are positively related to an exogenous variable γ,

$$\frac{d\hat{a}}{d\gamma} = \frac{-[C_{o\gamma} + C_{a\gamma}(1/O_a)]O_a}{L_{aa}} = \frac{-}{+} < 0. \quad (A6)$$

If R_o, R_p, and R_f are positively related and R_a negatively related to an exogeneous variable φ,

$$\frac{d\hat{a}}{d\varphi} = \frac{-[R_{o\varphi} + R_{a\varphi}(1/O_a)]O_a}{L_{aa}} = \frac{?}{+} \gtrless 0. \quad (A7)$$

The ambiguous sign of (A7) requires comment. The φ reflects an increase in the social loss accompanying unjust punishment. Strengthening the legal safeguards for accused persons will have two partially offsetting effects. First, for a given level of crimes and probability of apprehension, fewer innocent persons will be convicted. On the other hand, greater legal safeguards may encourage more crime. Other things being equal, with a higher level of crime, more innocent persons will be convicted. Thus, the sign of (A7) depends on which effect predominates. It seems reasonable to specify $-R_{a\varphi} > R_{o\varphi}$. Therefore, if O_a is small, the sign of

(A7) will be negative—the situation that would seem most likely to prevail in the real world.

If instead we take f and a to be fixed, the optimal value of p ($\hat{p}$) is determined by

$$L_p = \frac{\partial L}{\partial p} = \left[D' + C_0 + R_0 + (C_p + R_p)\frac{1}{O_p} + bpf\left(1 - \frac{1}{\epsilon_p}\right) \right]$$

$$O_p = 0, \qquad (A8)$$

providing

$$L_{pp} = \frac{\partial^2 L}{\partial p^2} = \left[D'' + C_{oo} + R_{oo} + 2(C_{op} + R_{op})\frac{1}{O_p} \right.$$

$$+ (C_{pp} + R_{pp})\frac{1}{O_p^2} + (C_p + R_p)\left(\frac{-O_{pp}}{O_p^3}\right)$$

$$\left. + bf\left(1 - \frac{1}{\epsilon_p}\right)\frac{1}{O_p} \right] O_p^2 > 0. \quad (A9)$$

All the terms in (A9) are positive except $R_{op}(1/O_p)$, providing $\epsilon_p < 1$. Assuming that (A9) holds, the following relationships between $\hat{p}$ and the exogenous parameters β, γ, and φ can be determined:

$$\frac{d\hat{p}}{d\beta} = \frac{D'_\beta O_p}{L_{pp}} = \frac{+}{+} > 0, \qquad (A10)$$

$$\frac{D\hat{p}}{d_\gamma} = \frac{[C_{o\gamma} + C_{p\gamma}(1/O_p)]O_p}{L_{pp}} = \frac{?}{+} \gtrless 0, \qquad (A11)$$

and

$$\frac{d\hat{p}}{d\varphi} = \frac{[R_{o\varphi} + R_{p\varphi}(1/O_p)]O_p}{L_{pp}} = \frac{?}{+} \gtrless 0. \qquad (A12)$$

The signs of both (A11) and (A12) are ambiguous for reasons similar to those for (A7). In general, it would seem reasonable that $C_{p\gamma} > C_{o\gamma}$ and $R_{po} > R_{o\varphi}$. If so, and if O_p is sufficiently small, the signs of (A11) and (A12) will be negative, which seems to be most likely.[6]

---

6. Becker avoided this problem of ambiguity by assuming that C_o was related to one exogenous variable, β, and C_p to another one, s. He then finds $dp/d\beta > 0$ and $dp/ds < 0$ (Becker 1968, p. 212). Convenient as this may be, it is hard to imagine what such exogenous variables might be. One would expect that something which increases the cost of apprehending a given fraction of a larger number of offenders would also affect the costs of apprehending a larger proportion of a given number of offenders and that the latter would tend to rise more sharply than the first.

Now taking p and a as fixed, the optimal value of f ($\hat{f}$) can be determined from

$$L_f = \frac{\partial L}{\partial f} = \left[D' + C_o + R_o + R_f \frac{1}{O_f} + bpf\left(1 - \frac{1}{\epsilon_f}\right) \right]$$
$$O_f = 0, \quad \text{(A13)}$$

providing

$$L_{ff} = \frac{\partial^2 L}{\partial f^2} = \left[D'' + C_{oo} + R_{oo} + 2R_{of} \frac{1}{O_f} + R_{ff} \frac{1}{O_f^2} \right.$$
$$\left. + R_f \left(\frac{-O_{ff}}{O_f^3}\right) + bp\left(1 - \frac{1}{\epsilon_f}\right)\frac{1}{O_f} \right] O_f^2 > 0. \quad \text{(A14)}$$

All terms of (A14) are positive with the exception $2R_{of}$ ($1/O_f$) providing $\epsilon_f < 1$. Assuming that (A14) is satisfied, the relationships between f and the exogenous parameters β, γ, and φ are:

$$\frac{d\hat{f}}{d\beta} = \frac{-D'_\beta O_f}{L_{ff}} = \frac{+}{+} > 0, \quad \text{(A15)}$$

$$\frac{d\hat{f}}{d\gamma} = \frac{-C_{o\gamma} O_f}{L_{ff}} = \frac{+}{+} > 0, \quad \text{(A16)}$$

and

$$\frac{d\hat{f}}{d\varphi} = \frac{-[R_{o\varphi} + R_{f\varphi}\,(1/O_f)]O_f}{L_{ff}} = \frac{?}{+} \gtreqless 0. \quad \text{(A17)}$$

Again, the opposing effects of fewer innocent victims at a given level of offenses and an increased number of offenses makes the sign of (A17) ambiguous. Using an argument similar to the one used previously, one would expect that the sign of (A17) would normally be negative.

It should be noted that the discussion in the text assumed that the signs of (A7), (A11), (A12), and (A17) are in fact negative. As argued, the restrictions necessary for this to be true appear reasonable a priori, but it must be kept in mind that the possibility exists of their being zero or positive.

Evaluation of changes in $\hat{a}$, $\hat{p}$, and $\hat{f}$ in response to shifts in β, γ, and φ when $\hat{a}$, $\hat{p}$, and $\hat{f}$ are allowed to vary simultaneously is not reported here. Most of the signs become ambiguous for the reasons that (A7), (A11), (A12), and (A17) are ambiguous. Changes in p, f, and a that *directly* reduce some social costs raise them indirectly through increasing the level of offenses. Reasonable arguments can be made that the signs of the derivatives reported above will also hold in the more general case.

REFERENCES

Becker, Gary: Crime and punishment: an economic approach. *J.P.E.*, *76*: 169-217, 1968.

Bretton, Henry: Political influence in southern Nigeria. In Spiro, H. J. (Ed.): *Africa: The Primacy of Politics*. New York, Random House, 1966.

Erikson, Kai T.: Notes on the sociology of deviance. In Becker, Howard S. (Ed.): *The Other Side: Perspectives in Deviance*. New York, Free Press, 1964.

Rosberg, Carl G., Jr., and Nottingham, John: *The Myth of Mau Mau: Nationalism in Kenya*. New York, Praeger, 1966.

Schwartz, Richard D., and Skolnick, Jerome H.: Two studies of legal stigma. In Becker, Howard S. (Ed.): *The Other Side: Perspectives in Deviance*, New York, Free Press, 1964.

Sklar, Richard L.: *Nigerian Political Parties*. Princeton, Princeton U. Pr., 1963.

————: Contradictions in the Nigerian political system. *J Modern African Studies*, 3:201-14, 1964.

Zolberg, Aristide R.: *Creating Political Order: The Party-States of West Africa*. Chicago, McNally, 1966.

Chapter 3

THE OPTIMUM ENFORCEMENT OF LAWS

GEORGE J. STIGLER

A LL PRESCRIPTIONS of behavior for individuals require enforcement. Usually the obligation to behave in a prescribed way
is entered into voluntarily by explicit or implicit contract. For
example, I promise to teach certain classes with designated frequency and to discuss matters which I, and possibly others, believe are relevant to the course titles. By negotiation, and in the
event of its failure, by legal action, I and my employer seek to
enforce the contract of employment against large departures from
the promised behavior. Performance of some kinds of behavior is
difficult or impossible to enforce—such as promises to be creative,
noble, or steadfast in crisis—and as a result such contractual
promises are either not made or enforced only when there is an
uncontroversially flagrant violation. The influence upon contract,
and upon economic organization generally, of the costs of enforcing various kinds of contracts has received virtually no study
by economists, despite its immense potential explanatory power.

When the prescribed behavior is fixed unilaterally rather than
by individual agreement, we have the regulation or law, and enforcement of these unilateral rules is the subject of the present
essay. Departures of actual from prescribed behavior are crimes
or violations, although one could wish for a less formidable description than "criminal" to describe many of the trifling offenses
or the offenses against unjust laws. My primary purpose is to
construct a theory of rational enforcement, a theory which owes
much to Gary Becker's major article on the subject (1968). In

Reprinted, with permission of the University of Chicago Press, from *Journal of Political Economy*, May/June 1970, pp. 526-536.

the conclusion the problem of explanation, as distinguished from prescription, will be commented upon.

THE GOAL OF ENFORCEMENT

The goal of enforcement, let us assume, is to achieve that degree of compliance with the rule of prescribed (or proscribed) behavior that the society believes it can afford. There is one decisive reason why the society must forego "complete" enforcement of the rule: enforcement is costly.

The extent of enforcement of laws depends upon the amount of resources devoted to the task. With enough policemen almost every speeding automobile could be identified. The success of tenacious pursuit of the guilty in celebrated crimes (such as the great English train robbery and the assassination of Martin King) suggests that few crimes of sane men could escape detection. We could make certain that crime does not pay by paying enough to apprehend most criminals. Such a level of enforcement would of course be enormously expensive, and only in crimes of enormous importance will such expenditures be approached. The society will normally give to the enforcement agencies a budget which dictates a much lower level of enforcement.

The cost limitation upon the enforcement of laws would prevent the society from forestalling, detecting, and punishing all offenders, but it would appear that punishments which would be meted out to the guilty could often be increased without using additional resources. The offender is deterred by the expected punishment, which is (as a first approximation) the probability of punishment times the punishment—$100 if the probability of conviction is $\frac{1}{10}$ and the fine $1,000. Hence, increasing the punishment would seem always to increase the deterrence. Capital punishment is cheaper than long term imprisonment; and seizure of all the offender's property may not be much more expensive than collecting a more moderate fine.

To escape from this conclusion, Becker introduces as a different limitation on punishment the "social value of the gain to offenders" from the offense. The determination of this social value is not explained, and one is entitled to doubt its usefulness as an explanatory concept: what evidence is there that society sets a positive value upon the utility derived from a murder, rape, or arson? In fact the society has branded the utility derived from such activities as illicit. It may be that in a few offenses some gain to the offender is viewed as a gain to society,[1] but such social gains seem too infrequent, small, and capricious to put an effective limitation upon the size of punishments.

Instead we take account of another source of limitation of punishment, which arises out of the nature of the supply of offenses. It is no doubt true that the larger the punishment, the smaller will be the expected net utility to the prospective offender from the commission of a given offense. But marginal decisions are made here as in the remainder of life, and the marginal deterrence of heavy punishments could be very small or even negative. If the offender will be executed for a minor assault and for a murder, there is no marginal deterrence to murder. If the thief has his hand cut off for taking five dollars, he had just as well take $5,000. Marginal costs are necessary to marginal deterrence.[2] The marginal deterrence to committing small crimes is also distorted if an otherwise appropriate schedule of penalties is doubled or halved.

One special aspect of this cost limitation upon enforcement is the need to avoid overenforcement. The enforcement agency could easily apprehend most guilty people if we placed no limits upon the charging and frequent conviction of innocent people. In any real enforcement system, there will in fact be conviction and punishment of some innocent parties, and these miscarriages of justice impose costs of both resources and loss of confidence in the enforcement machinery. The costs of defense of innocent parties, whether borne by themselves or by the state, are part

---

1. For example, the thief reduces the welfare expenditures of the state, or the arsonist warms the neighboring houses.

2. Becker writes the expected utility from an offense as $EU = pU(Y - f) + (1 - p)U(Y)$, where Y is the money value of the gain, p the probability of detection and conviction, and f the fine. (The income, Y, and fine, f, must be interpreted as average annual flows; for a single offense Y must be less than f.) If this expression is differentiated partially with respect to Y, $\delta EU/\delta Y = pU'(Y - f) + (1 - p)U'(Y) = U'(Y) - pfU''(Y)$, which is positive for all Y with diminishing marginal utility of income. Of course p and f will increase with Y to prevent this incitement to larger crime.

of the costs of enforcement from the social viewpoint. The conviction of innocent persons encourages the crime because it reduces the marginal deterrence to its commission.

The significance of an offense to society—the quantity of resources that will be used to "prevent" the offense—will in general increase with the gravity of the offense. The increase in resources, however, will not manifest itself only in an increase in punishments. The state will pursue more tenaciously the offender who commits a larger crime (or repetitive crimes) and thus increase also the probability of apprehending him.

There is a division of labor between the state and the citizen in the prevention of virtually every offense. The owner of large properties is required to do much of his direct policing: there are surely more watchmen and guards than policemen in a typical city. The larger accumulations of wealth, moreover, are to be guarded by the owner through devices such as nonnegotiability and custody of funds by specialists. Accordingly, the *public* punishments for crimes against property do not increase in proportion to the value of the property. In the protection of people, as distinguished from their property, the individual is required to protect himself from minor offenses or at least to detect their occurrence and assume a large part of the burden of prosecution (for example, shoplifting, insults, simple trespass), but he is allowed less discretion in prosecution for major assaults.

The relationship of duration and nature of penalties to age and sex of offender, frequency of previous offenses, and so forth is also explicable in terms of cost of enforcement. The first-time offender may have committed the offense almost accidentally and (given any punishment) with negligible probability of repetition, so heavy penalties (which have substantial costs to the state) are unnecessary. The probability of a repetition of an offense by a seasoned offender is also zero during his imprisonment, so the probability of repetition of an offense is relevant to the penalty also in his case.

Indeed, the problem of determining the efficient penalty may be viewed as one in statistical inference: to estimate the individual's average, durable propensity to offend (the population value) on the basis of a sample of his observed behavior and how this propensity responds to changes in penalties. As in other sequential sampling problems, one can estimate this propensity more accurately, the longer the individual's behavior is observed.

The society will be more concerned (because each individual is more concerned) with major than minor offenses in the following sense: There is increasing marginal disutility of offenses, so a theft of $1,000 is more than twice as harmful as a theft of $500. In the area of offenses to property, this result is implied by diminishing marginal utility of income. In the area of offenses to persons, it is more difficult to measure damage in any direct way, but a similar rule probably holds.

So much for prevention and punishment; let us turn to the offenses.

THE SUPPLY OF OFFENSES

The commission of offenses will be an act of production for income or an act of consumption. A consumption offense would be illustrated by speeding in an automobile used for recreation or assaulting a courtship rival (when the girl is poor). A production offense would be illustrated by theft, smuggling, and the violation of economic regulations. In the realm of offenses to property, income objectives are of course paramount, and we may recall Adam Smith's emphasis upon the economic nature of crime:

> The affluence of the rich excites the indignation of the poor, who are often both driven by want, and prompted by envy, to invade his possessions. It is only under the shelter of the civil magistrate that the owner of that valuable property, which is acquired by the labour of many years, or perhaps of many successive generations, can sleep a single night in security. He is at all times surrounded by unknown enemies, whom, though he never provoked, he can never appease, and from whose injustice he can be protected only by the powerful arm of the civil magistrate continually held up to chastise it. The acquisition of valuable and extensive property, therefore, necessarily requires the establishment of civil government. Where there is no property, or at least none that exceeds the value of two or three days labour, civil government is not so necessary [Smith 1937, p. 670].

The professional criminal seeks income, and for him the usual rules of occupational choice will hold. He will reckon the present value of the expected returns and costs of the criminal activity and compare their difference with the net returns from other criminal activities and from legitimate activities. The costs of failure in the execution of the crime correspond to the costs of failure in other occupations. The costs of injuries to a professional athlete are comparable to the costs to the offender of apprehension, defense, and conviction, but normally legal occupations have only monetary costs of failure.

The details of occupational choice in illegal activity are not different from those encountered in the legitimate occupations. One must choose the locality of maximum income expectation (and perhaps, like a salesman, move from area to area). One must choose between large, relatively infrequent crimes and smaller, more frequent crimes. One must reckon in periods of (involuntary) unemployment due to imprisonment. Earnings can be expected to rise for a time with experience.

The probability of apprehension (and therefore of conviction) is an increasing function of the frequency of commission of offenses. If the probability of detection is p for one offense, it is $1 - (1 - p)^n$ for at least one conviction in n offenses, and this expression approaches unity as n becomes large. In fact the probability of detection (p) rises after each apprehension because the enforcement agency is also learning the offender's habits. On this score alone, there is a strong incentive to the criminal to make very infrequent attempts to obtain very large sums of money. The probability of success is also affected by the precautions of the prospective victim: Fort Knox is more difficult to enter than a liquor store. The efforts of detection will also increase with the size of the offense.

We may postulate, in summary, a supply of offenses which in equilibrium has the following properties:

1. Net returns are equalized, allowance being made for risk and costs of special equipment required for various activities.

2. The determinants of supply which are subject to the control of society are: (a) the structure of penalties by offense; (b) the probability of detection for each offense; (c) certain costs of the conduct of the offending activity; for example,

the cost of making successful counterfeit money can be increased by complicating the genuine money.
3. The penalties and chances of detection and punishment must be increasing functions of the enormity of the offense.

Although it smacks of paradox, it may be useful to reinterpret the offending activity as providing a variety of products (offenses). These offenses are in a sense demanded by the society: My wallet is an invitation to the foot pad, my office funds to the embezzler. The costs of production of the offenses are the ordinary outlays of offenders plus the penalties imposed by the society. The industry will operate at a scale and composition of output set by the competition of offenders and the cost of producing offenses.

The structure of rational enforcement activities will have these properties:

1. Expected penalties increase with expected gains so there is no marginal net gain from larger offenses. Let the criminal commit in a year S crimes of size Q, where Q is the monetary value to the criminal of the successful completion of the crime. The fraction (p) of crimes completed successfully (or the probability of successful completion of one crime) is a decreasing function of the amount of expenditure (E) undertaken by society to prevent and punish the crime. (Punishment is used for deterrence, and is only a special form of prevention.) Hence $p = p(E, Q)$, or possibly $p = p(E, Q, S)$. The expected punishment is the fraction of crimes apprehended (and punished) times the punishment, F. The condition for marginal deterrence is, for all Q, $d(pSQ)/dQ \leqq d(1-p)SF/dQ$.

2. The expenditures on prevention and enforcement should yield a diminution in offenses, at the margin, equal to the return upon these resources in other areas. An increment of expenditures yields a return in reduced offenses,

$$\sum_{Q'} d(pSQ')/dE = \text{marginal return on expenditures elsewhere,}$$

where Q' is the monetary value of the offense to society.[3]

---

3. Currency has the same value to the criminal as to society, so $Q' = Q$. But for any commodity which does not have a market price independent of ownership, $Q < Q'$.

I do not include foregone lawful services of the criminal in the cost of his activity to society (= noncriminals) since he, not others, would receive the return (taxes aside!) if he shifted from crime to a lawful occupation.

THE ENFORCEMENT AGENCY: A NORMATIVE APPROACH

A law is enforced, not by "society," but by an agency instructed to that task. That agency must be given more than a mandate (an elegant admonition) to enforce the statute with vigor and wisdom: It must have incentives to enforce the law efficiently. There are at least two deficiencies in the methods by which most agencies are induced to enforce the laws properly.

The first deficiency is that the enforcement agency does not take into account, at least explicitly and fully, the costs it imposes upon the activity or persons regulated. In the area of ordinary criminal offenses, the society will, if anything, wish to increase (at no expense to itself) the costs of defense for guilty persons but it should not impose costs (and certainly not unnecessary costs) upon innocent parties. In fact, the administration of criminal justice should in principle include as a cost the reimbursement of the expenses of defense of people charged and acquitted. The compensation actually paid will not exactly compensate injured persons, because of the administrative costs of ascertaining exact compensation, but the taking of an innocent person's personal wealth, including foregone income, differs in no respect from the taking of some of his real estate (for which under eminent domain it is necessary to compensate him fully).[4]

In the area of economic regulation, guilt is often an inappropriate notion, and when it is inappropriate all costs of compliance must be reckoned into the social costs of enforcement. The utility's costs in preparing a rate case or Texas Gulf Sulfur's costs in defending itself against the Securities and Exchange Commission are social costs of the regulatory process. Reimbursement is now achieved by charging the consumers of the products and the owners of specialized resources of these industries: They bear the private costs of the regulatory process. This is at least an acci-

---

4. It is an interesting aspect of our attitudes in this area that many people believe that acquitted persons are probably guilty.

dental allocation of costs, and when the regulation seeks to aid the poorer consumers or resource owners, a perverse allocation.

The second deficiency in the design of enforcement is the use of inappropriate methods of determining the extent of enforcement. The annual report of an enforcement agency is in effect the justification of its previous expenditures and the plea for enlarged appropriations. The Federal Trade Commission will tell us, for example, that in fiscal 1966 as part of its duty to get truthful labeling of furs and textiles, it inspected 12,625 plants and settled 213 "cases" for $1,272,000 plus overhead. The agency may recite scandals corrected or others still unrepressed, but it neither offers nor possesses a criterion by which to determine the correct scale of its activities.

A rational measure of enforcement procedure could in principle be established in almost any area. Consider the fraudulent labeling of textiles. We could proceed as follows:

1. The damage to the consumer from the purchase of a mislabeled textile could be estimated, and will obviously vary with the mislabeling (assuming that the legal standards are sensible!). The difference between the market value of the true and alleged grades is one component of the damage. A second and more elusive component is the additional cost of deception (earlier replacement, skin irritation, and so forth): The consumer who would not have purchased the inferior quality at a competitive price had he known its inferiority has suffered additional damage. Thus the measure of damage is the amount a consumer would pay to avoid the deception, that is, the value of the *insured* correct quality minus the value of the actual quality.

2. As a matter of deterrence, the penalties on the individual mislabeler should be equal to a properly taken sum of the following items: (a) The damage per yard times the number of yards, say per year. Let this be H. (b) The costs of the enforcement agency, say E, per year. This sum should include reimbursement of the costs of those charged and acquitted. (c) The cost of defense (if detected) for the mislabeler, D. Where guilt is an appropriate notion, as

presumably in the case of mislabeling, the society may wish to ignore these costs, which is to say, resources devoted to this end deserve no return. Where guilt is inappropriate, these costs should be reckoned in. The sum of these penalties must be multiplied by $1/p$, where p is the probability of detection of the offense within the year. This probability is a function of E and H.

3. The enforcement agency should minimize the sum of damage plus enforcement costs, $(\Sigma H + E)$ or $(\Sigma H + \Sigma D + E)$.[5]

This goal will serve two functions. The first is to set the scale of enforcement, namely where marginal return equals marginal cost. If the scale of enforcement is correct, society is not spending two dollars to save itself one dollar of damage, or failing to spend one dollar where it will save more than that amount of damage. The second function is to guide the selection of cases: The agency will not (as often now) seek numerous, easy cases to dress up its record, but will pursue the frequent violator and the violator who does much damage.

This sort of criterion of enforcement is readily available in certain areas. The secret service, for example, reports that in fiscal 1967 the loss to the public from counterfeit money was $1,658,100.75 (an excellent instance of counterfeit accuracy). Perhaps half of the $17 million spent by this agency was devoted to the suppression of counterfeiting, and to this one must add the costs of legal actions, imprisonment, and so forth. The secret service should be asking whether the amount of counterfeit money passed would fall by a dollar if a dollar more were spent on enforcement costs minus the corresponding fines collected.

The penalty structure should incorporate the social appraisal of the importance of the suppression of the offenses. The law does not in general provide this scale of values, as can be shown by the list of maximum penalties for the violations of economic regulations listed in Table 3-I.

The use of criminal sanctions is erratic, and the implicit equivalence of fines and imprisonment varies from $1,000 per year to

---

5. The fines will be $\Sigma H/p$, but the fines per se are transfers rather than social costs; see Becker (1968), pp. 180–81.

TABLE 3-I

PUBLIC PENALTIES FOR VIOLATION OF ECONOMIC STATUTES

Offense	Enforcement Agency	Maximum Penalty	Statute
Restraint of trade	Antitrust Division	$50,000 + 1 year (+ triple damages and costs)	Sherman (1890, 1955)
Unfair methods of competition	FTC	Cease and desist order	FTC (1914)
Refusal to testify, or testify falsely, under same	FTC	$1,000-$5,000 + 1 year	Same
Price discrimination	FTC	Cease and desist (+ triple damages and costs)	Clayton (1914)
False advertisements of foods, drugs, or cosmetics	FTC	$5,000 + 6 months	Wheeler-Lea (1938)
Adulteration or misbranding of food	Secretary of Health, Education, and Welfare	$1,000 + 1 year, first offense; $10,000 + 3 years, later offense	Copeland Act (1938)
Exporting apples and pears without certificate of quality	Dept. of Agriculture	Denial of certificate for 10 days $100-$1,000 for knowing violation	Apples and Pears for Export (1933)
Exporting apples in improper barrels	Dept. of Agriculture	$1 barrel	Standard Barrels and Standard Grades of Apples Act (1912)
Exporting other fruit or vegetables in improper barrels	Dept. of Agriculture	$500 or 6 months if willful	Standard Barrels . . . for Fruits, Vegetables and Other Dry Commodities (1915)
Exporting grapes in improper baskets	Dept. of Agriculture	$25	Standard Baskets Act (1916)

Offense	Agency	Penalty	Act
Giving rebates in freight charges (trucks)	ICC	$200-$500 first offense; $250-$5,000 repeated offense	Motor Carrier Act (1935)
Same, water carriers	ICC		Transportation Act (1940)
Failure to disclose interest charges	FRB	$5,000 if willful Twice finance charge, within $100-$1,000; $5,000 and/or 1 year if willful	Consumer Credit Protection Act (1968)
Falsely certify a check	FBI	$5,000 and/or 5 years	62 Stat. 749 (June 25, 1948)
Failure to deliver gold or certificates to FR Bank when ordered	FRB	Twice the number of dollars	Federal Reserve Act (1913)
Evasion of excise taxes	Treasury	$10,000 and/or 5 years if willful; forfeiture of goods and conveyance	Revenue Act (1954)
Security Act violation	SEC	$5,000 and/or 5 years	Securities Act (1934)
Misbrand hazardous substances	Secretary of Health, Education, and Welfare	$500 and 90 days; $3,000 or 1 year if willful or repeated	Hazardous Substances Act (1960)

$10,000 per year. Many of the penalties are not even stated in the statutes: The penalty for drinking (industrial) alcohol which has not paid its beverage tax is sometimes blindness or death. The penalties for the essentially similar offense (if such it must be called) of reducing freight rates can be ten times as much for a barge operator as for a trucker. Of course these maximum penalties are not actual penalties, but one is not entitled to hope for much more rationality or uniformity in the fixing of penalties for specific offenses. (The lawyers have apparently not studied in adequate detail the actual sanctions for economic offenses.)

One may conjecture that two features of punishment of traditional criminal law have been carried over to economic regulation: the attribution of a substantial cost to the act of conviction itself, and the related belief that moral guilt does not vary closely with the size of the offense. Whatever the source, the penalty structure is not well designed for either deterrence or guidance of enforcement.

CONCLUSION

The widespread failure to adopt rational criteria of enforcement of laws has been due often and perhaps usually to a simple lack of understanding of the need for and nature of rational enforcement. The clarification of the logic of rational enforcement, and the demonstration that large gains would be obtained by shifting to a rational enforcement scheme, are presumably the necessary (and hopefully sufficient) conditions for improving public understanding of enforcement problems.[6]

There is, however, a second and wholly different reason for the use of what appear to be inappropriate sanctions and inappropriate appropriations to enforcement bodies: the desire of the public *not* to enforce the laws. The appropriations to the enforcement agency and the verdicts of juries are the instruments by which the community may constantly review public policy.

---

6. The peculiarities of the structure of sanctions in economic regulation are partially due also to the response of the regulated businesses. They may effectively lobby to limit appropriations to the regulatory body, but they can also impose costly activities upon the regulatory body which force it to curtail other controls.

If the society decides that drinking alcoholic beverages or speeding in automobiles is not a serious offense in their ordinary forms, they may curtail resources for enforcement and so compel the enforcement agency to deal only with a smaller number of offenses (perhaps offenses of larger magnitude, such as chronic drunkenness or driving at extremely high speeds). There is considerable inertia in the legislative process—inertia that serves highly useful functions—and it is much easier to make continuous marginal adjustments in a policy through the appropriations committee by varying the resources for its enforcement than it is to modify the statute. Variation in enforcement provides desirable flexibility in public policy.

REFERENCES

Becker, Gary: Crime and punishment: an economic approach. *J.P.E.,* 76: 169-217, 1968.

Smith, Adam: *The Wealth of Nations.* New York, Modern Library, 1937.

Chapter 4

CRIME AND THE COST OF CRIME: AN ECONOMIC APPROACH

Robert G. Hann

In the past few years there has been a considerable shift in the proportion of resources devoted to more operational or management-oriented approaches to criminological research and development. To a large extent this shift, with a few notable exceptions, has been accomplished by the influx of researchers or practitioners from outside the ranks of traditional criminological researchers.

Unfortunately, there seems to have been a lack of real understanding of both new and existing methods and approaches and, therefore, a reduction in the degree of acceptance and cooperation between the two groups.

By presenting an "economic" approach to a subject of past and present interest and relevance, namely "The Cost of Crime," this paper attempts to begin to alleviate this problem of communication as well as to summarize the work done in this area to date.

The paper first deals with problem definitions within an economic framework and then proceeds to develop economic guidelines relevant for a policy-maker in the Criminal Justice System. In so doing, it also lays a theoretical structure for evaluating existing or conducting future research into the cost of crime.

IN THE LAST TWO DECADES there has been a steady, persistent increase in the number of areas staked out by economists as being susceptible to economic research. The 1971 issues of the *Journal of Economic Literature* contain, in addition to the more "traditional" ones, sections on "Economics of War and Defense."[1]

This paper has been prepared as part of an Economic Analysis of Crime and Criminal Justice Project undertaken at the Toronto Centre of Criminology with a grant from the Canada Council. An earlier version was presented at the Sixth International Congress on Criminology in September, 1970, in Madrid. Reprinted, with permission of the National Council on Crime and Delinquency, from *Journal of Research in Crime and Delinquency*, January 1972, pp. 12-30.

1. See, for instance Hitch and McKean (1960); or Quade and Boucher (1968).

"Economics of Transportation,"[2] "Economics of Education,"[3] "Economics of Health,"[4] "Economics of Poverty,"[5] "Economics of Discrimination,"[6] and now, "Economics of Crime,"[7] It is still too early to assess the ultimate worth of these contributions, but it is already evident that their impact has been quite significant.

Criminology, like the other areas listed above, is a pursuit defined by its subject matter and not by any peculiar methodological approach. As such, it is and will continue to have its territorial imperative challenged by disciplines defined along methodological lines. Whether these "challenges" will result in a net cost or benefit to the criminal justice system will, of course, depend partly on the intrinsic merit of the particular contributions. The outcome, however, will also depend on the degree to which "native" criminologists can and will try to understand and accept them. Such is certainly the case for policy-oriented economic analysis. The understanding and acceptance of the latter discipline's efforts might be more efficiently achieved if economists were thoughtful enough to provide a summary prospectus or at least a memorandum of intent to noneconomists. Such is the intent of this paper.

The article makes no pretense at being all encompassing in regard to either the different approaches of economics or the potential areas of application—space certainly prohibits that. Instead, a much more specific strategy has been adopted. The paper has taken one particular problem of past and present[8] interest to criminologists, namely "the cost of crime," and has tried to demonstrate how economists would perceive and begin to set about

2. See, for instance, Kuhn (1962); or Winch (1963).
3. See, for instance, Becker (1964); or Judy, and Levine (1965).
4. See, for instance, Weisbrod (1960).
5. See, for instance, Bronfenbrenner (1969).
6. See, for instance, Raymond (1969).
7. See, for instance, Becker (1968); or Mishan (1969); or Tullock (1969); or Shoup (1964).
8. See, for instance, U.S. National Commission on Law Observance and Enforcement, *Report on the Cost of Crime* (1931); or Martin and Bradley (1964); or Martin (1965); or The President's Commission on Law Enforcement and Administration of Justice (1967) especially Chapter Three. Some of the existing literature is summarized in the proceedings of the Symposium on the "Cost of Crime and of Social Defense Against Crime," 1970, held by the International Centre of Comparative Criminology, Montreal.

dealing with the problem. The first and by far the largest section of the paper will be devoted towards defining the problem within an economic framework. It will be shown that the framework simultaneously provides an economic justification for (1) the existence of civil and criminal legislation and (2) the conclusion that some "crime" is in most cases necessary.[9] The economic justification of "socially bad crime" is then used to provide a theoretical base that should be adapted by any "cost of crime" study that might be subsequently undertaken. The paper then ends with certain additional methodological and operational guidelines that should be adapted by any cost of crime project—guidelines that would ensure their producing more than a lump-sum of accounting costs of rather dubious value.

Beccaria (1963) and Benthem[10] were perhaps representative of the "old wave" of economists contributing to criminology. Now, before the "new wave" gathers further momentum, it might be worthwhile to pause and speculate on what its effect on criminological research might be.

CRIME—AN ECONOMIC PHENOMENON
Economics and Problem Definition

The economic textbooks define economics as "the study of the use of limited resources for the achievement of alternative ends—more specifically as a social science which covers the actions of individuals and groups in the processes of producing, exchanging, and consuming goods and services," [Henderson and Quandt (1958)]. With a mandate as all encompassing as this, it is no wonder that economists feel very few qualms in applying their energies to problems in what sometimes seem to be the most unlikely areas. This is perhaps not so pompous an attitude as it first appears, because although an education in economics does develop a knowledge of the activities and functions of a particular segment of society, more importantly, it develops a rather peculiar

9. This conclusion has, of course, been reached by many scholars using completely different assumptions and approaches. See, for instance, Durkheim (1950).

10. See, for instance, numerous articles in *Bentham's Economic Writings* (1952-54).

and fruitful approach for analyzing a wide variety of human activities in general. Much the same, of course, can be said of sociology, philosophy, psychology, and systems analysis. Each, however, has an approach and tools of a unique enough nature to provide benefits and effects that might not be supplied by the other disciplines. One of the most operationally useful benefits might prove to be the economist's perception of crime *per se.*

The definition of economics given earlier seems to enjoy favor with the vast majority of economists. In contrast, a scan of the "criminological literature"[11] for a rigorous definition of crime or criminology produces no such consensus. It seems inappropriate for one discipline to presume to define another; but economics, specifically welfare economics, does in fact supply a definition which seems more than adequate for many types of criminological policy analyses. After a short summary of the general problem addressed by welfare economics, such a definition is proposed. It is, to be sure, one designed more for the normative question of deciding optimal private and public policy towards crime and criminal justice than for the positive problem of describing or explaining the actual activities of the existing agents in the system. It is more useful for showing what legislation, arrest quotas, or sentencing practices "should be" rather than what or why they "are." This tendency of economics to adopt and advocate a more equal balance between positive and normative problems within a consistent theoretical framework may represent one of the major influences of economists on criminological research.

Optimum Optimorum

Welfare economics has long been concerned with the problem of identifying the minimum conditions necessary to ensure an allocation of available resources among different production processes and individuals such that some sort of optimum of economic and/or social welfare would be achieved. In "Western" economics it has also been taken as "given" that one characteristic of this minimum set of conditions should be that it include a minimum

---

11. There are at least the two main groupings of Realists and Institutionalists implicit in the analysis of Biederman and Reiss (1967).

number of formal controls i.e. that maximum allowance be made for individual freedom.

Once such a minimum set of conditions has been identified, welfare economics is concerned with first, exploring the implications for levels and distribution of welfare of one or a group of the necessary conditions not being satisfied, and second, determining the set of minimum laws (or taxes and subsidies) that will bring the system back as close as possible to the *optimum optimorum.*

The position of this *optimum optimorum,* or "bliss point," is a function of two factors: the preferences of the community and the set of output combinations possible with the given quantities of resources available. The preferences of the community can be shown as a community welfare function.

$$W = W(U_1, U_2, \ldots U_m) \tag{1}$$

where W = the level of welfare of the community and U_i = the level of welfare (or utility) of the ith individual in an M individual community. The set of output combinations possible for a community can be shown by a community production function

$$P(X_1, X_2, \ldots X_n) = 0 \tag{2}$$

where X_j $(j = 1,n)$ is the quantity of the jth good produced or used up in production. The available technology defines the form of P.

It is assumed that,

$$U_i = U_i(X_{i1}, X_{i2} \ldots X_{in}) \quad i = 1,m \tag{3}$$

where X_{ij} is the quantity of the jth good consumed or given up by the ith individual and that,

$$X_j = X_j(X'_{j1}, X'_{j2}, \ldots X'_{jn}) \quad j = 1,n \tag{4}$$

where X'_{jk} is the amount of the kth good used as an input in the production of the jth good.

The problem then becomes one of maximizing W subject to

$$\sum_{j=1}^{n} X'_{jk} \leq \overline{X}'_k \quad k = 1,n \tag{5}$$

where $\overline{X}'_k$ is the total quantity of the kth good available for production.

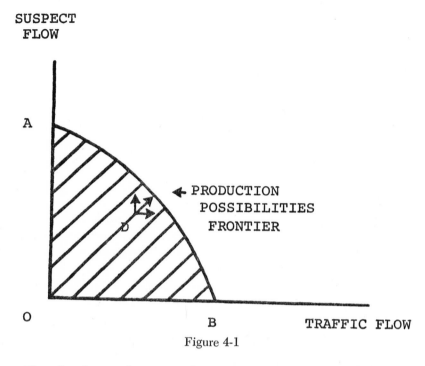

Figure 4-1

If we let the production and consumption quantities of all other goods and services remain fixed, the problem can be illustrated graphically for two goods. Assume the community has a certain amount of men, computers, radio transmitters, etc., that can be used either by its judicial department to improve the processing of suspected offenders in the courts or by its police to improve traffic flow in the city core. Let the vertical and horizontal axes in Figure 4-1 represent the different levels of these two activities. Each point in the graph then represents a particular combination of suspect flow and traffic flow that could be chosen. The problem, of course, is which point should the policy-maker choose—which combination of outputs corresponds with the highest level of community welfare. In the absence of any constraints the community would try to move as far as it could in the north-east direction producing more and more of both goods. There are, however, very real constraints imposed by the resources and technology available to the community. These two constraints define the production set, the set of combinations of suspect and traffic flow that can be produced. (This set is shown as the shaded area in Fig. 4-1.) Any point in the set can be produced but there is an important subset of output combinations that are of special interest to the policy-maker. These are the output combinations resulting from the most efficient use of the inputs. This subset forms the border (AB) of the production set and is called the "production possibilities frontier." The equation for this set is $P(X_1, X_2, \ldots X_n) = 0$ where all available resources are used, i.e.

$$\sum_{j=1}^{n} X'_{jk} = \overline{X}_k \quad k = 1,n$$

For any point on the production possibilities frontier, the quantity produced of one good is maximized given both the output levels of the other goods and the available resources and technology.

If we make the assumption of nonsatiation of the community (i.e. that more is preferred to less) at least within the production set, we can infer that the social welfare maximum we are seeking is one of the points on the production possibilities frontier. Our policy problem is narrowed down to deciding which one. This is where some economists stop because, to go further, what we have defined as a social or community welfare function (equation 1), a device showing how a community as a group ranks different output combinations in terms of their worth to the community, becomes necessary. The one we have shown is typical. The community welfare function is assumed to be some composite of the private welfare functions of the individual citizens. It has, however, been demonstrated[12] that even if all the individuals in the community act in a rational manner, such a community welfare function will not, in general, exhibit the usual characteristics of consistency and transitivity needed for rational consistent group decision-making. Without introducing a series of value judgements, it is, therefore, impossible to get an expression of community group preferences that will allow us to choose between

---

12. The first statement of the "Impossibility Theorem" was given by Arrow (1951).

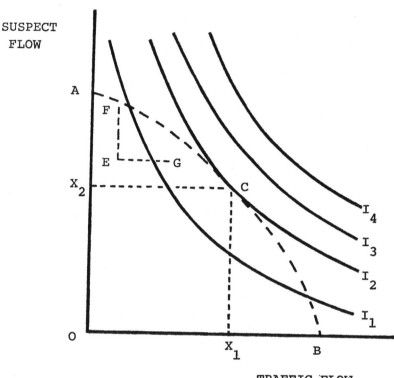

SUSPECT
FLOW

TRAFFIC FLOW

Figure 4-2

the different combinations of court and police activity located on the production possibility frontier. This leaves the policy-maker with two alternatives.

The first would be to assume responsibility for making the necessary value judgements[13] and working with whatever social welfare function evolved. In Figure 4-2 a well-behaved social welfare function has been shown. All combinations of suspect flow and traffic flow which enjoy the same ranking[14] in terms of com-

13. The "social welfare" function in this case could take various forms. Examples are a dictator's own private preferences, the preferences implicit after parliamentary debate and voting, or the preferences that evolve as the result of competing bribes from special interest lobbies.

14. An ordinal ranking is sufficient—a cardinal ranking is not necessary to derive most of the conclusions of welfare economic theory.

munity welfare have been joined to form one of a set of community welfare curves.

This gives us a set of curves each representing a certain level of community welfare. Again, assuming nonsatiation, it follows that a ray emanating from the origin will intersect curves l_1, l_2, l_3, and l_4, each representing higher and higher levels of community welfare.

If the production set and the community welfare function are shaped as in the diagram (i.e. are mathematically convex), then the point we are looking for is that point on the production possibilities curve which is also on the highest attainable community welfare curve. This point is the point of tangency of the production possibilities curve with a social welfare curve (i.e. at C). Point C becomes our social optimum or bliss point and all taxes and subsidies or rewards and punishments should be geared to ensuring that resources should be allocated so that X_2 flow of suspects in the courts and X_1 flow of traffic would be produced. In this case, the economists would then be able to proscribe economic "laws"[15] that must be followed to ensure the maximization of community welfare.

Some economists, however, either refuse to take responsibility for making these value judgements or alternatively wait until sociologists, politicians, and/or philosophers can supply an unambiguous formulation of such a community welfare function. These economists[16] are content to lower their sights and adopt a less ambitious concept of optimality, namely "Pareto optimality" or "Pareto efficiency," as their standard. In consumption space, an

---

15. These "laws" take the form of marginal conditions that must be met by producers and consumers. For example, economic policemen would have to enforce the rather complicated law that *at the margin* (the worth each consumer places on a good in terms of a second) must equal (the worth society attaches to that good in terms of the second) which must equal (the quantity of that good that each producer could produce if he cut back production of the second by one unit), which must equal (the quantity of that good society would want each producer to produce if he cut back production of the second by one unit) which must equal (the ratio of the price of that first good to the price of the second).

16. For a criticism of those who follow this second approach see, for instance, Wilson (1965).

allocation of goods and services is "Pareto optimal" if no one consumer can be made better off by reallocation without making at least one other consumer worse off. In production space, with a given quantity of inputs, a collection of goods and services is "Pareto efficient" if the quantity produced of any one good or service cannot be increased without reducing the quantity produced of at least one other good or service. This concept of optimality has the advantages of being value free[17] and its attainment is a necessary although certainly not sufficient prerequisite for most other concepts of optimality. It has the shortcoming, however, of defining a set of points rather than a single specific point. For instance, any point on the production possibilities frontier is Pareto efficient. We have, however, seen that only one of these points is optimal when a particular convex community welfare function can be defined.

In this second approach, the economic problem then becomes one of formulating rules for manipulating resources to ensure a movement towards the Pareto efficient production possibilities frontier from any point (say D in Fig. 4-1)[18] in the interior of the production set. The question in the particular case here becomes, "Given the amount of resources we have for improving suspect and/or traffic flow, how can we move closer to the most efficient use of our resources?" The algorithm used to ensure progress towards the production possibilities frontier is that each new combination of suspect and traffic flow must be "Pareto better" than the preceding or alternative one. Without specifying a community welfare function, economists or any policy-makers can do little more than point out the limitations of such an approach. For instance, if a welfare function exists but is unknown to us, it is evident from Figure 4-2 that after moving from an initial inefficient point, E, to a Pareto better point, F, on the production

---

17. "Value free" in the sense that it does not make "interpersonal comparisons of utility" i.e. that the policy-maker does not have to determine comparable cardinal measures of different individual's subjective evaluations of different goods. It is not "value free" if one includes as value judgments most economists' slavish acceptance of efficiency and growth as ultimate goals.

18. The economic laws to be enforced are those in footnote 15, after ignoring the terms in the first two sets of brackets.

possibilities curve, we might be worse off than if we had moved to some other Pareto better but still inefficient point, G, in the interior of the production set.[19] The choice must be made between the risk of misspecifying a community welfare function in the first approach and the risk of making a "value free" mistake using the second approach.

Pareto Optima and Economic Law

The preceding sections have shown that no matter which approach is adapted, the policy-maker will aim for some point that is Pareto efficient. The problem still remains of what rewards and punishments the policy-maker must mete out to provide incentive and/or to force citizens to cause the community to move towards the chosen objective. Welfare economists have been interested in two related aspects of this problem. First, is there any set of conditions that would be sufficient to ensure the achievement of a Pareto optimum with a minimum of formal controls? Second, what happens if these conditions are not met, and what tools are available to compensate for their absence? The following paragraphs will address both questions in order.

The particular set of conditions economists have been most interested in defines a state known as "perfect competition." This set includes assumptions of perfect mobility of resources, perfect knowledge of production and consumption possibilities, large numbers of competing consumers and producers in each activity, and no externalities. The last condition is the one most important for our purposes here and will be examined later. Perfect competition defines an environment such that when individuals freely pursue their own competitive ends in production and consumption, they will, as a by-product of their market activity, ensure a Pareto optimum of economic welfare for the individual as well as for the community as a whole. Adam Smith's "Invisible Hand" will prevail.

Moreover, besides perfect competition's describing a state of

---

19. For a discouraging but rigorous statement of this and other problems to be faced in making optimal policy decisions of this particular type with imperfect information about community preferences, see Samuelson (1950).

the world of interest in itself—a world where no laws would be needed to enforce a Pareto optimal level of economic welfare—it can also be shown[20] that the converse holds. For every allocation of goods that is Pareto optimal there is a perfectly competitive state leading to the same allocation of resources.

With one other result of welfare economists (that the reader is again asked to take on faith) we can tie this framework together and show what implications all this theory has for the legislator. This last "truth" is that the sole factor that determines which particular Pareto optimal equilibrium will be achieved by perfect competition is the initial distribution of resources or wealth that prevails among the citizens.

The implications then follow very simply. The problem of the lawmaker becomes one not of legislating for or against any particular activity or individual, but rather one of first choosing which one of the Pareto optimal configurations of outputs yields the highest level of social welfare (assuming the policymaker has some community welfare function he wishes to use) and then legislating the appropriate redistribution of wealth to achieve it. Thus, in a world of perfect competition both the legislator's problem and method of solution are precisely definable.

The world of perfect competition represents, in many senses, a utopia for the *laissez-faire* liberal. Once the initial redistribution of wealth has been accomplished at the beginning of the period, no more legislation is required to ensure that both an economic welfare optimum is obtained and that individuals are free to pursue their own self interests at their will. In fact, the latter ensures the former and the former justifies the latter.

Even though perfect competition is far from a description of the world in which we live, it is still a useful description of an ideal worth achieving. It also provides a useful model for evaluating a wide range of proposed and existing social policies—be they guidelines, laws, taxes, or subsidies.

If we first observe the level of social welfare existing when certain of the conditions for an optimum are not met, we can

20. See, for instance, the proof given in Chapter 14 of Dorfman, Samuelson, and Solow (1958).

then evaluate and compare alternative corrective policies by investigating how well they eliminate the gap between existing and potential levels of welfare. Legislation sponsoring subsidies to national railways and manpower retraining programs could be justified by their trying to offset the absence of the perfect mobility of resources conditions. Similarly, subsidies to education, national television, and radio networks help offset the absence of perfect knowledge of products and opportunities.

This line of analysis can also be readily applied to criminal justice programs. Hijackings, armed robberies, and pilferage, especially insofar as they cause preventative measures to be taken, can be seen as restricting the mobility of resources. Extortion, protection, and organized crime in general can, in many ways, be regarded as activities restricting the number of producers or consumers in an industry.[21]

Externalities and Crime

However, from an economic standpoint, criminal justice programs should more often be aimed at trying to compensate for the nonfulfillment of the last condition for perfect competition. They should be aimed at compensating for the presence of externalities. This point is important for "cost of crime" studies especially.

An externality[22] exists when an individual's utility (or happiness or well being) depends not only on the activities he, himself, is in control of, but also on activities others control. Viewed from the other side, externalities exist when an individual, through his activities, can impose some costs or benefits on other individuals. In mathematical terms, externalities exist if one or more activities under the control of B appear as arguments in the utility function of A, i.e. if

$$U_a = U_a(X_{a1}, X_{a2}, \ldots X_{an}, X_{bz})$$

where it is B's consumption of activity Z that affects A.

21. Some interesting attempts to treat certain criminal activities as industries supplying goods or services like any other industry and then asking what types of behavior on their part would be socially preferable are presented in T. C. Schelling, "Economic Analysis and Organized Crime," which appears as Appendix D of the President's Crime Commission *Task Force Report* (1967).

22. This definition is close to that given by Buchanan and Stubblebine (1962). Useful classification schemes for externalities are given there and Bator (1958).

If the effect of B's activity on A's utility or production is positive,

$$\text{i.e. if } \frac{\partial U_a}{\partial X_{bz}} > 0$$

then an external economy will exist. If the effect is negative,

$$\text{i.e. if } \frac{\partial U_a}{\partial X_{bz}} < 0$$

an external diseconomy will exist. A farmer, by growing more apple trees, and, therefore, more blossoms, indirectly but significantly increases the production of honey and the utility of bee-keepers, but the beekeeper does not control apple production. A thief robbing a bank affects the utility of the depositors but they have little control over his activities since he is not likely to take their utility into account in making his decision.

Before the externality assumption had been dropped, each individual's welfare depended only on activities over which he had control, and conversely, activities he controlled did not affect other individuals' welfare. Therefore, when individual B was making a choice of how much of an activity to engage in, he took into account all the community costs and benefits of his indulgence in the activity since he was the only one affected. In this case, the private and community[23] costs and benefits of his actions were identical. Therefore, what was optimal for him was also optimal for society. By allowing each individual in society to maximize his own utility, the "community" welfare was also maximized.[24]

However, as soon as externalities are allowed into the picture, private and community costs and benefits are no longer identical and the individual includes in his own decision calculus only those costs and benefits he himself feels. The result is that the level of his activity which yields a personal optimum will not necessarily yield a community welfare optimum. To attain a

23. The term "community welfare" has been used here instead of "social welfare"—the term usually used by economists. It seems the latter term would best be used to distinguish between "economic" and "social" welfare—even though many economists use "economic welfare" and "social welfare" interchangeably.

24. On the assumption that the existing income distribution is "optimal."

community optimum, the thief's activity, if it causes external diseconomies to his victim, *may* have to be restricted by the appropriate taxes or laws. (The importance of the *may* will be brought out later.)

We are now in a position to define crime within an economic framework. A crime simply becomes any activity that causes uncompensated external diseconomies. That is, if one of a thief's activities, e.g. a particular theft, appears in some other individual's, i.e. his victim's utility function with a negative effect and the victim is not compensated, then that theft is a criminal activity. We label it "crime" since the thief acting to maximize his own *private* utility by optimizing his own net *private benefits* may engage in thieving at a level that is not appropriate to a *community* welfare optimum which must also take the loss to the victims into account. A legislator trying to maximize community welfare might, therefore, wish to place a tax (i.e. increase the expected costs of conviction and punishment) on the thief's activity to restrict it to the "correct" level (or a subsidy to increase it to the "correct" level). The fact that the community welfare is not maximized is the justification for the government's intervention, while the optimization of community welfare becomes the constraint on government and individual activity.

Two points follow directly from this discussion. First, the set of activities defined by the presence of uncompensated external diseconomies is much larger than the set of what are now normally thought of as criminal activities. Most types of environmental pollution probably exhibit more significant uncompensated external diseconomies than do many of what we normally call crimes. The same can be said either about discrimination based solely on private prejudices or about many traffic offenses which, in Canada at least, are included in municipal or provincial statutes and not in the Federal Criminal Code proper. It would be overly optimistic to suppose that the initial legislative reaction, as the dangers of pollution become more evident, is due to the adoption of a similar expanded definition of crime. It is certainly consistent, however, with the main concept. On the other hand, there has been a movement of late to delete certain activities from the Criminal Code which fail, by and large, to exhibit these external diseconomies. For instance in Canada lately there has been slowly mounting pressure with various degrees of success to remove from the code or at least relax the enforcement of laws relating to activities such as homosexuality, abortion, and possession of certain of the "softer" drugs.

The second point comes out of an extension of the first. The definition of crime proposed may seem to include too many activities. It would include activities such as washing a child's chalk drawing off the sidewalk, giving a speech in favor of temperance near a pub, or coughing during a particularly tender and moving passage of a symphony. That these activities are crimes by our definition cannot be disputed. However, as is the case now, all activities designated as criminal do not have to be completely suppressed. No police force seriously tries to suppress all robberies. In some areas certain laws are not enforced at all. More important, in some cases this is as it should be. What needs to be factored out is that subset of criminal activities (or rather criminal activities carried out at certain levels) designated as "socially bad" crime. These are activities that, if a community welfare optimum is to be achieved, *should* be restricted.

It may not be immediately evident that activity X should not be *prima facie* restricted by the community when it causes harm to individual A, harm for which A does not receive compensation. The problem revolves around the reciprocal nature of externalities.[25]

To crystalize the issues, let us take two particular individuals, both of whom have decided to improve the furnishings in their respective dwellings, the first by redecorating sometime in the future, the second by decorating as soon as appropriate furniture becomes available. The second, B (who may become the villain in our story), has a set of preferences that put a relatively high value on possessing objects with some historical value and a low value on shopping in established overpriced antique stores. Our other individual, A (who will become the victim), has a quite

---

25. This reciprocal nature was first noted by Coase (1960).

different set of preferences that put a relatively high value on ultramodern furniture and a low value on the thrill of appearing in court in any capacity. Now, assume that the activity we are concerned with is B's appropriating A's old furniture from A's house before A had planned to dispose of it. The problem posed to our combination legislator and policeman is whether or not to restrict B's stealing from A. The important point is that although restrictions on B's activity will reduce the losses felt by A, such a restriction will, at the same time, force B to forego benefits he might otherwise have received—that is, our potential thief would suffer "internal" diseconomies. If the benefits foregone by the thief after any restrictions would be greater than the reduction of the losses felt by A,[26] the legislator-policeman would be economically wrong to restrict B in his thieving since this would cause a net reduction in total net benefits and potential community welfare.

The problem for those two individuals and this one activity is graphically represented in Figure 4-3. The number of thefts (counting one foray as one instance of theft being committed) produced by the criminal activity is measured on the horizontal axis while the money equivalent of both the marginal net gain to B (curve G^b) and the marginal net loss to A (curve L^a) from each additional unit increase in the levels of the activity of thieving are measured on the vertical axis. Figure 4-3 shows the simple case where each additional theft by B gives him positive (to a point) but decreasing marginal utility, perhaps because he chooses the items he values most on his earlier thefts or because as he makes more thefts he is more likely to get caught and his net benefits after deducting expected losses due to apprehension start to fall. However (after a point), each additional unit increase in the level of B's thieving causes A increasing marginal disutility. Although it is true A will eventually dispose of most of it anyway, as B steals more he is most likely to steal items that

---

26. Coase (1960) has also pointed out that there is a limit to the total compensation that should be expected—this limit being the maximum enjoyment that the original owner could experience from the furniture in the absence of this particular external diseconomy.

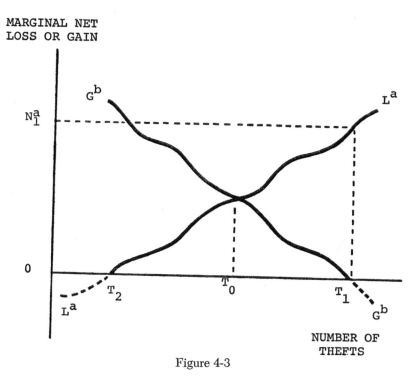

Figure 4-3

A needs in the meantime and, therefore, have a higher value to A at present. Also, as B steals more, the probability of A's having to resort to use of the police and the courts to stop him rises. Because of A's particular preferences this would involve an increased marginal cost to him. In summary then, B receives decreasing marginal internal economies while A suffers increasing marginal external diseconomies.[27]

The activity is a crime if it is carried out at a level greater than T_2. B's thieving is not a crime at a level below T_2, since it causes no external diseconomies to A, i.e. A's happiness is not negatively affected at those low levels of activity. (In fact, it might even be

---

27. These curves are drawn taking the income distribution as "given." The position of these "marginal evaluation" curves will shift as each individual's income changes. For instance, as money income rises, the individual will be more willing to pay a higher price than before for a good.

enhanced if he regards low levels of B's thieving as saving him cartage costs that he would have had to pay to dispose of furniture that has low resale value.) If B is left unrestricted he will produce T_1 thefts since every unit produced up to the T_1^{th} yields net additions to his wealth. However, at T_1, the marginal net gain to B (namely no gain) is less than the positive marginal loss to A, N^a. Both A and B could benefit by either A's bribing B with an amount less than N^a to restrict his activity or the government's forcing such a restriction and paying compensation.

In fact, at any level between T_0 and T_1 the activity of B is a "socially bad" criminal activity. It is "socially bad" because in that range, since the marginal external diseconomies are greater than the marginal internal economies, it is possible to increase the level of community welfare by restricting the level of operations and then effecting the appropriate transfer payments.[28] It is readily seen in this case that community welfare would be maximized by restricting B's activity from the level that he would choose to maximize his own private utility, ignoring the disutility to A. Furthermore, it should be restricted to the point where marginal net internal economies equal marginal net external diseconomies. Any further restriction could not yield Pareto better states since the required compensation to B would exceed the price A would be willing to pay for the restriction.

Thus, we reach the conclusion against total enforcement of all laws. For a Pareto optimal solution, external diseconomies should not be eliminated—only manipulated to the point where they are balanced off by internal economies (or in the general case, internal and external economies). Even in a Pareto optimum some people can profit at the expense of others—some crime is necessary. Thus, even though the activity of theft involves certain immediate external diseconomies to the initial victim and to the rest of society in terms of subsequent costs of prevention, en-

---

28. The costs of negotiating, legislating, and enforcing these transfers would, of course, be a significant cost to be considered when comparing the net benefits of moving to an alternative state. In fact, these costs often give an overwhelming advantage to the status quo. Mishan (1967) extends this argument to a position favoring the nonpermissive state where activities causing external diseconomies are in general forbidden. The onus then would lie with the "criminal" to prove some activity should be allowed.

forcement, drafting of new laws, and of potential effects on legal markets due to this illegal redistribution of goods, the presence of these externalities by themselves does not provide any prima facie economic argument for restricting the amount of theft. The externalities to the victims[29]—both direct and indirect—must first be weighed against the potential internal economies of the potential offender(s).

We have now arrived at the definition we desire. A criminal activity is a "socially bad" criminal activity if, by restricting its level, the government could achieve a Pareto better level of welfare for the community. It should be pointed out that we are talking about the potential for a Pareto better distribution of welfare. The definition is independent of whether the subsequent transfers are in fact carried out. We now have a definition that is independent[30] of the existing laws. We need not rely on the tautological definition of crime as "that which the law prohibits." It is also independent of any concept of intent. *Mens rea* may become a consideration in choosing the method for regulation but not in deciding whether to regulate in the first place. More generally, the definition is also independent of any theory of why

---

29. When the analysis is extended to cover more than one victim or offender affected by the same activity, the relevant marginal net loss curve is that one representing the sum of the marginal net losses to all victims at each level of theft. The relevant marginal net gain curve similarly is a vertical summation of individual marginal net gain curves. If $G_k{}^i$ ($L_k{}^i$) is the net marginal gain (loss) to the ith of m individuals who are affected by the kth activity, then the condition for the attainment of a Pareto optimum is

$$\sum_{i=1}^{m} G_k{}^i = \sum_{i=1}^{m} L_k{}^i \tag{1}$$

This is the classic optimality condition for a particular class of goods called "public goods" described first by Samuelson (1954).

30. These two points must be qualified to the extent that contrary to Coase (1960) the final Pareto optimal solution will depend on the law existing before as well as after the particular required change in social policy is introduced. See Mishan (1968). Briefly, the positions of A's and B's marginal curves depend on their changing levels of real income as they move from some initial point on the graph to the optimum. The law affects both their initial income (through income, property, and estate tax law) and their initial nonregulated nonoptimal starting position (through the criminal law's being initially permissive or non-permissive). The existing law, therefore, determines the positions of the marginal curves and, therefore, the final optimal position.

people commit crimes. Only in a restricted sense is it similar to the sociological definition of crime in terms of norms and deviations from norms. In that society's norms may determine the subjective evaluations that individuals attach to certain activities, and since these values are weighed one against the other in our decision calculus, norms may affect what we define as "socially relevant"[31] crime. It is, however, possible for an activity to be *de facto* "*normally*" thought of as a crime but when fresh information and analysis are brought to bear it may be a "socially irrelevant" crime or, as defined here, not a "crime" at all.

A related and equally important result arising out of our model is that an activity cannot, in general, be classified as criminal and noncriminal. The question of criminality becomes meaningful only if asked in relation to different levels of an activity. In our example shown in Figure 4-1, the activity, if carried out at a level between O and T_2, is not a crime at all. Indeed, in this case since the effect on A's utility is positive, it is instead an act of charity. Between T_2 and T_0 it is a crime but, again, should not be restricted. In these two areas the conclusion is strengthened even further since not only should "crime" not be restricted, it should be encouraged—we have "socially good" crime. Finally, above T_0 the activity is a "socially bad" crime and should be restricted. In fact, above T_1 it should be restricted for the criminal's own good.

The analysis, among other things, provides a rational justification for police ignoring (encouraging) some "crimes" if they remain below acceptable levels. More generally, the model provides a consistent criteria for deciding which activities should be regulated and to what degree—depending on whether the

---

31. "Socially relevant" is used here to represent a broader class of activities than those defined as "potentially relevant" by Buchanan and Stubblebine (1962). They define as "potentially relevant" any activity "to the extent that it is actually performed, generates any desire on the part of the externally benefited (damaged) party . . . to modify the behavior of the party enpowered to take action. . . ." For an activity to be "socially relevant" the possibility of improving community welfare need only exist, the parties do not have to be aware of it. This is especially important in cases of public goods where the costs of improving the situation might be prohibitive for each individual acting alone, but not for a government acting as their collective agent.

"crime" is now being carried out at a level that is "socially good" or "socially bad."

SOCIALLY RELEVANT CRIME AND COST OF CRIME STUDIES

There would, of course, be problems in operationalizing the evaluative criteria implicit in the foregoing—both problems of measurement[32] and problems of political acceptance. However, the difficulties seem no more insurmountable than those inherent in alternatives with a less palatable theoretical basis.

There have been many preliminary attempts in the measurement area. Both the Wickersham[33] in 1931 and the President's Crime Commission[34] in 1967 attempted measurement of the "cost of crime." These studies were, however, based on rather vague and tenuous definitions of what they were trying to measure.

The cost of crime, or rather the cost of "socially bad" crime, that studies should be measuring, in theory at least, is the potential difference between the level of community welfare before and after the "socially relevant" externalities have been removed. It is a measure of the potential improvement that could be made if the "correct" criminal legislation were drafted and enforced more efficiently. If we are going to continue funding projects which attempt to discover the "cost of crime," we must insist on more than the usual presentation of accounting costs collected with no consistent theoretical basis in mind.

The usual accounting costs seem useful for little else than "scare" value for the authorities. For instance, the market value of goods stolen bears only a tenuous relationship to the reduction in potential community welfare because of theft. The accounting value of bets placed in illegal gambling is more a measure of the benefits to society from bookmaking than of the cost. Tax revenue lost is a measure of the loss to the government—not to the community. If the government would have spent it less productively

32. Some useful comments on measurement, especially of criminal phenomena, can be found in Wilkins (1965), especially Chapter 9.

33. United States National Commission on Law Observance and Enforcement (1931).

34. The President's Commission on Law Enforcement and Administration of Justice (1967).

than the bookmakers, society might even have benefited from the bookmakers' tax evasion.

There is much work yet to be done in developing the necessary theoretical basis and operational tools for estimating any "cost of crime." This work would also seem to be preliminary to attempting any further rough estimates of dubious value.

The preceding concentrated on conceptually defining the problem. There are, however, a few economic problems of a more general nature that any cost of crime study must also meet before it undertakes any empirical analysis.

PRODUCTION AND COST FUNCTIONS

It is impossible to evaluate "cost of crime" research, or for that matter any research, without reference to the purpose for which it is undertaken. The justification for "cost of crime" studies would seem to lie in their usefulness in reducing the same "cost of crime." However, to be operationally useful to a policy-maker these studies, even if they have a strong conceptual base, must do more than present a point estimate of the magnitude of the crime problem. More important to the policy-maker is knowledge of how these costs were incurred and to what degree they are sensitive to different policy alternatives he might choose. Providing useful estimates of the cost of crime, then, involves a two-step procedure of which the first step has largely been ignored.

1. The first step is to estimate what economists would call the crime and anticrime supply and demand functions. These functions describe the quantitative behavioral relationship between the level of either criminal or anticriminal activity and the factors responsible for either of these levels being maintained. Knowledge of the significance of factors subject to control by the criminal justice system authorities such as apprehension, conviction, and sentencing practices would be of special interest. If the quantitative effect of these factors can be estimated, the policy-maker then has valuable information for formulating alternative strategies.

Connected very closely to the supply relationships are "production functions." These functions, in turn, describe the technological relationship between the levels of criminal or anticriminal activity and the resources needed to achieve those levels.

Each square mile per day of protective service might require two police cars, twelve drivers, two foot patrolmen, one receiver/dispatcher, one terminal to a criminal information storage "bank," and two hours service in an auto repair shop. These functions also perform the opposite task of providing information about what effect, for instance, varying the number of police cars would have on the amount of protection supplied.

Since the first of these two types of functions, the supply function, describes individual or group behavioral rather than technological relationships, the psychologist, sociologist, and economist will undoubtedly advocate widely differing specifications for each of the separate functions. If traditional economists control the research in this area, their models will differ from existing specifications in at least two major aspects. First and most important, the general model economists use to describe criminal behavior will probably be derived directly from their general economic theory of choice which assumes individuals act as if they possessed a much higher degree of rationality, intelligence, and consciousness than in most models peculiar to other disciplines. Economic models will no doubt regard the decision to commit a crime as being a choice between legitimate and illegitimate activities based on the perceived relative costs and benefits of each. As with any other activities, the individual is expected to engage in that action that offers the greatest potential increase in utility. This has certainly been the approach adopted by Becker,[35] Harris,[36] Ehrlich,[37] Fleischer (1966a; 1966b) and Schelling.[38] Even

---

35. Becker (1968) presents an attempt to develop optimal policy rules and implications using mathematically sophisticated but theoretically simplified models of the crime-criminal justice system. His model shows, for instance that optimal crime rates are in the region where offenders are risk preferers and, therefore, in an economic sense "crime does not pay." His economic model also shows that offenders should, under his assumptions, be more sensitive to probability of conviction than to value of punishment.

36. Harris (1970) extends Becker's analysis to include some of the costs felt by the community because of overenforcement of the laws.

37. Isaac Ehrlich has been attempting to empirically extend Becker's analysis at the National Bureau of Economic Research and Chicago University.

38. Schelling (1967) is concerned, among other things, with the probable effects on unorganized and organized criminal behavior of alternative policies designed to combat economic crimes.

the incorporation of uncertainty into the economic models still leaves a significant difference between the economic and other social science models. The second is in many ways a reflection of the first. Since they adopt a framework which emphasizes an optimizing calculus, the variables economists are likely to emphasize in their models are those measuring the costs and benefits of alternative opportunities. These variables likely to be tested are, for want of a better word, of a more "economic" nature. In crime supply functions we are thus likely to see emphasized explanatory variables such as wage rates, incomes, and unemployment rates for legitimate activities, and the probability of conviction, available wealth, and expected sentences of illegitimate activities. The worth of these economic models in this area has yet to be proven. Whether they are appropriate will be determined by how well they compare against and in conjunction with models preferred by the other disciplines.

2. We were, however, talking about a two-step procedure for estimating the cost of crime. Once the first step is completed and the necessary production and supply relationships have been empirically estimated, step two can be undertaken. This involves assigning unit costs[39] to the different factors of production within each activity and then showing how these individual and total costs vary with the level of each activity. It is important that these relationships showing how the costs of criminal and anticriminal activity vary with different levels of those activities, or "cost functions," denote first a precise linking of the cost estimates to the activities incurring them and second, denote not a point estimate but a schedule of estimates over different ranges of the

---

39. One of the more promising sources of data for both "costing out" operations and providing incentives for efficient formulation of policy will come as use of the accounting technique of "Planning Programming Budgeting Systems," "PPBS," becomes more widespread. *Program Budgeting,* David Novick, ed. (1967), presents a good introduction to the concepts of PPBS. P. L. Szanton, "Program Budgeting for Criminal Justice Systems," Appendix A of the President's Crime Commission, *Task Force Report: Science and Technology* (1967) presents a sample theoretical PPBS system for criminal justice operations. RAND publications describing their work for the New York City Police Department provide a practical example of what data can be gathered.

incurring activities. The main point in the foregoing is that all three relationships, supply, production,[40] and cost, must be provided if any future cost of crime estimates are to serve a useful purpose to policy-makers.

One of the difficulties in obtaining adequate specifications of any of the production, cost, or supply functions, one economists often encounter in analyzing subsectors of the economic system, arises from the nature of the milieu of most activities to be analyzed. Policemen do not operate in a separable system called a police system. They operate within the much larger criminal justice system with its intricate relationships and feedback mechanisms. Their activity is influenced by activities in other subsystems such as legislating done in the government subsystems or paroling done in the corrections subsystem. Similarly, the levels of activities in the police subsystem in turn affect the workload of the courts and corrections subsystems. It is unfortunately a law of statistics[41] that in order to ensure unbiased estimates of parameters in any relationship or equation describing one of the activities in a system, the researcher must conduct the estimation within a system of relationships or equations each of which describes the activities of a particular subsystem. Any parameters estimated using single equation techniques are certain to suffer often significant bias, and any policy based on such estimates will suffer accordingly. Suppose our policy-maker is interested in the effect that increasing the level of police activity will have on crime rates. To estimate this effect, his researcher may regress offense rates against police activity and get a strong *positive* regression coefficient indicating a positive relationship between the two. Does this imply that he should try to reduce the level of police activity to lower

---

40. Some examples of attempts to estimate these "production" relationships for police can be found in Martin, and Wilson (1969); McCormack; Moen; and Hoffman (1969); McEwen (1968); and Webster (1970).

Similar work for the courts has been done by J. A. Navarro and J. G. Taylor, "Data Analyses and Simulation of Court Systems in the District of Columbia for the Processing of Felony Defendants," President's Commission on Law Enforcement and the Administration of Justice, *Task Force Report: Science and Technology;* and Landes (1971).

41. For more on this see Goldberger (1964).

the offense rates? If he believes his researchers, that would seem the obvious course of action. What is more probable is that his researchers have caught not the supply function of crime but rather the reverse of the supply function of police activity which *a priori* at least would seem to bear a positive relation to the amount of crime. The moral is that in order to get unbiased estimates of the parameters of either of these functions and thereby separate the different processes, he must place the problem into a systems context and apply simultaneous estimation techniques to estimating parameters of both relationships at once. Otherwise, any parameters estimated will be meaningless for policy or any other purpose.

Any cost of a crime or criminal justice program should, therefore, ideally be derived from dynamic models of the criminal justice system and the relations in such a model must be estimated simultaneously. We are obviously still far from having such a model. Temporary recourse to Monte Carlo computer simulation techniques[42] may have to be made in order to circumvent many of the existing problems—not the least of which is the lack of data. This should, however, be regarded as only a temporary measure until more detailed models can be built. What is mandatory in the construction of these models for analyzing policy is a systems or macrocriminological approach rather than the more common narrower microcriminological approaches.

REFERENCES

Arrow, K. J.: *Social Choice and Individual Values.* New York, Wiley, 1951.

Bator, F.: The anatomy of market failure. *Quarterly Journal of Economics,* 72:351-379, 1958.

Becker, G. S.: *Human Capital.* New York, Columbia, 1964.

Becker, G. S.: Crime and punishment: an economic approach. *Journal of Political Economy,* 76(2):169-217, 1968.

Biederman, A., and Reiss, A., Jr.: On exploring the "Dark Figure" of crime. *Annals of the American Academy of Political and Social Science, 374:* 1-15, 1967.

Blumstein, Al, and Larson, R.: Models of a total criminal justice system. *Operations Research, 17*(2):199-232, 1969.

Bonesana, Cesare, and de Beccaria, Marchese: *Essay on Crime and Punishment.* Indianapolis, Liberal Arts Press, 1963.

---

42. See, for instance, Blumstein and Larson (1969); and Space General Corporation (1965).

Bronfenbrenner, M.: A working library on riots and hunger. *Journal of Human Resources,* 4(3):377-390, 1969.

Buchanan, J., and Stubblebine, W. C.: Externality. *Economica,* N.S., 29 (116):371-384.

Coase, R. H.: The problem of social cost. *Journal of Law and Economics,* 3:1-44, 1960.

Dorfman, R., Samuelson, P., and Solow, R.: *Linear Programming and Economic Analysis.* New York, McGraw-Hill, 1958.

Durkheim, E.: *Rules of Sociological Method,* 8th ed. Edited by G. Catlin. Translated by Sarah A. Solvay and John H. Mueller, Glencoe, Free Pr, 1950.

Fleisher, B. M.: *The Economics of Delinquency.* Chicago, Quadrangle, 1966a.

Fleisher, B. M.: The effect of income on delinquency. *American Economic Review,* 56(5):118-137, 1966b.

Goldberger, A. S.: *Systems of Simultaneous Linear Relationship, Economic Theory.* New York, Wiley, 1964, Ch 7.

Harris, J. R.: On the economics of law and order. *Journal of Political Economy,* 78(1):165-174, 1970.

Henderson, J. M., and Quandt, R. E.: *Microeconomic Theory: A Mathematical Approach,* New York, McGraw-Hill, 1958, p. 1.

Hitch, C. J., and McKean, R. N.: *The Economics of Defense in the Nuclear Age.* Cambridge, Harvard U Pr, 1960.

Hoffman, R.: *Technology and the Provision of Policing Service,* Working Paper Series, No. 26, 1969. School of Management, State University of New York at Buffalo.

Judy, R. W., and Levine, J. D.: *A New Tool for Educational Administrators.* Toronto, U of Toronto Pr, 1965.

Kuhn, T. E.: *Public Enterprise Economics and Transport Problems.* Berkeley, U of Cal Pr, 1962.

Landes, W.: An economic analysis of the courts. *Journal of Law and Economics,* 14(1):61-107, 1971.

Martin, J. P.: The cost of crime: some research problems. *International Review of Criminal Policy,* No. 23:57, 1965.

Martin, J. P., and Bradley, J.: Design of a study of the cost of crime. *British Journal of Criminology,* 6(4):591, 1964.

Martin, J. P., and Wilson, G.: *The Police: A Study in Manpower.* London, Hinemann, 1969.

McCormack, R. J., Jr., and Moen, J. L.: San Francisco's Mission Resource Allocation, unpublished, Berkeley, University of California.

McEwen, J. T.: *A Mathematical Model for the Prediction of Police Patrol Resources,* paper delivered to the Spring, 1968 meeting, Operations Research Society of America, San Francisco, California.

Mishan, E. J.: Pareto optimality and the law. *Oxford Economic Papers,* N.S., 19(3):255, 1967.

Mishan, E. J.: On the theory of optimum externality: comment. *American Economic Review*, 59(3):523-527, 1968.

Mishan, E.: A note on the costs of tariffs, monopolies, and thefts. *Western Economic Journal*, 7(3):230-233, 1969.

Novick, David (Ed.): *Program Budgeting*. Cambridge, Harvard U Pr, 1967.

President's Commission on Law Enforcement and Administration of Justice: "The Economic Impact of Crime," Task Force Report: *Crime and Its Impact—An Assessment*, 1967, Ch 3.

President's Commission on Law Enforcement and the Administration of Justice Task Force Report: *Science and Technology*.

President's Crime Commission Task Force Report: *Organized Crime*. Washington, U.S. Government Printing Office, 1967.

Quade, E. S., and Boucher, W. I. (Ed.): *Systems Analysis and Policy Planning: Applications in Defense*. RAND Publication No. R-439-PR. New York, Am Elsevier, 1968.

Raymond, R.: Changes in the relative economic status of nonwhites 1950-60. *Western Economic Journal*, 7(1):57-70, 1969.

Samuelson, P. A.: Evaluation of real national income. *Oxford Economic Papers*, N.S. 2(1):1-29, 1950.

Samuelson, P. A.: The pure theory of public expenditure. *Review of Economics and Statistics*, 36(4):387-389, 1954.

Schelling, Thomas C.: Economics and criminal enterprise. *The Public Interest*, 61-79, 1967.

Shoup, C. S.: Standards for distributing a free governmental service: crime prevention. *Public Finance*, 19(4):383, 1964.

Space General Corporation: *A Study of Prevention and Control of Crime and Delinquency*, Final Report PCCD-7, 1965.

Stark, W. (Ed.): *Bentham's Economic Writings*, 3 vols. New York, Burt Franklin, 1952-54.

Tullock, G.: An economic approach to crime. *Social Science Quarterly*, 50(1):59-71, 1969.

U.S. National Commission on Law Observance and Enforcement: *Report on the Cost of Crime*. Washington, U.S. Government Printing Office, 1931.

Webster, J.: Police task and time study. *The Journal of Criminal Law, Criminology, and Police Science*, 61(1):91-100, 1970.

Weisbrod, B. A.: *Economics of Public Health: Measuring the Economic Impact of Diseases*. Philadelphia, U of Pa Pr, 1960.

Wilkins, L. T.: *Social Deviance, Social Policy, Action and Research*. New York, Prentice-Hall, 1965.

Wilson, Thomas: Liberty as a problem of applied economics. *American Behavioral Scientist*, 8(19):34-37, 1965.

Winch, D. M.: *The Economics of Highway Planning*. Toronto, U of Toronto Pr, 1963.

Chapter 5

AN ECONOMIC APPROACH TO CRIME[1]

GORDON TULLOCK

A MONG THE VARIOUS APPROACHES to the study of crime, the economic perspective has been one of the least developed and
utilized.[2] The purposes of this article are to demonstrate the utility of the economic perspective and to present some simple computational tools in two areas of the law which the reader is likely
to have fairly extensive personal experience—motor vehicle code
violations and tax evasion. In the case of the former, we are not
only fully experienced, but we also have a very good and clear
idea in our own minds of the consequences of the violation. While
our knowledge and experience in regard to tax evasion are rather
less than those concerning violations of the traffic code, most of us
have at least contemplated padding our expenses on the income
tax form, and we find very little difficulty in understanding why
other people actually do it fairly regularly.

In addition to reader knowledge based on experience, there is
a further advantage to discussing motor vehicle offenses and tax
evasion. The customary element in such laws is extremely small.
Most of our laws on crime came down from great antiquity and
hence contain all sorts of quaint nooks and corners. The motor ve-

---

Reprinted, with permission of the Southwestern Social Science Association,
from *Social Science Quarterly,* Volume 50, 1969, pp. 59-71.

1. This article is part of a larger project in which efforts are made to apply
economic reasoning to many aspects of law including more serious crimes than
are discussed herein.

2. The approach is new only in terms of the 20th century. Bentham, Mill and
a number of other 19th-century scholars took a rather similar approach to crime.
Unfortunately, the modern apparatus of welfare economics or cost-benefit analysis
was not available to the 19th-century scholars and hence they were not able
to make as strong a case for their position as can now be made. For a recent
example of much the same approach see Becker (1968).

hicle law is almost entirely a creation of the 20th century and is periodically changed quite drastically. Similarly, the income tax code is largely a recent development, and in this case is being continuously changed by both legislative enactment and the actions of various administrative bodies. Thus, we do not have to deal with the weight of immemorial tradition when we turn to these problems.

ILLEGAL PARKING

To begin, let us consider the most common and simplest of all violations of the law, illegal parking. This is a new problem. In the days of yore, there were not enough idle vehicles to require special parking laws; when, however, common men began to buy automobiles, the number of vehicles was such that simply permitting people to park where they wished along the side of the street led to very serious congestion. The number of spaces was limited, and rationing on a first come, first served basis seems to have been felt to be unsatisfactory.[3] In any event, the proper governmental bodies decided that there should be a "fairer" distribution of parking space, and it was decided that individuals should vacate spaces at some specified time, frequently an hour, after they occupied them.

The question then arose as to how to assure compliance. The method chosen was to fine noncompliance. The police were instructed to "ticket" cars which parked beyond the time limit, and the owners of the ticketed cars were then fined a small sum, say ten dollars. Thus, the individual could choose between removing his car within the prescribed period or leaving it and running some chance of being forced to pay ten dollars. Obviously, the size of the fine and the likelihood that any given car owner would be caught would largely determine how much overparking was done. The individual would, in effect, be confronted with a "price list" to overpark, and would normally do so only if the inconvenience

---

3. We are now discussing the early development of parking regulations. The relatively recent invention of the parking meter has changed the situation drastically and will be discussed later.

of moving his car was greater than the properly discounted cost of the fine.[4]

Not all overparking is the result of a deliberate decision, however. Clearly a good deal of it comes from absentmindedness, and part is the result of factors not very thoroughly under control of the car owner. Nevertheless, we do not in general feel that the fine should be remitted. The absence of a criminal intent, or indeed of any intent at all, is not regarded as an excuse. When I was working in the Department of State in Washington, I served under a man who got several parking tickets a week. I think that I knew him well enough to be sure that all of these violations occurred without any conscious intent on his part. He would get involved in some project and forget that he was supposed to move his car. The District of Columbia was levying what amounted to a tax on him for being absentminded.

As far as I could tell, the police force of Washington, D.C., was not particularly annoyed with my superior. Apparently, they thought the revenue derived paid for the inconvenience of issuing tickets and occasionally towing his car away. Suppose, however, they had wanted to make him stop violating the parking laws. It seems highly probable that a drastic increase in the fines would have been sufficient. Absentmindedness about ten dollars does not necessarily imply absentmindedness about 100 or even 1,000 dollars. With higher fines he would have felt more pressure to train himself to remember, to avoid parking on the public streets as much as possible, and to arrange for his secretary to remind him. Thus, the fact that he was not engaging in any calculations at all when he committed these "crimes" does not indicate that he would not respond to higher penalties by ceasing to commit them.

So far, however, we have simply assumed that the objective is to enforce a particular law against parking. The question of whether this law is sensible, or how much effort should be put into enforcing it, has not been discussed. In order to deal with this

---

4. I am indebted to Professor Alexandre Kafka for the "price list" analogy. He insists, following his own professor, that the entire criminal code is simply a price list of various acts.

problem, let us turn to a more modern technology and discuss a metered parking area. In such areas the government in essence is simply renting out space to people who want to use it. It may not be using a market-clearing price because it may have some objectives other than simply providing the service at a profit, but this does not seriously alter the problem. For simplicity, let us assume that it is charging market-clearing prices. It would then attempt to maximize total revenue, including the revenue from fines and the revenue from the coins inserted in the parking meters minus the cost of the enforcement system. We need not here produce an equation or attempt to solve this problem, but clearly it is a perfectly ordinary problem in operations research, and there is no reason why we should anticipate any great difficulty with it.

Other Motor Vehicle Laws

However, parking is clearly a very minor problem; in fact, it was chosen for discussion simply because it is so easy. In essence, there is very little here except calculation of exactly the same sort that is undertaken every day by businessmen. For a slightly more complicated problem, let us consider another traffic offense—speeding. Presumably, the number of deaths from auto accidents, the extent of personal injuries and the material damage are all functions of the speed at which cars travel.[5] By enforcing a legal maximum on such speed, we can reduce all of them. On the other hand, a legal maximum speed will surely inconvenience at least some people, and may inconvenience a great many. The strictly material cost of lowering speeds is easily approximated by computing the additional time spent in traveling and multiplying this by the hourly earning power of an average member of the population. This is, of course, only an approximation, leaving out of account such factors as the pleasure some people get out of speed and the

---

5. Recently this relationship has been somewhat obscured by the publication of Ralph Nader's *Unsafe at any Speed*. It is undoubtedly true that cars can be designed to reduce fatalities in accidents and, for that matter, that highways can be designed to reduce accidents. Recent discoveries of methods of reducing skidding by improved highway surfaces probably indicate that there is more potential in highway improvement than in car redesign. Nevertheless, for a given car and highway, speed kills.

diversion of economic activity which would result from the slowing of traffic. Nevertheless, we could use this approximation[6] and the costs of deaths, injuries and material damage from auto accidents to work out the optimal speed limit, which would be simply the limit which minimized total costs in all of these categories. The computation would be made in "social" terms because the data would be collected for the whole population. Individuals, however, could regard these figures as actuarial approximations for their personal optima.

To the best of my knowledge, no one has ever performed these calculations in a reasonably direct and precise way. Presumably the reason for the omission is an unwillingness to consciously and openly put a value on deaths and injuries which can then be compared with the strictly material costs of delay. When I point out to people that the death toll from highway accidents could be reduced by simply lowering the speed limit (and improving enforcement), they normally show great reluctance to give any consideration to the subject. They sometimes try to convince themselves that the reduction would not have the predicted effect, but more commonly they simply shift quickly to another subject. They are unwilling, for reasons of convenience, to approve a substantial lowering of the speed limit, but they do not like to consciously balance their convenience against deaths. Nevertheless, this is the real reasoning behind the speed limits. We count the costs of being forced to drive slowly and the costs of accidents, and choose the speed limit which gives us the best outcome. Since we are unwilling to do this consciously, we probably do a bad job of computing. If we were willing to look at the matter in the open, consciously to put a value on human life, we could no doubt get better results.

As an example of this reluctance to think about the valuation we are willing to put upon deaths and injury in terms of our own convenience, a colleague of mine undertook a study of the methods used by the Virginia Highway Commission in deciding how to improve the roads. He found that they were under orders to

---

6. For those who object to approximation, more elaborate research, taking into account much more of the costs of slowing down traffic, could be undertaken.

consider speed, beauty, and safety in presenting projects for future work. The beauty was taken care of by simply earmarking a fixed part of the appropriations for roadside parks, etc. For speed they engaged in elaborate research on highway use and had statistical techniques for predicting the net savings in time from various possible changes. It was the possibility of improving these techniques which led them to invite my colleague to make his study. For safety, on the other hand, they had no system at all.

It was clear that they did take safety into account in designing roads, and spent quite a bit of money on various methods of reducing the likelihood of accidents. They did not, however, have any formula or rule for deciding either how much should be spent on safety or in what specific projects it should be invested. They must have had some trade-off rule which they applied. This rule, however, remained buried in their subconscious even though they used fairly elaborate and advanced techniques for other problems. This is particularly remarkable when it is remembered that, given any exchange value, the computations of the amount to be spent on safety would be fairly easy.

If, for example, it is decided that we will count one fatal accident as "worth" $500,000 in inconvenience to drivers (measured in increased travel time), then, with statistics on accidents and volume of traffic, it would be possible to work out how much should be spent on safety and how much on speed. Since the Highway Commission did not spend all of its money on safety, some such "price" for accidents must have taken some part of its reasoning, but rather sophisticated engineers were unwilling to admit, probably even to themselves, that this was so. Perhaps more surprising, my colleague fully approved of their attitude. Basically a "scientific" type, with a great interest in statistical decision theory, he felt that here was one place where careful reasoning was undesirable. He did not want to consider ratios between deaths and convenience himself, did not want the people who designed the highways on which he drove to consciously consider them, and did not want to discuss the subject with me.

But even if we do not like to critically examine our decision process, clearly the decision as to the speed limit is made by bal-

TABLE 5-I

EFFECTS OF SPEED LIMITS

Speed Limit (mph)	Deaths per 100,000,000 Miles	Costs of Delay
10	1	$50,000,000,000.00
20	2	35,000,000,000.00
30	4	22,500,000,000.00
40	8	15,500,000,000.00
50	16	5,000,000,000.00
60	32	2,000,000,000.00
70	64	500,000,000.00

ancing the inconveniences of a low limit against the deaths and injuries to be expected from a high one. The fact that we are not willing to engage in conscious thought on the problem is doubly unfortunate, because it is difficult enough so that it is unlikely that we can reach optimal decisions by any but the most careful and scientific procedures. The problem is stochastic on both sides since driving at a given speed does not certainly cause an accident; it only creates a probability of an accident. Similarly, our convenience is not always best served by exceeding the speed limit, so we have only a stochastic probability of being inconvenienced. There will also be some problems of gathering data which we do not now have (mainly because we have not thought clearly about the problem) and making reasonable estimates of certain parameters. In order to solve the problem we need a table of probabilities rather like Table 5-I. Obviously, with this table, and one more thing, a conversion factor for deaths and delay, we could readily calculate the speed limit which would minimize the "cost" of using the road.[7]

Equally obviously, no direct calculation of this sort is now undertaken, but our speed limits are set by a sort of weighing of ac-

7. Note that I am ignoring all consequences of accidents except deaths and that it is assumed that the speed limit is the only variable. These are, of course, simplifying assumptions introduced in order to make my table simple and the explanation easy. If any attempt were made to explicitly utilize the methods I suggest, much more complex data would be needed. The figures are, of course, assumed for illustrative purposes only.

cident prevention against inconvenience. The only difference between our present methods and the ones I have outlined is that we are frightened of having to admit that we use a conversion ratio in which lives are counted as worth only some finite amount of inconvenience, and we refuse to make the computations at a conscious level and hence are denied the use of modern statistical methods.

Having set a speed limit, we now turn to its enforcement. If, for example, the limit is 50 MPH, then it does not follow the people who drive over that speed will automatically have accidents. Nor does it follow that driving at 51 MPH is very much more likely to lead to an accident than driving at 50 MPH. The use of a simple limit law is dictated by the problems of enforcement rather than the nature of the control problem itself. If we had some way of simply charging people for the use of the streets, with the amount per mile varying with the speed,[8] this would permit a better adjustment than a simple speed limit. In practice, the police and courts do something rather like this by charging much higher fines for people who greatly exceed the speed limit. Let us, however, confine ourselves to the simple case where we have a single speed limit, with no higher fines for exceeding it by a sizable amount.

Our method of enforcing this law is in some ways most peculiar. In the first place, if a citizen sees someone violating this law and reports it, the police will refuse to do anything about it. With one specific exception, which we will footnote in a moment, you cannot be penalized for speeding unless a police officer sees you do it. Think what burglars would give for a similar police practice in their field of endeavor.

A second peculiarity is that the penalty assessed is unconnected with the attitude of mind of the person who violates the speed limit.[9] Driving at 70 MPH may get you a fine of 100 dollars or a

---

8. Needless to say, the cost of driving 50 MPH in a built-up area would be higher than in the open countryside.

9. There is a partial and imperfect exception to this for certain special cases. The man who speeds to get his wife to the hospital before the birth of their child is perhaps the one who gets the most newspaper attention.

ten-year sentence, depending upon the occurrence of events over which you have no control. Suppose, for example, two drivers each take a curve in the highway at 70. The first finds a police car on the other side, gets a ticket and pays a fine. The second encounters a tractor driving down his side of the road and a column of cars on the other side. In the resulting crash, the tractor driver is killed, and the outcome may be a ten-year sentence for the driver of the car.[10] We can assume both men exceeded the speed limit, for the same motives, but the second had bad luck. Normally we like to have penalties depend upon what the defendant did, not on external circumstances beyond his control. (The only other situation in which this kind of thing is done involves the rule which makes a death caused while committing a felony murder regardless of the intent.)

The peculiarity of this procedure is emphasized when it is remembered that the man who risks being sent up for ten years for killing someone in an accident almost certainly had no intent to do so. He was driving at high speed in order to get somewhere in a hurry, an act which normally leads to a moderate fine when detected. The heavy sentence comes not from the wickedness of this act, but from the fact that he drew an unlucky number in a lottery. The case is even clearer in those not terribly rare cases where the accident arises not from conscious violation of the law but from incompetence or emotional stress (losing one's head). In ordinary driving we frequently encounter situations where a small error in judgment can cause deaths. A man who has no intent to drive carelessly may simply be a bad judge of distance and try to pass a truck where there is insufficient room. An excitable person may "freeze" when some emergency arises, with the result that there is an accident which could easily have been prevented. Both of these cases might well lead to prison terms in spite of the complete lack of "criminal intent" on the part of the defendant. "If a driver, in fact, adopts a manner of driving which the

10. Note that the rule that a traffic offense is prosecuted only if seen by a police officer is not followed in the event of a serious accident. A third driver may be imagined who took the curve at the same speed and met neither the police nor the tractor. He would, of course, go off scot-free even if his offense were reported to the police.

jury thinks dangerous to other road users . . . then on the issue of guilt, it matters not whether he was deliberately reckless, careless, momentarily inattentive, or doing his incompetent best."[11]

As anybody who has studied game theory knows, a mixed strategy may pay off better than a pure strategy. It may be, therefore, that the combination of three different treatments is better than a simpler rule providing a single and fairly heavy penalty for speeding, regardless of whether you hit anyone or happen to encounter a policeman while engaged in the criminal act. But, although we must admit this possibility, it seems more likely that a single penalty based on the intent of the individual would work better in preventing speeding. The probable reason for the rather peculiar set of rules I have outlined is simply the functioning of the court system. If someone who disliked me alleged that he had seen me speeding and I denied it, the court would have to decide who was lying without much to go on except the expressions on our faces. Since "dishonesty can lie honesty out of countenance any day of the week if there is anything to be gained by it," this is clearly an uncertain guide. Thus, under our current court system, permitting people to initiate prosecutions for speeding by stating that they had seen someone doing so would almost certainly mean that innumerable spite cases would be brought before the courts, and that the courts would make many, many mistakes in dealing with them.

Similarly, the use of two sets of penalties for speeding, depending on factors not under the defendant's control, is probably the result of judicial performance. Charging a very heavy fine or relatively brief imprisonment for every speeding conviction would very likely be resisted by judges who do not really think speeding is very serious unless it kills somebody. That this is the restriction cannot strictly be proven but at least some evidence can be provided for it. In Virginia, as in many states, multiple convictions for traffic offenses can result in removal of the driving license. The state has encountered real difficulty in getting its judges to carry out this provision. Under the conditions of modern life the deprivation of a driver's license is a real hardship, and judges appar-

---

11. Hill v. Baxter, 1 *QB* (1958), p. 277.

ently do not like to impose it for a speeding offense simply because the offender has been convicted twice before. Similarly, if a license is suspended, the courts are unlikely to inflict a very heavy penalty on the man who drives anyhow, provided he avoids killing someone.[12]

It is probable that problems of judicial efficiency account for another peculiarity of the motor traffic code; i.e. it is almost impossible for an individual to defend himself against the accusation. Normally the police officer's testimony is accepted regardless of other evidence. Further, in general, the penalty exacted for the average minor violation of the code is small if the defendant pleads guilty, but high if he does not. Parking offenses, for example, may very commonly be settled for one or two dollars on a guilty plea, but cost ten to twenty if you choose to plead not guilty. This amounts to paying the defendant to plead guilty. As almost anyone who has had any experience with a traffic court is aware, most of the people who get tickets are indeed guilty, but those who are not guilty normally plead guilty anyway because of this system of enforcement.

Obviously we could apply the same line of reasoning to deal with all other parts of the traffic code. The problem is essentially a technological one. By the use of some type of exchange value and evidence obtained from statistical and other sources, we could compute a complete traffic code which would optimize some objective function. In practice we do not do this because of our reluctance to specify an exchange value for life. Nevertheless, we get much the same result, albeit with less accuracy and precision, by our present methods.

TAX EVASION

Turning now to the income tax law, we must begin by noting that apparently almost anybody can get special treatment. The

12. Possibly, given the difficulties of enforcement, a restriction of the license rather than a removal might be wise. Restricting the license of a multiple offender to a limited area, including his home, a couple of shopping centers and his place of employment, together with a low speed limit, say 30 MPH, might appeal to judges who would be unwilling to remove the license totally. Judges might also be more inclined to give heavy sentences to people who violate such restrictions than to people who continue to drive to work in spite of the lack of a license.

present laws and regulations are a solid mass of special rules for special groups of people. There are innumerable cases where some particularly wealthy man or large corporation has succeeded in obtaining special tax treatment. Nevertheless, we can consider how the existing tax code should be enforced.

Unfortunately, even the enforcement is full of loopholes. In the first place, there are a great many people (special classes that readily come to mind are doctors, waitresses, and farmers) who have special facilities for evading the income tax. It is also widely believed that certain groups (the farmers in particular) have been able to make use of their political power to see to it that the Internal Revenue Service does not pay as much attention to detecting evasion by them as by other groups. Nevertheless, we can assume that the tax code contains within it both a set of special privileges for individuals and instructions for evasion which apply only to certain classes, and hence that the true tax law is residual after we have knocked all these holes in what was originally a rather simple piece of legislation.

There are further difficulties. The individual presumably is interested in the taxes being collected from other people because he wants the government services which will be purchased by them. He would prefer to be left free of tax himself, but this is unfortunately not possible. He, in a sense, trades the tax on his own income for the benefit which he obtains from the purchase of government services by the entire community. It is by no means clear that for everyone the present amount of government services is optimal. If I felt that the total amount of government services being purchased today was excessive (i.e. that lower tax rates and lower levels of service were desirable), presumably I would feel relatively happy about systematic evasion of a tax law on the part of everyone. On the other hand, if I felt that the present level of government services was too low and the taxes should be higher, I might conceivably feel that "overenforcement" is desirable.

Even if I am happy with the present level of government expenditures, it is by no means obvious that I should be terribly much in favor of efficient enforcement of the revenue code. I might favor a revenue code which sets rates relatively high and

TABLE 5-II

DEFINITIONS OF SYMBOLS

C_P	= Private cost of enforcement (includes cost of incorrect tax penalties)
C_R	= Cost of revenue protection service
I	= Income
I'	= Some part of income
L_C	= Likelihood of compliance
L_D	= Likelihood of detection of evasion
N	= Social return on tax (excess burden not subtracted)
P	= Penal rate for detected noncompliance
R	= Tax rate
T_R	= Tax revenue (net of direct enforcement costs)

an enforcement procedure which permits a great deal of evasion to lower rates and better enforcement procedures which brought in the same revenue. Surely I would prefer the former if I had some reason to believe that I would be particularly able to evade the taxes. But even if I assume that everyone will have about the same ability to evade, I might still prefer the higher rates and higher level of evasion. Nevertheless, it seems to me that most people would prefer the lowest possible level of tax for a given net return. I have been unable to prove that this is optimal,[13] but it does seem to me to be reasonable that this would be the appropriate social goal. In any event, that is the assumption upon which our further calculations are built. It would be relatively easy to adjust these calculations to any other assumption on this particular matter.

Under these circumstances and on these assumptions, the return in taxation to the government from various levels of enforcement can be seen by Equation 1, which is fairly lengthy but really simple. (See Table 5-II for definitions of symbols.)

$$T_R = L_C \cdot R \cdot I + (1 - L_C) \cdot I' \cdot L_D \cdot P - C_R \qquad (1)$$

The first term on the right of the equal sign is the likelihood that individuals will fully comply with tax laws, multiplied by the tax rate and income. Note that this is deliberately somewhat ambiguous. It can be taken as any individual's tax payments or the payment

---

13. I sincerely hope that some of my readers may be able to repair this admission.

for the economy as a whole, depending on which definition we choose for income. We add to this the probability that an individual will attempt to evade payment of taxes on all or part of his income, times the probability of detection of his evasion, times the penalty he will be compelled to pay on the evasion. This gives us the total return which the community will receive. There is, of course, the cost of maintaining the inspection and revenue collection system, which is subtracted from this output in the final term C_R.

Ignoring, for the moment, the taxpayer's propensity toward accepting risks, the condition for a favorable decision to attempt *to evade* the tax legally payable on some particular portion of his income is

$$L_D \cdot P \cdot I' < R \cdot I' \qquad (2)$$

That is to say, if the likelihood of detection times the penalty he must pay on detection is less than the rate that he would legally pay, he would appropriately attempt to evade. It will be noted that both in this inequality and in the previous equation there is an implicit assumption that the individual will be able to pay a fine if he is found to have evaded the tax law. The reason that the individual is normally able to pay a fine is simply that in general those who get into income tax difficulties are well off.

Nevertheless, although this is a very good approximation, it is not entirely accurate. The income tax authorities do sometimes attempt to put people in prison for tax evasion. In general, the Internal Revenue Service has a dual system. If you make a "tax saving" which is relatively easy for them to detect, they will normally adjust your return and charge you a relatively modest interest payment. If, on the other hand, you do something which is quite hard to detect, which normally means a directly dishonest statement, they assess a much heavier penalty. From their standpoint no doubt this is sensible as a way of minimizing enforcement costs.

There is another peculiarity of the income tax policing process. Usually the policeman himself (i.e. the Internal Revenue man) simply assesses a deficiency on the face of the form if he does not suspect what is technically called evasion. This is usually the complete legal proceeding. In small cases the individual normally pays, although he may complain to the person making the assessment. It is highly probable that in this matter, as in other small claims litigation, there is a great deal of inaccuracy on both sides. Since these are small matters, the use of a cheap but relatively inaccurate procedure is optimal. For major matters, however, very elaborate legal proceedings may be undertaken. These proceed at first through the administrative channels of the Internal Revenue Service and turn to the regular courts only if all administrative methods are exhausted. Here one would anticipate a great deal more care and far fewer errors, and there is no doubt that this is the case.

Returning, however, to our basic equations, it will be noted that the likelihood of quiet compliance (i.e. the likelihood of the income-tax payer's making no effort to evade) is a function of the likelihood of detection of evasion as shown in Equation 3:

$$L_C = g(L_D) \qquad (3)$$

The likelihood of detection of evasion in turn is a function of two things, as shown in Equation 4:

$$L_D = h_1(C_R) + h_2(C_P) \qquad (4)$$

One of these, of course, is simply the amount of resources that we put into the revenue service. The second, however, is the resources that we force the private taxpayer to put into keeping records and filing returns and doing other things which make it easier to enforce the tax revenue code. Thus, Equation 1 was incomplete. Equation 5 shows the net social benefit, or loss from the tax, including the factor C:

$$N = L_C \cdot R \cdot I + (1 - L_C) \cdot I' \cdot L_D \cdot P - C_R - C_P \qquad (5)$$

It will be noted that I have, for these computations, ignored problems of excess burden.

The term C_P is interesting and very comprehensive. It not only includes the troubles involved in filling out the income tax forms, which we all know may be considerable, but also the necessity of keeping our accounts in such form that the Internal Revenue Service may survey them. It includes the possibility that we will be audited even if we have not violated the law. It does not include any penalty which we might incur if we have violated the law, because that is included under P. It includes a number of other things which are somewhat less obvious, however. It includes the inconvenience we might suffer occasionally when the Internal Revenue Service is investigating a potential violation of the internal revenue code by someone other than ourselves; we might, for some reason, have some evidence which the Internal Revenue Service wants and be compelled to furnish it. It also includes the possibility that the Internal Revenue Service will wrongly suspect us and will then assess an incorrect fine upon us. Lastly, of course, it includes legal expenses involved in all of the above. Thus, it is by no means a small figure.

Still, the problem is relatively easy. We should simply maximize N.[14] Examination of this equation indicates some superficially not terribly probable consequences. We could, for example, be in favor of increasing enforcement even though we know it is likely to raise our own payments. It will be noted that there is nowhere in the equation the assumption that we will obey the law and others will not. If we really believe that the government money is being spent for something worthwhile, then we make a net gain of some nature from increasing N. It is true that the N in our equation represents this net gain very crudely, since it takes a total figure rather than a marginal figure, but we need not worry about this.

As noted above, we might feel it desirable to include some kind of risk aversion factor. If the penalty for evasion of the tax code is quite large, let us say 25 times the tax that is evaded, and if we feel that there is a fair probability of the Internal Revenue Service going wrong in assessing such penalties, then our term C_P could be large. This might still maximize the value of N, but if we are risk avoiders, we might prefer a lower value of N in order to avoid the risk of being assessed such a very large penalty.

But these are refinements. Basically we could calculate an op-

14. J. Randolph Norsworthy (1965) has studied present-day Internal Revenue procedures on the assumption that they behave somewhat in accord with the instruction of maximizing T_R. His methods are quite different from ours, but his doctoral dissertation is well worth studying.

timum tax enforcement policy from a set of equations such as those here. I think that if the reader considers his own reactions he will realize that his own attitude towards the income tax authorities is based upon something like this form of reasoning. He does, of course, hope that the income tax authorities will give him special treatment and does his best to obtain it. But insofar as this special treatment has already been taken into account, his behavior would be appropriately described by Equation 2. His behavior with respect to general social policy in this period would then be described more or less by a desire to maximize N in Equation 5. There may be some people who have strong moral feelings about their own payments under the income tax, but I have never run into them. Most of my friends will talk about the desirability of the income tax, but I also find them discussing in detail what they can get away with. In fact, I suspect that moral considerations are less important in tax enforcement than any other single part of the law.

SUMMARY

In this article we have discussed two areas of the law with which the reader is likely to have fairly great personal experience. We have demonstrated in both cases the very simple computational tools for defining an "optimum law." Application of these computational tools would, it is true, require the development of certain empirical information we do not now have, but they are nevertheless suitable guides to further work. Further, our computational tools in this respect are simply formalizations of the thought processes now used by most people in dealing with these matters.

REFERENCES

Becker, Gary: Crime and punishment: an economic approach. *Journal of Political Economy*, 74:169-217, 1968.

Norsworthy, J. Randolph: *Tax Evasion*, doctoral dissertation, University of Virginia, 1965.

Section II

EMPIRICAL STUDIES OF
THE ECONOMICS OF
CRIMINAL BEHAVIOR

Chapter 6

PARTICIPATION IN ILLEGITIMATE ACTIVITIES: A THEORETICAL AND EMPIRICAL INVESTIGATION

ISAAC EHRLICH

INTRODUCTION

MUCH OF THE SEARCH in the criminological literature for a theory explaining participation in illegitimate activities seems to have been guided by the predisposition that since crime is a deviant behavior, its causes must be sought in deviant factors and circumstances determining behavior. Criminal behavior has traditionally been linked to the offender's presumed unique motivation which, in turn, has been traced to his presumed unique inner structure, to the impact of exceptional social or family circumstances, or to both (for an overview of the literature see, e.g. Taft and England, 1964).

A reliance on a motivation unique to the offender as a major explanation of actual crime does not, in general, render possible predictions regarding the outcome of objective circumstances. We are also unaware of any persuasive empirical evidence reported in the literature in support of theories using this approach. Our alternative point of reference, although not necessarily incompatible, is that even if those who violate certain laws differ systematically in various respects from those who abide by the same laws, the former, like the latter, do respond to incentives. Rather than resort to hypotheses regarding unique personal characteris-

This study has been supported by a grant for the study of law and economics from the National Science Foundation to the National Bureau of Economic Research.

Reprinted, with permission of the University of Chicago Press, from *Journal of Political Economy*, May/June 1973, pp. 521-564.

tics and social conditions affecting respect for the law, penchant for violence, preference for risk, or in general preference for crime, one may separate the latter from measurable opportunities and see to what extent illegal behavior can be explained by the effect of opportunities given preferences.

In recent years a few studies attempted to investigate the relation between crime and various measurable opportunities. For example, Fleisher (1966) studied the relation between juvenile delinquency and variations in income and unemployment conditions via a regression analysis, using inter- and intracity data relating to the United States in 1960. Smigel-Leibowitz (1965) and Ehrlich (1967) used several regression methods to study the effect of probability and severity of punishment on the rate of crime across states in the United States in 1960. In his significant theoretical contribution to the study of crime in economic terms, Becker (1968) has developed a formal model of the decision to commit offenses which emphasizes the relation between crime and punishment. Stigler (1970) also approaches the determinants of the supply of offenses in similar terms. Following these studies, and particularly my 1970 study, an attempt is made in this paper to formulate a more comprehensive model of the decision to engage in unlawful activities and to test it against some available empirical evidence. My analysis goes beyond that of Becker and other previous contributions in several ways. First, it incorporates in the concept of opportunities both punishment and reward—costs and gains from legitimate and illegitimate pursuits—rather than the cost of punishment alone, and attempts to identify and test the effect of their empirical counterparts. Specifically, it predicts and verifies empirically a systematic association between the rate of specific crimes on the one hand, and income inequality as well as law enforcement activity on the other. Second, it links formally the theory of participation in illegitimate activities with the general theory of occupational choices by presenting the offender's decision problem as one of an optimal allocation of resources under uncertainty to competing activities both inside and outside the market sector, rather than as a choice between mutually exclusive activities. The model developed can be used to predict not only the *direction*, but also the relative *magnitude* of the response of specific offenders to changes in various observable opportunities. In addition, the analysis distinguishes between the deterrent and preventive effects of punishment by imprisonment on the rate of crime (by the latter is meant the reduction in criminal activity due to the temporary separation of imprisoned offenders from potential victims) and enables an empirical verification of the former effect alone. Finally, in the context of the empirical implementation, I analyze the interaction between offense and defense—between crime and (collective) law-enforcement activity through police and courts—and employ a simultaneous-equation econometric model in estimating supply-of-offenses functions and a production function of law-enforcement activity. The results of the empirical investigation are then used to provide some tentative estimates of the effectiveness of law enforcement in deterring crime and reducing the social loss from crime.

THE CRIMINAL PROSPECT

In spite of the diversity of activities defined as illegal, all such activities share some common properties which form the subject matter of our analytical and empirical investigation. Any violation of the law can be conceived of as yielding a potential increase in the offender's pecuniary wealth, his psychic well-being, or both. In violating the law one also risks a reduction in one's wealth and well-being, for conviction entails paying a penalty (a monetary fine, probation, the discounted value of time spent in prison and related psychic disadvantages, net of any direct benefits received), acquiring a criminal record (and thus reducing earning opportunities in legitimate activities), and other disadvantages. As an alternative to violating the law one may engage in a legal wealth- or consumption-generating activity, which may also be subject to specific risks. The net gain in both activities is thus subject to uncertainty.

A simple model of choice between legal and illegal activity can be formulated within the framework of the usual economic theory of choice under uncertainty. A central hypothesis of this theory is that if, in a given period, the two activities were mutually exclusive, one would choose between them by comparing the expected utility associated with each alone.[1] The problem may be formulated within a more general context, however, for the decision to engage in illegal activity is not inherently an either/or choice, and offenders are free to combine a number of legitimate and illegitimate activities or switch occasionally from one to another during any period throughout their lifetime.[2] The relevant object of choice to an offender may thus be defined more properly as his optimal activity mix: the optimal allocation of his time and other resources to competing legal and illegal activities.[3] Allowing explicitly for varying degrees of participation in illegitimate activity, we then develop behavioral implications concerning entry into, and optimal participation in, such activity.

Optimal Participation in Illegitimate Market Activities: A One-Period Uncertainty Model

For the sake of a simple yet general illustration, assume that an individual can participate in two market activities: i, an illegal activity, and l, a legal one, and must make a choice regarding his optimal participation in each at the beginning of a given period. No training or other entry costs are required in either activity, neither are there costs of movement between the two. The returns in both activities are monotonically increasing functions of work-

---

1. Such formulation is used in Ehrlich (1967) and Becker (1968).

2. The standard literature on occupational choices usually assumes specialization in a single activity, rather than multiple-job holding. An important incentive for such specialization arises from time dependencies generated by specific training, for wages in activities involving training stand in some positive relation to the total amount of time previously spent there training or learning by doing. Multiple-job holding also entails various costs of movement between jobs that may offset potential gains due, say, to the increased returns on time spent in each. Specialization in a single market activity may thus be optimal, at least during periods of intensive training. Nevertheless, in the case of market activities involving a large measure of risk, there may be an incentive for diversifying resources among several competing activities. We propose that such an incentive exists in the case of illegitimate activities, especially those that do not require specific training.

3. In addition, an offender's probability of being apprehended and convicted of a specific charge is not determined by society's actions alone, but is modifiable through his deliberate actions (self-protection). For an analysis of an offender's simultaneous decision to allocate resources to illegal and legal activities as well as to self-protection, see Ehrlich (1970).

ing time. Activity l is safe in the sense that its net returns are given with certainty by the function $W_l(t_l)$, where t denotes the time input. Activity i is risky, however, in the sense that its net returns are conditional upon, say, two states of the world: a, apprehension and punishment at the end of the period, with (subjective) probability p_i and b, getting away with crime, and probability $1-p_i$. If successful, the offender reaps the entire value (pecuniary and nonpecuniary) of the output of his illegitimate activity, net of the costs of purchased inputs (accomplices' and accessories' services) $W_i(t_i)$.[4] If apprehended and punished, his returns are reduced by an amount $F_i(t_i)$: the discounted (pecuniary and nonpecuniary) value of the penalty for his entire illegitimate activity and other related losses (including the possible loss of his loot). It is assumed that the probability of apprehension and punishment is independent of the amount of time spent in i and l,[5] and that time is proportionally related to any other direct inputs employed in the production of market returns.

The individual is assumed to behave as if he were interested in maximizing the expected utility of a one-period consumption prospect.[6] For analytical convenience, let the utility in any given state of the world s, be given by the function

$$U_s = U(X_s, t_c), \tag{1.1}$$

4. In large measure, the pecuniary returns from crime are positively related to the amount of transferable goods and assets and other wealth possessed by potential victims. More important, these returns may be subject to uncertainty due to varying degrees of self-protection provided by potential victims. (For a theoretical analysis of private self-protection, see Ehrlich and Becker, 1972.) For analytical simplicity, and in view of the limited data available for an empirical estimation of illegitimate returns, we here treat W_i as a single-valued function of t_i.

5. This assumption is relaxed in Ehrlich (1970), where we have allowed p_i to be a positive function of t_i (or the number of offenses committed), and a negative function of the degree of self-protection provided by the offender, which, in turn, is expected to be positively related to t_i. The behavioral implications of our model are shown to hold in this more general case, as well.

6. This may be compatible with the assumption that the individual wishes to maximize the expected utility of his lifetime consumption, since it is possible, in general, to represent his decision problem at any given period in terms of maximizing a derived one-period utility function, which is explicitly a function of current variables, but which also summarizes realized past consumption and the results of optimal decisions at relevant subsequent periods for all possible future events. For an elaborate discussion of this proposition, see Fama (1970).

where X_s denotes the stock of a composite market good (including assets, earnings within the period and the real wealth equivalent of nonpecuniary returns from legitimate and illegitimate activity), the command over which is contingent upon the occurrence of state s; t_c is the amount of time devoted to consumption or nonmarket activity; and U is an indirect utility function that also converts X_s and t_c into consumption flows. Denoting all earnings within the period in real terms, that is, in terms of the composite good X, there exists under the foregoing assumptions regarding the earning functions in i and l only two states of the world with respect to X. Either

$$X_b = W' + W_i(t_i) + W_l(t_l) \tag{1.2}$$

is obtained with probability $1 - p_i$, or

$$X_a = W' + W_i(t_i) - F_i(t_i) + W_l(t_l) \tag{1.3}$$

is obtained with probability p_i, where W' denotes the market value of the individual's assets (net of current earnings), including his borrowing opportunities against earnings in future periods, and is assumed to be known with certainty, given the state of the world in the beginning of each period. The expected utility which is generally given by

$$EU(X_s, t_c) = \sum_{s=a}^{n} \pi_s U(X_s, t_c) \tag{1.4}$$

where π_s denotes the probability of state s, reduces in this case to

$$EU(X_s, t_c) = (1 - p_i)U(X_b, t_c) + p_i U(X_a, t_c). \tag{1.4a}$$

The problem thus becomes that of maximizing equation (1.4a) with respect to the choice variables t_i, t_l, and t_c, subject to the wealth constraints given by equations (1.2) and (1.3), a time constraint,

$$t_0 = t_i + t_l + t_c, \tag{1.5}$$

and nonnegativity requirements,

$$t_i \geq 0; \; t_l \geq 0; \; t_c \geq 0. \tag{1.6}$$

Substituting equations (1.2) and (1.3) in equation (1.4a), the

Kuhn-Tucker first-order optimality conditions can be stated as follows:

$$\frac{\partial EU}{\partial t} - \lambda \leq 0,$$

$$\left(\frac{\partial EU}{\partial t} - \lambda \right) t = 0, \qquad (1.7)$$

$$t \geq 0,$$

where t stands for the optimal values of each of t_i, t_l, and t_c, and λ is the marginal utility of time spent in consumption. It can easily be shown that given the amount of time allocated to consumption t_c, the optimal allocation of working time between i and l, in case of an interior solution, must satisfy the first-order condition,

$$- \frac{w_i - w_l}{w_i - f_i - w_l} = \frac{p U'(X_a)}{(1 - p) U'(X_b)}, \qquad (1.8)$$

where $w_i = (dW_i/dt_i)$, $f_i = (dF_i/dt_i)$ and $w_l = (dW_l/dt_l)$. The term on the left-hand side of equation (1.8) is the slope of an opportunity boundary, the production transformation curve of the composite good X between the two states of the world considered in this example (by condition [1.6] it is defined only between points A and B in Fig. 6-1), and the term on the right is the slope of an indifference curve (defined along $dU^* = 0$). In an equilibrium position involving participation in both i and l, they must be the same. Clearly, a necessary prerequisite for equation (1.8) is that the potential marginal penalty, f_i, exceed the differential marginal return from illegitimate activity, $w_i - w_l$, for otherwise the marginal opportunities in i would always dominate those in l.[7] The imposition of concurrent imprisonment terms for several offenses committed by the same offender is thus shown to create an incentive for offenders to specialize in illegitimate activity. Equation (1.8) would be necessary and sufficient for a strict global maximum involving participation in both i and l if the indifference curve is strictly convex to the origin (which implies

7. This paraphrases and modifies a well-known argument that "the evil of punishment must be made to exceed the advantage of the offense" (see Bentham 1931, p. 325).

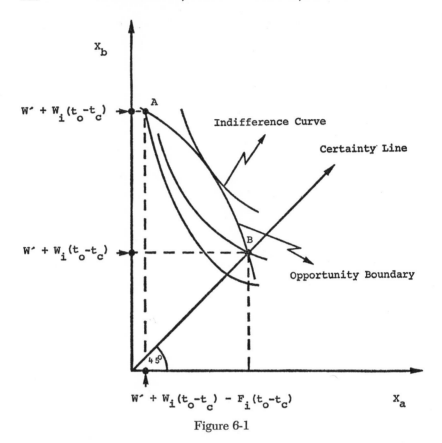

Figure 6-1

diminishing marginal utility of real wealth) and the opportunity boundary is linear or strictly concave (which is consistent with, say, diminishing marginal wages and constant or increasing marginal penalties).[8]

Figure 6-1 and equation (1.7) can be used to analyze the range of possible combinations of illegitimate and (safe) legitimate activities. A *sufficient* condition for entry into i—regardless of attitudes toward risk—is that the absolute slope of the oppor-

8. The second-order condition for a (strict) local maximum in this case is

$$\Delta = (1 - p)U''(X_b)(w_i - w_l)^2 + pU''(X_a)(w_i - f_i - w_l)^2 \tag{1.8a}$$

$$+ (1 - p)U'(X_b)\left(\frac{dw_i}{dt_i} + \frac{dw_l}{dt_l}\right) + pU'(X_a)$$

$$\left(\frac{dw_i}{dt_i} - \frac{df_i}{dt_i} + \frac{dw_l}{dt_l}\right) < 0.$$

tunity boundary exceed the absolute slope of the indifference curve at the position where the total working time is spent in legitimate activity (point B on the certainty line) or $-(w_i - w_l)/(w_i - f_i - w_l) > p_i/(1 - p_i)$. This requires, in turn, that the marginal expected return in i exceed that in l. For risk avoiders or risk-neutral persons, this is also a necessary condition for entry into i, and its converse would imply their specialization in l.

If the opportunity boundary were concave to the origin, as in Figure 6-1 (or if the probability of apprehension and punishment were a positive function of t_i), participation in both legitimate and illegitimate activity may be consistent with constant or increasing marginal utility of wealth. Assuming that the opportunities available to offenders were independent of their attitudes toward risk, it can then be shown that a risk-neutral offender will spend more time in illegitimate activity relative to a risk avoider, and a risk preferrer will spend more time there relative to both.[9] Moreover, if the opportunity boundary were linear (and p_i were constant), *offenders* who are risk preferrers would necessarily specialize in illegitimate activity, since the optimality conditions imply a corner solution in this case. In contrast, offenders who are risk avoiders are likely to combine a relatively safe legitimate activity with their illegitimate activity to hedge against the relatively greater risk involved in a full-time pursuit of the latter. Whether offenders are likely to specialize in illegitimate activity thus becomes an aspect of their attitudes toward risk, as well as their relative opportunities in alternative legitimate and illegitimate activities.[10] Also, whether in equilibrium, crime pays or does

---

9. By equation (1.8) in an equilibrium position, $- (1 - p_i)(w_i - w_l)/p_i(w_i - f_i - w_l) \gtrless 1$; that is, $E(w_i) = (1 - p_i)w_i + p_i(w_i - f_i) \gtrless w_l$, as $U'' \lessgtr 0$. Since the opportunity boundary is concave to the origin, the equilibrium position of a risk preferrer must be to the left of that of a risk neutral, and even further to the left of that of a risk avoider (i.e. closer to the X_b axis).

10. At present, there are no reliable statistics on how many crimes are committed by full-time criminals. Studies of prisoners in federal, state, and local correctional institutions in the United States show that a majority of these offenders did have legitimate occupational experience—mainly in unskilled occupations—prior to their apprehension, and that only a small fraction never worked (see Ehrlich, forthcoming, NBER). Other available data indicate that professional criminals are responsible for a large proportion of major thefts (see PCL, p. 47).

not pay in terms of expected (real) marginal returns is simply a derivative of an offender's attitude toward risk, since in equilibrium the expected marginal returns from crime would exceed, be equal to, or fall short of the marginal returns from legitimate activity, depending on whether the offender is a risk avoider, risk neutral, or risk preferrer, respectively.[11]

Although our model has been illustrated for two states of the world, the analysis generally applies to *n* states—various combinations of contingencies in legitimate and illegitimate activities. For example, if returns in *i* and *l* are (each) subject to a binomial probability distribution due to success or failure in *i* and employment or unemployment in *l* throughout a given period, the necessary condition for an interior solution with respect to the allocation of working time between *i* and *l* that maximizes equation (1.4) becomes

$$(1 - p_i)(1 - u_l)U_a'(w_i - w_l) + (1 - p_i)u_lU_b'w_i \\ + p_i(1 - u_l)U_c'(w_i - f_i - w_l) + p_iu_lU_d'(w_i - f_i) = 0, \quad (1.9)$$

where u_l is the probability of unemployment in *l* and *a, b, c,* and *d* are the four relevant states of the world.[12] The basic implications of the preceding analysis hold with some modifications in this more general case as well (see Ehrlich 1970).

The model developed in this section can be used to explain why many offenders, even those convicted and punished, tend to repeat their crimes. Given the offender's opportunities and preferences, it may be optimal for him to commit several offenses in any given period. Moreover, even if there were no systematic variations in preferences for crime from one period to another (these may in fact intensify), an offender is likely to repeat his illegitimate activity if the opportunities available to him remain

---

11. A proof is given in n. 9. Some evidence as to whether crime pays in the monetary sense alone is discussed below in n. 49.

12. In deriving eq. (1.9), we have implicitly assumed that legitimate wage rates in case of unemployment are zero. Note that losses from unemployment may be insured via market insurance, whereas no such insurance is available against punishment for crime. This is one reason for expecting *l* to be a safer activity relative to *i*.

unchanged. Indeed, legitimate earning opportunities of convicted offenders may become much more scarce relative to their illegitimate opportunities because of the criminal record effect and the effect of long imprisonment terms on legitimate skills and employment opportunities. Recidivism is thus not necessarily the result of an offender's myopia, erratic behavior, or lack of self-control, but may rather be the result of choice dictated by opportunities.

Some Behavioral Implications

Equation (1.7), and, more specifically, equations (1.8) or (1.9), identify the basic factors determining entry into and optimal participation in illegitimate activities. We now turn to derive some comparative statics implications associated with these factors and start by considering their effects on the (relative) allocation of working time $(t_0 - t_c)$ between competing legitimate and illegitimate activities in the market sector.

An increase in either p_i or f_i with no change in the other variables entering equation (1.8) or (1.9) reduces the incentive to enter and participate in illegitimate activity because it increases the expected marginal cost of punishment, $p_i f_i$. If an offender had a neutral attitude toward risk, and was only interested in the expected value of his wealth prospect, the magnitude of his response to a 1 percent increase in either p_i or f_i would be the same, for equal percentage changes in each of these variables have the same effect on $p_i f_i$. Equal percentage changes in p_i and f_i may have quite different effects on the expected utility from crime, however, if one has nonneutral attitudes toward risk. The deterrent effect of a 1 percent increase in the marginal or average penalty per offense can be shown to exceed or fall short of that of a similar increase in the probability of apprehension and punishment if the offender is a risk avoider or a risk preferrer, respectively. Moreover, if the offender was a risk preferrer and yet partly engaged in legitimate activity, an increase in the average penalty per offense might not deter his participation in crime.

Such participation might even increase.[13] This result is not inconsistent with an assertion often made by writers on criminal behavior regarding the low, or even the positive effect of punishment on the criminal propensities of *some* offenders. Such behavior is here found to be consistent with preference for risk and need not be interpreted as evidence of an offender's lack of response to incentives.

Similarly, an increase in the marginal or average differential return from illegal activity, $w_i - w_l$, resulting from an increase in (real) illegitimate payoffs or a decrease in (real) legitimate wages with no change in the other variables entering equations (1.8) or (1.9), can generally be shown to increase the incentive to enter into or allocate more time to illegitimate activity: since the opportunity boundary in Figure 6-1 becomes steeper about point B, some persons who initially specialized in legitimate activity would now find it optimal to allocate some time to an illegitimate activity (more general proofs are given in Ehrlich, 1970 under some restrictive assumptions regarding absolute risk aversion). However, an increase in the *probability* of unemployment, u_l (if unemployment is viewed as an uncertain event in the beginning of a given period), has a more ambiguous effect on the incentive to

---

13. The effect of a 1 percent increase in p_i on the optimal fraction of working time allocated to i, t_i^*—W', w_i, w_l, f_i, and t_c held constant—can be found, for example by differentiating eq. (1.8) with respect to $\ln p_i$: $(\partial t^*_i / \partial p_i) p_i = (1/\Delta)$ $[-U_a'(w_i - f_i - w_l)p_i + U_b'(w_i - w_l)p_i] = (+)/(-) < 0$, where Δ is defined in eq. (1.8a) in n. 8. Similarly, the partial effect of a 1 percent increase in all the penalty rates, f_i, hence in the average rate, $f = (F/t_i)$, would be given by $(\partial t_i^* / \partial f)f$ $= (1/\Delta) [U_a'p_i f_i + U_a''(w_i - f_i - w_l)p_i f t_i^*]$. If $U'' \leqq 0$, the preceding equation would always be negative. The result would be ambiguous, however, if $U'' > 0$, and would depend on opposite wealth and substitution effects. Moreover, it can easily be verified that

$$-\frac{\partial t_i^*}{\partial p_i} \ p_i \gtreqless -\frac{\partial t_i^*}{\partial f} f, \text{ as } U'' \gtreqless 0, \tag{1.10}$$

where the right-hand side of eq. (1.10) represents the effect of a 1 percent change in either the marginal or the average penalty for crime. This result can also be shown to apply under some restrictive assumptions to the relative effects of probability and severity of punishment on the *absolute* amount of time allocated to i. Moreover, it holds unambiguously for the relative effects of these variables on the incentive to enter (or exit from) illegal activity (a mathematical proof is given in Ehrlich, 1970).

assume the greater risk involved in additional illegitimate activity if offenders are risk avoiders.[14]

A pure wealth effect may be defined as the effect of an equal proportional increase in wealth in every state of the world with no change in the probability distribution of states. Such may be the case when legitimate and illegitimate returns increase by the same proportion, and punishment for crime is by imprisonment (an empirical implementation of this case is considered below). Whether the optimal allocation of working time between i and l changes would then depend on whether an offender has increasing or decreasing relative risk aversion.[15] Increasing relative risk aversion thus implies that the rich have a lesser incentive to participate in crimes punishable by imprisonment relative to the poor.

Note, finally, that a decrease in the amount of time allocated to nonmarket activities (including schooling), due to a change in factors other than those considered in the preceding analysis, is likely to generate a positive scale effect on participation in i and l: since more time is spent in market activities, more time would be spent in both legal and illegal market activities, provided that the reduction in t_c did not affect one's relative preferences for wealth in different states of the world (that is, provided the indifference map depicted in Fig. 6-1 were invariant to changes in t_c).

We have so far considered the effects of changes in various indicators of the opportunities available in legitimate and illegitimate activities on the fraction of working time allocated to these activities. The behavioral implications of the preceding analysis would strictly apply to the absolute level of participation in i and l if changes in market opportunities did not affect the demand for time in nonmarket activities due, say, to offsetting wealth and

---

14. The reason is that the increase in the probability of the least desirable state of the world (unemployment in l and failure in i) increases the demand for wealth in this state and might decrease the incentive to participate in i since the latter decreases the potential wealth in this state (see Ehrlich, 1970, appendix 1). However, the partial effect of an increase in u_l on entry into i is unambiguously positive and symmetrical to that of an increase in p_i.

15. For an elaborate discussion of this result, see Ehrlich and Becker (1972).

substitution effects. This may not be true in general. For example, wealth-compensated changes in legitimate and illegitimate opportunities generate a pure substitution effect on the demand for consumption time. A partial increase in w_i is then expected to increase both the fraction of working time devoted to i as well as its absolute level, due to a complementary scale effect on working time. In contrast, a partial increase in w_l would lead to a decrease in the absolute level of participation in i only if the resulting substitution effect within the market sector exceeds an opposite scale effect on working time. This analysis shows that the effect of compensated and even uncompensated changes in legitimate market wages on the extent of participation in i may be lower than that of changes in illegitimate payoffs. Another important result is that the effect of uncompensated changes in various legitimate and illegitimate opportunities on the extent of participation in illegitimate activities is generally expected to be greater on offenders who participate in such activities on a part-time basis than on those who specialize in such activities. To illustrate, if an offender specializes in i—a boundary solution obtains—his objective opportunities will not be affected at all by small changes in legitimate employment opportunities, and he may not respond even to changes in illegitimate opportunities if such uncompensated changes have no effect on the demand for consumption time.[16] Thus, the extent of (initial) participation in illegitimate activity may be an important determinant of the *magnitude* of the response of specific offenders to changes in various market opportunities. Full-time or hard-core offenders may be less deterred in absolute magnitude by, say, an increase in law-enforce-

---

16. More generally, let the total time spent in illegitimate activity be given by the identity $i \equiv t_0 - c - l$, where i, c, and l denote the number of hours an offender spends in i, c, and l, respectively. Let the subscripts p and f distinguish between relatively part-time and full-time offenders. By assumption, then, $i_f > i_p$ $l_p > l_f \geq 0$. If a is a parameter that improves the relative opportunities in i, the effect of an uncompensated increase in a on i_p and i_f will be denoted by $E_{pa} = (\partial i_p/\partial a)(a/i_p)$ and by $E_{fa} = (\partial i_f/\partial a)(a/i_f)$, respectively. Assuming, now, that the partial elasticities of l and c with respect to a, $\sigma_{la} = -(\partial l/\partial a)(a/l)$ and $\sigma_{ca} = -(\partial c/\partial a)(a/c)$, are the same for both groups of offenders, then it can easily be shown that $D \equiv E_{pa} - E_{fa} = \sigma_{la}(l_p/i_p - l_f/i_f) + \sigma_{ca}(c_p/i_p - c_f/i_f)$ is necessarily positive if $\sigma_{la} \geq \sigma_{ca} \geq 0$.

ment activity, relative to part-time or occasional offenders, simply because of their greater involvement in illegitimate activity.

Market Opportunities and Crimes Against the Person

Unlike crimes involving material gains that may be motivated largely by the offender's desire for self-enrichment, crimes against the person may be motivated primarily by hate or passion: phenomena involving interdependencies in utilities among individuals whereby the utility of one is systematically affected by specific characteristics of another.[17] It may thus be appropriate to consider crimes against the person nonmarket activities, that is, activities that directly meet needs, as distinct from market or wealth-generating activities.

Since those who hate need not respond to incentives any differently from those who love or are indifferent to the well-being of others, the analysis of the preceding sections would apply, with some modifications, to crimes against the person as well as to crime involving material gains. Specifically, an increase in the probability and severity of punishment would deter crimes against the person for the same reasons it was expected to deter participation in crimes against property. Moreover, independent changes in legitimate market opportunities may also have a systematic effect on participation in crimes against the person. For example, given the total time spent in nonmarket activities, t_c, an increase in w_l that was fully compensated by a reduction in other income would reduce the demand for time-intensive consumption activities (for this concept, see Becker 1965) because of the increase in their relative costs; some crimes against the person might fit into this category.[18] In contrast to crimes against property, how-

---

17. Indeed, the empirical evidence lends support to such a proposition, for it shows that crimes against the person, unlike crimes against property, occur most frequently among people known to exercise close and frequent social contact and whose utilities are likely to be interdependent. For a more elaborate discussion, see Ehrlich (1970).

18. This is likely particularly in view of the prospect of imprisonment associated with these crimes. If the length of incarceration, rather than the full cost of imprisonment, f_i, is held constant, as in the empirical implementation of our model, an increase in w_l is likely to increase the cost of crimes against persons relative to legitimate consumption activities.

ever, a decrease in t_c due to specific exogenous factors is likely to produce a negative scale effect on participation in crimes against the person simply because less time could then be spent on all nonmarket activities, legitimate, as well as illegitimate. It also follows that an improvement in legitimate earning opportunities that increases the total amount of time spent at work may reduce participation in crimes against the person even if it did not increase the cost of such crimes relative to other nonmarket activities (some empirical evidence pertaining to these implications is discussed on pp. 180-184).

THE SUPPLY OF OFFENSES

The Behavioral Function

Given the validity of our analysis and the behavioral implications developed in the preceding section, we may now specify a behaviorial function relating a person's actual participation in illegal activity in a given period to its basic determinants. Since in many illegal activities crime is comprised of discrete actions, or offenses, the dependent variable could be generally specified in terms of the directly observable number of offenses one commits, q_{ij}, rather than as the amount of time and other resources one devotes to such activities, assuming that the latter are monotonically related:

$$q_{ij} = \Psi_{ij}(p_{ij}, f_{ij}, w_{ij}, w_{lj}, u_{lj}, \pi_j). \qquad (2.1)$$

The argument π_j is introduced in equation (2.1) to denote other variables that may affect the frequency of offenses committed by a specific individual, j, in addition to those discussed in the preceding section. These include his personal or family level of wealth, his efficiency at self-protection, the amount of private insurance provided by his family (or a criminal organization), and other factors that may affect the demand for time spent in nonmarket activities. In addition, the variable π includes costs and gains in other specific illegal activities which are close substitutes or complements to the illegal activity, $(_i)$.[19] Finally, π ac-

---

19. We have already considered the choice between single legitimate and illegitimate activities, but the analysis could easily be extended and applied to a choice among several competing legitimate and illegitimate activities. Participation in i might , in general, be affected by the opportunities available in some related illegal activities, as well as in l.

counts for the form of the penalty: imprisonment, a fine, or their combination. (The importance of this distinction is discussed below.)

The Aggregate Function

If all individuals were identical, the behavioral function (2.1), except for change in scale, could also be regarded as an aggregate supply function in a given period of time. In general, however, none of the variables entering (2.1) is a unique quantity, since people differ in their legitimate and illegitimate earning opportunities and hence in their opportunity costs of imprisonment (if punishment assumes such form). Therefore, the behavioral implications derived earlier apply here for independent changes in the level of the entire distributions of these variables, or for changes in the mean variables within specific communities, holding all other parameters of the distributions constant:

$$Q_i = \Psi_i(P_i, F_i, Y_i, Y_l, U_l, \Pi_i), \qquad (2.2)$$

where P_i, F_i, etc., denote the mean values of p_{ij}, f_{ij}, etc., and Π includes, in addition to environmental variables, all the moments of the distributions of p, f, etc., other than their means.

Our general expectations concerning the effect of exogenous shifts in various opportunities on the number of offenses committed may hold with fewer qualifications in the aggregate than in the case of individual offenders. The aggregate supply curve of offenses can be conceived of as the cumulative distribution of a density function showing variations across persons with respect to the minimum expected net gain that is sufficient to induce them to enter an illegal activity (their entry payoffs) as well as the extent of response of active offenders to changes in net gains. Variations in entry payoffs across persons reflect different attitudes toward risk (as well as different psychic net benefits if the net gain is defined to include monetary elements only). People with preference for risk or a penchant for violence may enter crime even when their expected monetary gains are negative. Others, risk averters or law abiders, may enter crime only when the expected monetary gains are very high. A positive elasticity of the aggregate supply of offenses with respect to an increase in net gains from an offense may thus be expected, even if all individual supply curves were infinitely elastic—that is, if all offenders specialized in illegitimate activity and did not respond to such change at all—because the higher net gains would induce the entry of new offenders to illegitimate activity.

The Preventive Effect of Imprisonment

The set of hypotheses spelled out on pages 151-156 regarding the effect of various opportunities on individuals', and hence the aggregate, supply of offenses, follows from our basic thesis that offenders respond to incentives. However, an increase in the probability and severity of punishment by imprisonment might reduce the total number of offenses even if it did not have any deterrent effect on offenders, because at least those imprisoned are temporarily prevented from committing further crimes. While both deterrence and prevention may serve equally well the basic purpose of law enforcement, which is to reduce total crime, they involve different costs. Moreover, the preventive effect of imprisonment may be partly offset by the enhanced incentive for recidivism generated through the possible adverse effect of imprisonment on legitimate relative to illegitimate skills and employment opportunities. It is therefore important (and challenging) to establish the existence of an independent deterrent effect of imprisonment on crime, both to verify the validity of our theory and to determine the effectiveness of penal modes that may have a deterrent effect only.

An estimation of the preventive effect of imprisonment can be derived through the following reasoning. Suppose that offenders constituted a noncompeting group that does not respond to incentives, the constant proportion of which $\overline{S} = S/N$, is determined by nature, and let punishment be imposed solely in the form of imprisonment. In this model, where no deterrent effect of imprisonment (or other factors) is assumed, the rate (per capita) of flow of offenses in any given period, $k = Q/N$, would be a positive function of the rate of offenders at large (those free to commit offenses), $\overline{\theta} = \theta/N$, or

$$k_t = \zeta \overline{\theta}_t, \tag{2.3}$$

where ζ is the number of offenses committed by an average offender in a given period and is assumed to be constant. The rate of offenders at large in the population is in turn identically equal to the rate of the offenders' subpopulation net of the rate of those in jail, or

$$\bar{\theta}_t = \bar{S}_t - \bar{J}_t. \tag{2.4}$$

Let the fraction of offenders apprehended and imprisoned in any period (the probability that an offender is apprehended and jailed in t) be P, and let the average duration of time spent in jail by each convict be T periods. It can then be shown that in a steady state the rate of offenders in jail would be

$$\bar{J} = \frac{\bar{S}\, P \displaystyle\sum_{\tau=1}^{T} (1+g)^{-\tau}}{1 + P \displaystyle\sum_{\tau=1}^{T} (1+g)^{-\tau}}, \quad \text{for } P < 1, [20] \tag{2.5}$$

where g is a constant rate of growth (per period) of both the total

---

20. The number of offenders jailed in the beginning of each period is identically equal to the total number of offenders apprehended and jailed in the preceding T periods, or

$$J_t \equiv \sum_{\tau=1}^{T} P(S_{t-\tau} - J_{t-\tau}).$$

Given that $S_t = S_0(1+g)^t$ and $N_t = N_0(1+g)^t$, the identity above can be expressed as a linear difference equation of the Tth degree,

$$\bar{J}_t + P(1+g)^{-1}\bar{J}_{t-1} + \ldots + P(1+g)^{-T}\bar{J}_{t-T} = P\bar{S} \sum_{\tau=1}^{T} (1+g)^{-\tau}. \tag{2.5a}$$

Equation (2.5) is the particular integral of eq. (2.5a). The condition $P < 1$ (if $g \geq 0$) can be shown to be a sufficient condition for the general solution of (2.5a) to converge toward the equilibrium value of its particular integral.

population and the offender subpopulation. Substituting equations (2.6) and (2.5) in (2.4) yields

$$k = \frac{\zeta \overline{S}}{1 + p \sum_{\tau = 1}^{T} (1 + g)^{-\tau}} \approx \frac{\zeta \overline{S}}{1 + PT} \text{ for } g \approx 0. \quad (2.6)$$

Since ζ, g, and $\overline{S}$ are assumed given constants, the rate of offenses committed in a steady state would be a negative function of PT, the expected length of imprisonment for an offender. In particular, the absolute value of the elasticity of the rate of offenses per period with respect to changes in probability and severity of imprisonment would be approximately the same:[21]

Clearly, σ is independent of the value of ζ and is positively related to PT.[22] Therefore, the preventive effect of imprisonment may be relatively small for less serious crimes. Equation (2.7) establishes the important point that the preventive effect of P and T is in principle distinguishable from the deterrent effect: Not only is the latter compatible with, say, $\sigma_{kT} \geq 1$, it is also compatible with $\sigma_{kT} \gtrless \sigma_{kP}$.[23] The existence of a deterrent effect can thus be inferred from empirical estimates of the absolute and relative values of σ_{kP} and σ_{kT}.

21. An increase in P may have a greater preventive effect than an equal proportional increase in T in the short run, however, because the latter does not have any immediate impact on the number of offenders at large, whereas an increase in P does. Indeed, that may have led some criminologists to believe the probability of punishment to be of greater importance than severity of punishment in preventing crime (see Becker 1968, p. 176 n. 12). A comparison of the exact values of σ_{kP} and σ_{kT} in eq. (2.7) shows that a relatively greater effect of P may persist, to a limited extent, even in a steady state, if $g > 0$ and $T > 1$.

$$\sigma_{kP} \approx \sigma_{kT} \approx \frac{PT}{1 + PT} \text{ for } g \approx 0. \quad (2.7)$$

22. This implies a potential variation across states in the coefficients (elasticities) b_1 and b_2 of the regression eq. (3.2), for states with relatively higher values of PT might have higher elasticities of offenses with respect to P and T. However, the variation in PT of specific crimes across states is found to be quite small in practice.

23. In terms of our model (see eq. [1.10] in n. 13), $\sigma_{kF} > \sigma_{kP}$ indicates risk aversion on the part of the average offender. Since $\sigma_{kT} \leqq \sigma_{kF}$ (see Appendix, item 3), this conclusion may be strengthened if $\sigma_{kT} > \sigma_{kP}$.

An Econometric Specification of the Model

The Supply-of-Offenses Equation

The variables entering the behavioral function (2.1) have been generally defined in terms of the real wealth equivalent of both monetary and psychic elements. Since psychic elements cannot be accounted for explicitly in an empirical investigation, it will be useful to modify equations (2.1) and (2.2) by separating quantifiable from nonquantifiable variables. A simple form of a mean (group) supply-of-offense function which is consistent with this modification is

$$\left(\frac{Q}{N}\right)_i = P_i^{b_{1i}} F_i^{b_{2i}} Y_i^{c_{1i}} Y_l^{c_{2i}} U_i^{d_i} V^{c_i} Z_i, \tag{3.1}$$

where (Q/N_i) denotes the number of offenses in crime category i committed by the average person in a community (crime rate); F_i, Y_i and Y_l are arithmetic means of the monetary components of f_{ij}, w_{ij}, and w_{lj} in eq. (2.1); V is a vector of environmental variables; and Z summarizes the effect of psychic and other nonquantifiable variables on the crime rate.[24]

To the extent that individuals' taste for crime was either proportional to some of the quantifiable variables affecting crime, or uncorrelated in the natural logarithms with all the explanatory variables, it is possible to specify a stochastic function of the form

$$\left(\frac{Q}{N}\right)_i = A P_i^{b_{1i}} F_i^{b_{2i}} Y_i^{c_{1i}} Y_l^{c_{2i}} U_i^{d_i} V^{e_i} \exp(\mu), \tag{3.2}$$

---

24. The mean supply-of-offenses function given by eq. (3.1) can be derived by integrating individual supply-of-offenses functions of the same form if the individual elasticities b_{1ij}, b_{2ij}, etc., are the same for all. The variables entering eq. (3.1) would then be the geometric means of the corresponding variables entering eq. (2.1). However, if the density function of, say, p_{ij}—$g(p_{ij}P_i)$—were equal across states and homogeneous of degree minus one in p_{ij} and P_i (the arithmetic mean), and similarly for all the explanatory variables entering eq. (2.1), then eq. (3.1) could be specified in terms of arithmetic rather than geometric means, with an appropriate modification of the constant term Z (for proofs see Tobin, 1950 or Chow, 1957). Note, however, that to the extent that the variation in the rate of crime across communities is due to changes in the average offender's participation in crime, and not only to entry and exit of offenders, the coefficients of eq. (3.2) may vary systematically with Q/N; the regression equation may not, then, be strictly linear in the parameters. This problem is ignored in our analysis.

where A is a constant, and μ stands for random errors of measurement and other stochastic effects and is assumed to have a normal distribution. In this paper we apply equation (3.2) in a cross-state regression analysis.[25]

Crime, Income Inequality, and Affluence

It was shown earlier that the extent of individual participation in crime, and hence the crime rate in each state, is a positive function of the absolute differential returns from crime $(Y_i - Y_l)$.[26] Information concerning such monetary differential returns is at present unavailable on a statewide basis, and alternative income opportunities cannot be estimated unless one is able to identify a control group representing potential offenders and study its alternative income prospects. The difficulty may be met, in part, by making some plausible assumptions regarding the occupational characteristics of activities such as robbery, burglary, and theft, which are actually investigated in our empirical analysis. We postulate that payoffs on such crimes depend, primarily, on the level of transferrable assets in the community, that is, on opportunities provided by potential victims of crime, and to a much lesser extent on the offender's education and legitimate training. The relative variation in the average potential illegal payoff, Y_i, may be approximated by the relative variation in, say, the median value of transferrable goods and assets or family income across states which we denote W.[27] The preceding postulate also implies that

25. The cross-state regression analysis does not control spillovers or displacement effects due to a possible migration of individuals from one state to another in response to differences in opportunities across states. To the extent that such effects exist, the estimated coefficients associated with P_i, F_i, and Y_i would be overstated, while those associated with Y_l and U would be understated, relative to their values in closed communities. We implicitly assume, however, that there is no perfect mobility of resources across states because of considerable costs of migration. Different states can thus be viewed essentially as different markets.

26. The *elasticity* of offenses with respect to Y_i need not be equal to that with respect to Y_l. We have therefore introduced both variables in eq. (3.2) (rather than the difference $Y_i - Y_l$), allowing for their coefficients c_1 and c_2 to be different.

27. More precisely, the assumption is that, given the relative distribution of family income in a state, variations in average potential payoffs on property crimes can be approximated by the variation in the level of the *entire* distribution. If the income distribution were of the log-normal variety, it can be shown that variation

those in a state with legitimate returns well below the median have greater differential returns from property crimes and, hence, a greater incentive to participate in such crimes, relative to those with income well above the median. The variation in the mean legitimate opportunities available to potential offenders across states, Y_l, may therefore be approximated by that of the mean income level of those below the state's median. Partly because of statistical considerations, we have chosen to compute the latter somewhat indirectly by the percentage of families below one half of the median income in a state, which we denote X (income inequality).[28]

Since X is a measure of the *relative* distance between legitimate and illegitimate opportunities, changes in W, X held constant, would amount to equal percentage changes in the absolute wage differential, $Y_i - Y_l$. Given the probability and severity of punishment, an increase in W might have a positive effect on the rate of property crimes similar to that of X. In our empirical implementation, the severity of punishment, F, is measured by the

---

in its level would be reflected by an equal proportional variation in its *median* value. Note that the relative variation in *potential* payoffs on property crimes may be an unbiased estimator of the relative variation in the realized gross payoffs if self-protection (of property) by potential victims were proportionally related to their wealth.

28. Let the average legitimate income of those with income below and above the average be w_p and w_r, respectively. Our measure of income inequality X (originally used by Fuchs, 1967, as an index of poverty) can be regarded as inversely related to w_p/W. If median income, W, were held constant, the effect of an increase in X on the rate of property crimes $k = Q/N$ would be given by $\sigma_x = -d\ln k/d\ln(w_p/W) = \eta_p + \eta_r \, d\ln w_r/d\ln w_p$, where $\eta_p = -\partial\ln k/\partial\ln(w_p/W)$ and $\eta_r = -\partial\ln k/\partial\ln(w_r/W)$. By our assumptions η_r is much smaller than η_p. A 1 percent increase in X might therefore have approximately the same effect as a 1 percent decrease in legitimate opportunities available to potential offenders, or $\sigma_x \approx \eta_p$. In contrast, if the income effect on the supply of malice and acts of hate were the same for rich and poor alike, $\eta_p = \eta_r = \eta$, then an increase in income inequality—mean and median income held constant—can be shown to have a positive effect on the incidence of crimes against the person only if the income effect were negative ($\eta > 0$), for then $\sigma_x = \eta \, [1 - (w_p/w_r)] > 0$. Precisely the same result applies in reference to the impact of an increase in X on crime through its opposing effects on self-protection by potential victims. One reason for employing X rather than w_p in the regression analysis is that its correlation with W is relatively lower.

effective incarceration period of offenders, T. If punishment were solely by imprisonment, an increase in W, X and T held constant, might increase $Y_i - Y_l$ and F (the opportunity cost of imprisonment) by the same proportion, and its net effect could be nil (see our discussion of pure-wealth effects on pg. 153). In contrast, an increase in X would imply in this case a decrease in both Y_l and F. In practice, however, a major proportion of offenders is punished by means other than imprisonment (see Ehrlich 1970, Table 1). Consequently, we may expect the median income level (affluence) as well as income inequality to be positively related to the incidence of property crimes. Note that one advantage of introducing W and X in equation (3.2) in lieu of $Y_i - Y_l$ is that the former can be treated as exogenous variables, whereas the actual differential gain from crime may be a function of both the crime rate and private expenditure on self-protection (see our discussion in nn. 4 and 29).

Crime and Law Enforcement: A Simultaneous-Equation Model

Equation (3.2) defines the rate of a specific crime category $(Q/N)_i$ as a function of a set of explanatory variables, including the probability and severity of punishment. In general, both P and F may not be exogenous variables, since they are determined by the public's allocation of resources to law-enforcement activity and, as will be argued below, by the level of crime itself. The expenditure on law enforcement, in turn, is likely to be affected by the rate of crime and the resulting social loss. In order to insure consistent estimates of equation (3.2), it is desirable to construct a simultaneous-equation model of crime and law enforcement.[29]

To simplify matters, we assume that the severity of punishment is in practice largely unaffected by the joint determination of Q/N

---

29. Simultaneous relations may also exist between the rate of crime, the average payoff from crime, Y_i, and *private* self-protection against crime that can be expected to have an adverse effect on both (see our discussion in n. 4). We do not elaborate on these relations here because in our empirical investigation we use indirect estimates of Y_i that can be considered largely exogenous to our system of equations and because of the lack of reliable data on private self-protection.

and P.[30] Our model consists of a supply-of-offenses function discussed above, a production function of direct law-enforcement activity by police and courts, and a (public) demand function for such activity.

An increase in expenditure on police and courts, E/N, can be expected to result in a greater proportion of offenders apprehended and convicted of crime. However, the productivity of these resources is likely to be lower at higher levels of criminal activity because more offenders must then be apprehended, charged, and tried in court in order to achieve a given level of P. Thus, with a given level of expenditure devoted to law-enforcement activity, the rate of crime and the probability of apprehension and punishment for crime might be negatively related, but the causality runs in an opposite direction from the one predicted by our analysis; for example, in a riot, the probability of apprehension of individual rioters, as well as of offenders committing other crimes, decreases considerably below its normal level due to the excessive load on local police units. (This is a source of external economies in criminal activity.) The population size and density may also be negatively related to P because of the relative ease with which an offender could elude the police in densely populated areas. A natural way to summarize these relations is via a production function of the Cobb-Douglas variety:

$$P = B \left(\frac{E}{N}\right)^{\beta_1} \left(\frac{Q}{N}\right)^{\beta_2} Z^\delta \exp(\xi) \qquad (3.3)$$

---

30. Bureau of Prisons statistics from 1940, 1951, 1960 and 1964 show little variation in the median time served in state prisons by felony offenders over the past few decades. For example, the median time served for burglary (T_b) in the United States in 1940 and 1964 was virtually identical: 20.6 and 20.1 months, respectively, even though the national burglary rates in those 2 years (based on unpublished FBI data) were 285.6 and 630.3 per 100,000 civilian population, respectively, and the number of prisoners received from court in federal and state institutions for the crime of burglary (based on unpublished Bureau of Prisons data) rose from 7,434 in 1942 to 21,600 in 1962. Furthermore, there had been relatively little change in the distribution of T_b across states: in 35 out of 44 states in our sample, changes in T_b between 1940 and 1964 were in the order of magnitude of ± 6 months, with the number of increases approximately matching the number of declines.

with $\beta_1 > 0$ and $\beta_2 < 0$,[31] where B is a constant, Z is a vector of environmental variables (productivity indicators), and ξ is a random variable.[32]

The demand for law-enforcement activity is essentially a negative demand for crime or a positive demand for defense against crime. In general, potential victims may wish to self-protect against victimization, both privately and collectively. Our present discussion is confined to collective self-protection via law-enforcement activity and ignores private self-protection and other collective methods of combating crime, since data exigencies rule out a comprehensive analysis of social defense against crime. (A theoretical analysis of self-protection by victims is implicit, however, in Ehrlich and Becker, 1972.) For a sample exposition, assume a binomial probability distribution of losses from crime to the ith person in a given period: he has either a potential real wealth I_i^e with probability $1-k_i$, or a lower wealth, $I_i^e\text{-}L_i$, with probability k_i, where L_i is his potential loss from crime and k_i the probability of victimization. If the number of persons in the community were large enough, and their probabilities of victimization largely independent, their actual per capita wealth would be known with certainty and would equal the expected personal wealth, $Y = I - kL$, where

$$k = \frac{1}{N} \sum_{i=1}^{N} k_i = \frac{Q}{N}, \; I = \frac{1}{N} \sum_{i=1}^{N} I_i \text{ and } L =$$

$$\frac{\displaystyle\sum_{i=1}^{N} k_i L_i}{\displaystyle\sum_{i=1}^{N} k_i}. \tag{3.4}$$

---

31. The elasticity of P with respect to Q/N, β_2, is not likely to be lower than -1, however, since this would imply that, given E/N, an increase in Q/N reduces the absolute number of offenses cleared by conviction, and not only their proportion among all offenses.

32. Since $0 < P < 1$, the natural logarithm of P is bounded between $-\infty$ and

Effective law enforcement by police, courts, and legislative bodies is expected to reduce the crime rate (i.e. the objective probability of victimization to a person) via increasing the probability and severity of punishment for crime. In addition, it may also reduce the actual loss to victims by recovering stolen property, guarding property, and other related actions. Consequently, we may write $k = k(r, j)$ and $L = L(r, j)$, where $r = E/N$ is real per capita expenditure on direct law enforcement and j represents expenditure on the determination and actual implementation of imprisonment or other punitive measures, private expenditure on self-protection against crime, and other outlays affecting the level of criminal activity in a state. Both k and L are assumed to have continuous first- and second-order derivatives with respect to r, so that $k'(r)$ and $L'(r)$ are negative and $k''(r)$ and $L''(r)$ are positive in sign. To further simplify matters, we ignore any functional dependence between r and j and treat j as an exogenous variable. If the public were interested in maximizing the expected utility of the average person,[33] optimal per capita expenditure, r^*, would be derived under the foregoing assumptions by maximizing the expected personal wealth,

$$Y = I - k(r)L(r) - r - j, \qquad (3.5)$$

with respect to r. The first-order optimality condition can be written

0, and its distribution cannot be assumed normal. Nevertheless, the normal distribution may approximate that of $\ln P$ over its observed range of variation. For example, the observed mean and standard deviation of our measures of $\ln P$ of all offenses in 1960 are -3.1670 and 0.5365, respectively. Moreover, since our regression estimates are derived by method of two-stage least-squares, they are asymptotically unbiased.

33. Collective self-protection may be viewed as a voluntary pooling of resources by potential victims of crime (all members of the community) to provide a common service—decreasing the probabilities of (private) states of the world involving victimization—the benefits of which are to be divided among all members. Maximization of the utility of an average member would then be the appropriate decision rule. Note that the loss to a victim of crime, even in the case of property crimes, is a net social loss, not just a transfer payment: if criminal activity were competitive, and offenders' risk neutral, then the potential marginal payoff to an average offender would equal the marginal value of the foregone resources he would devote to achieve it, including his marginal expected opportunity costs of imprisonment.

$$r^* = (e_1 + e_2)L(r^*)k(r^*), \qquad (3.6)$$

where $e_1 = -k'(r^*)(r^*/k)$ and $e_2 = -L'(r^*)(r^*/L)$ are assumed constant. Optimal expenditure on apprehending and convicting offenders, $r^* = (E/N)^*$, is thus seen to be proportional to the resulting crime rate and potential loss to a victim of crime. The latter may be forecast in practice as the actual crime rate and the average loss to a victim. The demand function for (expenditure on) law-enforcement activity may thus be specified as

$$\left(\frac{E}{N}\right)^* = \Gamma \frac{Q}{N} L. \qquad (3.7)$$

Equation (3.7) shows the level of per capita expenditure on law enforcement that would be desired in the absence of adjustment costs. In practice, one may expect a partial adjustment of public expenditure on law enforcement to its desired level in a given period due to positive costs of adjustment in a relatively short run. If the ratio of current to lagged expenditure were a power function of the ratio of the desired to lagged expenditure, the relevant demand function could easily be shown equal to

$$\frac{E}{N} = \Gamma L^\gamma \left(\frac{Q}{N}\right)^\gamma \left(\frac{E}{N}\right)_{t-1}^{1-\gamma} \exp(\epsilon), \qquad (3.8)$$

where $0 < \gamma < 1$ is an adjustment coefficient and ϵ is assumed a normally distributed random variable. Equations (3.2), (3.3), and (3.8)[34] form the structure of our simultaneous-equation model of law enforcement and crime.[35]

---

34. Available information regarding expenditure on police relates to fiscal years, whereas the other variables used in the regression analysis relate to calendar years. The appropriate forecasts of $k(r^*)$ and $L(r^*)$ may therefore be defined as weighted geometrical means of current and lagged crime rates and average losses. At present no data on losses to victims of crime are available on a statewide basis, and no serious attempt has been made to estimate eq. (3.8). Lagged crime rates are included in the reduced form regression equations.

35. Stability conditions associated with this system of equations require that the product of the elasticities b_1 and β_2 in eqs. (3.2) and (3.3)—both assumed negative in sign—does not exceed unity. This is because when solving for the value of Q/N in terms of reduced-form variables, lagged expenditure $(E/N)_{t-1}$, for example, is raised to the power $[(1 - \gamma)b_1\beta_1]/(1 - b_1\beta_2 - \gamma b_1\beta_1)$. This coefficient would be negative for all possible values of γ—the simultaneous-equation system would have a stable solution—if the denominator were positive. A sufficient

TABLE 6-I

LIST OF VARIABLES USED IN REGRESSION ANALYSIS

$\left(\dfrac{N}{Q}\right)_i, \left(\dfrac{Q_i}{N}\right)_{t-1}$		= current and 1-year lagged crime rate: the number of offenses known per capita
$\left(\dfrac{C}{Q}\right)_i = P_i$		= estimator of probability of apprehension and imprisonment: the number of offenders imprisoned per offenses known
T_i		= average time served by offenders in state prisons
W		= median income of families
X		= percentage of families below one half of median income
NW		= percentage of nonwhites in the population
A_{14-24}		= percentage of all males in the age group 14-24
U_{14-24}, U_{35-39}		= unemployment rate of civilian urban males ages 14-24 and 35-39
L_{14-24}		= labor-force participation rate for civilian urban males ages 14-24
Ed		= mean number of years of schooling of population 25 years old and over
$SMSA$		= percentage of population in standard metropolitan statistical areas
$\dfrac{E}{N}, \left(\dfrac{E}{N}\right)_{t-1}$		= per capita expenditure on police in fiscal 1960, 1959
M		= number of males per 100 females
D		= dummy variable distinguishing northern from southern states (south = 1)

Note—Variables are time and state-specific; i denotes a specific crime category.

ANALYSIS OF CRIME VARIATIONS ACROSS STATES IN THE UNITED STATES

We have applied the economic and econometric framework developed in the preceding sections in a regression analysis of variations of index crimes across U.S. states in 1960, 1950, and 1940.[36] A short description of the variables used in the empirical investigation as counterparts of the theoretical constructs entering equations (3.2), (3.3), and (3.8) is given in Table 6-I, and the

condition is $b_1\beta_2 < 1$. Note that unlike Becker's optimality conditions for the minimization of the social loss from crime (see Becker, 1968, pp. 181-83), our stability conditions do not require that $|b_2| < 1$ or that $|b_2| < |b_1|$: we do not require that in equilibrium offenders must be, on balance, risk preferrers. Indeed, some of our empirical estimates of $|b_{2i}|$, exceed those of $|b_{1i}|$.

36. Due to data exigencies, the empirical investigation deals with only seven felony offenses (index crimes) punishable by imprisonment. The data on (and definitions of) these crimes are available in the *Uniform Crime Reports* of the FBI. Samples from 1960 include 47 state observations and those from 1950 include 46. The 1940 sample sizes vary between 36 and 43.

interested reader is referred to the Appendix for a more elaborate analysis and discussion of this list. Since data on police expenditure across states are available for 1960, but not for 1950 and 1940, crime statistics relating to the latter two years are only used to derive ordinary-least-squares (OLS) estimates of supply-of-offenses functions. Data from 1960 are also used to derive two-stage least-squares (2SLS) and seemingly unrelated (SUR) estimates of supply-of-offenses functions and a production function of law-enforcement activity.

Supply-of-Offenses Functions: The Effect of Probability and Severity of Punishment, Income and Income Inequality, and Racial Composition

Despite the shortcomings of the data and the crude estimates of some of the desired variables (see the Appendix), the results of the regression analysis lend credibility to the basic hypotheses of the model. The major consistent findings are:

1. The rate of specific crime categories, with virtually no exception, varies inversely with estimates of the probability of apprehension and punishment by imprisonment, $P = C/Q$, and with the average length of time served in state prisons, T.

2. Crimes against property (robbery, burglary, larceny, and auto theft) are also found to vary positively with the percentage of families below one half of the median income (income inequality), X, and with the median income, W; in contrast, these variables are found to have relatively lower effects on the incidence of crimes against the person (particularly murder and rape). Also, the regression coefficients associated with X and W have relatively high standard errors in the case of crimes against the person.

3. All specific crime rates appear to be positively related to the percentage of nonwhites in the population, NW. (For the reasons for including this, and other demographic variables, see the Appendix.) These findings hold consistently across samples from 1960, 1950, and 1940, independently of the regression technique employed or the specific set of (additional) variables introduced

in the regression analysis. We therefore present them separately from other results.[37]

OLS ESTIMATES

Tables 6-II and 6-III present a summary of weighted OLS estimates of elasticities associated with P, T, W, X, and NW. The regression equation used is a natural logarithmic transformation of equation (3.2):

$$\ln\left(\frac{Q}{N}\right)_i = a + b_{1i}\ln P_i + b_{2i}\ln T_i + c_{1i}\ln W + c_{2i}\ln X +$$
$$e_{1i}\ln NW + \mu_i,^{38} \qquad (4.1)$$

and the weighting factor is the square root of the population size.[39]

The OLS estimates of the elasticity of offenses with respect to P_i and T_i, $\hat{b}_{1i}$, and $\hat{b}_{2i}$, respectively, are generally lower than unity in absolute value. Also, the difference $|b_{1i}| - |b_{2i}|$ exceeds twice its standard error in regressions dealing with murder, rape, and robbery, while the converse holds in the case of burglary in

---

37. The FBI's estimates of crime rates across states in 1950 and 1940 relate to urban areas, whereas no such data are available in 1960. Also, our estimates of income inequality in 1940 are derived from a sample of wage and salary workers, whereas in 1960 they are derived from a census of family income. Because of these differences we have not integrated the three samples for a more comprehensive regression analysis. Also, the point estimates of the regression coefficients are not exactly comparable across the different samples.

38. When grouping specific crime categories in broader classes, the probability and severity of punishment, P_g and T_g, were measured as weighted averages of the P's and T's associated with the single categories:

$$P_g = \left(\sum_{i=1}^{g} C_i\right) \Big/ \left(\sum_{i=1}^{g} Q_i\right) \text{ and } T_g = \sum_{i=1}^{g} C_i T_i \Big/ \sum_{i=1}^{g} C_i.$$

It should be pointed out that the coefficient b_{2i} in eqs. (4.1) and (4.3) below is expected to be lower than b_{2i} in eq. (3.2) by a positive constant factor (see our discussion in the Appendix, item 3).

39. A residual analysis of unweighted regressions generally showed a negative correlation between the absolute value of estimated residuals and the population size. This apparent heteroscedasticity is consistent with the assumption that unspecified random variables which affect participation in crime are homoscedastic at the individual level. Thus, $\sqrt{N}$ may be an appropriate weighting factor.

TABLE 6-II

OLS (WEIGHTED) REGRESSION ESTIMATES OF COEFFICIENTS
ASSOCIATED WITH SELECTED VARIABLES IN 1960, 1950, AND 1940:
CRIMES AGAINST THE PERSON AND ALL OFFENSES
(Dependent variables are specific crime rates)

Offense and Year	a Intercept	b_1 with ln P_i	b_2 with ln T_i	c_1 with ln W	c_2 with ln X	e_1 with ln NW	Adj. R^2
			Estimated Coefficients Associated with Selected Variables				
Murder:							
1960	−0.6644*	−0.3407	−0.1396*	0.4165*	1.3637*	0.5532	.8687
1950†	−0.7682*	−0.5903	−0.2878	0.6095*	1.9386	0.4759	.8155
Rape:							
1960†	−7.3802*	−0.5783	−0.1880*	1.2220	0.8942*	0.1544	.6858
Assault:							
1960	−13.2994	−0.2750	−0.1797*	2.0940	1.4697	0.6771	.8282
1950	−0.7139*	−0.4791	−0.3839	0.5641*	0.9136*	0.5526	.8566
1940	−0.2891	−0.4239	−0.6036	0.7274*	0.5484*	0.7298	.8381
Murder and rape:							
1960†	−1.8117	−0.5787	−0.2867	0.6773*	0.9456	0.3277	.6948
Murder and assault:							
1950†	1.0951*	−0.7614	−0.3856	0.3982*	1.1689*	0.4281	.8783
Crimes against persons:							
1960†	−4.1571*	−0.5498	−0.3487	1.0458	0.9145	0.4897	.8758
All offenses:							
1960	−7.1657	−0.5255	−0.5854	2.0651	1.8013	0.2071	.6950
1950	−1.5081*	−0.5664	−0.4740	1.3456	1.9399	0.1051	.6592
1940	−5.2711	−0.6530	−0.2892	0.5986	2.2658	0.1386	.6650

Note—The absolute values of all regression coefficients in Tables 6-II and 6-III, except those with *, are at least twice those of their standard errors; † indicates regressions in which the absolute difference $(\hat{b}_1 - \hat{b}_2)$ is at least twice the value of the relevant standard error $S(\hat{b}_1 - b_2)$.

1960. However, estimates of b_{1i} are likely to be biased in a negative direction relative to those of b_{2i} (provided that the true absolute values of b_{1i} were lower than unity) because of a potential negative correlation between $(Q/N)_i$ and $P_i = (C/Q)_i$ arising from errors of measurement in Q_i[40] (see our discussion in the Appendix). In addition, the OLS estimates of b_{1i}

40. Since the variances of errors of measurement in Q_i are likely to be greater in 1950 and 1940 relative to 1960, the bias in the difference between b_{1i} and b_{2i}

TABLE 6-III

OLS (WEIGHTED) REGRESSION ESTIMATES OF COEFFICIENTS
ASSOCIATED WITH SELECTED VARIABLES IN 1960, 1950, AND 1940:
CRIMES AGAINST PROPERTY
(Dependent variables are specific crime rates)

Offense and Year	*a* Intercept	*b₁* with $\ln P_t$	*b₂* with $\ln T_t$	*c₁* with $\ln W$	*c₂* with $\ln X$	*e₁* with $\ln NW$	Adj. R^2
Robbery:							
1960[†]	−20.1910	−0.8534	−0.2233*	2.9086	1.8409	0.3764	.8014
1950[†]	−10.2794	−0.9389	−0.5610	1.7278	0.4798	0.3282	.7839
1940	−10.2943	−0.9473	−0.1912*	1.6608	0.7222	0.3408	.8219
Burglary:							
1960[†]	−5.5700*	−0.5339	−0.9001	1.7973	2.0452	0.2269	.6713
1950	−1.0519*	−0.4102	−0.4689	1.1891	1.8697	0.1358	.4933
1940	−0.6531*	−0.4607	−0.2698	0.8327*	1.6939	0.1147	.3963
Larceny:							
1960	−14.9431	−0.1331	−0.2630	2.6893	1.6207	0.1315	.5222
1950	−4.2857*	−0.3477	−0.4301	1.9784	3.3134	−0.0342*	.5819
1940	−10.6198	−0.4131	−0.1680*	0.6186	3.7371	0.0499*	.6953
Auto theft:							
1960	−17.3057	−0.2474	−0.1743*	2.8931	1.8981	0.1152	.6948
Burglary and robbery:							
1960	−9.2683	−0.6243	−0.6883	2.1598	2.1156	0.2565	.7336
1950	−3.0355*	−0.5493	−0.4879	1.3624	1.6066	0.1854	.5590
Larceny and auto theft:							
1960	−14.1543	−0.2572	−0.3339	2.6648	1.8263	0.1423	.6826
1950	−3.9481*	−0.3134	−0.4509	1.9286	2.9961	−0.0290*	.5894
Crimes against property:							
1960	−10.1288	−0.5075	−0.6206	2.3345	2.0547	0.2118	.7487
1950	−2.8056	−0.5407	−0.4792	1.5836	2.2548	0.0755	.6253

Note—Same references as in Table 6-II.

and b_{2i} may be subject to a simultaneous-equation bias. More reliable estimates are therefore provided by our simultaneous-equation estimation methods.

The estimated elasticities of specific crimes against property

---

is likely to be relatively large in regressions using data from the former two years. Indeed, this may explain why the differences $|b_{2i}| - |b_{1i}|$ in regressions concerning burglary and larceny in 1960 are positive and significant, while in 1940 they are negative but insignificant.

with respect to both W and X, $\hat{c}_{1i}$ and $\hat{c}_{2i}$, respectively, are positive, statistically significant, and generally greater than unity. Note, however, that $\hat{c}_{1i}$ may reflect, in part, the effect of "urbanization" (the percentage of the population in standard metropolitan statistical areas, SMSA), since W and SMSA are highly correlated.[41] This may explain why the absolute values of $\hat{c}_{1i}$ in regressions using 1940 and 1950 data are lower than their estimates in the 1960 regressions: the dependent variables in the 1940 and 1950 regressions are urban crime rates, while in 1960 they are state crime rates. The fact that variations in X and W are found to have a lower effect on the incidence of crimes against the person relative to crimes against property supports our choice of them as indicators of the relative opportunities associated with these latter crimes. Moreover, the introduction of X and W in the regression analysis helps to obtain significant results concerning the effect of T, which is to be expected since variations in these variables presumably account for the variation in the opportunity costs of imprisonment.

The positive correlation between the percentage of nonwhites, NW, and the rate of specific crimes is found to be independent of a regional effect tested via the introduction of a dummy variable distinguishing northern and southern states: the dummy variable loses its statistical significance when NW is also introduced in the regression analysis. Moreover, virtually the same elasticities of crime rates with respect to NW have been derived in an OLS regression analysis including northern states only. The significant effect of NW on the rate of specific crimes may essentially reflect the effect of the relatively inferior legitimate market opportunities (and lower opportunity cost of imprisonment) of nonwhites, since our measures of average relative legitimate opportunities in a state do not fully reflect opportunities available to nonwhites.

The simple multiple regressions appear to account for a large

---

41. Urbanization may serve as a measure of accessibility to (lower direct costs of engaging in) various criminal activities due, for example, to the concentration of business activity, the massive communication networks, and the density of the population in metropolitan areas. The positive simple-regression coefficient associated with SMSA becomes insignificant, however, when P and W are also introduced in regressions concerning specific crimes against property.

part of the variation in crime rates across states: the adjusted R^2 statistics range from .87 for murder to .52 for larceny in 1960. Apparently, the ranking of the R^2 statistics by crime categories is negatively related to the ranking of these crimes by the extent of their underreporting errors and by the extent to which they involve punishment other than imprisonment. The R^2 statistics may partly reflect, however, the extent of negative correlation between $(Q/N)_i$ and P_i, due to measurement errors in Q_i. This may explain why the R^2 statistics associated with the 1940 regressions are not lower than those associated with the 1960 ones.

The 2SLS and SUR Estimates

The set of equations (4.1) has also been estimated via a 2SLS procedure, applying our simultaneous-equation model and using data from 1960. The set of exogenous and predetermined variables introduced in the reduced-form regression analysis has been

$$\ln P_i = a_0 + a_{1i}\ln T_i + a_{2i}\ln \left(\frac{E}{N}\right)_{t-1}$$

$$+ a_{3i}\ln \left(\frac{Q_i}{N}\right)_{t-1} + a_{4i}\ln W + a_{5i}\ln X$$

$$+ a_{6i}\ln U_{35\text{-}39} + a_{7i}\ln NW + a_{8i}\ln A_{14\text{-}24} \qquad (4.2)$$

$$+ a_{9i}\ln SMSA + a_{10i}\ln M$$

$$+ a_{11i}\ln N + a_{12i}D + a_{13i}\ln Ed + u_i.^{42}$$

Estimates of specific regression equations are presented in Tables 6-IV, A and 6-V, A.

The 2SLS estimates do not take account of disturbance correlations. However, random changes (disturbance terms) relating to the rate of, say, burglary may be positively associated with those

---

42. It should be pointed out that the coefficients associated with $(E/N)_{t-1}$ in the reduced-form regressions are generally found to be statistically insignificant (a few having wrong signs), presumably because of a multicollinearity between $(E/N)_{t-1}$ and $(Q_i/N)_{t-1}$. Similar weak results were obtained in the reduced-form regression analysis when $\ln(Q/N)_i$ were regressed on the set of independent variables included in eq. (4.2). The presumed existence of multicollinearity in these regressions should not bias the computed (expected) values of both $(Q/N)_i$ and P_i, however, and should not affect the consistency of the estimates of our structural coefficients.

TABLE 6-IV

2SLS AND SUR (WEIGHTED) REGRESSION ESTIMATES OF
COEFFICIENTS ASSOCIATED WITH SELECTED VARIABLES IN 1960:
CRIMES AGAINST PROPERTY

		Coefficient (β) Associated with Selected Variables				
	a	b_1 with	b_2 with	c_1 with	c_2 with	e_1 with
Offense	*Intercept*	*ln $\hat{P}_i$*	*ln T_i*	*ln W*	*ln X*	*ln NW*
			A. *2SLS Estimates*			
Robbery:						
β	−11.030	−1.303	−0.372	1.689	1.279	0.334
$\beta/S\beta$	(−1.804)	(−7.011)	(−1.395)	(1.969)	(1.660)	(4.024)
Burglary:						
β	−2.121	−0.724	−1.127	1.384	2.000	0.250
$\beta/S\beta$	(−0.582)	(−6.003)	(−4.799)	(2.839)	(4.689)	(4.579)
Larceny:						
β	−10.660	−0.371	−0.602	2.229	1.792	0.142
$\beta/S\beta$	(−2.195)	(−2.482)	(−1.937)	(3.465)	(2.992)	(2.019)
Auto theft:						
β	−14.960	−0.407	−0.246	2.608	2.057	0.102
$\beta/S\beta$	(−4.162)	(−4.173)	(−1.682)	(5.194)	(4.268)	(1.842)
Larceny and auto:						
β	−10.090	−0.546	−0.626	2.226	2.166	0.155
$\beta/S\beta$	(−2.585)	(−4.248)	(−2.851)	(4.183)	(4.165)	(2.603)
Property crimes:						
β	−6.279	−0.796	−0.915	1.883	2.132	0.243
$\beta/S\beta$	(−1.937)	(−6.140)	(4.297)	(4.246)	(5.356)	(4.805)
			B. *SUR Estimates*			
Robbery:						
β	−14.800	−1.112	−0.286	2.120	1.409	0.346
$\beta/S\beta$	(−2.500)	(−6.532)	(−0.750)	(2.548)	(1.853)	(4.191)
Burglary:						
β	−3.961	−0.624	−0.996	1.581	2.032	0.230
$\beta/S\beta$	(−1.114)	(−5.576)	(−4.260)	(3.313)	(4.766)	(4.274)
Larceny:						
β	−10.870	−0.358	−0.654	2.241	1.785	0.139
$\beta/S\beta$	(−2.52)	(−2.445)	(−1.912)	(3.502)	(2.983)	(1.980)
Auto theft:						
β	−14.860	−0.409	−0.233	2.590	2.054	0.101
$\beta/S\beta$	(−4.212)	(−4.674)	(−1.747)	(5.253)	(4.283)	(1.832)

Note—The underlying regression equation is

$$\ln\left(\frac{Q}{N}\right) = a + b_{1i}\ln\hat{P}_i + b_{2i}\ln T_i + c_{1i}\ln W + c_{2i}\ln X + e_{1i}\ln NW + u_i. \quad (4.3)$$

TABLE 6-V

2SLS AND SUR (WEIGHTED) REGRESSION ESTIMATES OF
COEFFICIENTS ASSOCIATED WITH SELECTED VARIABLES
IN 1960: CRIMES AGAINST THE PERSON AND
TOTAL OFFENSES

	Coefficient (β) Associated with Selected Variables					
	a	b_1 with	b_2 with	c_1 with	c_2 with	e_1 with
Offense	Intercept	$\ln \hat{P}_i$	$\ln T_i$	$\ln W$	$\ln X$	$\ln NW$
		A. 2SLS Estimates				
Murder:						
β	0.316	−0.852	−0.087	0.175	1.109	0.534
$\beta/S\beta$	(0.085)	(−2.492)	(−0.645)	(0.334)	(1.984)	(8.356)
Rape:						
β	−0.599	−0.896	−0.399	0.409	0.459	0.072
$\beta/S\beta$	(−0.120)	(−6.080)	(−2.005)	(0.605)	(0.743)	(0.922)
Murder and Rape:						
β	2.703	−0.828	−0.350	0.086	0.556	0.280
$\beta/S\beta$	(0.732)	(−6.689)	(−3.164)	(0.172)	(1.188)	(5.504)
Assault:						
β	−7.567	−0.724	−0.979	1.650	1.707	0.465
$\beta/S\beta$	(−1.280)	(−3.701)	(−2.301)	(2.018)	(2.111)	(3.655)
Crimes against the person:						
β	1.635	−0.803	−0.495	0.328	0.587	0.376
$\beta/S\beta$	(0.380)	(−6.603)	(−3.407)	(0.570)	(1.098)	(4.833)
All offenses:						
β	−1.388	−0.991	−1.123	1.292	1.775	0.265
$\beta/S\beta$	(−0.368)	(−5.898)	(−4.483)	(2.609)	(4.183)	(5.069)
		B. SUR Estimates				
Murder:						
β	−1.198	−0.913	−0.018	0.186	1.152	0.542
$\beta/S\beta$	(−0.033)	(−3.062)	(−1.710)	(0.361)	(2.102)	(8.650)
Rape:						
β	0.093	−0.930	−0.436	0.333	0.425	0.065
$\beta/S\beta$	(0.019)	(−6.640)	(−2.318)	(0.502)	(0.692)	(0.841)
Assault:						
β	−6.431	−0.718	−0.780	1.404	1.494	0.460
$\beta/S\beta$	(−1.103)	(−4.046)	(−2.036)	(1.751)	(1.871)	(3.801)

Note—Same reference as in Table 6-1V.

relating to the rate of robbery if these crimes were complements. To derive efficient estimates of the supply-of-offenses functions we have also employed an asymptotically efficient simultaneous-equation estimation method proposed by Zellner (1962) for estimating seemingly unrelated regression equations (SUR).[43] Such estimates have been derived separately for crimes against property and crimes against the person and are presented in Tables 6-IV, B and 6-V, B.

The results of the 2SLS and SUR regression analyses strongly support the qualitative results of the simple regressions analyzed in the preceding discussion. They show that the rates of all specific crimes are inversely and significantly related to the appropriate P_i and T_i and directly related to NW, the estimated regression coefficients generally exceeding twice their standard errors. Crimes against property are found to be positively and significantly related to W and X, whereas the estimated elasticities of crimes against the person with respect to these variables are relatively lower—and their standard errors relatively higher—especially those associated with W in the regressions concerning murder and rape.[44] Moreover, estimates derived via the 2SLS and SUR methods are similar in magnitude, the latter generally having lower standard errors. However, these estimates only have the desirable large-sample property of consistency, and their small-sample properties are for the most part unknown.[45]

Unlike the OLS estimates of the elasticities of specific crimes with respect to P_i, the elasticities derived via 2SLS and SUR methods are expected to be free of a potential negative bias (due to measurement errors in Q_i) between current values of $(Q/N)_i$

43. We have not attempted to derive 3SLS or FIML estimates of eq. (4.1) because of the absence of data that would be needed to estimate eqs. (3.3) and (3.8) in the case of specific crime categories; in particular, data concerning police expenditure on combating *specific* crimes and average losses from crime to victims.

44. To some extent crimes against the person may be complementary to crimes against property since they may also occur as a by-product of the latter. This is particularly true in the case of assault, for it is generally agreed that some incidents of robbery are classified in practice as assault. This may be one reason why assault exhibits a greater similarity to crimes against property in its estimated functional form.

45. See Zellner, 1970. A more elaborate analysis of this problem in the context of this study is given in Ehrlich, 1970.

and $P_i = (C/Q)_i$, since $\hat{P}_i$ is a linear combination of a set of variables that does not include (current) $(Q/N)_i$.[46] Nevertheless, estimates of both b_{1i} and b_{2i} appear even higher than those reported in Tables 6-III and 6-IV. It is interesting to note that the absolute values of the estimated elasticities of crimes against the person with respect to probability and severity of punishment are not lower on the average than those associated with crimes against property. This suggests that law enforcement may not be less effective in combating crimes of hate and passion relative to crimes against property.[47]

The absolute values of b_{1i} in Tables 6-IV and 6-V are found to exceed those of b_{2i} in the case of murder, rape, and robbery, while they fall short of b_{2i} in the case of burglary and larceny (the differences exceeding twice the value of their standard errors). It should be emphasized, however, that the various T_i are less than proportionally related to the discounted cost of imprisonment and, therefore, our estimates of b_{2i} necessarily understate the true elasticities of the various crimes with respect to severity of punishment, F_i—especially in the case of crimes punishable by long imprisonment terms (see our discussion in item 3 of the Appendix). In view of these results we may venture the conclusion that burglars and thieves are risk avoiders (see the analysis on pg. 151). Whether other offenders are risk preferrers cannot be determined unambiguously, however, without knowledge of offenders' discount rates: the higher the latter, the larger would be the absolute values of our revised estimates of b_{2i}.[48] Following our earlier analysis (Optimal Participation in Illegiti-

---

46. The 2SLS estimates might still be affected by spurious correlation if errors of measurement in $(Q/N)_i$ were serially correlated in each state. We have therefore derived alternative 2SLS estimates of the supply-of-offenses functions by excluding $(Q_i/N)_{t-1}$ from the reduced-form regressions. The results, reported in Ehrlich (1970, Table 15 of appendix R), are nevertheless highly consistent with those reported in Tables 6-IV and 6-V.

47. Note, however, that this may be partly due to the preventive effect of imprisonment which is expected to be generally higher for crimes against the person.

48. We have computed estimates of correction factors $1/\lambda$ (where λ is defined in the Appendix) based on arithmetic mean values of T_i and alternative arbitrary discount rates. We find that only when using a yearly rate of 36 percent do the revised estimates of b_{2i} for murder and rape (but not for robbery) approach our estimates of b_{1i} associated with the same crimes.

mate Market Activities: A One-Period Uncertainty Model), we can, therefore expect that in a real income sense, crime does pay at the margin to burglars and thieves, while it may not pay to robbers.[49]

It is difficult to determine accurately on the basis of available data to what extent the estimated values of b_{1i} and b_{2i} are attributable to a preventive effect of imprisonment (see eq. [2.7]) because the absolute values of our estimates of P_i may not be accurate.[50] Since our 2SLS and SUR cross-states estimates of b_{1i} and b_{2i} appear to be significantly different in the case of murder, rape, robbery, burglary, and larceny (some of these estimates approach or even exceed unity in absolute value), the independent deterrent effect of law enforcement appears to be confirmed because the preventive effect of probability and severity of imprisonment, P_i and T_i, is expected to be virtually identical, and, in view of the available information regarding average values of T_i and reasonable estimates of P_i in the United States, considerably lower than unity.

Supply-of-Offenses Functions: The Effect of Unemployment, Labor-Force Participation, and Age Composition

We have also investigated in our regression analysis the partial effects of unemployment and labor-force participation rates of urban males in the age groups 14 to 24, U_{14-24} and L_{14-24}, respectively, as well as the effect of the variation in the proportion of all males belonging to that age group, A_{14-24}, by adding these vari-

---

49. We have attempted to test these implications directly by calculating the net monetary gains associated with an average robbery, burglary, larceny, and auto theft. Surprisingly, our crude estimates of the expected net gains are compatible with their predicted values according to the regression results discussed above, for the net gain is estimated to be negative in the case of robbery and positive in the case of burglary and larceny (see Ehrlich, 1970, pp. 128-31 ["Does Crime Pay?"]).

50. Estimates of σ based on our estimates of P and T are found to account for less than 10 percent of the magnitude of the 2SLS estimates of b_1 and b_2 associated with all offenses. The latter may be regarded as estimates of steady state elasticities of the crime rate with respect to P and T, because the variation in these variables across states is likely to exhibit persistent differences.

TABLE 6-VI

ALTERNATIVE ESTIMATES OF ELASTICITIES OF OFFENSES WITH RESPECT TO UNEMPLOYMENT AND LABOR-FORCE PARTICIPATION OF YOUNG AGE GROUPS IN 1960

(Dependent variables are specific crime rates)

| Crime Category | Ordinary Least-Squares (OLS) | | | | | | Two-Stage Least-Squares (2SLS) | | | | | |
| | Unweighted | | | Weighted | | | Unweighted | | | Weighted | | |
	d_1	d_2	e_2	d_1	d_2	e_2	d_1	d_2	e_2	d_1	d_2	e_2
Robbery:												
β	0.148	−0.346	...	−0.297	−0.431	...	−0.634	−0.793	...	−0.749	−0.920	...
$\beta/S\beta$	(−0.383)	(−1.145)	...	(−0.838)	(−1.208)	...	(−1.281)	(−2.006)	...	(−1.968)	(−1.754)	...
Burglary:												
β	−0.078	0.059	0.9092	−0.084	0.216	...	−0.306	−0.136	...	−0.033	0.334	...
$\beta/S\beta$	(−0.333)	(0.301)	(1.4150)	(−0.380)	(0.944)	...	(−1.115)	(−0.559)	...	(−0.154)	(1.107)	...
Larceny:												
β	0.186	0.573	...	0.091	0.430	...	0.214	0.487	...	−0.103	−0.033	...
$\beta/S\beta$	(0.955)	(2.056)	...	(0.326)	(1.395)	...	(0.711)	(1.188)	...	(−0.306)	(−0.067)	...
Auto theft:												
β	0.147	0.435	1.062	−0.137	0.373	...	0.516	0.401	...	−0.315	0.174	...
$\beta/S\beta$	(0.534)	(1.984)	(1.328)	(−0.553)	(1.360)	...	(0.188)	(1.396)	...	(−0.365)	(0.519)	...
Murder:												
β	−0.132	−0.656	1.803	−0.178	−0.602	1.622	−0.151	−1.510	2.072	−0.324	−0.822	1.293
$\beta/S\beta$	(−0.388)	(−2.264)	(1.875)	(−0.636)	(−2.018)	(2.043)	(−0.268)	(−2.456)	(1.298)	(−0.227)	(−1.966)	(1.698)
Rape:												
β	0.238	−0.728	1.339	0.222	−0.654	1.605	0.286	−0.851	1.430	0.209	−0.576	2.043
$\beta/S\beta$	(0.853)	(−3.232)	(1.660)	(0.828)	(−2.363)	(2.080)	(0.428)	(−3.366)	(1.603)	(0.774)	(−1.902)	(2.583)
Assault:												
β	−0.073	−0.325	2.792	−0.083	−0.314	2.164	−0.132	−0.162	3.403	−0.389	−0.168	1.345
$\beta/S\beta$	(−0.219)	(−1.044)	(2.885)	(−0.268)	(−0.903)	(2.431)	(−0.283)	(−1.370)	(2.492)	(−0.938)	(−1.272)	(1.938)
All offenses:												
β	0.037	0.159	1.044	0.049	0.275	1.157	−0.129	−0.481	1.386	−0.169	0.004	...
$\beta/S\beta$	(0.172)	(0.768)	(1.709)	(0.262)	(1.264)	(2.051)	(−0.421)	(−1.288)	(1.606)	(−0.806)	(0.012)	...

ables to the regression equations (4.1) and (4.3). The expanded regression equation is

$$\ln\left(\frac{Q}{N}\right)_i = a_i + b_{1i}\ln P_i + b_{2i}\ln T_i + c_{1i}\ln W + c_{2i}\ln X + d_{1i}\ln U_{14\text{-}24}$$

$$+ d_{2i}\ln L_{14\text{-}24} + e_{1i}\ln NW + e_{2i}\ln A_{14\text{-}24} + \mu_i, \qquad (4.4)$$

and the results concerning these variables are shown in Table 6-VI.[51]

The partial effect of age is found to be inconclusive in the regressions dealing with crimes against property. The signs of e_{2i} vary across different crimes and their values fall short of their standard errors, especially when estimates are derived via a 2SLS procedure. Possibly, then, not age per se, but the general opportunities available to offenders determine their participation in crimes against property. The percentage of young age groups does appear to be positively correlated with the rate of crimes against the person in 1960, independently of the regression method employed.

The results concerning the partial effect of the unemployment rate $U_{14\text{-}24}$ are generally disappointing: the signs of d_{1i} are not stable across different regressions and do not appear significantly different from zero. One reason may be that variations in $U_{14\text{-}24}$ across states reflect considerable variation in voluntary unemployment due to the search for desirable employment, since this source of unemployment is particularly important among young workers. Indeed, we have achieved somewhat better results when using the unemployment rates of urban males in the age group 35 to 39 in lieu of $U_{14\text{-}24}$. Another reason may be that the effect of variations in the true probability of involuntary unemployment is impacted in the effect of income inequality, X, since a decline in legitimate market opportunities leading to an increase in involuntary unemployment is likely to affect disproportionately

51. We have generally excluded $A_{14\text{-}24}$ from eq. (5.4) whenever the ratio of e_2 to its standard deviation fell short of 1. In the 2SLS regressions, P_i were replaced by estimates of specific probabilities of imprisonment, $\hat{P}_i$, derived through a modified version of the reduced-form regression eq. (4.2), including $U_{14\text{-}24}$ and $L_{14\text{-}24}$, in addition to the explanatory variables entering eq. (4.2), and excluding $U_{35\text{-}39}$.

those with lower schooling and training and may therefore increase income inequality. It may finally be noted that our theoretical analysis indicates some ambiguity regarding the effect of an increase in the probability of unemployment on offenders engaging in both legitimate and illegitimate activities, if unemployment is regarded as an uncertain event (see n. 14).

Interesting results have been obtained with respect to the partial effect of labor-force participation on the rate of specific crimes. The effect of $L_{14\text{-}24}$ is somewhat inconclusive in the case of crimes against property but is found consistently negative and significantly different from zero in the case of specific (as well as all) crimes against the person. Are these results compatible with the theory developed in the first section of this paper?

One important question is what do variations in labor-force participation rates indicate in the context of this investigation? On the one hand, if all offenders specialized in crime and also chose to register as not in the labor force, then $L_{14\text{-}24}$ could be viewed as a rough index of time spent in *legitimate* market activities by young persons in a state: movements in $L_{14\text{-}24}$ would then be likely to reflect opposite movements in the rate of participation in crimes against property. On the other hand, if most offenders were partly engaged in legitimate market activities, $L_{14\text{-}24}$ would be an index of time spent by the average young person in *all* market activities, legitimate as well as illegitimate.

Traditional economic theory predicts that labor-force participation is a function of real income, the market wage rate if employed, and the probability of unemployment. If variations in these variables were effectively accounted for by the variation in W, X, and $U_{14\text{-}24}$, the variation in $L_{14\text{-}24}$ would mainly capture the effect of exogenous factors determining labor-force participation of young age groups (e.g. the rate of school enrollment or the degree of enforcement of child labor laws). Assuming that $L_{14\text{-}24}$ is an index of total time spent in market activities by the average young person, variations in $L_{14\text{-}24}$ would then produce a pure scale effect on participation in crime. We have expected such a scale effect to be positive in the case of crimes against property and negative in the case of crimes against the person.

However, since variations in legitimate wage rates available to potential young offenders are only indirectly accounted for by the variation in family income inequality, X, they, too, are likely to be reflected by the variation in $L_{14\text{-}24}$. Specifically, with the distribution of family income held constant, an increase in legitimate wages available to young workers is expected to reduce their incentive to participate in all crimes. This negative substitution effect is likely to offset the positive scale effect of an increase in $L_{14\text{-}24}$ on the rate of crimes against property, but may reinforce the negative scale effect of an increase in $L_{14\text{-}24}$ on the rate of crimes against the person. The results reported in Table 6-VI are compatible with these expectations.

It should be pointed out that the introduction of $A_{14\text{-}24}$, $U_{14\text{-}24}$, and $L_{14\text{-}24}$ in the regression analysis has had virtually no effect on the estimated elasticities and only a marginal impact on the extent of the R^2 statistics reported in Tables 6-II and 6-III.[52]

The Effectiveness of Law Enforcement: Some Tentative Estimates

Is law enforcement effective in combating crime? Is there at present too much or too little enforcement of existing laws against felonies? The answer to these questions can be obtained, in principle, by considering two related issues. First, what would be the effect of an increase in the probability and severity of

---

52. The regression models employed thus far have implicitly assumed that specific illegal activities, i, were independent of each other. Specific crimes may be substitutes (or complements) in the sense that an increase in opportunities available in one crime would have opposite (or similar) effects on the rate of related crimes. (For example, offenders charged for robbery are often convicted of burglary; an increase in the penalty for burglary might then deter participation in both crimes.) To test interdependencies among specific crimes, we have introduced in the regression eq. (4.3) the (estimated) probability and severity of imprisonment relating to subsets of these crimes, $\hat{P}_g$ and T_g, respectively, in addition to own variables. The 2SLS estimates of the regression coefficients associated with $\hat{P}_g$ and T_g indicate that robbery and burglary are complements, and that burglary and theft are substitutes, but the absolute values of the coefficients associated with these variables are found to be quite low relative to their standard errors. Moreover, the estimated coefficients of the explanatory variables introduced in eq. (4.3) are virtually unaffected by the introduction of these other variables (see Ehrlich, 1970, pp. 86-89).

punishment on the level of felony offenses and the resulting social loss? Second, to what extent would an additional expenditure on law-enforcement agencies increase their effectiveness in apprehending and punishing felons?

Our empirical estimates of supply-of-offenses functions provide consistent results pertaining to the first issue. In addition, an attempt has been made to estimate the effectiveness of public outlays on police in determining the probability of apprehending and punishing felons, P, by estimating an aggregate production function of law-enforcement activity (eq. [3.3] defined for all felony offenses) via a 2SLS weighted-regression procedure using state data from 1960. In the first stage of the analysis, the rate of all felony offenses, Q/N, and per capita expenditure on police, E/N, were regressed on the set of exogenous and predetermined variables specified in the reduced-form regression equation (4.2). In the second stage, P was regressed on values of $\hat{Q}/N$ and $\hat{E}/N$ computed from the estimated reduced-form regression equations, and on other environmental variables, some of which were discussed in connection with equation (3.3). The results are given in equation (4.5) below (the numbers in parentheses denote the ratios of the regression coefficients to their standard errors).

$$\ln P = 0.963 + 0.305 \ln \left(\frac{\hat{E}}{N}\right) - 0.908 \ln \left(\frac{\hat{Q}}{N}\right) \quad (4.5)$$
$$ (0.371) \quad (0.827) \qquad (-3.895)$$

$$- 0.212 \ln N - 0.0617 \ln SMSA + 1.409 \ln X + 0.289 \ln NW + 2.45 \ln Ed$$
$$(-2.516) \quad (-1.496) \qquad (2.274) \quad (2.908) \qquad (2.616)$$

$$- 0.686 \ln A_{14\text{-}24} + 1.454 D.$$
$$(-1.837) \qquad (1.349)$$

As expected, the probability of apprehending and convicting felons is found to be positively related to the level of the current expenditure on police and negatively related to the crime rate, the estimated elasticities being $\hat{\beta}_1 = 0.305$ and $\hat{\beta}_2 = 0.908$, respectively. The productivity of law-enforcement activity is found to be negatively affected by the size and density of the population, as indicated by the negative signs of the coefficients associated with N and SMSA, and positively affected by the extent of relative poverty, the schooling level of the adult population, and the proportion of nonwhites, as indicated by the positive signs of the coefficients associated with X, Ed, and NW.[53] Also, P appears to be greater in southern states and lower in states with a greater proportion of juveniles.[54] Note, however, that the standard error of the coefficient associated with E/N is 0.368, which implies, for example, that the lower and upper 90 percent confidence limits of $\hat{\beta}_1$ (calculated from the normal distribution) are -0.428 and 1.037, respectively. Put differently, the probability that $\hat{\beta}_1$ takes on a *positive* value, given that β_1 is normally distributed with mean 0.305 and standard deviation 0.368, is only .7959. This somewhat weak result may be attributed to both measurement errors in E/N and aggregation biases involved in estimating an aggregate production function of law-enforcement activity. First, E/N measures all expenditures on police activity, including, for example, traffic control, but not on criminal courts. The latter is presumably an important determinant of felony conviction rates. (Also see our discussion of item 6 in the Appendix.) Second, monetary expenditure on police is an imperfect measure of the real outlays on police activity across states because of possible regional differences in the rates of pay to policemen across states that are not due to differences in productivity. Finally, to the extent that the coefficients of the production function of law-enforcement activity against *specific* crimes differ for different crime categories (in particular, crimes against the person as against crimes against property), the estimated coefficients in equation (4.5) may be subject to aggregation biases, since the distribution of specific crimes among total felonies (especially crimes

---

53. The positive association between P and both X and NW indicates that those with lower income spend less resources on legal counsel and legal defense. The positive (partial) effect of Ed on P, given E/N, is interesting, for it may reflect the degree and effectiveness of private self-protective efforts and other assistance provided by victims and law-enforcement agents in bringing about the apprehension and conviction of offenders (also see the Appendix, item 6).

54. One reason why P—the probability of punishment by imprisonment—may be negatively related to A_{14-24} is that many young convicts are sent to reformatories and other correctional institutions rather than to state and federal prisons.

against property) varies significantly across states.[55] This implies, of course, that all the estimated coefficients in equation (4.5), not only $\hat{\beta}_1$, must be viewed with caution.

Assuming for a methodological purpose the validity of our estimates of the aggregate production function (4.5), we may now combine these with estimates of the aggregate supply-of-offenses function to derive a preliminary estimate of the effectiveness of public expenditure on law enforcement in a given year in reducing the rate of crime in that year. Substituting equation (3.3) in equation (3.2), it is easily seen that the elasticity of the crime rate, Q/N, with respect to current expenditure, E/N, is $e = (b_1\beta_1)/(1 - b_1\beta_2)$. In terms of our 2SLS estimates of b_1, β_1, and β_2, e is, then, estimated at -3.04: a 1 percent increase in expenditure on direct law enforcement would result in about a 3 percent decrease in all felony offenses. However, the standard error of this estimate calculated through a Taylor's series approximation of e as a function of b_1, β_1 and β_2 is found to be 11.2. This implies that the probability that $\hat{e}$ takes on a negative value, given that e is asymptotically normally distributed with mean -3.04 and standard deviation 11.2, is only .61812.

The total social loss from crimes against property and crimes against the person in 1965 has been estimated in monetary terms at $5,968 million (see PCL, p. 44), which is probably an underestimate of the true social loss due to these crimes. On the other hand, total expenditure on police, courts, prosecution, and defense in 1965 was $3,178 million (see PCL, p. 54), which obviously is an overestimate of the public expenditure devoted to combating these crimes alone. Nevertheless, if one accepted the tentative estimate of $e = -3$, one would conclude that in 1965 the marginal cost of law enforcement against felonies fell short of its marginal revenue, or that expenditure on direct law enforce-

---

55. Indeed, the value of the coefficient associated with E/N is found to exceed twice the value of its standard error in a regression analysis estimating a production function of law-enforcement activity that relates to crimes against the person only (see Ehrlich, 1970, p. 92).

ment was less than optimal.[56] In view of the imperfections inherent in our estimate of *e*, however, this result cannot be considered very reliable. More accurate and specific data on expenditure on various kinds of law-enforcement activity, on private self-protection against crime, and on the social losses from crime would be required in order to derive more reliable simultaneous-equation estimates of production functions of law-enforcement activities and the effectiveness of these activities in reducing specific crimes and the resulting social losses.

CONCLUSION

The basic thesis underlying our theory of participation in illegitimate activities is that offenders, as a group, respond to incentives in much the same way that those who engage in strictly legitimate activities do as a group. This does not necessarily imply that offenders are similar to other people in all other respects, or that the extent of their response to incentives is the same. Indeed, our theory suggests that the extent of individual offenders' response to incentives may vary (negatively) with the extent of their specialization in illegitimate activity and so may not be uniformly high or low. We do emphasize, however, the role of opportunities available in competing legitimate and illegitimate activities in determining the extent of an offender's participation in the latter and thus, indirectly, also the extent of his response to incentives.

The results of our regression analysis of variations in the rate

56. Assuming that the social loss from crime is proportionally related to the number of offenses committed, an increase in the expenditure on police and courts in 1965 by $32 million (1% of $3,178 million) could have reduced the loss from felonies by about $180 million (3% of $5,968 million). Furthermore, our tentative estimates of β_1 and e indicate that a 1 percent increase in the expenditure on police and courts might have reduced the flow of offenders committed to prisons, $C/N = P (Q/N)$ and thus the total costs of their imprisonment by $\beta_1 + e = 2.7$ percent. Since expenditures on state adult institutions in 1965 amounted to $385 million (see PCL, p. 54; this represents approximately the total costs of imprisonment of a yearly flow of offenders committed to state prisons throughout their effective prison terms), the additional cost of law enforcement associated with a 1 percent increase in the expenditure on police and courts in 1965 might have amounted to about $22 million only ($32 million less $10 million savings in imprisonment costs).

of index crimes across states in the United States are not inconsistent with this basic thesis. In spite of the shortcomings of the crime statistics used, the indirect estimates of some of the theoretical constructs and the somewhat stringent econometric specification of functional relationships, the signs and alternative point estimates of the coefficients of specific regression equations exhibit a remarkable consistency with the theoretical predictions, as well as with one another, across independent samples. The rate of specific felonies is found to be positively related to estimates of relative gains and negatively related to estimates of costs associated with criminal activity. In particular, and contrary to some popular arguments, the absolute magnitudes of the estimated elasticities of specific crimes with respect to estimates of probability and severity of punishment are not inconsistent with the hypothesis that law-enforcement activity has a deterrent effect on offenders, which is independent of any preventive effect of imprisonment. Moreover, the elasticities associated with crimes against the person are not found to be lower, on the average, than those associated with crimes against property.

Viewing the decision to participate in crimes involving material gains as an occupational choice is not inconsistent with the evidence concerning the positive association between income inequality and the rate of crimes against property. Moreover, the relative magnitude of estimates of the elasticities of burglary and larceny with respect to probability and severity of punishment indicate that burglars and thieves are risk avoiders. These findings indicate, in turn, that many crimes against property, not unlike legitimate market activities, pay in the specific sense that their expected gains exceed their expected costs at the margin. This approach may be useful in explaining not only variations in the rate of felonies and many other types of crime across states or over time, but also a variety of specific characteristics associated with individual offenders: for example, why many appear to be relatively young males with little schooling and other legitimate training; why some are occasional offenders who combine legitimate and illegitimate market activities, while others specialize in crime; and why many continue their participation in illegitimate activities even after being apprehended and punished. Such characteristics may be largely the result of the relative opportunities available to offenders in legitimate and illegitimate activities rather than the result of their unique motivation.

More important, the analytical and econometric framework developed in this paper seems useful in evaluating the effectiveness of public expenditure on law-enforcement activity. Some tentative estimates of the effectiveness of police and court activity against felonies in 1965 indicate that such activity paid (indeed, "overpaid") in the sense that its (partial) marginal revenue in terms of a reduced social loss from crime exceeded its (partial) marginal cost. Our empirical investigation also indicates that the rates of all felonies, particularly crimes against property, are positively related to the degree of a community's income inequality, and this suggests a social incentive for equalizing training and earning opportunities across persons, which is independent of ethical considerations or any social welfare function. Whether it would pay society to spend more resources in order to enforce existing laws would then depend not only on the effectiveness of such expenditure in deterring crime, but also on the extent to which alternative methods of combating crime pay. Our ability to analyze these important issues would undoubtedly improve as more and better data concerning the frequency of illegitimate activities, self-protection by both offenders and victims, and alternative private and collective methods of combating crime become available.

APPENDIX

THE EMPIRICAL COUNTERPARTS OF OUR THEORETICAL CONSTRUCTS

The empirical counterparts of our constructs can be itemized as follows:

1. $(Q/N)_i$, the crime rate of a specific crime category, is measured as the number of offenses known to the police to have occurred in a given year per 100,000 (state) population. Statistics of offenses known are based on a count of complaints of crimes filed with the police by victims and other sources and subsequently substantiated. Since reporting a crime is time consuming and may

involve psychic and other disadvantages, an underreporting of crime is expected, especially in the case of milder offenses where the various costs of reporting may exceed its benefits (the potential recovery of stolen property, the collection of insurance benefits, or vengeance).[57] If relative underreporting of specific crimes did not differ systematically across states and percentage reporting errors were random, the relative variation in the rate of offenses known would serve as an unbiased approximation to that of the true crime rate (see Ehrlich 1970, pp. 120-25).

2. P_i, an average offender's subjective probability that he will be apprehended and punished for his engagement in a specific crime category in a given year, may be approximated by the objective probability that a single offense will be cleared by the conviction of an offender.[58] At present, no judicial statistics on the number of convictions are available on a statewide basis. Instead, we have computed the ratio of the number of commitments to state (and in the case of auto theft also federal) prisons in a given state to the number of offenses known to have occurred in the same year, $(C/Q)_i$.[59] Of course, not all those convicted are committed to prisons; some (especially young offenders) are sent to correctional institutions or released on probation. To the extent that the proportion of such convicted offenders did not differ systematically across states, the relative variation in $(C/Q)_i$ could serve as an efficient approximation to that in P_i.

It is possible that a purely statistical exaggeration of the expected negative sign of the regression coefficient associated with

57. Evidence consistent with this argument is presented in PCL, pp. 18, 19.

58. If the probability that an offender will be apprehended and convicted of his criminal activity in a given year were independent of the amount of time he devoted to illegal activity, as our model has assumed for simplicity, an objective measure of P would be the ratio of the number of offenders convicted, C', to the number of active offenders in the same year, or $P_i = (C'/\theta)_i$. This ratio would be the same as the ratio of offenses cleared by conviction to the total number of offenses committed, or K/Q, if those convicted committed the same number of offenses per period ζ, as other offenders in the same state, or $(K/Q) = (\zeta C'/\zeta \theta)$.

59. Data for both this and the following variable, T_i, are collected from the National Prisoner Statistics. These variables were first used by Smigel-Leibowitz (1965).

$(C/Q)_i$ in equation (4.1), b_{1i}, would result from spurious correlation. Recall that the dependent variable is $(Q/N)_i$. If Q_i were not measured appropriately, the errors in the numerator of the dependent variable and in the denominator of the probability measure would move in the same direction. This spurious correlation would bias b_{1i} to a higher (absolute) value if and only if the absolute value of the true regression coefficient were lower than unity (a proof is given in Ehrlich, 1970, pp. 120-25).[60] A spurious correlation may also exist in an opposite direction, however, for if the recovery of stolen merchandise or vengeance played an important role in determining the reporting of an offense, or if the fraction of reported offenses were positively related to law enforcement activity, a low probability of apprehending and convicting offenders would be associated with a low rate of *reported* crimes, thus biasing the correlation between $(Q/N)_i$ and $(C/Q)_i$ toward a positive value. A similar argument can be made regarding the correlation between the severity of punishment and reported crime.

3. F_i, the average cost of punishment for a specific crime category, is measured by the average time actually served by offenders in state prisons for that crime before their first release, T_i. As with our measure of P_i, if the relative variation in T_i also reflected the relative variation in the severity of other punitive measures imposed for the same crime, then T_i would serve as an efficient indicator of F_i. Note, however, that T_i is not proportionally related to F_i. For example, the opportunity costs of imprisonment, F', which may be assumed to be proportionally related to the total cost of punishment, would be measured under a continuous discounting process as $F' = \int_0^T \omega\, e^{-rt}\, dt$, where ω denotes an average prisoner's (constant) foregone value of time per period of imprisonment and r is the relevant discount rate. The elasticity of crime rates with respect to T, σ_{kT}, can therefore be expected to be consistently lower than that with respect to F, σ_{kF}, the differ-

---

60. If the number of offenses committed by the average offender, ζ, were positively related to the crime rate, then our probability measure C/Q would underestimate the relative level of the true probability in states with higher crime rates. This might inject a further negative bias on the regression estimates of b_1.

ence being particularly significant in the case of crimes punishable by long imprisonment terms.[61]

4. As indicators of differential returns in property crimes we use W and X.

5. U, the average probability of unemployment in legitimate activities in a given year, is measured by census estimates of yearly unemployment rates in the civilian labor force. The variation in unemployment rates may not fully capture the variation in the average unemployment duration across states, for which data were not available in our sample years, and thus it may not reflect the true variation in the relevant probability of unemployment with sufficient accuracy. One way to minimize potential biases is by narrowing the base of the unemployment index to apply to relatively homogeneous groups of labor-force participants. Alternative estimates used have been the unemployment rate of urban males in the age group 14 to 24, $U_{14\text{-}24}$, and 35 to 39, $U_{35\text{-}39}$. Another way is by introducing census estimates of labor-force participation rates jointly with unemployment rates. We have actually used the labor-force participation rate of civilian urban males in the age group 14 to 24, $L_{14\text{-}24}$.

6. E/N, the per capita amount of resources allocated to law-enforcement activity in a given year, is measured as the per capita yearly expenditure on police activity by state and local governments (collected from *Governmental Finances in 1960*). Data on expenditures on courts by local governments, which bear the bulk of these expenditures, are not available on a statewide basis. To the extent that the proportion of total expenditure on direct law enforcement devoted to courts did not differ systematically across states (the production functions [3.3] were homogeneous with

---

61. Assuming that losses due to the criminal record effect and other disadvantages of punishment for crime are proportionally related to F', it is easily shown that $(d\ln F)/(d\ln T) = (rTe^{-rT})/(1 - e^{-rT}) = \lambda < 1$. This implies that the coefficient b_{14} in eqs. (4.1) and (4.3) is lower than b_{14} in eq. (3.2) by a constant proportion, λ. Clearly, λ tends to zero as T tends to infinity. Another difficulty with the use of T is that it measures the average penalty per offender, not per offense. To the extent that the number of offenses committed by the average offender were positively related to the crime rate across states, estimates of b_2 may be biased toward positive values.

respect to police and court activity[62] and the ratio of factor costs were constant), and if, in addition, the absolute prices of the relevant factors were constant, the relative variation in our measure of E/N would approximate its true variation. However, the absence of data on private expenditure on self-protection might bias our estimates of equation (3.3) if the former had a direct effect on apprehending and convicting offenders and were not related proportionally to the per capita expenditure on police. To some extent, we may have accounted for the variation in private self-protection by the variation in the schooling level of the adult population across states, Ed. The latter can be shown to be positively related to optimal expenditures on the former (see Ehrlich and Becker, 1972).

7. The percentage of young males aged 14 to 24, $A_{14\text{-}24}$, and the percentage of nonwhites in the population, NW, are introduced in the regression analysis to account for variations in the demographic composition of the population. One reason for standardizing the observations for age and racial composition is to increase the efficiency of our estimators of probability and severity of punishment. For example, there is likely to be a positive correlation between the age of offenders and the use of punitive methods other than imprisonment across states. In addition, since the variation in differential returns from criminal activities is only indirectly accounted for in the regression analysis via X and W, the effect of both $A_{14\text{-}24}$ and NW may partly reflect the effect of such differential returns, or a lower opportunity cost of imprisonment, for the legitimate employment opportunities of young age groups and nonwhites are well below the average, whereas their returns from illegitimate activity may not be significantly different. (For a more detailed discussion of schooling, age, race, and crime, see Ehrlich [forthcoming, NBER].) Given P and T, both NW and $A_{14\text{-}24}$ may thus be positively related to all crime rates. Other

---

62. By definition, the probability of apprehension and conviction is $P \equiv P_a \cdot P_{c|a}$, where P_a is the probability of apprehension and $P_{c|a}$ is the conditional probability of conviction, given apprehension. If $P_a = g(E_p')$ and $P_{c|a} = h(E_c')$ were homogeneous with respect to real per capita expenditure on police (E_p') and courts (E_c'), so would P be with respect to both.

demographic variables used in some of the cross-state regressions are listed in Table 6-1.

REFERENCES

Becker, G. S.: A theory of the allocation of time. *Econ J*, 75:493-517, 1965.
———: Crime and punishment: an economic approach. *J.P.E.*, 76, no. 2: 169-217, 1968.
Bentham, J.: *Theory of Legislation*. New York, Harcourt Brace, 1931.
Chow, G. C.: *The Demand for Automobiles in the United States—a Study in Consumer Durables*. Amsterdam, North-Holland, 1957.
Ehrlich, I.: The Supply of Illegitimate Activities. Unpublished manuscript, Columbia Univ., 1967.
———: *Participation in Illegitimate Activities: An Economic Analysis*, Ph.D. dissertation, Columbia Univ., 1970.
———: On the relation between education and crime. In Juster, F. T. (Ed.): *Education, Income, and Human Behavior*. New York, Nat. Bur. Econ. Res. (forthcoming).
Ehrlich, I., and Becker, G. S.: Market insurance, self-insurance and self-protection, *J.P.E.*, 80, no. 4:623-48, 1972.
Fama, E. F.: Multiperiod consumption-investment decisions. *A.E.R.*, 60, no. 1:163-74, 1970.
Fleisher, B. M.: *The Economics of Delinquency*. Chicago, Quadrangle, 1966.
Fuchs, V. R.: Redefining poverty and redistributing income. *Public Interest*, no. 8 (Summer 1967).
President's Commission on Law Enforcement and Administration of Justice (PCL): *Crime and Its Impact—an Assessment*. Task Force Reports. Washington, Government Printing Office, 1967.
Smigel-Leibowitz, Arlene: *Does Crime Pay? An Economic Analysis*. M.A. thesis, Columbia Univ., 1965.
Stigler, George J.: The optimum enforcement of laws. *J.P.E.*, 78:526-36, 1970.
Taft, D. R., and England, R. W., Jr.: *Criminology*, 4th ed. New York, Macmillan, 1964.
Tobin, J.: A statistical demand function for food in the U.S.A. *J Royal Statis Soc*, Ser. A, *113*:113-40, 1950.
U.S., Department of Commerce, Bureau of the Census: *Prisoners in State and Federal Prisons and Reformatories*. Washington, Government Printing Office, 1943.
———: *Governmental Finances in 1959*. Washington, Government Printing Office, 1960.
———: *Governmental Finances in 1960*. Washington, Government Printing Office, 1961.

U.S., Department of Justice, Bureau of Prisons: *Prisoners in State and Federal Institutions, 1950.* National Prisoner Statistics. Washington, Government Printing Office, 1956.

———: *Prisoners Released from State and Federal Institutions, 1951.* National Prisoner Statistics. Washington, Government Printing Office.

———: *Characteristics of State Prisoners, 1960.* National Prisoner Statistics. Washington, Government Printing Office.

———: *Federal Prisons, 1960.* Washington, Government Printing Office.

———: *Prisoners Released from State and Federal Institutions, 1960.* National Prisoner Statistics. Washington, Government Printing Office.

———: *Prisoners Released from State and Federal Institutions, 1964.* National Prisoner Statistics. Washington, Government Printing Office.

U.S., Department of Justice, Federal Bureau of Investigation: *Uniform Crime Reports for the U.S.* (UCR) Printed annually 1933 to date. Washington, Government Printing Office.

Zellner, A.: An efficient method of estimating seemingly unrelated regressions and tests for a regression bias. *J American Statis Assoc 57:*348-68, 1962.

———: Estimation of regression relationships containing unobservable independent variables. *Internat Econ Rev, 11,* no. 3:441-55, 1970.

CHAPTER 7

PROPERTY CRIME AND ECONOMIC BEHAVIOR: SOME EMPIRICAL RESULTS

DAVID LAWRENCE SJOQUIST*

BELTON FLEISHER AND GARY BECKER have previously suggested that crime may be explainable, at least in part, by economic theory. This paper will consider this possibility for the crimes of robbery, burglary, and larceny over $50.[1] The hypothesis to be tested is that under some conditions, criminals can be treated as rational economic beings, assumed to behave in the same economic manner as any other individual making an economic decision under risk.

AN ECONOMIC MODEL OF CRIMINAL BEHAVIOR

Given a fixed amount of time, t, an individual must choose between those various activities which consume time. For our purposes, let us assume there are two time-consuming activities or forms of behavior, one of which is legal,[2] i.e. work, and the other illegal, i.e. crimes against property. Our task is to explain how the individual allocates his time between the two activities. It is expected that this depends on the gains and costs involved in the two activities.

---

* I wish to thank the National Institute of Law Enforcement and Criminal Justice for financial support of this paper, a fact which does not necessarily indicate the concurrence of the Institute in the statements or the conclusions contained herein.

Reprinted, with permission of the American Economic Association, from *The American Economic Review*, June 1973, pp. 439-446.

1. For a definition of these crimes, see Federal Bureau of Investigation (FBI), *Reports*, pp. 13-26.

2. If leisure and work are equally valued at the margin then we need only consider one of them as the legal activity.

Participation in the two activities is expected to result in psychic and financial gains and costs. The gain per unit of time from legal activity is measured by the individual's wage rate, g_w, which is assumed to be constant and to include any psychic gain. The individual's total gain from legal activity, $\bar{g}_w$, therefore equals the time allocated to that activity, t_w, times the wage rate. We assume that g_w is generated with certainty with all associated costs both financial and psychic included.

Participation in illegal activities results in a psychic and/or financial gain. The psychic gain is measured by that quantity of money which the individual is willing to pay to obtain the psychic gain. The financial gain is measured directly by the dollar value to the criminal of the assets stolen.[3]

Since a crime could be unsuccessful, the gain from illegal activity, particularly the financial gain, is random with the individual normally possessing a subjective probability distribution of the possible gains. We will simplify however, by assuming that the gain is generated with certainty. We will also assume that the wage rate from crime, g_c, is constant and includes any psychic gain so that the total gain from illegal activity, $\bar{g}_c$, is equal to the time spent in illegal activity, t_c, times the wage rate from crime.[4] All costs of illegal activity, both financial and psychic, other than those associated with arrest, conviction, and punishment, are included in g_c.

Besides any expenditures for tools, etc., illegal activity involves the possibility of costs resulting from arrest, conviction, and punishment. These include public scandal, loss of freedom, the distaste of prison life, lawyer fees, possible reduction in potential income, since individuals possessing criminal records find it more difficult to obtain employment, and loss of earnings while imprisoned, measured by the discounted value of income foregone while in prison less any benefits received, such as room and board and vocational training.

The psychic and financial costs associated with arrest and con-

3. Since nonfinancial assets are normally distributed through a black market, the value to the criminal will not necessarily be the same as the loss of the victim.

4. Assume t_w, $t_c \geq 0$, $t > 0$ and $t_w + t_c = t$.

viction are assumed to be quasi-fixed costs, that is, if arrested and convicted, the cost is the same regardless of the time the individual spent in illegal activity.[5]

The costs associated with imprisonment are variable and depend upon the length of the sentence served and the individual's legal wage rate. Assuming that the expected length of the sentence received is positively related to the time spent in illegal activity,[6] and that the length of the sentence received is positively related to the length of the sentence actually served, we can conclude that the expected cost of imprisonment depends upon the legal wage rate and the time spent in illegal activity. (There is a substantial amount of evidence indicating that variance in sentencing is large,[7] implying the existence of a probability distribution of possible costs from imprisonment, given that arrest and conviction have taken place. We will, however, disregard this and assume that there is no uncertainty as to the sentence received.)

We then have the total cost of illegal activity, $\bar{p}$, composed of a quasi-fixed cost component, p^*, and a variable cost component, $\hat{p} = \hat{p} (g_w, t_c)$. Thus, $\bar{p} = p^* + \hat{p} (g_w, t_c)$. Assume for simplicity that $\partial \hat{p}(g_w, t_c)/\partial t_c = p$ and is constant.

All crimes do not result in arrest and conviction, meaning that the cost of illegal activity occurs according to some probability distribution. Individuals are assumed to possess a subjective evaluation of the probabilities of arrest, of conviction, and of imprisonment. Although these probabilities no doubt depend upon the time spent in illegal activity, we will assume they are constant. Since nothing is lost in the analysis by doing so, we will also assume temporarily that the probability of conviction and punishment, conditioned on arrest, is one. Thus the joint probability of arrests, conviction, and punishment equals the probability of arrest.

The gains and costs from legal and illegal activities are evalu-

---

5. If the quasi-fixed costs are large, then an increase in the length of the sentence increases total cost by a small percent. The effect then would be for variations in the length of the sentence to have little influence on the amount of time spent in illegal activity.

6. For a study of sentencing which yields this result, see Edward Green.

7. See Glendon Schubert.

ated by the individual according to his preference ordering, taking into account the various probabilities. We assume that this preference ordering is a Von Neumann-Morgenstern measurable utility function, that is, under conditions involving risk, individuals will choose between alternatives so as to maximize the expected value of utility.

There exist two possible states of nature, the individual will either be arrested and therefore convicted and punished, or not arrested. Let $U(\bar{g}_w + \bar{g}_c)$ represent the ordinal utility if not arrested, and $U(\bar{g}_w + \bar{g}_c - \bar{p})$ represent the ordinal utility if arrested, where the utility index is appropriately chosen in accordance with the Von Neumann-Morgenstern axioms. Let r represent the probability of arrest, conviction, and punishment; that is, the probability of incurring those financial and psychic costs associated with arrest, conviction, and punishment. The expected total utility is thus:

$$E(U) = (1 - r)U(\bar{g}_w + \bar{g}_c) + rU(\bar{g}_w + \bar{g}_c - \bar{p}) \qquad (1)$$

which is to be maximized subject to the constraint $t = t_w + t_c$.

The first-order conditions for maximization require that

$$\frac{g_w - g_c}{g_c - g_w - p} = \frac{(1 - r)U_1'}{rU_2'} \qquad (2)$$

where

$$U_1' = \frac{dU(\bar{g}_w + \bar{g}_c)}{d(\bar{g}_w + \bar{g}_c)}$$

and

$$U_2' = \frac{dU(\bar{g}_w + \bar{g}_c - \bar{p})}{d(\bar{g}_w + \bar{g}_c - \bar{p})}$$

Assuming U_1', $U_2' > 0$, then condition (2) holds if

$$g_c - g_w < p \qquad (3)$$

It should be pointed out that a corner solution at $t_w = t$ is quite possible because of the quasi-fixed cost of illegal activity.

The second-order condition requires that

$$(1 - r)U_1'' [g_c - g_w]^2 + rU_2'' [g_c - g_w - p]^2 < 0, \qquad (4)$$

where U_1'', U_2'' refer to the second derivatives. A sufficient condition for (4) to hold is that the individual is risk averse, i.e. U_1'',

$U_2'' < 0$. If an individual has a strong enough preference for risk the indifference curves will be concave, in which case the individual will either specialize in work or crime.

The question we wish to ask is: How do people respond to changes in risk, wages, and punishment? If the individual is risk averse, then given our previous assumptions, it can be shown that $dt_w/dr > 0$, i.e. an increase in r reduces the time spent in illegal activity. However if the indifference curves are concave then a person who was specializing in work will now specialize in crime, if the change in r is large enough. Likewise it can be shown that for an individual who is risk averse we would have $dt_w/dg_c < 0$, $dt_w/dg_w > 0$, and $dt_w/dp > 0$.

TESTING THE MODEL

The time spent in criminal activity by the ith individual, t^i_c, can be expressed as a function of the variables specified in the previous section, namely,

$$t^i_c = f^i\left(r^i, p^i, g^i_w, g^i_c; x^i\right) \tag{5}$$

where x^i is an index of variables which "measures" tastes, and the other variables are as previously defined.

Assume that this function has the following explicit form:

$$t^i = a_0\, r^{ia_1^i}\, g_w^{ia_2^i}\, g_c^{ia_3^i}\, p^{ia_4^i}\, x^{ia_5^i} \tag{6}$$

The model is specified in terms of individual behavior, while the available data are community aggregates. Taking the natural *logs* of (6) and replacing individual values by community means we have

$$ln\,(TC/I) = ln\,a_0 + a_1\,ln\,r + a_2\,ln\,GW \tag{7}$$

$$+\; a_3\,ln\,GC + a_4\,ln\,P + a_5\,ln\,X$$

where (TC/I), GW, GC, P, and X represent population means of t_c, g_w, g_c, p, and x, respectively, TC is the total time spent in illegal activity and I is the community population. The values of the parameters of (7) will be the same as the parameters of (6) if we assume that the values of the parameters of (6) are the same for all individuals in a given community[8] and that the density function between individual values and the community mean of the variable are homogeneous of degree one with respect to changes in the individual values and community means.[9]

A cross-sectional sample of 53 municipalities with 1960 populations of 25,000 to 200,000 was selected on the basis of the following criteria:

1. We eliminated communities with 1960 populations of less than 25,000 because of a lack of data, and of more than 200,000 in order to use communities which were internally homogeneous.

2. To minimize spillover effects, any community with neighboring communities of 25,000 or more was eliminated, as well as any community with less than 50 percent of the population of its Standard Metropolitan Statistical Area *(SMSA)*.

Of the 75 communities which fulfilled these criteria, 22 had to be dropped for lack of information on arrests.

Since it is not possible to directly measure the time spent in illegal activity, we measured the amount of illegal activity by the total number of property crimes committed, *N*. This in turn was measured by the total number of the three types of property crimes recorded by the local police department as reported in the 1968 FBI *Reports*.

The data on reported crimes is subject to strong criticism[10] and hence one must be very cautious in drawing implications using this data.

The FBI supplied unpublished information, collected yearly from local police departments, which we used to measure arrests and convictions at the local level for the year 1968. The number of convictions was similarly estimated[11] for 1968 from this in-

---

8. For a proof see Henri Theil, p. 142.

9. See James Tobin, p. 126.

10. For a discussion of the problems with crime data see Thorsten Sellin and Marvin E. Wolfgang, pp. 71-86, and The National Opinion Research Center *Report*.

11. Convictions were determined in the following manner: A conviction rate was found using the ratio of persons guilty to the sum of persons guilty and acquitted. This ratio was then applied to those cases not yet brought to court. The number of convictions was then the sum of this product, the number guilty and the number sent to juvenile court.

formation.[12]

We employed three separate measures of r: the ratio of arrests to the number of crimes; the ratio of convictions to the number of crimes; and the ratio of convictions to arrests. These measure, respectively, the probability of arrest, $r(A)$, the probability of conviction, $r(AC)$, and the probability of conviction given arrest, $r(C|A)$.

When the ratio of arrests or convictions to reported crimes is used to measure r, reported crimes appear in both the dependent and the independent variable. Thus to the extent that there are errors in the measure of reported crimes, we expect a bias in the coefficients of that equation.

The net gain from legal activity, GW, was measured by the annual labor income to manufacturing workers in 1968. These are county-wide data and were obtained from the 1968 *County Business Patterns*.[13]

It is not possible to differentiate the incomes of criminals from the incomes of victims, which poses a problem in measuring the gain from legal activity. To the extent that crimes against high income individuals yield greater returns to the criminal, we would expect a positive correlation to exist between income and the number of crimes. If this is true then use of mean community income is not a good measure of the opportunity cost of committing crime. In addition to mean income therefore, we also employed substitute variables: the 1968 labor force unemployment rate, derived from information published by the Bureau of Labor Statistics, and the percent of families with income below $3,000, taken from the 1960 *Census of Population*. An unemployed person has more time to allocate to illegal activity and since his current income is low, he would have a greater incentive

12. Using the number of arrests and convictions and the number of crimes for the same period does not take into account time lag between the criminal act and the arrest and the resulting conviction. This may result in erroneous measures of r.

13. The size of the city and the method of selection of the sample resulted in a sample for which differences between the city and the rest of the county was minimized, so that the problem of using county-wide data is minimal.

to commit crimes. The same reasoning can be applied to a family with a low income.

We have been unable to find any information on the financial loss of the public from criminal activity, other than a national average for each classification of crime. As a substitute variable we used retail sales per establishment reasoning that the size of the expected gain depends upon the size of the establishment a criminal chooses to rob or burglarize.

We assumed that the only variable cost of illegal activity is the cost of punishment, which depends upon the income foregone while in prison, less benefits, and any psychic costs. The discounted value of the foregone earnings is highly correlated with current earnings, thus we cannot use both in our regression equation. Given the mean income for the community, the foregone earnings will be proportional to the length of the sentence served. Thus the length of the sentence served can be used to reflect the cost of illegal activity. (Since we had no measure of the psychic costs, we had to ignore them.)

To measure the average sentence served, we used the reported state-wide average time served by inmates released from state and federal prisons in 1960, for the crimes we are considering, as published by the Federal Bureau of Prisons. Figures other than state-wide averages or beyond 1960 were not available.[14]

A number of variables was employed to reflect economic and demographic differences between communities as well as to reflect possible differences in the evaluation of the psychic gains and costs. The percent of the population which is nonwhite reflects the income distribution and regional differences, since in our sample the percent nonwhite decreases as one moves from the South to the Northeast, to the West, to the Midwest. The mean number of school years completed reflects both cultural

---

14. We feel the assumption that the same sentence is served by all criminals for a particular crime in a given state regardless of the community is not unreasonable. We know that the variance in the sentence served across states is substantially less than the variance in the sentence imposed. In addition, since paroles are normally granted by one agency for all state prisons in a particular state, we expect even more uniformity in the sentence served than in the sentence imposed.

differences and differences in expectations of future incomes. We employed population density to reflect the fact that the closer the opportunities are, the greater the likelihood the individual can acquire the information necessary to perform a crime. Finally, we included population as a factor because of possible differences in the social make-up of residents of different sized cities.

Thus we arrive at the equation we estimated:

$$(N/I) = \beta_0 r^{\beta_1} S^{\beta_2} GW^{\beta_3} E^{\beta_4} NW^{\beta_5} SY^{\beta_6} D^{\beta_7} I^{\beta_8} \phi \qquad (8)$$

where N, r, GW, and I are as previously defined, S is the average prison sentence served, E is retail sales per establishment, NW is the percent nonwhite, SY is the mean school years completed, D is population density, and ϕ is a random error term assumed to have a lognormal distribution.

RESULTS OF THE STATISTICAL ANALYSIS

Using multiple regression analysis, we estimated the parameters of equation (8) using the total of the reported property crimes in the three categories, robbery, burglary, and larceny over $50 to measure N and employing three different measures of risk: $r(A)$, $r(AC)$, and $r(C|A)$. (We are assuming that if convicted the individual is punished.) The results of the regressions are presented in Table 7-I.

It was implied from our model that the coefficients of the measure of risk should be negative and as seen in Table 7-I the coefficients are of that sign. However, when r is measured by $r(A)$ and $r(AC)$ the coefficients are biased, as indicated above. Note though, that the coefficient for convictions per arrest, which is not biased, is also negative.

According to the theory, an increase in r reduces the amount of crime because it increases the expected cost and therefore lowers expected utility from crime. Separate increases in the three measures of risk result in increases in different costs. We thus expect the elasticity of N with respect to risk to be higher for $r(AC)$ than for $r(A)$ given $r(C|A)$, and for $r(C|A)$ given $r(A)$. It is also expected that the elasticity for $r(C|A)$ would be less than the elasticity for $r(A)$, given our discussion of cost.

Equation (4) of Table 7-I presents the results of a regression in

TABLE 7-I

REGRESSION EQUATIONS USING N TO MEASURE NUMBER OF CRIMES

(*t*-statistics in parentheses)

1) $ln\ N/I = -1.09 - .342\ ln\ r(A) - .212\ ln\ S + .167\ ln\ E + .142\ ln\ GW + .179\ ln\ I$
$(-3.374)^* \quad (-1.070) \quad (.547) \quad (.526) \quad (1.402)^*$

$\quad + .126\ ln\ NW + .702\ ln\ SY + .051\ ln\ D$
$\quad (3.627)^* \quad (1.255) \quad (.438)$

$R^2 = .506$

2) $ln\ N/I = -1.46 - .354\ ln\ r(AC) - .292\ ln\ S + .071\ ln\ E + .205\ ln\ GW + .084\ ln\ I$
$(-3.759)^* \quad (-1.438)^* \quad (.229) \quad (.746) \quad (.636)$

$\quad + .140\ ln\ NW + 1.159\ ln\ SY + .087\ ln\ D$
$\quad (3.987)^* \quad (2.062)^* \quad (.776)$

$R^2 = .565$

3) $ln\ N/I = -2.00 - .678\ ln\ r(C|A) - .467\ ln\ S - .111\ ln\ E + .349\ ln\ GW + .275\ ln\ I$
$(-1.502)^* \quad (-2.076)^* \quad (-.310) \quad (1.132) \quad (2.028)^*$

$\quad + .121\ ln\ NW + .129\ ln\ SY + .208\ ln\ D$
$\quad (3.006)^* \quad (1.944)^* \quad (1.590)^*$

$R^2 = .440$

4) $ln\ N/I = -1.39 - .365\ ln\ r(A) - .267\ ln\ r\ (C|A) - .285\ ln\ S + .088\ ln\ E + .200\ ln\ GW$
$(-3.316)^* \quad (-.634) \quad (-1.368)^* \quad (.272) \quad (.719)$

$\quad + .082\ ln\ I + .142\ ln\ NW + 1.222\ ln\ SY + .077\ ln\ D$
$\quad (.616) \quad (3.887)^* \quad (1.886)^* \quad (.626)$

$R^2 = .556$

* Significant at the 10 percent level with a one-tailed test.

N = Total number of robberies, burglaries and larcenies over \$50 in 1968 reported to the FBI by local police.

A = Number of arrests in 1968 for the crimes of robbery, burglary and larceny over \$50 as reported to the FBI by local police departments.

C = Number of convictions in 1968 for the crimes of robbery, burglary, larceny over \$50 as reported by the local police to the FBI.

$r(A) = A/N$

$r(AC) = C/N$

$r(C|A) = C/A$

GW = Yearly income in thousands of dollars from the 1968 *County Business Patterns;* county wide.

E = Yearly sales per retail establishment in thousands of dollars taken from the 1967 *Census of Business.*

S = The average sentence served by inmates released from State and Federal Institutes who had been charged with either robbery, burglary, or larceny over \$50. This is state wide.

I = Community population, in thousands, taken from the estimates of 1968 population made by Rand McNally and published in their *Commercial Atlas and Marketing Guide.*

NW = The percent of the city population which was nonwhite in 1960, taken from the 1960 *Census of Population.*

SY = Mean school years completed by residents of the community in 1960 taken from the 1960 *Census of Population.*

D = Population density, persons per square mile, for the community taken from the 1960 *Census of Population.*

TABLE 7-II

REGRESSION EQUATIONS USING *PCBT* AND *UE*[a]

(*t*-statistics in parentheses)

1) $\ln N/I = -1.13 - .384 \ln r(A) - .268 \ln S + .137 \ln E + .175 \ln GW + .085 \ln I$
             (-3.601)*   (-1.280)*   (.431)   (.550)   (.634)

   $+ .150 \ln NW + 1.011 \ln SY + .050 \ln D - .021 \ln PCBT$
     (3.202)*   (1.772)*   (.434)   (-.121)

                                               $R^2 = .561$

2) $\ln N/I = -1.15 - .388 \ln r(A) - .253 \ln S + .204 \ln E + .083 \ln I + .158 \ln NW$
             (-3.686)*   (-1.231)   (.707)   (.622)   (3.560)*

   $+ 1.031 \ln SY + .052 \ln D - .066 \ln PCBT$
     (1.827)*   (.450)   (-.439)

                                               $R^2 = .558$

3) $\ln N/I = -1.33 - .354 \ln r(A) - .200 \ln S + .103 \ln E + .239 \ln GW + .185 \ln I$
             (-3.649)*   (-1.046)   (.357)   (.938)   (1.452)*

   $+ .137 \ln NW + .826 \ln SY + .002 \ln D + .343 \ln UE$
     (4.156)*   (1.580)*   (.015)   (2.822)*

                                               $R^2 = .637$

4) $\ln N/I = -1.65 - .368 \ln r(A) - .186 \ln S + .220 \ln E + .184 \ln I + .137 \ln NW$
$\quad\quad\quad\quad\quad (-3.857)^* \quad\quad (-.981) \quad\quad (.850) \quad\quad (1.452)^* \quad (4.161)^*$

$\quad + .857 \ln SY + .004 \ln D + .336 \ln UE$
$\quad\quad (1.644)^* \quad\quad (.040) \quad\quad (2.772)^*$

$\quad\quad\quad\quad\quad\quad\quad\quad\quad\quad\quad\quad\quad R^2 = .629$

5) $\ln N/I = -1.47 - .356 \ln r(A) - .204 \ln S + .101 \ln E + .273 \ln GW + .189 \ln I$
$\quad\quad\quad\quad\quad (-3.608)^* \quad\quad (-1.051) \quad\quad (.347) \quad\quad (.927) \quad\quad (1.453)^*$

$\quad + .130 \ln NW + .820 \ln SY + .001 \ln D + .347 \ln UE + .383 \ln PCBT$
$\quad\quad (2.964)^* \quad\quad (1.546)^* \quad\quad (.006) \quad\quad (2.794)^* \quad\quad (.240)$

$\quad\quad\quad\quad\quad\quad\quad\quad\quad\quad\quad\quad\quad R^2 = .638$

6) $\ln N/I = -1.49 - .364 \ln r(A) - .184 \ln S + .207 \ln E + .181 \ln I + .142 \ln NW$
$\quad\quad\quad\quad\quad (-3.709)^* \quad\quad (-.956) \quad\quad (.773) \quad\quad (1.398)^* \quad (3.432)^*$

$\quad + .858 \ln SY + .005 \ln D + .334 \ln UE - .033 \ln PCBT$
$\quad\quad (1.627)^* \quad\quad (.043) \quad\quad (2.708)^* \quad\quad (-.237)$

$\quad\quad\quad\quad\quad\quad\quad\quad\quad\quad\quad\quad\quad R^2 = .629$

* Significant at 10 percent level with a one-tailed test.
a In addition to the variables defined in Table 7-I, Table 7-II includes:
PCBT = Percent of the families in the community who had incomes below $3,000 in 1959 taken from the 1960 *Census of Population.*
UE = The labor force unemployment rate in 1968 generated from data published by the Bureau of Labor Statistics.
The sample size for both regressions is 53, as is reported in the text.

which both $r(C|A)$ and $r(A)$ were used. Comparing equation (4) with equation (2), we see that the elasticity for $r(C|A)$ is smaller than the elasticity for $r(AC)$ as expected, though not significantly. The elasticity for $r(A)$, however, is slightly larger than the elasticity for $r(AC)$. We note also from equation (4) that elasticity for $r(C|A)$ is less than the elasticity for $r(A)$, but again not significantly.

The coefficient for average sentence served, S, is negative for all equations in Table 7-I, a result our theory leads us to expect.

In equation (4), we note that the elasticity of N/I is greater with respect to $r(A)$ than with respect to S, but not significantly. If we assume risk aversion, i.e. that the expected loss of utility is less than the utility of the expected loss, and that the cost of arrest is large, it follows that the change in the expected loss of utility will be greater for a 1 percent increase in $r(A)$ than for a 1 percent increase in the cost of punishment. This implies that more crimes will be prevented by increasing $r(A)$ than by increasing the cost of punishment or that the elasticity of N/I with respect to $r(A)$ should be greater than with respect to S, which is our measure of the cost of punishment.

The coefficient of E, retail sales per establishment, is positive in three of the four equations in Table 7-I. Retail sales per establishment is admittedly a very crude measure of the gain to criminal activity, a statement which is borne out by the low values of the t-statistic.

The only result of the analysis which appears to be in conflict with the theory is the coefficient for income, which we find to be positive, whereas a negative coefficient is anticipated. If it is true, as previously suggested that GW is a measure of the gain to both legal and illegal activity, the coefficient of income could be either positive or negative.

To test our theory further, we ran regressions employing two additional variables, the labor force unemployment rate, UE, and the percent of families with incomes below \$3,000, $PCBT$, for which we would expect positive coefficients. As seen in Table 7-II, the coefficients for UE are all positive while the coefficients for $PCBT$, however, are mixed.

Let the two roles that income plays in our model be designated as the "gain effect," i.e. as a measure of the gain from crime, and the "need effect," i.e. as a measure of the gain from legal activity. The results presented in Table 7-II provide some evidence that the coefficient of income is picking up the gain effect. When *PCBT* and/or *UE* are used with *GW*, part of the need effect should be removed from the coefficient of *GW*, resulting in a larger coefficient for *GW* which we find when comparing equation (1) of Table 7-I with the equations in Table 7-II. Likewise, when *GW* is removed from the equation, the coefficients for *UE* and *PCBT* fall, since they are now picking up the gain effect. This would also explain two of the negative coefficients for *PCBT*.

We also note that the coefficient for *E* moves in the opposite direction of the movement of the coefficient of *GW*, providing further evidence for our explanation of the positive coefficient for income.

CONCLUSIONS

Following the lead of Becker and Fleisher, we have postulated an economic theory of property crime. Employing a Von Neumann-Morgenstern utility function we developed a model in which an individual must allocate his time between legal and illegal activities so as to maximize expected utility. We tested the model by running regressions on a cross-sectional sample of communities.

The empirical results give at least tentative credence to our hypothesis. We find that an increase in the probability of arrest and conviction and an increase in the cost of crime (punishment) both result in a decrease in the number of major property crimes committed.

Given our results, further work in this area does not appear to be out of order, particularly more sophisticated work employing better data.

REFERENCES

Becker, G. S.: Crime and punishment: an economic approach. *J Polit Econ*, 76:169-217, 1968.

Fleisher, B.: *The Economics of Delinquency*. Chicago, Quadrangle, 1966.

Green, E.: *Judicial Attitudes in Sentencing*. London, 1961.

Schubert, G.: *Judicial Behavior: A Reader in Theory and Research*. Chicago, 1964.

Sellin, T. and Wolfgang, M.: *The Measurement of Delinquency.* New York, 1964.

Theil, H.: *Linear Aggregation of Economic Relations.* Amsterdam, 1954.

Tobin, J.: A statistical demand function for food in the U.S.A. *J Royal Statist Soc,* Series A, Part II, *113:*113-45, 1950.

Federal Bureau of Investigation: *Uniform Crime Reports—1968.* Washington, 1969.

Federal Bureau of Prisons: *Inmates Released from State and Federal Institutions 1960.* Washington, 1960.

National Opinion Research Center: *Criminal Victimization in the United States: A Report of a National Survey.* Washington, 1967.

Rand McNally and Company: *1968 Commercial Atlas and Marketing Guide,* 99th ed. New York, 1968.

U.S. Bureau of the Census: *Census of Business, 1967,* Vol. II, *Retail Trade, Area Statistics.* Washington, 1970.

———: *County Business Patterns, 1968.* Washington, 1969.

———: *U.S. Census of Population: 1960,* Vol. I, *Characteristics of the Population.* Washington, 1963.

U.S. Bureau of Labor Statistics: *Employment and Earnings.* Apr. 1968, *14.*

CHAPTER 8

CRIME AS A DISECONOMY OF SCALE

ISRAEL PRESSMAN AND ARTHUR CAROL

THE PROCESS OF URBANIZATION occurs for one thing because there exist external economies of scale. A greater density of population allows for specialization of labor, extension of markets, availability of joint resources and so on. The mere fact of the urbanization process is evidence that people place a value on at least some of the consequent advantages. In recent decades, while people in the United States continue to leave rural for urban areas, there has developed a counter trend to leave the most densely populated urban centers for the suburban surroundings. Manhattan, the most densely populated county in the nation, has been losing population steadily since the turn of the century. This suggests the possibility that there may be external diseconomies of size whose costs now exceed the corresponding benefits, e.g. pollution and the very press of numbers.[1]

It would be desirable to be able to obtain measures of both external economies and diseconomies of urbanization. Such measures might provide an indication of optimal degrees of urbanization. That is, they might be indicative of a range within which the economies and diseconomies were roughly in balance. The purpose of this paper is much more modest. It seeks to investigate whether crime is a manifestation of an external diseconomy of urbanization. Crime has a cost. In the case of burglary, for example, the cost might be estimated fairly readily based on the market value of the goods burglarized.[2] Where the crimes are against person rather than property, costs become more difficult

Reprinted, with permission of The Association for Social Economics, from *Review of Social Economy*, March 1971, pp. 227-236.

1. The move to the suburbs has other causes besides the creation of diseconomies of size. To some extent it may be an attempt to maintain racial separation.
2. One could argue, Robinhood-like, that some types of crime are simple transfer payments and that the net value to society is unchanged, or increased.

to estimate, but not impossible. Consequently, if the frequency of certain crimes is a function of urbanization, it is at least conceptually possible to estimate the cost of these crimes as a function of urbanization.

The belief is widely held that crime rates will be high where there exists a high population density. But the matter is by no means settled. Psychologists, sociologists and anthropologists are not all agreed. The following report of a partial correlation study provides fresh evidence which, although unfortunately far from conclusive, is suggestive of further avenues of investigation which might prove fruitful.

CROSS SECTIONAL ANALYSIS

Recent increases in reported crime rates have been attributed in part to more complete reporting procedures. Also, there are other statistical difficulties with time series data. Consequently, a cross sectional study was preferred. The most recent year for which all the desired data could be obtained was 1965.[3] That was prior to the more recent widespread urban riots and therefore not subject to any confusions or inconsistencies in crime data reporting the riots may have engendered.

Initially each of the Standard Metropolitan Statistical Areas in the United States was selected for inclusion in the analysis. But various problems in data incomparability and the exclusion of atypical cases reduced the number to ninety-five. In addition, the study was performed separately using data from each of the fifty states. This means that there is an undesirable amount of aggregation. For instance, two SMSAs could each have the same population density, but entirely different density patterns. One might consist of a highly urbanized center with a sparsely populated surrounding suburban area, and the other could be of relatively uniform density throughout. But the study relied on existing Department of Commerce and Department of Justice data as reported in the Statistical Abstract of the United States. No new data were generated.

Correlations were obtained between crime rates and population density and net in-migration rates. The latter factor was chosen

3. See footnotes to tables.

since it has been suggested that large movements of population might be related to crime. That is, the unsettling effect of influxes of people into an area, even one not already densely populated, results in that type of social disruption which leads to criminal acts. But correlations between crime and these two measures of urbanization are influenced by numerous other factors. For example, a positive correlation between crime and in-migration might obscure underlying relationships between affluence and in-migration (people may move to areas in which economic prospects are good), and between affluence and crime (more wealthy people are better prospects for the burglar). In this way, the true relationships could yield a specious correlation between crime rates and in-migration rates.

Several factors were selected for analysis. The primary purpose was to weed out any misleading relationships as indicated above. A secondary purpose was also served in that these factors are of interest in their own right. These factors were as follows: Family income level in area as measured by median income for all SMSAs, and percent of families with incomes over $10,000 and under $3,000 for SMSAs with populations over 250,000 (available only for those areas); educational level as measured by median number of school years completed; racial mix as measured by percent of population classified as nonwhite; percent of population residing in poverty areas, by race; climate as measured by mean annual temperature; number of full time police officials as a percent of center city population. The reasons for the inclusion of these particular factors were largely dictated by their availability. Obvious modifications easily could be argued for.

Correlations were found between crime rates and each of the factors mentioned. In those instances in which the results were at all significant, the factors were retained for a partial correlation analysis. The purpose of a partial correlation study is to assess the relationship between any two variables holding certain other variables constant. In the preceding illustration, partial correlations could be found between crime rates and in-migration rates holding the level of affluence as a constant. That is to say, in those areas in which the level of affluence is the same, we seek the relationship between crime rates and in-migration rates.

RESULTS

The correlations between educational levels and crime indicated no relationships. We hasten to stress that we do not take this as conclusive, merely that using the data available and the chosen analytical technique, no relationship was found.

The correlations between number of police per capita and crime rates were positive and significant (at the .05 confidence level in most instances). This is most probably explained by the hypothesis that in an area with high crime rates, more police are employed.[4] Changes in the number of police from one year to the next yield no correlations with changes in crime rates one and two years subsequently. This is suggestive that more police may not be the answer to high crime rates and that larger expenditures on police protection are not cost effective in combating crime.

Correlations between mean annual temperature and crime, especially crimes against persons, is positive and significant. But the partial correlation between these variables, holding the racial factor constant, is not significantly different from zero. It is difficult to unscramble the interrelationships here. That there is a relation between climate and crime, and between racial composition and crime, there is no question. But the concentration of nonwhites in areas with a high mean annual temperature makes it difficult to discern underlying factors. There are only a few areas with warm climates and few nonwhites (e.g. Santa Barbara, California), still fewer areas with cold climates and a high proportion of nonwhites. Insofar as the evidence allows, the racial factor is the more potent, but this is highly tentative. What is wanted is a comparison of crime rates among whites in different climates.[5]

The major results of the study are summarized in Tables 8-I and 8-II. The correlation between crime rates and each of the other factors is a partial correlation, showing the relationship between crime and each factor holding the other factors listed in the table

---

4. The primary objective of a police force may not be to minimize the total crime index. See "Round Table on Allocation of Resources in Law Enforcement," *American Economic Review*, May, 1969, p. 504-5.

5. The phenomenon is world wide. The nonwhite population is concentrated in warmer climates.

TABLE 8-I

TABLES OF PARTIAL CORRELATION COEFFICIENTS

	Crimes Against Persons	Crimes Against Property
Population density	.09	.09
Net migration	.21	.35*
Percent of population—nonwhite	.66*	.43*
Median family income	−.05	.19
Multiple correlation coefficient	.70*	.59*

* t-test level of significance: .01.

Notes:

1. Data upon which the correlations are based are taken from the Statistical Abstract of the United States and the supplement thereto. The data concerning crime rates and population density are for the year 1965; the net migration rates are for the years 1960 through 1965; the nonwhite data are for the year 1960; the income data are based on the years 1960, 1962, and 1965.

2. The correlations are based only on Standard Metropolitan Statistical Area data. Thus, sparsely populated areas are excluded from consideration.

3. Although, as in the case of the other variables tested, population density and median family income did not prove to be significant, they are included here because of the widely held belief to the contrary.

constant. Table 8-I is based on data from SMSAs of all population sizes. Since the SMSAs with population of less than 250,000 group all crimes into the general categories of "crimes against persons," and "crimes against property," the table reflects only this breakdown. Table 8-II portrays the results of a more detailed analysis of criminal category, but fails to reflect the SMSAs with under 250,000 population and any peculiar characteristics they may have. For one thing, they are in general less densely populated. Also, the larger SMSAs allow a more detailed analysis of the effect of family income.

The most striking result is the lack of correlation between crime rates and population density. Tentatively, the conclusion would be that urbanization, at least by this measure, does not lead to an increased crime rate.[6]

---

6. If there is no evidence to support the hypothesis that crime is an external diseconomy of urban size, there is evidence that urbanization may provide external economies. Among the SMSAs, the correlation between median family income and population density is .45. Among the States, the correlation between family income and percent of population residing in urban areas is .67. Both are significant at the .99 level of confidence.

TABLE 8-II

	Crimes Against Persons				Crimes Against Property		
	Murder	Forcible Rape	Robbery	Aggravated Assault	Burglary	Larceny	Auto Theft
Population density	−.09	−.02	.15	−.04	.03	−.03	.40†
Net migration	.20	.35	.25	.22	.44†	.39†	.21
Percent of population—NW .	.77*	.47†	.47†	.63*	.47†	.35	.35
Percent of population:							
Family income over $10,000	−.03	.09	.18	−.09	.15	.12	.20
Family income under $3,000	.32	.20	.02	.12	−.10	−.02	.06
Multiple correlation							
coefficient	.86*	.63*	.59*	.68*	.68*	.55*	.60*

* t-test level of significance: .01.
† t-test level of significance: .05.
Notes:
1. See note 1, Table 8-I.
2. The correlations are based on data for SMSAs with populations over 250,000 only. These areas tend to be more densely populated. The correlations are based on a more restricted range than those shown in Table 8-I. The smaller sample size explains the lower levels of significance than in Table 8-I.
3. Murder includes non-negligent manslaughter. Larceny includes only cases involving fifty dollars or more.

This is certainly contrary to widespread belief and must not be accepted uncritically.

Three questions concerning this conclusion will be raised here. The first has already been indicated. An SMSA is a large area aggregating many communities. An SMSA could have a high crime rate because its center was densely populated, and yet because of sparsely populated suburban surroundings, show up with a low overall population density. The analysis would be insensitive to such a phenomenon. It should be noted, though that a perusal of the data did not support such a caveat. Jersey City, as an example, has a staggering population density of over 13,000 people per square mile in just forty-seven square miles, yet its crime rates are about average. This would tend to support the general result that crime and density are not necessarily correlates.

A second possible qualification arises after analyzing State data.

In general such an analysis is less promising since the degree of aggregation is still greater. But it does have the advantage of including the effects of nonurbanized areas. There was no significant correlation between population density and crime rates. But in the case of crimes against property, there was a suggestive partial correlation (holding income and racial factors constant) between degree of urbanization and crime rate. Population density for a State as a whole is not a meaningful figure. But if in States with a low degree of urbanization crime rates are low, it may be that very sparsely populated areas do correlate with low crime rates.

A final question concerns the nature of density itself. Density is defined by the number of people per square mile. Is this what we should really mean by density? High-rise apartment houses in a sense reduce density. Given two areas with the same number of people per square mile, one with large numbers of high-rise apartment houses, the press of population will not be the same. Consequently, the measure of density employed may not be appropriate. Perhaps the concept of population density requires elaboration before a useful test can be devised. It may be noted, however, that a casual inspection of high crime areas indicates that they also may be those with large numbers of high-risers and vice versa in the low crime areas.

To turn now to the other measure of urbanization, in-migration rates, the picture is entirely changed. Here the evidence seems to be clear—the process of urbanization is related to crime rates. This is especially the case in crimes against property. One could speculate, therefore, that people migrate in search of economic gain, and not finding it to their satisfaction, resort to a criminal approach. Also, various interpretations concerning the psychology of people who migrate are possible, they may be less subject to conventional social morality, and so forth. Or it simply may be that in an area with a static population people tend to know each other better and therefore are less apt to steal from or harm one another. We leave such speculations to the psychologists.

It is of interest to note that these findings are consistent with what we believe to be true in Western Europe. Crime rates there

TABLE 8-III

	Crimes Against Persons	Crimes Against Property
Percent of white families below poverty level	−.20	−.39
Percent of white families residing in poverty areas ..	−.02	−.24
Percent of nonwhite families below poverty level	.11	−.23
Percent of nonwhite families residing in poverty areas	.18	−.19

are generally lower than they are here. Yet Western Europe is more densely populated than the United States, and experiences less internal migration.

Correlations are suggestive, but not statistically significant, that crimes against persons are inversely related to family income and that crimes against property are directly related to family income. Murder and non-negligent manslaughter in particular seem to occur at the highest rate in areas in which the proportion of poor people is highest. Rape and assault also may occur more frequently in these areas. Robbery, which is really a hybrid (a crime against person and property), may be more prevalent in wealthier areas. There appears to be a certain economic rationality in criminal behavior as evidenced by the positive correlations between high family income and crimes against property. Where people have more, there is more reason to steal. The analysis of the State data revealed similar patterns, but again were not statistically significant.

Table 8-III requires some interpretation. The figures shown are total correlations, not partials. The two factors thus neglected are population density and in-migration rates. Since the factors indicated in the table were available in a consistent fashion for only a small sample of the SMSAs, a partial correlation analysis would have reduced sharply the significance of any results. Nevertheless, if it can be asumed that the relationships between density migration and racial factors remained consistent with the earlier analysis, it would follow that the correlation values shown for the nonwhites would be closer to those shown for whites.[7]

7. This would be so because there were positive correlations between migration rates and nonwhites as well as between migration rates and crime.

Other interactions as might be revealed by a partial correlation analysis escape casual detection.

Two possibilities may be inferred from the correlations in Table 8-III. One is that residing in poverty areas is more conducive to crime than being poor. This is indicated by each of four comparisons, e.g. a −.20 correlation between crimes against persons and percent of white families below poverty level versus a −.02 correlation between crimes against persons and percent of white families residing in poverty areas. This might indicate that crime could be reduced by attempting to integrate the poor into the non-poor community; that, of course, would present problems of its own. The second inference to be drawn from Table 8-III is that in an area with a high incidence of poverty, crimes against persons are more to be expected than crimes against property (compare the first and second columns), tending to confirm the earlier analysis.

Before proceeding to any conclusions, it might be well to restate the purpose of the study. We wished to see if there was evidence which related certain measures of urbanization, population density and in-migration rates, to crime rates. To do this, it was desirable to control for any factors which might obscure the relationships we sought. One such factor was family income, another was racial mix. The resulting high correlations between the racial factor and crime rates should not be misinterpreted. Many hidden factors may be mediated through racial manifestations. Climate was seen to be such an example. There may be any number of others and no causal connection between crime and race can be safely assumed. It is the relation between urbanization and crime which allows for policy recommendations.

CONCLUSIONS

No relationship was discerned between population density and crime rates. This is contrary to frequent casual commentary and requires more intensive investigation. Should the conclusion withstand further analysis, it would mean that crime is not an external diseconomy of urbanization.

It was pointed out that an area might have a high crime rate because it contained extremely high-density pockets, although its overall density was low. This is apparently not the case, and at all events, the evidence is fairly clear that high average densities are not related to the incidence of crime. Thus, an area with a uniform population density as high as the average of the most densely populated SMSAs is not more likely to experience a high crime rate than any other SMSA. New York, for example, has several times the population density of the other major SMSAs and has a lower crime rate than most of them. At the other end of the scale, no data were available for the crime rates in the sparsely populated areas outside the SMSAs. It may be that at very low levels of density, crime rates are lower as well, and the analysis of the State data did lend some support to such a conjecture.

The process of urbanization, as measured by net in-migration rates, does appear to be directly related to crime rates. A community might seek to reduce the costs of crime by instituting arrangements which would discourage in-migration.[8] For such arrangements to be most cost-effective, they would have to be directed more specifically to the precise relationship between in-migration and crime. If it were discovered, for instance, that crimes were committed most often by migrants without employment, such people could be arrested as vagrants and escorted out of the area. On the other hand, if migrancy itself were related to crime, in-migration might be discouraged by placing a tax on the first house purchase or rental of migrants. All this is merest theorizing. First the exact relationship between in-migration and crime would have to be firmly established, then a careful cost-effective scheme should be thoughtfully developed.

---

8. This could raise a serious constitutional issue.

APPENDIX
CRIME PER 100,000 POPULATION, 1965

	Crimes Against Persons, Ten SMSAs With Highest and Lowest Rates
Galveston-Texas City	594
Chicago	461
Los Angeles	458
Flint, Mich.	438
Greensboro-Winston Salem-High Pt., N.C.	407
Savannah, Ga.	404
Miami	400
Fort Lauderdale-Hollywood, Fla.	395
Washington, D.C.	388
Baltimore	386
Utica-Rome, N.Y.	37
Johnston, Pa.	35
Cedar Rapids, Iowa	32
Altoona, Pa.	31
Springfield-Chicopee-Holyoke, Mass.	31
Manchester, N.H.	30
Provo-Orem, Utah	29
Binghamton, N.Y.-Pa.	27
Madison, Wisc.	27
Fargo, N.D.-Morehead, Minn.	26

	Crimes Against Property, Ten SMSAs With Highest and Lowest Rates
Los Angeles	3,109
Miami	2,513
Fresno, Cal.	2,382
Lexington, Ky	2,326
San Francisco-Oakland	2,258
Phoenix	2,218
San Bernardino-Riverside, Calif.	2,156
Atlantic City	2,150
Anaheim-Santa Ana-Garden Grove	2,133
Las Vegas	2,117
Manchester, N.H.	562
Utica-Rome, N.Y.	560
Reading, Pa.	559
Provo-Orem, Utah	558
Altoona, Pa.	532
Monroe, La.	530
Wheeling, W.Va.-Ohio	500
Wilkes Barre-Hazelton, Pa.	461
Lancaster, Pa.	412
Johnston, Pa.	347

	Ten Largest SMSAs Crime Against Persons	Crimes Against Property
1. New York	256	1,726
2. Chicago	461	1,588
3. Los Angeles	458	3,109
4. Philadelphia	231	1,065
5. Detroit	362	1,837
6. San Francisco-Oakland	281	2,258
7. Boston	115	1,595
8. Pittsburgh	162	1,141
9. St. Louis	295	1,622
10. Washington, D.C.	388	1,783

CHAPTER 9

ECONOMIC FACTORS AND THE RATE OF CRIME

JOHN P. ALLISON

A S THE WEALTH of our society increases, more emphasis is being placed on correcting various social ills which affect the quality of life. This paper is directed toward one of these problems; that is, the concern over the growing crime rates and the economic and social factors which may have a causal and direct relationship to them. A representative list of these social and economic factors is found in the Introduction of the Federal Bureau of Investigation publication, *Uniform Crime Reports:* density and size of the community's population and the metropolitan area of which it is a part; composition of the population with reference particularly to age, sex, and race; economic status and mores of the population; relative stability of population including commuters, seasonal, and other transient types; climate, including seasonal weather conditions; educational, recreational, and religious characteristics; effective strength of the police force; standards governing appointments to the police force; policies of the prosecuting officials and the courts; attitude of the public toward law enforcement problems; the administrative and investigative efficiency of the local law enforcement agency, including the degree of adherence to crime reporting standards.

The selection of these factors is supported by the findings of the Commission on the Causes and Prevention of Violence. Using this list as a foundation, plus data from the 1960 census, statistically measurable relationships were tested to determine the usefulness of the factors as predictors of the level of crime of a city.

Reprinted, with permission of the Board of Regents of the University of Wisconsin System, from *Land Economics,* May 1972, pp. 193-196.

The data used were for the city of Chicago and those communities within a forty-mile radius which had a 1960 population of 25,000 or greater. The apparatus used to process the data and to test the factors was a stepwise linear regression program. The variables used in the regression equation were:

X_1 = actual crime rate of the community

X_2 = population of the community

X_3 = distance in miles between the community and core of the city

X_4 = population density (population divided by land area measured in square miles)

X_5 = percentage of the community's population which is fifteen through twenty-four years of age

X_6 = percent of male civilian members of the work force over fourteen years of age which are unemployed

X_7 = number of persons in the community per police department employee

X_8 = mean number of years of education completed by males twenty-five years old and older in the community

X_9 = percentage of nonwhites in the community's population

X_{10} = difference between the percent of females and males in the population of the community

X_{11} = expenditure by the community for police protection per capita

X_{12} = expenditure for parks and recreation per 1,000 persons in the community

X_{13} = per capita income for the community

X_{14} = expenditure per student for education by the community

X_{15} = percentage change in the population of the community between 1950 and 1960.

The equation resulting from the regression accounted for 85 percent of the variance between the crime rates of the various communities. However, 78 percent of the variance was attributable to the six most significant variables, which most effectively explained why the crime rates differ.

In order of their importance, the six variables are: (1) the rate of unemployment, (2) the percentage of males in the population, (3) expenditures for parks and recreation by the community, (4) the mean number of years of schooling of the population, (5) the proportion of the population age fifteen through twenty-four, and (6) the distance the community is from the core of the city.

The correlation between the rate of unemployment of the community and the crime rate for the community was significant, accounting for 57 percent of the variance. The correlation of the variable which related the proportion of males in the population was also high, explaining an additional 10 percent of the variance. These two variables have relatively high T values, 3.782 and 2.760 respectively (at the sixth step of the regression), indicating only a very slight chance that the coefficient of either variable is minute or zero. Each of the last four variables accounted for about three additional percentage points. The T values for these variables ranged from 1.074 to 1.912 which indicates that the chances of these variables being of some importance is still good, especially for those with the larger T values. Therefore, the data indicate that the crime rate of a community is highly related directly to the rate of unemployment and to the proportion of males in the community's population. The crime rate is also somewhat related to the percentage of young people in the population and to the years of schooling, and somewhat inversely related to the expenditures on parks and recreation by the community and to the distance the community is from the core of the city. The crime rate = f(U, M, A, S, P, D) where U = unemployment rate, M = pro-

TABLE 9-I

RESULTS OF THE REGRESSION RELATING CRIME RATES TO THE
SIX MOST SIGNIFICANT FACTORS: CHICAGO AND ENVIRONS

Variable	Intercept	Regr. Coef.	Standard Error	T Value
—	−5895	—	3321	−1.775
X_3	—	− 14.71	13.70	−1.074
X_5	—	155.4	99.46	1.563
X_6	—	846.3	223.8	3.782
X_8	—	455.3	238.1	1.912
X_{10}	—	−208.9	75.69	−2.760
X_{12}	—	− 26.00	15.10	−1.722

portion of males, A = proportion of young people, S = mean number of years of schooling, P = expenditures for parks and recreation, and D = distance from the city.

These results are what would be expected except for the variable measuring the educational level of the community—the mean number of years of schooling. The sign associated with this variable indicates that the community with the higher proportion of educated people will have the higher crime rate. This direct relationship has some significant policy implications in that increasing expenditures for education as a preventative measure for crime may not be successful. This, of course, cannot be accepted based only on this small sample, but it does suggest that perhaps education is not the panacea for our social problems. This result also indicates the problem with interpreting the results of statistical analysis. Processing the regression with the unemployment and the proportion of males variables with most of the other variables omitted resulted in the correlation of the years of schooling to the crime rate to be high and with the more logical sign. The variable explained 34 percent of the variance and had a T value of 2.951. Most of the variance that might have been accounted for by the years of education variable was explained by the rate of unemployment variable. It could be concluded that the rate of unemployment is a function of the level of education, and, therefore, the two variables might be highly related.

The fact that some variables did not appear to be significant in the analysis is as important if not more important than those that did show significance. The less significant variables were considered important and did not prove to be so while the significant variables proved to be important as expected. These less significant variables included the two measures of police protection, the population density, and the measures of the community's income including the variable which expressed the proportion of the population which is non-white. It should be noted that the highest correlated variable, the unemployment rate, may be directly related to the proportion of non-whites in the population since they have the highest levels of unemployment. Therefore, the relationship of the nonwhite variable to the crime rate may be concealed by the influence of the unemployment variable.

The lack of correlation between the crime rate and police department expenditures and personnel can be explained by the unbalanced growth model developed by William J. Baumol (1967) in which he concludes that the cost of externalities rises more rapidly than the population. Chicago, which has an extremely large population, has disproportionately large expenditures per capita for police protection and a large number of police department employees compared to the population, coupled with a very high rate of crime. As the city increased in population, the crime rate rose more rapidly than the population according to the Baumol model. The addition of more police officers and increased police protection expenditures became less and less effective. The cost of preventing crime rose faster than the population. What resulted was both high expenditures for police protection and also a high crime rate accounting for the lack of correlation between the level of police protection expenditures and the rate of crime.

The conclusion from the analysis of the Chicago area indicates a strong relationship between the rate of crime and the rate of unemployment in the community as well as the proportion of males in the community. The other possible factors which might affect crime showed little or no correlation with the rate of crime. This suggests that causal factors indicated by the FBI and the National Commission on the Causes and Prevention of Violence are basically correct but the data go one step further by indicating which factors are relatively more important. The data also suggest, at least partially, that the model of unbalanced growth does answer the question of why the effectiveness of increasing police protection expenditures as a means of preventing crime is decreasing.

REFERENCES

Baumol, William J.: Macroeconomics of unbalanced growth: the anatomy of urban crisis. *American Economic Review*, June 1967, pp. 415-426.

CHAPTER 10

THE EFFECT OF INCOME ON DELINQUENCY

Belton M. Fleisher

R ECENT GOVERNMENT POLICY is evidence of considerable public interest in the relationship of young people to the labor market. Delinquency problems arise in this context because decisions to engage in illegitimate activity seem interconnected with decisions about schooling, labor force participation, and even occupational choice. Thus a study of factors affecting delinquency is of interest not only to criminologists and to crime prevention agencies, but to all those concerned with the allocation of youth's time among alternative pursuits.

This study is an attempt to discover whether low income is a cause of juvenile delinquency, and if so, to present evidence of its importance. Economists have often investigated relationships between income and expenditures—Engel's being perhaps the earliest well-known work of this type; in addition they have recently begun studying quantitatively the effects of income on other behavior. Two novel analyses of income-behavior relationships are the recent studies of Becker (1960) on fertility and of Mincer (1962) on the labor force participation of married women. So, while my subject matter may seem strange to economists, it is not really deviant from an important tradition involving the application of economic analysis to a rather wide variety of social phenomena.

The literature on delinquency contains a wide range of estimates (both negative and positive) of the effect of income. How-

Research for this paper was carried out under United States Department of Health, Education and Welfare Grant No. 62216 at the University of Chicago.

Reprinted, with permission of the American Economic Association, from *The American Economic Review*, March 1966, pp. 118-137.

ever, there is little consensus regarding their meaning. This lack of consensus is largely due to the absence of an accepted theoretical framework for analyzing delinquency and to a lack of agreement about which empirical observations best represent the analytical concepts that have been employed. I think the approach to the problem employed in this study can eventually promote considerable progress toward an understanding of the effect of economic conditions upon delinquent behavior.

AN ECONOMIST'S VIEW OF DELINQUENCY

Most studies of the effect of income on behavior purport to present estimates of demand or supply functions, and this study is no exception because it is an attempt to estimate a net causal relationship running from income to delinquent behavior. The economist's ordinary tools of supply and demand appear useful in constructing a model for the empirical investigation of delinquency. I shall use the concept of demand to mean a causal relationship between economic and other characteristics of persons on the one hand and their tendencies to commit delinquent acts on the other. But the number of delinquent acts committed should depend also on the number or value of delinquency opportunities. I assume that the supply of delinquency opportunities depends on the economic and social characteristics of the environment. I further assume the interaction of these two forces—the propensity to be delinquent and the opportunities available—determines the number of delinquent acts actually committed. The use of an economist's tools to analyze delinquency does not in any way presuppose that "economic" variables such as income are the most important factors determining delinquency rates. It still remains to estimate their importance in the context of a model which allows us to view separately the possible effects of income, opportunities, and other factors.

The question of just what constitutes these "other" factors is of crucial importance. Intuitively one believes that personality traits and family characteristics must play an important role in determining delinquent behavior within rather broad economic and social constraints. It is these to which I refer in the concept of "taste for delinquency." Insofar as these tastes are correlated with incomes, it is necessary to specify them correctly so that their influence is not included in the estimates of the effect of income, and vice versa. Also at the intuitive level, one suspects that those personal traits which cause some individuals, other things the same, to earn more than others—stability, industriousness, etc.— also contribute to low delinquency rates. It therefore appears likely that taste for delinquency and income levels will be rather highly correlated.[1]

While tastes are undoubtedly important determinants of legitimate vs. illegitimate behavior, it is intuitively appealing, and casual inspection leads one to suspect that economic factors are also an important cause of delinquency. The principal theoretical reason for believing that low income increases the tendency to commit crime is that it raises the relative cost of engaging in legitimate activity. In the first place, youngsters probably view their families' income as an index of their own long-run legitimate earning possibilities. Thus, so long as there is not substantial positive covariation between the expected returns to legitimate and illegitimate activity, individuals with low incomes (or whose parents have low incomes) probably expect relatively large payoffs for committing delinquent acts. To such individuals, the probable cost of getting caught is relatively low, since because they view their legitimate lifetime earning prospects dis-

---

1. It is perhaps risky for someone trained in economics to try to explain what has been going on in another discipline, such as sociology. However, it is desirable to attempt to relate the "economist's view" of delinquency to the "sociologist's view." In my opinion, the concept of taste is closely related to sociological concepts such as "anomie." When sociologists argue the relative merits of "commitment to the existing social structure" vs. "opportunities" or "material well-being" as variables explaining delinquency, they refer to questions which I hope to be able to answer at least partially with a model taking into explicit consideration both tastes and economic variables. The problem that criminologists and sociologists have not solved, and for which it will become apparent that I have not provided the definitive solution, is the identification of those observable phenomena which are the operational equivalents of conceptual tastes for delinquency. In statistical jargon, we are not reasonably certain how to specify properly a model of delinquency. Consequently all interpretations of the results of empirical investigations are weakened by our not knowing whether we are observing the effects of the variable we conceive as relating to delinquency or whether we are observing the effects of misspecification of the model of delinquency.

mally they may expect to lose relatively little earning potential by acquiring criminal records; furthermore if legitimate earnings are low, the opportunity cost of time actually spent in delinquent activity, or in jail, is also low. A related possible effect of income on delinquency is due to the lifetime pattern of income. Since most legitimate careers entail lower earnings during their earlier stages (especially during formal schooling) than in their later stages, youngsters who can rely upon little help from parents or other family members in providing desired goods and services may well be tempted to engage in illegitimate activities on a "part-time" basis.

As stated above, casual observation also leads one to suspect that poverty causes high delinquency rates. Particularly within cities, it has long been observed that areas of low incomes, high unemployment, and the like are the areas of highest delinquency rates.[2] It is also true that a disproportionately large number of serious crimes for which youth are arrested are crimes against property. In 1961, for instance, 93 percent of the serious arrests of people aged less than 25 were for the crimes of robbery, burglary, larceny, and auto theft (Fleisher, 1963, p. 544). Although this age group constituted only 43 percent of the 1960 population of the United States, in 1961 it accounted for almost 90 percent of the arrests for auto theft and over 60 percent of arrests for the remaining property crimes (Fleisher, 1963, p. 544).[3]

---

2. A classic study is Shaw and McKay (1942).

3. I think it is advisable to point out that it is by no means inconsistent with the above discussion of the relationship between economic factors and delinquency rates to observe that incomes and crimes of violence are also negatively correlated. Insofar as violent activity has entertainment value, or whatever, to those who engage in it, the economic cost of such activity in terms of the penalties associated with apprehension will be low if youths expect only minor effects on their lifetime earnings. A youngster who aspires to become a lawyer cannot afford to have a police record for assault or rape. However, such a record would probably be relatively unimportant to a potential manual laborer. It is also conceivable that any pleasure derived from violent crimes may be a substitute for market goods and services. They may also be complements, however, as one supposes that higher incomes are associated with increased consumption of alcoholic beverages, and through this medium may be positively associated with crimes of violence. Finally, one should not ignore the possibility that crimes of violence and property crimes may be complements in the economic sense.

While incomes are conceptually negatively related to the cost of engaging in delinquent activity, they are positively related to the expected gains. This is true of crimes against property, at least, which constitute a disproportionately large number of the delinquent acts of youth. The greater the income or wealth of potential victims, the greater will be the expected value of theft. Consequently, income has two conceptual influences on delinquency which operate in opposite directions, although they are not necessarily equal in strength. Thus it is desirable to attempt to estimate these influences separately. In terms of an economist's view of delinquency, the expected negative relation between income and delinquency can be expressed as a demand relationship, and the expected positive relation as supply.

A SIMPLE MODEL OF DELINQUENCY

Variables Employed

I present now the list of variables employed in the empirical investigation. I shall discuss what theoretical concepts the variables are thought to represent, how they fit into a simple model of delinquency, and some biases that may be included in their estimated effects.

1. The dependent variables employed are not, by necessity, actual juvenile crimes or crime rates. Since it is necessary to know the ages of offenders in order to identify crimes of youth, arrest and court-appearance data are used in forming dependent variables. It is generally thought to be a fault of arrest and court data that the probability of one's appearing in these statistics, given one's actual offense record, is negatively correlated with economic and social standing. Thus the use of arrest and court data may impart a negative bias to the estimated (demand) effect of income on delinquency. Since this economic or social bias is thought to be stronger, the farther removed is the measure of crime from the actual commission of the crime, arrest data may yield more reliable estimates of the income effect than do court-appearance data. The influence of social standing on the number of reported arrests and court appearances is probably greatest

within police and court jurisdictions, as it is probably relative levels of income and social influence that are important.

I think one must beware of exaggerating the importance of socioeconomic bias in arrest and court-appearance data. Undoubtedly one of the causes of bias is that the influence of parents of relatively high socioeconomic standing on the behavior of their children is generally thought to lead toward legitimate behavior. Thus, the probability of a child's being punished at home on account of a complaint from the police is thought to be smaller, the lower the social or economic standing of the family from which he comes. It is therefore probable that the low-status child who gets into trouble will commit more crimes in the future if he is not brought to justice formally when he is apprehended. I do not mean to pass judgment at this point on the efficacy of our methods of dealing officially with juvenile offenders; I merely wish to point out that biases in arrest and court-appearance data may well reflect real differences in the tendencies toward delinquency of different segments of the population.

The actual dependent variables used in this study depend upon the sample from which they were taken. They are:

Y_{cc}, the number of court appearances of males, aged 12 through 16 years, during the years of 1958 to 1961, for the census tract communities in the city of Chicago. (Census tract communities are aggregates of census tracts which purport to represent useful subdivisions of the city into areas of rather stable community structure.)[4] The number of appearances is expressed as an annual average number, per thousand males aged 12 through 16.

Y_{cs}, the same as Y_{cc} for 45 suburbs of Chicago in Cook County with populations in excess of 10,000. These data were provided by Henry D. McKay in the State of Illinois Institute for Juvenile Research.

Y_{usp}, the number of arrests of males, aged less than 25 years, for crimes of robbery, burglary, larceny, and auto theft, in each of 101 cities of the United States with populations greater than

---

4. The Chicago delinquency and other variables are taken from Kitagawa and Taeuber (1963).

25,000. The number is expressed as the rate per thousand males less than 25 years of age. Information is available for most of the cities for the years 1960, 1961, and 1962, but not for all of them. The data are expressed as annual average rates.[5]

Y_{usv}, the same as Y_{usp}, except that the arrests are the crimes of violence, namely, homicide, rape, and assault.

2. Although a number of income variables were experimented with in this study, only three of them are used in the results reported here. Two variables represent income as usually conceived.

MEINC2 is the mean family income of the second lowest quartile of families which receive income. This variable is intended to stand for the economic level of a community as it affects the tendency to commit delinquent acts.

MEINC4 is the mean income of the highest quartile of families. This variable represents an attempt to measure the payoff for certain kinds of delinquent behavior. These two measures of income are generally used together in the regressions, as follows:

$$Y = a + b\ MEINC2 + c\ MEINC4 + \ldots \qquad (1)$$

Equation (1) can be rewritten by adding and subtracting c $MEINC2$ to the right-hand side, yielding

$$Y = a + b\ MEINC2 + c\ MEINC4 + c\ MEINC2 - c\ MEINC2 + \ldots \qquad (2)$$

When equation (2) is rearranged, we find that (1) is the equivalent of

$$Y = a + (b + c)\ MEINC2 + c(MEINC4 - MEINC2) + \ldots \qquad (3)$$

Thus, the sum of the coefficients of the two income variables yields an estimate of the effect of family income on delinquency. The coefficient of the fourth quartile yields an estimate of the income dispersion on delinquency. The sum $(b + c)$ can be thought of as the demand relation between income and delinquency, and

---

5. These data are based on information provided by the United States Federal Bureau of Investigation. They are not published, as the FBI assures reporting cities of the anonymity of the information provided by them. While they do not represent an exhaustive list of all U.S. cities with more than 25,000 population, they do represent all size classes in this range.

the coefficient c can be thought of as the supply relation. Other measures of family income and dispersion yielded regression results so close to those obtained using equation (3) that it does not seem worthwhile to present them.

The income data are all taken from the 1960 Census of Population and refer, of course, to incomes during the calendar year 1959.[6]

3. In attempting to estimate the effect of income on delinquency, it is important to consider the effects of both normal family incomes and deviations from normal due to unemployment. Both normal income and deviations from normal may affect delinquency, but the effects may be different.

UNEMMC is the male civilian unemployment rate taken from the 1960 Census of Population.

4. Four variables are employed to represent tastes. *SPDVFM* is the proportion of females over 14 years of age who are separated or divorced. This is supposed to reflect the proportion of broken families in the community. I shall refer to it as the family-structure variable. There are several means by which family structure may influence delinquency. An obvious means is that families with only female heads tend to have lower incomes (by about 50%) than do families with both male and female heads. However, the multiple regression technique, which estimates the effects of income and family structure simultaneously, is an attempt to remove the income component from the estimated effect of family structure on delinquency. Another means by which family structure may affect delinquent behavior is through parental supervision and guidance. This works in two ways, both of which are related to the fact that children in broken families usually live with only their mothers as adult family members. The first is that the mother is likely to have to supplement the family's income with her own earnings if the father is not present. This means that

---

6. Mean income of the lowest quartile is not employed, as it is most likely to be influenced by family structure and other characteristics of the samples which are highly correlated with taste. Since low-income groups tend to be more delinquent than others, *MEINC* 2 is probably a good measure of the economic opportunities of potential delinquents.

she has less time to supervise the activities of her children. Secondly, it is a widely held belief that boys (who constitute the bulk of delinquents and with whose behavior we are exclusively concerned in this paper) learn about the economic facts of life primarily through their relationship with the father and his connection with the economic system. To the extent that legitimate endeavor requires a longer time horizon—a clear view of relatively distant payoffs—than does illegitimate behavior, absence of a male family head probably works in favor of delinquency. Of course, the male family head probably helps reduce delinquency by participating in the pure supervisory role, along with the female head.

It is important to consider whether, supervisory roles and labor market connections aside, the family-structure variable has still an additional influence on delinquency. If this variable truly reflects what I have referred to as the taste for delinquency, it will affect behavior not only through the means discussed in the preceding paragraph, but also because, given the amount of supervision, etc., parents are able to provide their children, the attitudes of broken families will be oriented less toward what is generally regarded as legitimate behavior and more toward delinquent behavior. If the family-structure variable does reflect such a taste factor it may serve the purpose of holding tastes constant so that the true income effect may be estimated. The supervision and market connection phenomena are analogous to tastes in this context and are additional reasons for including the family-structure variable in the regression analysis.

But there is an important way in which family structure may be related to delinquency which would be a reason for excluding it from the regression analysis. Suppose that causation runs from delinquency to divorce, rather than vice versa. For instance, consider the possibility that delinquency is partly caused by economic variables, which are included in the regression analysis. Suppose also that delinquent populations tend to have higher divorce rates than others. Then by putting the family-structure variable in the regression we may rob the economic variables of their effects; which variable "wins" may depend principally upon which has the least serious errors of measurement.[7] I can do no more than point out this possible source of error in interpreting the regression results and then go on; without a well-developed theoretical model of delinquency and a great deal of testing, the probability is always high that empirical work will be hampered by doubts regarding specification.

MOBILR is the proportion of the population over five years of age that lived somewhere other than the community of current residence five years previous to the 1960 census. The variable is an attempt to capture, and to hold constant, the effect on delinquent behavior of residing in a strange community. Presumably new residents are less likely to observe the established codes of behavior of the community than old residents. While the mobility variable may also reflect any temporary losses of income associated with moving, this effect should be mostly eliminated by the presence of the income variables in the regression equations. The expected influence of mobility is to increase delinquency, except for one possibility.

If a large proportion of a community's recent in-migrants arrived only in the year before the census, then the income variable for these people will in part reflect income of a previous job which, if the in-migrants are moving toward improved economic

---

7. It is possible, but factually less appropriate, to apply this same argument to the income variable. It could be held, for instance, that delinquent populations have lower legitimate earnings than do other populations, and that this is reflected in reported family incomes. However, the income variables used reflect income of the whole community; it seems likely that more conventional economic factors outweigh any effects of delinquency on the measured family incomes of communities. This, I think, is even true of the Chicago census tract communities, which are likely to be more homogeneous than the suburbs or 101 cities. In any event I would argue that the use of the taste variables in the regressions tends to hold constant the effect of delinquency on earnings.

In the extreme case that both the income and taste variables are "caused" by delinquency, we are in the unfortunate situation of not having a properly specified model of delinquency at all. We are merely doing correlation analysis in the most literal sense.

I feel that it is likely that some element of reverse causation is present and confounds the regression results presented here. However, I think the importance of this is greatest for the family-structure variable and of negligible importance for the income variables.

TABLE 10-I

SELECTED SAMPLE STATISTICS OF SAMPLE GROUPS AND SUBGROUPS USED IN THE REGRESSION ANALYSIS

Group	SPDVFM		Delinquency		MEINC 2		MEINC 4		UNEMMC	
	Mean	Std. Dev.	Mean	Std. Dev.	Mean	Std. Dev.	Mean	Std. Dev.	Mean	Std. Dev.
101 Cities	.062	.019	17	8.7	5,172	881	14,091	2,892	.052	.017
101 Cities (High)	.083	.011	24	8.8	4,659	686	13,827	1,886	.056	.015
101 Cities (Medium)	.060	.0042	14	5.6	5,234	774	14,107	3,096	.053	.016
101 Cities (Low)	.040	.0070	12.8	6.7	5,650	902	14,354	3,540	.046	.019
Chicago Com.	.070	.057	25	20	5,940	1,430	15,721	5,854	.051	.036
C. Com. (High)	.13	.054	46	19	4,491	1,196	13,968	5,702	.085	.043
C. Com. (Med.)	.046	.0065	18	7.4	6,187	543	15,803	5,890	.039	.012
C. Com. (Low)	.027	.0043	11	4.1	7,236	818	17,534	5,645	.027	.009
Chicago Suburbs	.027	.012	7.4	4.4	8,214	2,043	22,563	11,530	.017	.009

List of independent variables employed in the regressions:

MEINC 2—Mean income of the second lowest quartile of income recipients (1959).

MEINC 4—Mean income of the highest quartile of income recipients (1959).

UNEMMC—Male civilian unemployment rate (1960).

NWHITE—Proportion of the population that is nonwhite (1960).

MOBILR—Proportion of population of five-year-olds that lived in another county in 1955 (1960).

SPDVFM—Proportion of females over 14 who are separated or divorced (1960).

NSDUMM—Regional dummy variable equal to one for Southern cities, zero otherwise.

opportunities, may be lower than current income. In this case, the mobility variable may pick up the tendency of current income to be higher than measured income; this influence on delinquency rates should be negative.

NWHITE is the proportion of the population that is nonwhite. Its use is an attempt to pick up any taste factors, associated with race, which are not reflected in the other taste variables. One hardly need mention that the racial composition of a community is correlated with its income and family characteristics.

NSDUMM is a regional dummy variable, equal to one for Southern cities and equal to zero for all other cities. It is employed only in the 101 cities analysis.

The independent variables and their symbols are listed in Table 10-I.

The source of all variables not specified elsewhere is the 1960 Census of Population.

RESULTS OF THE REGRESSION ANALYSIS

Since the delinquency rate is conceptually bounded by zero and one thousand, it is not unlikely that a nonlinear relationship exists between the rate and some of its causes. Also, it has been suggested that the influence of incomes on delinquency will be greater in the presence of a high proportion of separation and divorce. That is to say, the response of potential delinquents to economic incentives may be greater in communities that have high tastes for delinquency than in communities with strong tendencies toward legitimate behavior.

Thus, for purposes of estimating the effects of the income and taste variables, the two largest samples (101 cities and Chicago communities) were divided into three subgroups of approximately equal size, according to the values of the family-structure variable. The observations in a high subgroup have the highest proportions of separated and divorced females, and so on. The regressions were estimated using both the entire samples and the subgroups. The division into subgroups is an attempt to capture any effects of nonlinearity in the true relationships and/or interactions between variables and effects that may exist. It is also a method of holding constant tastes as reflected in the family-structure variable. I

TABLE 10-II

101 U.S. CITIES > 25,000

Regression	Variable	Dependent Variable Y_{usp} Regression Coefficient	t-Ratio	Elasticity	Multiple R^2
101 Cities					
#1	MEINC 2	− .0044	−2.5	−1.3	
	MEINC 4	+ .00061	+1.5	+ .51	
	UNEMMC	+108	+1.7	+ .33	.20
	MOBILR	+ 27	+1.9	+ .13	
	NSDUMM	− 3.0	−1.0		
#2	MEINC 2*	− .00094	−0.6	− .28	
	MEINC 4*	− .00016	−0.4	− .13	
	UNEMMC	+ 16.0	+0.3	+ .05	
	NWHITE	+ 6.9	+0.7	+ .05	.48
	MOBILR	+ 8.2	+0.6	+ .04	
	SPDVFM	+279	+4.6	+1.0	
	NSDUMM	− 5.9	−2.4		
#3	MEINC 2	− .0014	−1.2	− .42	
	UNEMMC	+ 18.7	+0.4	+ .06	
	NWHITE	+ 5.8	+0.6	+ .04	.48
	MOBILR	+ 8.0	+0.6	+ .04	
	SPDVFM	+278	+4.6	+1.0	
	NSDUMM	− 6.0	−2.5		
Grouped by SPDVFM					
High	MEINC 2	− .0093	−2.6	−1.8	
	MEINC 4	+ .0013	+1.4	+ .77	
	UNEMMC	− 80	−0.9	− .19	
	NWHITE	− 13.5	−0.9	− .14	.59
	MOBILR	− 48.0	−1.9	− .20	
	SPDVFM	+548	+4.0	+1.9	
	NSDUMM	− 11.8	−3.1		
Medium	MEINC 2	− .0011	−0.6	− .43	
	MEINC 4	− .00012	−0.2	− .12	
	UNEMMC	+130	+1.5	+ .49	
	NWHITE	+ 12.2	+0.7	+ .08	.34
	MOBILR	+ 31.9	+2.2	+ .21	
	SPDVFM	+227	+0.9	+ .97	
	NSDUMM	− 2.8	−0.8		
Low	MEINC 2	− .00026	−0.1	− .12	
	MEINC 4	− .00031	−0.6	− .35	
	UNEMMC	+ 36	+0.4	+ .13	
	NWHITE	− 31.9	−0.9	− .07	.36
	MOBILR	+ 43.2	+1.3	+ .23	
	SPDVFM	+322	+1.6	+1.0	
	NSDUMM	− 15.2	−2.0		

* The sum of coefficients of *MEINC* 2 and *MEINC* 4 is −.0011; the *t*-ratio is 0.83.

TABLE 10-III

101 CITIES REGRESSIONS FOR AGES 17 AND UNDER

Regression	Variable	Regression Coefficient	t-Ratio	Elasticity	Multiple R^2
Property Crimes					
	MEINC 2 ...... – .0021		–1.5	–.75	
	UNEMMC ..... – 9.6		–0.2	–.03	
	NWHITE ...... + 9.7		+0.8	+.08	.34
	MOBILR ...... + 18.2		+1.2	+.11	
	SPDVFM ...... +213		+2.9	+.89	
	NSDUMM ..... – 8.6		–2.9		
Violence Crimes					
	MEINC 2 ...... – .000051		–0.8	–.61	
	UNEMMC ..... – .31		–0.10	–.04	
	NWHITE ...... + 1.6		+2.7	+.46	.35
	MOBILR .... + .72		+0.9	+.14	
	SPDVFM ...... + 5.4		+1.5	+.76	
	NSDUMM ...... – .23		–1.6		

think it is realistic to consider the Chicago suburbs as corresponding to either of the lowest subgroups of the two other samples. Table 10-I presents some of the sample statistics for the samples and their subgroups. There are substantial differences among the subgroups in the level and variance of the family-structure variable. There are also notable differences in the levels of delinquency and income.

The regression results are shown in Tables 10-II through 10-VI. Most of the regression coefficients are large enough to be interesting from the economic or sociological point of view, and most of the coefficients of economic variables are statistically significant.[8] If one is interested in comparing the size of the effects of

8. I think it is appropriate to apply a one-tailed test of significance to the regression estimates. With 19 degrees of freedom (the smallest number for any of the regressions) a t-ratio of .86 indicates statistical significance at the 20 percent level.

A one-tailed significance test seems appropriate because of the a priori considerations which suggest the signs of the regression coefficients. While a 20 percent level of significance is high by some standards, I believe it is not inappropriate, considering the desirability of reducing both "type I" and "type II" errors. The reader is of course free to establish whatever criteria for statistical significance he chooses.

The Economics of Crime and Law Enforcement

the variables included in the regressions, the elasticities, which are calculated at the mean values of the variables, are of interest. These are estimates of the percentage change in the dependent variable which occurs when there is a 1 percent change in the independent variable.

Table 10-II shows the regression results for the 101 cities sample and subgroups. Examination of the results of the regressions based on the entire 101 cities sample shows that adding the family structure variable to the regression has a substantial effect on the multiple R^2 and on the estimated coefficients of the other variables. The results of regressions including the family-structure variable imply that there is a nonnegligible negative effect of in-

TABLE 10-IV

101 CITIES REGRESSIONS

Regression	Variable	Dependent Variable Y_{usv} Regression Coefficient	t-Ratio	Elasticity	Multiple R^2
Communities Grouped by SPDVFM					
High	MEINC 2 ...... + .00033		+0.46	+ .80	
	MEINC 4 ...... + .000018		+0.10	+ .13	
	UNEMMC ...... −13.1		−0.76	− .38	
	NWHITE ...... + 3.4		+1.1	+0.45	
	MOBILR .... − 0.81		−0.17	− .04	.21
	SPDVFM ...... +31.4		+1.2	+1.4	
	NSDUMM ..... − 0.21		−0.28		
Medium	MEINC 2 ...... − .00020		−0.85	−1.1	
	MEINC 4 ...... + .000039		+0.66	+0.60	
	UNEMMC ..... + 7.7		+0.78	+0.45	
	NWHITE ...... + 2.8		+1.5	+0.3	
	MOBILR*				
	SPDVFM ...... +33.0		+1.2	+2.2	.30
	NSDUMM ..... + 0.64		+1.7		
Low	MEINC 2 ...... + .000060		+0.28	+ .73	
	MEINC 4 ...... − .000022		−0.50	− .69	
	UNEMMC ..... − 2.3		−0.33	−. 22	.21
	NWHITE ...... + 5.0		+1.7	+0.31	
	MOBILR .... − 3.5		−1.3	−0.51	
	SPDVFM ...... + 6.9		+0.42	+0.60	
	NSDUMM ..... + .094		+0.15		

* F-level in stepwise regression < .0001.

TABLE 10-V

74 CHICAGO COMMUNITIES

Regression	Variable	Dependent Variable Y_{cc} Regression Coefficient	t-Ratio	Elasticity	Multiple R^2
All 74 Communities					
	MEINC 2* ...... − .0051		−2.8	−1.2	
	MEINC 4* ...... + .00038		+1.9	+ .24	
	UNEMMC ...... +187		+2.3	+ .38	
	NWHITE .... + 2.69		+0.4	+ .02	.85
	MOBILR .... +160		+3.5	+ .32	
	SPDVFM .... + 22.5		+0.31	+ .06	
Communities Grouped by SPDVFM					
High	MEINC 2 .... − .0053		−1.0	− .57	
	MEINC 4 .... + .00039		+0.6	+ .12	
	UNEMMC ...... +215		+1.0	+ .40	
	NWHITE .... + 1.40		+0.1	+ .02	.60
	MOBILR .... +166		+1.4	+ .30	
	SPDVFM .... − 15.9		−0.1	− .05	
Medium	MEINC 2 .... − .0074		−2.4	−2.6	
	MEINC 4 .... + .00029		+1.5	+ .26	
	UNEMMC ...... +186		+1.5	+ .41	
	NWHITE .... + 10.9		+0.7	+ .02	.63
	MOBILR .... +126		+0.8	+ .26	
	SPDVFM .... −111		−0.4	− .28	
Low	MEINC 2 .... − .0021		−0.9	−1.4	
	MEINC 4 .... + .000037		+0.1	+ .06	
	UNEMMC ...... +259		+2.1	+ .64	.72
	NWHITE .... + 1.1		+0.1	+ .0009	
	MOBILR .... + 21.9		+0.4	+ .06	
	SPDVFM .... −116		−0.6	− .28	

* The sum of coefficients of *MEINC* 2 and *MEINC* 4 is −.0047. The *t*-ratio is −2.7.

come on delinquency, but they fail to show the predicted effect of the income dispersion, or supply variable. Removing mean income of the highest quartile (*MEINC4*) from the regression results in an increase in the statistical significance of mean income of the second lowest quartile (*MEINC* 2) and in the size of the income (demand) effect.[9] The estimated effect and statistical significance of unemployment are small, as are the estimated

9. This is true even when the coefficient and standard error of *MEINC* 2 estimated alone are compared with the sum of the coefficients of *MEINC* 2 and *MEINC* 4 and the standard error of the sum.

TABLE 10-VI

45 CHICAGO SUBURBS > 10,000

Regression	Variable	Dependent Variable Y_{cs} Regression Coefficient	t-Ratio	Elasticity	Multiple R^2
All suburbs					
#1	MEINC 2 .... – .000085		–0.08	–.09	
	MEINC 4 .... – .000069		–0.4	–.21	
	UNEMMC ...... +25.8		+2.7	+.61	
	NWHITE .... +12.2		+1.0	+.045	.48
	MOBILR .... + 7.07		+0.8	+.11	
	SPDVFM .... + 5.60		+0.07	+.02	
#2	MEINC 2 .... – .00047		–1.6	–.53	
	UNEMMC ...... +25.0		+3.4	+.59	
	NWHITE .... +11.9		+1.2	+.04	.48
	MOBILR .... + 7.11		+0.9	+.11	

effects of the proportion nonwhite *(NWHITE)* and mobility *(MOBILR)*. The North-South dummy variable *(NSDUMM)* co-efficient indicates that, other things the same, delinquency tends to be lower in the South than it is in the North.

Rather different inferences can be drawn when the subgroup results are examined. Since a priori considerations suggest that stratifying the samples will improve the specification of the model, I shall base further interpretation of the results primarily on the stratified regressions. The highest subgroup yields large, significant estimates of both the supply and demand aspects of income. The family structure variable and *NSDUMM* have esti-mated effects absolutely larger than those in the aggregate sample. The estimated effects of *MOBILR* and *NWHITE* are negative. The lower groups yield estimated effects of income dispersion similar to the combined sample. The estimated effect of income declines in value and in statistical significance as one moves from high to low subgroups.[10]

10. Table 10-III shows the regression results for the 101 cities' property crimes, individuals aged 17 and under. Since the coefficient of *MEINC 4* was insignificant, I have shown only the results with *MEINC 4* eliminated from the regressions. This regression may be compared with regression number 3 in Table 10-II. The principal difference is that the regression for the younger age group has a lower R^2, and the coefficients are less significant statistically. A possible interpretation

Examination of the Chicago communities reveals a striking difference from the 101 cities; the estimated effect of *SPDVFM* is relatively small and tends to be insignificant. The estimated effect of income dispersion is positive in all subgroups, but highest in the medium. Similarly, the effect of income appears highest in absolute terms in the medium group. The statistical significance of both income variables is also highest there. Since the difference between the coefficients of the income variables in the two highest Chicago subgroups is small compared with the standard errors of either subgroup, it seems fair to conclude that the evidence of the Chicago subgroups does not contradict the 101 cities evidence that income effects are most pronounced in the highest subgroups. The estimated effect of unemployment is positive in all three subgroups. Its size is large, and the coefficients are statistically significant. The estimated effect of mobility in the Chicago subgroups is positive and significant, and the effect of racial composition appears to be negligible.

I now turn to the regressions based on the Chicago suburbs sample, once again drawing attention to the similarity between this sample and the lowest subgroups of the Chicago communities and 101 cities samples. The effect of income on delinquency appears negative. The estimated effect is much more sensitive than in the other samples to the covariation between the two income variables, and when *MEINC* 4 is removed, the estimated effect is similar in significance to the lowest 101 cities subgroup.[11]

---

is that the variables included in the regressions affect delinquency of both age groups in a similar manner; however, the response of the younger age group is less consistent.

Table 10-IV shows the regression results for the 101 cities subgroups violence crimes, individuals aged 24 and under. The violence-crimes regression for the 101 cities sample, individuals aged 17 and under, is reported in Table 10-III. The statistical significance of economic factors is lower in the violence-crimes regressions than in those for property crimes; the coefficients sometimes have the "wrong" signs as well. This is evidence consistent with the hypothesis that the estimates of the income effects do not include the effects of tastes.

11. The regression results in Table 10-IV show the effect of *MEINC* 2 alone, *UNEMMC*, *NWHITE*, and *MOBILR* in the *absence* of *SPDVFM*. However, inclusion of *SPDVFM* appears to have only a negligible effect on the regression coefficients derived from this sample.

It is smaller than the estimate in the lowest Chicago communities subgroup. The estimated effect of unemployment is both substantial and significant. The estimated effect of mobility is positive, but of low significance, and the effects of race and family structure appear to be negligible.

I think one can discern a general pattern of behavior that is reflected in these regression estimates. The over-all effect of income on delinquency appears to be negative and more pronounced among "delinquency prone" groups than among others. The negative effect of income on delinquency may be somewhat offset by the positive influence of income on the payoff for property crimes. The offsetting effect also appears to be most pronounced in the most-delinquent groups. Unemployment appears to be a cause of delinquent behavior, but the inter-subgroup pattern of the unemployment effect does not seem to be the same as the pattern of income effect. That is, there is no tendency for the high subgroups to exhibit an especially strong response to temporary deviations from normal incomes as measured by unemployment.

This study is mainly concerned with the effects of economic factors on delinquency, but it is interesting to note that holding economic and taste factors constant, the addition of a racial variable *(NWHITE)* adds almost nothing to the explanatory power of the regression model in any of the samples.

EVALUATION AND CONCLUSION

Specification of the Model

In evaluating the results of these regressions, probably the most important question is whether the model has been correctly specified. In fact, there is not a great deal of evidence that it has. The erratic behavior of the family-structure variable is not strong evidence of its appropriateness in the regressions. Furthermore, *SPDVFM* is correlated with the income variables, *MOBILR* and *NSDUMM*, in much the same way as delinquency. Compare the regression results in Table 10-VII with those of Table 10-II (Regression #1); the elasticities are similar, and the multiple R^2 is higher. Thus it is impossible to rule out the possibility that *SPDVFM* is either caused by delinquency or is so closely related as to be virtually the same phenomenon. While there is no sug-

TABLE 10-VII

101 COMMUNITIES

Variable	Dependent Variable SPDVFM Regression Coefficient	t-Ratio	Elasticity	Multiple R^2
MEINC 2	−.000010	−3.1	−.88	
MEINC 4	+.0000023	+2.9	+.53	
UNEMMC	+.30	+2.5	+.26	.38
MOBILR	+.070	+2.6	+.10	
NSDUMM	+.0076	+1.4		

gestion at present regarding which alternate taste variable would improve the estimates, my experience with the effect of employing alternate taste variables indicates that there is little effect on the estimated income effects.[12] Thus, it is possible that, although we still cannot profess to know all the important variables that should be included in a model of delinquency, we nevertheless have obtained "reasonable" estimates of the effect of economic conditions.

The Effect of Income

Given the reliability of the estimates of the effect of economic conditions on delinquency, I should now like to explore some of their implications. To begin with, it appears that the effect of income on delinquency is not a small one. In extremely delin-

---

12. The literature on delinquency contains a number of empirical studies in which alternate taste variables have been used. This is not to say that the writers of these studies used such terminology; I am imposing my own framework on what I think these authors were attempting to do. Three important studies were those of Lander for Baltimore (1954), Bordua for Detroit (1959), and Chilton for Indianapolis (Chilton, 1964). Variables which were used, I think, primarily to hold tastes constant were proportion nonwhite, proportion foreign-born, proportion of homes owner-occupied, proportion of homes substandard, and the proportion of unrelated individuals to families plus unrelated individuals. These studies never reported regression coefficients, but only partial correlation coefficients and/or beta coefficients. Usually, variables explicitly representing incomes did not pass a conventional *t*-test for significance. However, I have performed regression analyses of the data for Detroit census tracts (1950) and for Indianapolis census tracts (1960; the Indianapolis data were provided by Roland Chilton). The effect of income appears similar in both the Indianapolis and Detroit samples; I virtually duplicated the Detroit study, obtaining an estimated income effect of −.0018 (elasticity = −.50), and a standard error of .00091.

quent areas, a 1 percent rise in incomes may well cause a 2.5 percent decline in the rate of delinquency. The effect of income dispersion—the supply effect of income—probably operates only in very delinquent areas, and it is probably not large relative to the demand effect of income.

Remember that the estimated income effects are net of the effects of other variables in the regressions. If it is true, as seems likely, that family structure is a function of income, then changes in income not only will operate directly upon delinquency rates, but indirectly through family structure, as well. One must not be too mechanical in applying the indirect relationship to policy questions, however. It is unlikely that changes in income transfer payments, such as unemployment compensation, ADC payments, and the like, would have the same effect on family structure as would changes in the earning power of individuals—especially males. Nor would all the indirect income effects be desirable ones. Increased community income would probably attract in-migrants, and through this means rising incomes would probably cause delinquency to increase.

To illustrate the possible influence of economic conditions upon delinquency, consider the following simple example based on the regression estimates of the high 101 cities subgroup. Suppose that the average family income in this subgroup is raised by $500 per year for all income classes. (The effect of the change in income of the first and third quartile is assumed to be reflected in the coefficients for the second and fourth.) The pure income effect on delinquency would be $(-.0093 + .0013) 500 = -4.00$, which is to say that the rate would fall by 4 arrests per thousand population, a reduction of somewhat more than 15 percent of the average rate in the sample. Now suppose that the increase in income has an effect on family structure equivalent to one-half the estimated effect shown in Table 10-VII. I assume only half, because income changes cannot be expected to change tastes for delinquency, but to operate on delinquency through family structure via the supervision and market connection effects. From Table 10-VII, we can estimate that a $500 increase in family income will cause a decline in the number of women over fourteen who are separated or divorced of about 2.7 per thousand women. One half of this effect times the estimated impact of family structure on delinquency would imply a decline in the delinquency rate of one. This is 25 percent of the direct impact of income. In addition, I estimate that the delinquency rate will be reduced by still another one half of 1 percent because normal families have higher incomes than broken ones. These rough calculations indicate that a 10 percent rise in income may be expected to reduce delinquency rates by between 15 and 20 percent when the income change occurs in highly delinquent areas and is of the type that will reduce the number of broken families as well.

The Effect of Unemployment

The estimated elasticities of the unemployment-delinquency relationship are in general smaller than those of the effect of income. However, aside from the highest 101 cities subgroup estimate, they are all positive and between .05 and .60; this range includes most of the estimates from a previous time-series analysis of the effect of unemployment on delinquency (Fleisher, 1963). There is no evidence that the effect of unemployment is higher in the high delinquency subgroups than in the low, as is the effect of income. One may only speculate at this point as to why this may be. Two possible explanations come to mind. One is that, in the groups which have high rates of separation and divorce, high unemployment substantially increases the amount of parental supervision. I think this is intuitively an unappealing explanation. For one thing, the high separation and divorce group probably has high tastes for delinquency; it is problematical whether increased parental supervision in such circumstances would do much to reduce delinquency rates. For another, it seems likely that family morale is low during periods of high unemployment and that parental discipline is not likely to be vigorous.

What seems a more plausible explanation arises from the correlation between family structure and income. Broken families occur more frequently among low-income groups than among high.[13] There are two implications of this observation: (1) unemployment compensation is likely to be a more powerful offset to the effects of unemployment for low-income families because there are ceilings on unemployment benefits; (2) in the high subgroup families, unemployment is likely in part to constitute a permanent feature of earnings; this means that differences in unemployment among observations may not consistently reflect differences in deviations of actual income from normal income.[14]

It would be misleading, I feel, to conclude on the basis of the relatively low estimated elasticities of the relationship between unemployment and delinquency that unemployment is consequently a less important explanatory or policy variable than income. For instance, the speculations of the preceding paragraph (and the regression estimates) are consistent with a positive effect on delinquency of changes in the general level of unemployment, even for the high subgroups. Another important consideration is that the variation (as measured by the coefficient of variation) of the unemployment rates is much higher than the variation of incomes. This is true in the samples used in this study, and I think it is true in general for these kinds of samples. Thus, to the extent that the "normal" variation of the variable is an index of the constraints within which policy-makers must operate, there is more scope for changing unemployment than for changing income levels directly. Perhaps the most important consideration is that social policy which permanently reduces unemployment will also raise normal levels of income, and reducing unemployment in

---

13. This is not only because broken families usually have only one principal earner. It is also because broken families would have lower incomes, on the average, even with two principal earners. A rough indication that this is true is that the differences in mean incomes (as measured by *MEINC* 2) among the subgroups in Table 10-I are considerably larger than can be explained by the hypothesis that the differences are solely due to differences in family structure, assuming that families with only female heads have incomes equal to one-half those of families with both male and female heads.

14. Another possibility is that, since current income is being held constant in the regressions, residual unemployment among observations is therefore negatively correlated with permanent income. This could lead to a negative coefficient for unemployment if the permanent income effect were strong relative to the unemployment effect.

high-delinquency areas will probably have relatively large effects on normal income levels. This is because unemployment rates in these areas are high to begin with and probably constitute part of the environment determining normal earnings; a 50 percent reduction in unemployment rates in an area where nearly 10 percent of the labor force is unemployed may raise average incomes by as much as 5 percent (perhaps less if the chronically unemployed are less productive than other earners). In the light of the numerical example illustrating the income effect, such a reduction of the unemployment rate could possibly reduce the delinquency rate by 10 percent.

Finally, while changes in incomes alone do not explain the behavior of delinquency over time, if one assumes an elasticity of the relationship between income and unemployment of .15 (which is consistent with the estimates presented in this paper and with those of a previous study of the relation between delinquency and unemployment over time) (Fleisher, 1963) one can "explain" about 15 percent of the measured increase in juvenile delinquency from 1952 through 1960.[15]

REFERENCES

Becker, Gary S.: An Economic Analysis of Fertility. *Demographic and Economic Change in Developed Countries,* a Conference of the Universities—National Bureau Committee for Economic Research. New York, 1960, pp. 209-31.

Bordua, David J.: Juvenile delinquency and "anomie"—an attempt at replication. *Social Problems,* 6:230-38, 1959.

Chilton, Roland J.: Continuity in delinquency area research: a comparison of studies for Baltimore, Detroit, and Indianapolis. *Am Soc Rev,* 29:71-83, 1964.

Fleisher, Belton M.: The effect of unemployment on juvenile delinquency. *Jour Pol Econ,* 71:543-55, 1963.

Kitagawa, Evelyn M. and Taeuber, Karl E. (Eds.): *Local Community Fact Book Chicago Metropolitan Area 1960.* Chicago, 1963.

Lander, Bernard: *Towards an Understanding of Juvenile Delinquency.* New York, 1954.

---

15. This statement is based on the change in unemployment rates over this period and changes in per capita juvenile arrests for property crimes, according to United States Federal Bureau of Investigation.

Mincer, Jacob: Labor force participation of married women: a study of labor supply. *Aspects of Labor Economics,* a Conference of the Universities-National Bureau Committee for Economic Research, Princeton, 1962, pp. 63-97.

Shaw, Clifford R. and McKay, Henry D.: *Juvenile Delinquency and Urban Areas.* Chicago, 1942.

United States Federal Bureau of Investigation: *Uniform Crime Reports* (various issues), Washington, annually.

CHAPTER 11

CRIME, YOUTH, AND THE LABOR MARKET

LLAD PHILLIPS, HAROLD L. VOTEY, JR.
AND DAROLD MAXWELL

INTRODUCTION

ARREST DATA SHOW that crime is predominantly an urban, youthful male phenomenon with nonwhites more than proportionately involved.[1] We investigate the hypothesis that increasing crime rates for youth can be explained by their deteriorating economic opportunities. This hypothesis has been tested, in part, by Belton Fleisher who postulates that fluctuations in civilian employment affect youthful crimes rates.[2] Our study focuses on four of the seven FBI index crimes for which an economic motive would be expected: larceny, burglary, robbery, and auto theft.[3]

This paper makes two contributions. One is the formulation of

Reprinted, with permission of the University of Chicago Press, from *Journal of Political Economy*, May/June 1972, pp. 491-504.

This study was supported by the National Institute of Law Enforcement and Criminal Justice, U.S. Department of Justice.

1. The observation that economic crimes may be regarded essentially as a male phenomenon is attested to by the fact that over 94 percent of those arrested for the crimes of burglary, robbery, and auto theft in the eighteen- to nineteen-year-old age group were males. For larceny the percentage was 75. Consequently, this study was limited to youthful males. The study concentrated on urban crime because urban crime rates are highest, and because the earlier *Uniform Crime Reports* data only tabulated urban crime statistics.

2. See Fleisher (1963, 1966a, 1966b). Theories relating criminal behavior to economic conditions have a long and distinguished history. For examples, see Bonger (1916), Vold (1958), Sutherland and Cressey (1966), and Becker (1968). For other studies relating crime rates to economic conditions see Glaser and Rice (1959) and Votey and Phillips (1969).

3. The four felonies account for approximately 87 percent of arrests in city areas for the seven index crimes (U.S. Department of Justice, FBI 1967) and also have had the highest rates of increase since 1952.

a model which permits alternative partitions of the population, classified on the basis of labor-market activity, showing how each of the subsets is linked to youthful crime.

The second contribution, which follows directly from the model, is the proposition that labor-force participation may be a crucial element in the explanation of youthful crime. Our econometric analysis demonstrates that the model explains variations in crime rates for youth. In the process it reveals the importance of including participation rates as explanatory variables. Finally, our results are consistent with and extend Fleisher's earlier work.

THE HYPOTHESIS

The hypothesis linking youthful crime rates and economic opportunities is suggested by a perusal of crime and labor-market data spanning the past two decades. These data show that arrest rates (per person) for the four economic felonies have been growing at exponential annual rates ranging from 4.7 percent for larceny to 3.0 percent for robbery, and that youth play a particularly important role in these crimes. Arrest rates for the four major felonies are one or two orders of magnitude higher for the fourteen- to twenty-four-year-age groups than for males a generation older. Furthermore, trends in crime rates by age show that youth have a higher rate of increase than older age groups, except for burglary.

The high rate of increase in aggregate arrest rates can be explained, in part, by the post-World War II baby boom and the consequent shift in the age distribution of the population toward a more youthful population.[4] For example, if arrest rates by age are held constant at the 1952 levels, the shift toward a younger population accounts for 15 percent of the rise in the aggregate arrest rate for larceny over the years 1952 to 1967. This leaves a considerable rise in arrest rates over this period to be explained by other factors.[5] Our study analyzes crimes by individual age

4. The median age of the population was 30.3 years in 1952 and had fallen to 27.7 years by 1967 (see U.S. Department of Commerce, Bureau of the Census [1965] Ser. P-25, no. 321).

5. This has been pointed out by others including the President's Commission (1967) where estimates of the impact of changes in several demographic variables

groups in order to abstract from the effect of the secular shift in the age distribution of the population. It is interesting to observe that while crime rates were skyrocketing for youth, unemployment rates for eighteen- to nineteen-year-old white males rose from a low of 7.0 percent in 1952 to a peak of 16.5 percent in 1958, and were still at 9.0 percent in 1967. For nonwhite males the situation was even worse. In 1952 their level of unemployment was 10.0 percent; it rose to a high of 27.2 percent in 1959, and recovered to the level of 20.1 percent in the prosperity year of 1967.[6] During the same period, the aggregate unemployment rate started at 2.8 percent, rose to a peak of 6.8 percent in 1958, and fell to 3.1 percent by 1967. Thus, by comparison, youth in general and nonwhites in particular, were clearly in a disadvantaged position in our society. Examination of labor-force participation rates reinforces this view. For white youth eighteen to nineteen years old, this rate declined from 72.9 percent in 1952 to a low of 65.4 percent in 1966, then rose somewhat to 66.1 percent in 1967. For nonwhites, the 1952 figure was 79.1 percent and dropped steadily to 62.7 percent in 1967. In relating labor-market opportunities for youth to their arrest rates, it is particularly important to consider labor-force participation as well as unemployment rates. It is necessary to take account of the fact that since youth have low participation rates, unemployment rates will have less weight because of the considerable fraction of youth outside the labor force. In addition, while unemployment rates reflect cyclical and short-run conditions in the labor market, participation rates capture secular changes, including the influence of past unemployment rates.

The high incidence of crime by nonwhites is underlined by the

on the change in the magnitude of arrests from 1960 to 1965 are presented (pp. 25, 207-10). Our more detailed calculation for 1952-67 was required as a starting point for the analysis of the effects of economic variables on age-specific crime rates. The period 1952-67 was chosen because of specific data limitations. Prior to 1952, the FBI had based its *Uniform Crime Reports* on fingerprint records. Subsequent information has been based on reports of individual police agencies. Consequently there is little relationship between earlier data and the present series (see n.12 below).

6. Labor force data are from U.S. Department of Labor (1970).

fact that in 1967, for youths under eighteen, the urban arrest rate (per 10,000 population) for larceny was 268.0 for nonwhites while the comparable figure for whites was 93.1. For the remaining FBI index crimes, the differences are of a comparable or greater magnitude. It would be desirable to study crime rates by race as well as age, but the arrest rates by race are only available annually since 1962, and then only for the broad categories of under eighteen, and eighteen and over. Consequently, it is only feasible to analyze crime by race on the causal side.

The nature of the information in the crime data suggests how the hypothesis linking crime rates and economic opportunities can be translated into a formal model. The approach followed was to postulate that the crime rate for eighteen- to nineteen-year-old males is a weighted average of crime rates for various subsets of this population group, classified by labor-force status and by race.[7] This proposition is formally developed in the next section.

THE MODEL

The age-specific crime rate y_i for a particular economic crime may be viewed as a weighted average of the crime rates r_{ijk} in each class into which the population (white or nonwhite) is partitioned. Thus we can write

$$y_i = \sum_{j=1}^{m} \sum_{k=1}^{2} r_{ijk} W_{jk}, \ (i = 1, 4),\qquad(1)$$

where $i = 1$—larceny, 2—burglary, 3—robbery, 4—auto theft (hereafter the i subscript is dropped for simplicity), and the W_{jk} are the fractional distributions of the population by class.

The most detailed breakdown of males our data will permit is to consider the population subsets $j = 1$—other males and all females, 2—employed males, 3—unemployed males, 4—males not in the labor force.[8] Since the weights add to one we have

7. This age group was selected as satisfying the two criteria of having a high crime rate (characteristic of youth) while being at the threshold of choosing among further education, the labor force, or other alternatives.

8. For detailed definitions of each category refer to Wolfbein (1964) or U.S. Bureau of Labor Statistics (1969).

$$\sum_{j=1}^{4} \sum_{k=1}^{2} W_{jk} = 1 \qquad (2)$$

where the weight for each color, W_k, is

$$\sum_{j=1}^{4} W_{jk} = W_k, \ (k = 1, 2).$$

Substituting for W_{1k} and collecting terms,

$$y = \sum_{k=1}^{2} r_{1k} W_k + (r_{2k} - r_{1k}) W_{2k} + (r_{3k} - r_{1k})W_{3k}$$
$$+ (r_{4k} - r_{1k}) W_{4k}. \qquad (3)$$

The population class weights may be written in terms of the unemployment rate and the civilian labor-force participation rate by expanding the weights in terms of the employed (E), the unemployed (U), the civilian labor force (CLF), the civilian noninstitutional population $(CNIP)$, and the total population (POP). For example, the ratio W_{3k} of the unemployed for a given color to the total population (POP) may be expanded to

$$W_{3k} = \frac{U_k}{POP} = \frac{U_k}{CLF_k} \cdot \frac{CLF_k}{CNIP_k} \cdot \frac{CNIP_k}{TNIP} \cdot \frac{TNIP}{POP}. \qquad (4)$$

Substituting the definitions for the unemployment rate, the civilian labor-force participation rate, and the weights $\mu_k = U_k/CLF_k$, $\rho_k = CLF_k/CNIP_k$, $\theta_k = CNIP_k/TNIP$, and $\phi = TNIP/POP$ $(\cong 1)$, we obtain[9]

$$W_{3k} = \mu_k \ p_k \ \theta_k. \qquad (5)$$

Similarly, we obtain

$$W_{2k} = \frac{E_k}{POP} = (1 - \mu_k) \ p_k \ \theta_k \text{ and } W_{4k} = \frac{NLF_k}{POP} = (1 - p_k) \ \theta_k. \qquad (6)$$

Substituting equations (5) and (6) in equation (3), rearranging terms, and recalling that $W_1 + W_2 = 1$, we obtain

9. The ratio of male, civilian, noninstitutional population for each color (k) over the total noninstitutional population for both races and sexes is $CNIP_k/TNIP$.

$$y = r_{12} + (r_{11} - r_{12})\ W_1 + \sum_{k=1}^{2} (r_{4k} - r_{1k})\ \theta_k$$

$$+ (r_{2k} - r_{4k})\ \theta_k\ (1 - \mu_k)\ p_k + (r_{3k} - r_{4k})\ \theta_k\ \mu_k\ p_k. \quad (7)$$

In this formulation, the age-specific crime rate is a function of seven population weights. These weights varied during this period in a manner reflecting both economic and social changes. The fraction of white males in the eighteen- to nineteen-year-old civilian, noninstitutional population, θ_1, is sensitive to variations in the armed services.[10] The corresponding fraction for nonwhites, θ_2, does not appear to be as sensitive to fluctuations in the armed services. The unemployment rates, μ_1 and μ_2 for whites and nonwhites, respectively, and the participation rates, ρ_1 and ρ_2, reflect changing labor-market and educational opportunities for eighteen- and nineteen-year-old males. The specification of various partitions of the population, hypothesized to be distinguishable with regard to criminal activity, can be formulated with subsets of these seven population weights.

The use of age-specific arrest rates as the dependent variable is necessary since offense rates are not available by age. However, we can obtain a proxy for age-specific offense rates. This is achieved by dividing the age-specific arrest rates by the ratio of offenses cleared by arrest for the population as a whole, assuming that the clearance ratio for eighteen- to nineteen-year-olds is proportional to the clearance ratio for the population.[11]

---

10. The correlation coefficient between θ_1 *(CNIP/TNIP)* and the fraction of the total noninstitutional population classified as male armed services *(AS/TNIP)* is −.99. This variation in the armed services is a major factor creating variance in the independent variables. It is interesting to note that while increases in the armed services decrease the white male civilian noninstitutional population, the impact on the nonwhite male civilian noninstitutional population is negligible. The correlation coefficient between θ_2 and *AS/TNIP* is −.19, insignificant at the 5 percent level. The correlation coefficient between the civilian labor force participation rate for male white (ρ_1) and *AS/TNIP* is .83 (significant at the 5% level). As noted above, increases in the armed services decrease *CNIP*, the denominator of ρ_1.

11. Note that offenses $\equiv$ arrests/(arrests/offenses). If we assume that arrests/offenses (eighteen- to nineteen-year-olds) $\cong$ k arrests/offenses (total), then we can write offenses (eighteen- to nineteen-years-olds) = arrests (eighteen to nine-

EMPIRICAL RESULTS

Population Partitions: Employed, Unemployed, Not in the Labor Force, Others

The estimation of equation (7) is illustrated for larceny.[12] The variance explained for the other three crimes was also high with the same signs on the variables and comparable *t*-values obtained for burglary and robbery, but two very low *t*-values for auto theft.

$$
y_1 = \underset{(0.98)}{37.0} - \underset{(-0.78)}{34.1W_1} + \underset{(0.33)}{8.9\theta_1} + \underset{(1.21)}{166.6\theta_1} - \underset{(-.55)}{54.7\mu_1\rho_1\theta_1} - \underset{(-.30)}{91.3\mu_2\rho_2\theta_2}
$$

$$
\underset{(-0.67)}{- 33.0\ (1 - \mu_1)\rho_1\theta_1} \underset{(-1.07)}{- 186.5\ (1 - \mu_2)\rho_2\theta_2} \qquad \begin{array}{l} \bar{R}^2 = \quad .84 \\ F_{7,\,7} = 11.0 \\ \text{D-W} = 2.19 \end{array}
$$

(*t*-values are shown in parentheses). These results are indicative of several propositions which are reinforced by additional statistical analysis. First, the model has great explanatory power as reflected by the high $\bar{R}^2$ and the *F*-statistic, significant at the 1 percent level. Second, when the population is as finely partitioned as in equation (7), multicollinearity between the independent variables detracts from the significance of the individual variables.[13] Third, the economic interpretation of the results is consistent with expectations with the exception that fluctuations in unemployment apparently have less impact for whites than non-

---

teen)/*k* arrests/offenses (total). Consequently we divide the age-specific arrest rate by the proportion of offenses cleared by arrest to obtain a proxy for age-specific offense rates. We thank one of the referees for suggesting this improvement in the dependent variable.

12. The model was estimated for the period 1953-67 since data for the weights θ_1 and θ_2 were only available from 1953 to date, and the years 1968, 1969, and 1970 were reserved to test the predictive power of the model. The figures for 1970 were preliminary, unofficial figures released to us by the FBI.

13. An acceptable test for multicollinearity (see Farrar and Glauber, 1967) is to regress each of the independent variables on the remaining set. A high R^2 in each of these regressions indicates that each of the variables is collinear with the remaining group. This was done for the variables in equation (7) with the result that the R^2 in each case was greater than .9. Further tests indicated that as variables are successively dropped from the set the degree of collinearity is reduced.

whites. The partial change in the age-specific larceny crime rate with respect to the participation rate for each color is negative.[14] The change in the crime rate with respect to the unemployment rate is positive for nonwhites but negative for whites. In the latter case, the difference between the coefficients for employed and unemployed whites is small and probably reflects no major difference between the two groups.

To reduce the multicollinearity, we estimated two alternative partitionings of the population: not working (unemployed and not in the labor force combined) and others; and labor force, not in the labor force, and others. This reduces the number of collinear variables. However, the variables representing these partitions are still collinear for whites and nonwhites. This arises because of the proportionality between nonwhites and whites in the population and because their labor-force statistics move proportionally. For example, the fraction of male nonwhites in the population not working is 20 percent of the fraction of male whites in the population not working.[15] As a consequence, it is difficult to improve on equation (7) in significantly distinguishing the effects of whites and nonwhites on crime rates. At best we can only measure (in a statistically significant way) their joint effects on the crime rate using either white or nonwhite variables.

Population Partitions: Not Working and Others

A reasonable specification of the model is to differentiate those not working (unemployed plus not in the labor force) for both colors from the remaining population:

$$POP = (U_1 + NLF_1) + (U_2 + NLF_2) + R \qquad (8)$$

---

14. From the estimates in equation (7) we find that the arrest rate for males "not in the labor force" is higher than for males employed for both colors. This implies that the higher the participation rate the lower the arrest rate. This follows because of the dominant weight in the labor force of those employed and can be confirmed by calculating the partial derivatives of the crime rate with respect to the participation rates by color.

15. Running canonical correlation between the white variables as a group and the nonwhite variables is a further indication of collinearity between the variables by color.

and dividing by *POP*

$$1 = W_{NW1} + W_{NW2} + W_R, \qquad (8a)$$

where $W_{NWk} = \mu_k \rho \theta_k + (1 - \rho_k) \theta_k$. Thus, the crime rate is a weighted average of the crime rates for these three groups:

$$y = r_{NW1} W_{NW1} + r_{NW2} W_{NW2} + r_R W_R, \qquad (9)$$

substituting for W_R

$$y = r_R + (r_{NW1} - r_R) W_{NW1} + (r_{NW2} - r_R) W_{NW2} \qquad (9a)$$

Since the proportion not working for nonwhites, W_{NW2}, is linearly related to the proportion not working for whites, W_{NW1},

$$W_{NW2} = a + \beta W_{NW1}, \qquad (10)$$

we have upon substitution for W_{NW2}

$$y = [r_R + a(r_{NW2} - r_R)] + [(r_{NW1} - r_R) + \beta(r_{NW2} - r_R)] \, W_{NW1}, \qquad (11)$$

or, alternatively, substituting for WN_1

$$y = \frac{[\beta r_R - a(r_{NW1} - r_R)]}{\beta}$$
$$+ \frac{[(r_{NW1} - r_R) + \beta(r_{NW2} - r_R)]}{\beta} W_{NW2}. \qquad (12)$$

Consequently, if the white and nonwhite rates cannot be significantly differentiated in equation (9a), the coefficients estimated in equations (11) and (12), using either white or nonwhite variables, combine the effects of both groups. The ratio of the coefficients for the white and nonwhite variables (in eqs. [11] and [12]) is simply β, the regression coefficient in equation (10), which reflects the proportionality between the weights. The results for equation (9a) are reported in Table 11-I. The coefficients for not-working whites (NW1) are not significant when estimated jointly with the nonwhites. However, the signs of the coefficients for both colors indicate that the crime rate increases with the unemployment rate and decreases with the participation rate except for whites in the case of larceny. (Note: $\delta y / \delta \mu_k = [r_{NWk} - r_R] \rho_k \theta_k$ and $\delta y / \delta \rho_b = - [r_{NWk} - r_R] [1 - \mu_k] \theta_k$.) Observe that the intercept is insignificant. If equation (9a) is reestimated

TABLE 11-I

REGRESSION ESTIMATES OF THE AGE-SPECIFIC CRIME RATES:
NOT-WORKING FORMULATION

Crime	Intercept	W_{NW1}	W_{NW2}	$\bar{R}^2$	F	D-W
	White and Nonwhite					
Larceny	0.66	–4.53	167.66	.67	15.5 (2, 12)	1.02
	(0.62)	(–0.41)	(3.94)			
Burglary	–0.57	5.33	69.44	.46	6.9 (2, 12)	0.60
	(–0.64)	(0.58)	(1.96)			
Robbery	0.01	0.79	12.68	.18	2.5 (2, 12)	0.60
	(0.050)	(0.30)	(1.24)			
Auto theft	–0.03	1.54	39.33	.39	5.6 (2, 12)	0.57
	(0.05)	(0.30)	(1.96)			
	Nonwhite					
Larceny	0.32	. . .	154.47	.70	33.0 (1, 13)	1.06
	(0.49)		(5.74)			
Burglary	–0.16	. . .	84.97	.48	14.30(1, 13)	0.52
	(–0.30)		(3.78)			
Robbery	0.07	. . .	14.98	.24	5.4 (1, 13)	0.57
	(0.47)		(2.32)			
Auto theft	0.01	. . .	43.82	.44	12.0 (1, 13)	0.57
	(0.30)		(3.47)			

Note—The t-values of the coefficents are in parentheses; the R^2 are corrected for degrees of freedom; the estimate of equation (10) is:

$$W_{NW2} = .005 + .197 \ W_{NW1}$$
$$(-.73) \quad (4.18)$$

$$R^2 = .54$$
$$F_{1,\,13} = 17.5$$

without the intercept, the coefficients for both races are all positive with slightly better t-values for nonwhites but still insignificant results for whites.

The results for equation (12), using not working for nonwhites, are reported in Table 11-I. The equations for all four crimes are significant at the 5 percent level or better. Equation (12), using not working for whites, was also estimated, yielding positive coefficients significant at the 5 percent level or better, with lower coefficients of determination.

Population Partitions: Labor Force, Not in the Labor Force, Others

A reasonable alternative specification of the model is to postulate that the difference between working and others may not be as critical to the criminality of eighteen- and nineteen-years-olds as the distinction among the labor force, not in the labor force and others. It is possible that unemployed may be more similar to the employed than to those not in the labor force in terms of criminality for this age group. In this formulation, population is partitioned by color into in the labor force, not in the labor force, and the remaining population:

$$POP = LF_1 + LF_2 + NLF_1 + NLF_2 + R, \qquad (13)$$

and dividing by POP,

$$1 = W_{L1} + W_{L2} + W_{N1} + W_{N2} + W_R, \qquad (13a)$$

where $W_{LK} = \rho_k \theta_k$ and $W_{Nk} = (1 - \rho_k) \theta_k$. The crime rate is a weighted average of the crime rates for these five groups:

$$y = r_{L1}W_{L1} + r_{L2}W_{L2} + r_{N1}W_{N1} + r_{N2}W_{N2} + r_R W_R, \qquad (14)$$

and substituting for W_R and rearranging terms,

$$y = r_R + (r_{N1} - r_R) \theta_1 + (r_{L1} - r_{N1})p_1\theta_1 \\ + (r_{N2} - r_R) \theta_2 + (r_{L2} - r_{N2})p_2\theta_2. \qquad (15)$$

The results for equation (15) are reported in Table 11-II. The coefficients for nonwhites are significant and have the expected signs (at the 5% level or better) indicating a higher criminality for those not in the labor force than for those in the labor force or in the remaining population. Once again, when the equation is run jointly for whites and nonwhites, the white coefficients are insignificant. This formulation was estimated using only white variables and only nonwhite variables. (We recall from the discussion above that using the variables for either color estimates the combined effect for both.) The results are reported in Table 11-II. Using the variables for either color, the coefficients are significant at the 5 percent level or better and have the expected signs.

The labor-force/not-in-the-labor-force formulation of the model has more explanatory power than the working/not-working formulation for all crimes, even though the former equation does not explicitly involve the unemployment rate as an explanatory variable. This may be because the participation rate in part re-

TABLE 11-II

REGRESSION ESTIMATES OF THE AGE-SPECIFIC ARREST RATES:
NOT-IN-THE-LABOR-FORCE VERSUS LABOR-FORCE FORMULATIONS

Crime	Intercept	θ_1	$\rho_1\theta_1$	θ_2	$\rho_2\theta_2$	$\overline{R}^2$	F	D-W
White and Nonwhite								
Larceny	6.86 (1.66)	-4.74 (-0.44)	-20.22 (0.93)	257.82 (4.73)	-260.95 (4.09)	0.87	24.5(4, 10)	2.16
Burglary	3.00 (0.97)	2.26 (0.28)	-9.41 (0.58)	122.10 (2.98)	-162.17 (3.38)	0.82	17.3(4, 10)	1.52
Robbery	-0.34 (-0.29)	-0.72 (-0.24)	3.22 (0.53)	33.25 (2.16)	-41.30 (-2.30)	0.55	5.3(4, 10)	1.19
Auto theft	-0.10 (-0.06)	-1.87 (-0.39)	7.63 (0.80)	76.01 (3.15)	-107.70 (-3.81)	0.79	14.0(4, 10)	2.07
White								
Larceny	14.77 (2.65)	36.06 (3.90)	-95.22 (-4.16)	...	...	0.61	12.0(2, 12)	1.51
Burglary	5.79 (1.71)	26.80 (4.78)	-54.61 (-3.93)	...	...	0.66	14.3(2, 12)	1.29
Robbery	0.49 (0.46)	5.58 (3.16)	-8.37 (-1.91)	...	...	0.38	5.3(2, 12)	0.99
Auto theft	1.47 (0.69)	14.33 (4.09)	-22.20 (-2.56)	...	...	0.53	9.1(2, 12)	1.35
Nonwhite								
Larceny	0.04 (0.01)	...	...	256.29 (5.06)	-259.46 (- 7.71)	0.84	38.1(2, 12)	2.06
Burglary	1.62 (0.89)	...	...	130.56 (4.07)	-178.51 (- 8.37)	0.84	39.6(2, 12)	1.84
Robbery	0.15 (0.22)	...	...	30.48 (2.54)	- 35.92 (- 4.50)	0.61	12.1(2, 12)	0.92
Auto theft	1.00 (0.91)	...	...	69.16 (3.60)	- 94.32 (7.38)	0.81	30.8(2, 12)	1.68

flects the impact of present and past unemployment rates and as an indicator of labor-market opportunities is less transitory than the unemployment rate for the current period.

Forecasts for 1968, 1969, and 1970

The model was used to forecast the arrest rates for each crime for three years beyond the period used for estimation. Equation (7) was used to make the forecasts. Eight of the twelve forecasts fall within plus or minus 2 SE of the regression (a more stringent test than 95 percent confidence intervals). The two earlier years for robbery are within 3 SE. Only for larceny for the latter two

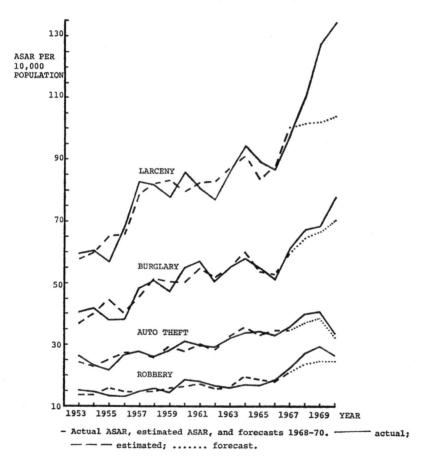

- Actual ASAR, estimated ASAR, and forecasts 1968-70. ———— actual;
— — — estimated; .... forecast.

Figure 11-1

years does the model fail to accurately foretell the pattern of crime. Plots of the actual, estimated, and forecast values are displayed in Figure 11-I. One can observe that the overall pattern of crime is matched by the model particularly with respect to major changes in pattern such as take place in 1958 and 1966. Forecasts follow the pattern remarkably well for all the crimes but larceny. The fact that all the forecasts fall below the actual figures suggest an increase in criminality in the last three years not explained by equation (7).[16]

CONCLUSIONS

We conclude that changing labor-market opportunities are sufficient to explain increasing crime rates for youth.

To test this hypothesis, we constructed a model which includes all of the population subsets, classified by labor-market activity and color, for a particular population age group. This formulation of the model has explanatory and predictive power but is plagued by collinearity between the independent variables, particularly between the colors. For purposes of analysis, two alternative formulations of the model are tested: classification of the population as not working (unemployed plus not in the labor force) and others, and as in the labor force or not in the labor force and others. The estimates of the not-working formulation indicate that an increase in the unemployment rate and/or a decrease in the participation rate for either color will increase the crime rate. Collinearity between the explanatory variables by color is such that one can only obtain significant estimates of the impact of changing labor-market conditions for both colors jointly using either the white or the nonwhite variables.

The labor-force/not-in-the-labor-force formulation has greater explanatory power than the not-working formulation, demonstrating the importance of participation rates relative to unemployment rates in explaining crime rates. This point is reinforced when one observes that during the middle and latter sixties, crime rates rose while unemployment rates declined. It is the decline in the

---

16. The marked increase in felony drug offenses in recent years may account, in part, for the increase in property crime not explained by the model.

participation rate which provides an explanation for the rise in crime during this period.

We propose that our findings indicate that a successful attack on rising crime rates must consider the employment problems facing young people.

REFERENCES

Becker, Gary S.: Crime and punishment: an economic approach. *J.P.E. 76:* 169-217, 1968.

Bonger, W. A.: *Criminality and Economic Conditions.* New York, Agathon, 1916.

Farrar, Donald E., and Glauber, Robert R.: Multicollinearity in regression analysis: the problem revisited. *Rev Econ and Statis,* 49:92-107, 1967.

Fleisher, Belton M.: The effect of unemployment on juvenile delinquency. *J.P.E.,* 71:543-53, 1963.

————: *The Economics of Delinquency.* Chicago, Quadrangle, 1966a.

————: The effect of income on delinquency. *A.E.R.* 56:118-37, 1966b.

Glaser, Daniel, and Rice, Kent: Crime, age, and employment. *American Soc Rev,* 24:679-86, 1959.

President's Commission on Law Enforcement and Administration of Justice: *Task Force Report: Crime and Its Impact—an Assessment.* Washington, Government Printing Office, 1967.

Sutherland, Edwin H., and Cressey, Donald R.: *Principles of Criminology,* 7th ed. Philadelphia, Lippincott, 1966.

U.S. Bureau of Labor Statistics: *Employment and Earnings.* Washington, Government Printing Office, September 1969.

U.S. Department of Commerce, Bureau of the Census: *Current Population Reports.* Series P-20, P-25. Washington, Government Printing Office, September 1969.

U.S. Department of Justice, Federal Bureau of Investigation. *Uniform Crime Reports.* Washington, Government Printing Office, September 1969.

U.S. Department of Labor. *Manpower Report of the President.* Washington, Government Printing Office, 1970.

Vold, George B.: *Theoretical Criminology.* New York, Oxford Univ. Press, 1958.

Votey, Harold L., Jr., and Phillips, Llad. *Economic Crimes: Their Generation, Deterence, and Control.* Springfield, U.S. Clearinghouse Federal Sci. and Tech. Information, 1969.

Wolfbein, Seymour L.: *Employment and Unemployment in the United States.* Chicago, SRA, 1964.

CHAPTER 12

THE RETURNS TO BURGLARY

Michael Sesnowitz

THE MAGNITUDE of theft crimes has increased at a rapid rate throughout the United States.[1] The purpose of this note is to explore the monetary return to burglary, the most prevalent type of crime in the F.B.I. index crimes against property. For Pennsylvania in 1967, it is found that such returns were negative.[2]

Burglary is a risky activity, since the individual's return depends upon whether or not he is apprehended and convicted. Accordingly, the monetary return is an expected value and can be expressed as

$$R = (1 - p)S + p(S - D)$$

where p is the probability that the individual is caught and penalized; S is the monetary component of the income from the act—or simply the amount stolen;[3] and D is the dollar equivalent of the penalty imposed on those apprehended.

The Gain Component (S)

In 1967 the average market value of stolen property yielded by a burglary in Pennsylvania was $288 (Commonwealth of

---

Reprinted, with permission of the Western Economic Association, from *Western Economic Journal*, December 1972, pp. 477-481.

1. The FBI reports that the population-adjusted index, crimes against property (burglary, larceny of $50 or more and auto theft), increased by 147 percent from 1960 to 1970 (*Crime in the United States*, 1971, p. 1).

2. The returns calculated are for adult burglaries only. Juveniles are excluded for two reasons. First, the motivation for burglaries may differ between the two groups. Second, juveniles are treated differently in both the prosecution and punishment process. As a result, the returns probably differ for the two groups.

3. If intermediate goods are employed by burglars, then R will overstate the true return. This can be corrected for by netting out the cost of intermediate goods from S.

Pennsylvania, Board of Parole, 1969a). However, the gain to the burglar generally falls short of this amount since he is unable to dispose of his nonmonetary ill-gotten gains at their market value. Although there are no reliable data concerning the percentage of the market value of stolen items actually received by burglars, the President's Commission on Law Enforcement and Administration of Justice (1967) provides an estimate of from ⅕ to ⅓ of the actual value. If a figure of ¼ is used, S is reduced to approximately $137, since 70 percent of burglarized property represents loot in kind.

The Penalty Component (pD)

To compute the probability of conviction, the number of adult convictions for burglary in Pennsylvania is divided by twice the number of reported adult burglaries. The number of reported adult burglaries is found by assuming that the ratio of burglaries committed by adults to that committed by juveniles is equal to the ratio of burglary arrests of adults to burglary arrests of juveniles. Twice the number of adult burglaries is used in the denominator to allow for unreported burglaries.[4] This method of computation yields a probability of conviction of .058.[5]

Calculation of the dollar value of the penalty will include only those direct costs resulting from incarceration and the confiscation of stolen property. To be sure, there are many additional costs associated with the prosecution process (time, attorney's fees, etc.) and the penalty (time on probation or parole, decreased potential earnings in the legitimate sector, etc.). These costs are difficult to measure, however, and the assumptions necessary to

4. An estimate of unreported burglaries is given in Ennis (1967). For home burglaries, it was found that 70 percent of such acts go unreported. However, one would expect that underreporting among organizations would be considerably less than among individuals. Based upon FBI data for the total burglary rate (U.S. Department of Justice, 1967), the total amount of underreporting would be only 50 percent if all organizations reported all burglaries. This figure is probably closer to the true figure and is therefore employed in this study.

5. While this may not be the true probability of conviction, since it ignores both the possibility of multiple crimes being committed by individuals and the use of accomplices in the commission of a single crime, its use will not bias R, since such factors will affect the other components of R in an offsetting manner.

calculate them from existing data would make their inclusion of dubious value. Furthermore, the return calculated by including only those components of the penalty cost indicated above is already negative, thereby making the return from an estimation of other components of minor value. The exclusion of such costs should, however, strengthen the case for the negative sign found for R.

To allow for the confiscation of stolen property, S is reduced by 13 percent, the percentage of stolen property (excluding autos) that is recovered (Commonwealth of Pennsylvania, Board of Parole, 1969a). The result is that S falls from $137 to $119.[6]

The measure of the value of the burglar's time while incarcerated will be his net foregone earnings, less the value of his consumption and earnings, if any, while in prison. The personal discomfort associated with prison life is a subjective element which will be negative for most, if not all, inmates. No attempt will be made to measure this factor, but its exclusion once again strengthens the case for believing that the returns are in fact negative.

The measure of foregone earnings will be the present value of the average after-tax earnings of individuals with characteristics similar to those of burglars, over the length of imprisonment. In the absence of appropriate data for Pennsylvania, or for the nation as a whole, use will be made of survey data collected by the President's Commission on Crime in the District of Columbia in 1965, to calculate the legitimate sector earning opportunities of incarcerated burglars. The survey indicated that adult whites convicted of property crimes in the District of Columbia had, on the average, completed approximately nine years of school, while nonwhites had completed approximately eight.[7] On the average, convicted burglars were 26 years of age. All were male. The age,

---

6. This calculation assumes either that all property is recovered before the burglar disposes of it or that once the property is recovered the burglar is caught and made to return the proceeds. It also assumes that the distribution of the stolen property between money and goods is similar among all crimes involving the theft of property, and that the distribution of recovered property is similar to the distribution of stolen property.

7. The survey data were reported by classes. The calculations here were made by assigning the value of the mean to each class and closing the last class at grade 14.

sex and educational characteristics of persons committing property crimes in the District of Columbia are assumed similar to those of persons who commit burglaries in Pennsylvania.

Wage rates for 1967 by race, sex, age, education and geographic area are available from the Survey of Economic Opportunity and have been refined by R. E. Hall (1970). Whites in the 25 to 34 year age group with 7 to 9 years of school completed earned $2.41 per hour in the Pittsburgh S.M.S.A.[8] If each individual worked forty hours per week for 52 weeks, the gross earnings of whites would be $5,013 and that of nonwhites $4,285. While the average individual will not work forty hours per week for 52 weeks per year, his leisure time may still be valued by his wage rate. If he voluntarily forgoes work for leisure, then his forgone earnings may be taken as an estimate of the value of his leisure time. Since all 52 weeks are spent in prison, the full year would appear to be the relevant time consideration. After adjustment for the federal income tax, yearly forgone earnings of whites is $4,510, while that of nonwhites is $3,856.[9] Since the racial composition of burglars in Pennsylvania is 71.1 percent white and 28.9 percent nonwhite,[10] average forgone earnings is $4,321.

One might argue that persons who turn to crime have legitimate earnings potentials below others with similar characteristics and that the forgone earnings estimated above therefore overstate the true costs to the incarcerated burglar. There is no way, presently, to evaluate the merit of such an argument. Is the unemployment rate in the legitimate sector high because they choose to be burglars? Or do they choose to be burglars because they are un-

8. This figure was calculated from Hall (1970). The Pittsburgh S.M.S.A. is taken as representative of the state.

9. This calculation involves the following assumptions: (a) all individuals file joint returns, (b) all individuals claim two dependents, (c) all individuals take the standard deduction, and (d) income from sources other than wages is zero. The after-tax earnings cited above will overstate the true net income if assumptions (a) and (d) are violated, will understate the true figure if (c) is violated, and will either overstate or understate the true net earnings if assumption (b) is violated.

10. Because of a lack of alternative data, the racial composition employed is that of the total group of burglars released from state prisons in Pennsylvania from June 1 to December 31, 1964 (Commonwealth of Pennsylvania, Board of Parole, 1965).

employed in the legitimate sector? We are tempted to argue that, if anything, our estimate understates the true cost of incarceration to burglars, since it implicitly values leisure time at a price of zero.

While the burglar forgoes $4,321 per year while in prison, he is provided with consumption goods and may be paid for work he performs. Twenty-three percent of all burglars sentenced to prison in Pennsylvania serve their time in state institutions, the remainder being sentenced to county institutions. The value of the consumption of a state prisoner is $980 per year and that of a county prisoner is $444.[11] The expected yearly value of consumption, then, to a burglar sentenced to prison is $567. Since 30 percent of those sentenced to state prisons and none of those sentenced to county prisons can be expected to work for pay, and since the average wage paid to inmates is $.50 a day, the expected prison earnings for a burglar sentenced to prison is $12.59 per year ($.23 \times .3 \times \$.5 \times 365$).

The estimated time served by imprisoned burglars is forty months.[12] The expected cost to him, in present value terms is, therefore, $9,323.[13] Since 3.39 percent of all burglars are sentenced to prison (approximately 58% of those convicted), the expected cost of imprisonment to the burglar is approximately $316. Sub-

11. These estimates were made from prison allotment sheets provided by the Pennsylvania Bureau of the Budget. Included are such items as food, rent on property, repairs, maintenance, etc. Such expenditures accounted for approximately 20 percent of all expenditures. Since no allotment sheets were available for the county prisons, the assumption was made that 20 percent of total county prison expenditures represented consumption items.

12. This estimate is obtained from interval data of the distribution of time served by incarcerated burglars before release on parole and was provided the author by the Pennsylvania Board of Probation and Parole. The midpoint was assigned to each class interval and a weighted average obtained. Since approximately 90 percent of all burglars are paroled, the result was adjusted to account for the 10 percent who serve a full term. While separate data for county prisoners not released in the custody of the State Parole Board were unavailable, the author was informed in private correspondence with Dominick J. Pastore, Director of the Pennsylvania Bureau of the Budget, that the terms served by burglars in county jails is believed similar to that served in state institutions.

13. The discount rate employed is the approximate rate on consumer credit, 1.5 percent per month.

tracting this from the adjusted gain component, we find the monetary return to be −$197.

REFERENCES

Ennis, P. H.: *Criminal Victimization in the United States: A Report of a National Survey.* Chicago, 1967.

Hall, R. E.: Wages, Income and Hours of Work in the U.S. Labor Force, Unpublished paper, Mass. Inst. of Tech., Aug., 1970.

Pastore, D. J.: Personal correspondence, Harrisburg, Apr. 15, 1970.

Commonwealth of Pennsylvania, Board of Parole: Characteristics of Persons Arrested for Burglary, Unpublished report, June 1, 1965.

————: Department of Justice, *Pennsylvania Judicial Statistics:* 1967, Report J-11, Harrisburg, Oct., 1968.

————: Pennsylvania Crime Commission, *Task Force Report: Assessment of Crime and Criminal Justice in Pennsylvania,* Harrisburg, Jan., 1969a.

————: *Task Force Report: Corrections in Pennsylvania,* Harrisburg, July, 1969b.

President's Commission on Crime in the District of Columbia: *Report of the President's Commission on Crime in the District of Columbia: Appendix.* Washington, 1966.

President's Commission on Law Enforcement and Administration of Justice: *Task Force Report: Narcotics and Drug Abuse.* Washington, 1967.

U.S. Department of Justice, Federal Bureau of Investigation: *Crime in the United States: Uniform Crime Reports—1967.* Washington, 1968.

Crime in the United States: Uniform Crime Reports—1970. Washington, 1971.

Section III
LAW ENFORCEMENT OUTPUT AND EXPENDITURES

CHAPTER 13

STANDARDS FOR DISTRIBUTING
A FREE GOVERNMENTAL SERVICE:
CRIME PREVENTION

CARL S. SHOUP*

A GOVERNMENT DISTRIBUTING services free of direct charge must decide how much of each service each household or firm is to receive.

If, indeed, no one can be excluded from enjoyment of a service when it is rendered, and the amount received is the same for all, the decision is made when the level of service is determined.

Often, however, some degree of exclusion is practicable, or varying intensities of service may be rendered to different households or firms. Here, questions of equity and efficiency emerge, similar to those encountered in taxation. Shall a certain service, say police protection, be distributed equally among the residents of a city? What does "equally" imply? If a service is not distributed equally, what other standards, perhaps implicit, are employed?

In fact, little is known about distribution of government services by location, race, religion, income class, or other category. Usually, no record is made, no estimate attempted. The laws providing for the service are silent in this respect; the authorizing or appropriating committees of legislatures do not discuss it; budgets submitted by the executive say nothing about how a given service is to be distributed among the users. This silence reflects in part a social propensity to discriminate covertly in ways that are not tolerable in taxation, where the pattern of impact is more obvious. For example: education has been distributed unequally, by

* Originally published in *Public Finance/Finances Publiques*, Vol. 19, No. 4/ 1964, pp. 383-394.

social class, race, or color, in communities that would not think of distributing the tax bill by those indicia.

Sometimes a fixed amount of free service is offered on a first-come or queuing basis; rationing is by time and patience, which are more evenly distributed than money income. More often, administrators allot a service in the light of what they infer of the legislator's or executive's aims.

The pattern of initial distribution can be evaluated only if the extent to which benefits from the service are passed forward or backward is known, or at least assumed. Again, the problem is similar to that faced in appraising taxes. The present analysis bypasses the issue of "shifting and incidence" of benefits from government service by assuming that the benefits remain with the original recipients.

The service chosen here, for illustrative purposes, is protection of persons against crime in residential districts of a city (the analysis does not cover business districts); urban "police protection," for short, thus abstracting from all other uses of the police force, such as controlling traffic or maintaining an oppressive regime in power. To simplify the argument, all crimes are considered of equal importance. The rate of crime per capita, for a given period of time, is imagined as being computed for each residential district in the city. Equality of crime rates per capita among residential districts is taken to signify equal probability, for any person in one district compared with any person in any other district, that he will be the victim of a crime in a given time period. Such probability is taken as a measure of the product, police protection; the lower the probability, the greater is the product. If every person faces the same probability, the service, police protection, is said to be distributed evenly, or equally.

It need not be assumed that equal distribution of free police protection is an optimum distribution. Even those who favor equal distribution of income need not apply this standard for any one commodity, say food, or clothing, or housing, in view of differences in consumer tastes. Still, equal distribution of police protection has enough intuitive appeal to warrant an examination of its implications, especially its implication for another intuitively attractive rule, minimization of total number of crimes in the city as a whole.

This second goal, minimization of crime, with a fixed amount of police resources available, is achieved when an increment of police input will reduce the number of crimes by the same amount no matter where it is placed within the city, or at what time of day. The marginal cost of preventing one more crime will then be the same everywhere in the city. But achievement of this goal will usually leave some of the city's districts more crime-ridden than others, that is, the rate of crime per capita will be higher in some districts than in others. Crime will have been minimized at the cost of distributing police protection unequally.

In part this inequality might be the result of differences in population of districts. Let us suppose that one of the city's districts has three times the population of another, and that initially the crime rate per capita is the same in the two districts. Let us further suppose that transfer of one policeman to the more populous district from the less populous district would prevent two more crimes in the more populous district while allowing one more crime in the less populous district. This assumption might be reasonable, because the absolute number of crimes is, of course, larger in the more populous district. The assumption becomes especially reasonable if the two districts cover about equal areas. Under these conditions, the policeman should be transferred, if number of crimes in the city as a whole is to be minimized. But after the transfer has been made, the crime rate per capita in the less populous district will be higher than before, that in the more populous district will be lower, and the crime rates per capita will therefore be unequal in the two districts. It will now be more risky to live in the less populous district than in the more populous district.

Even if the two districts are equal in population, minimization of crime will commonly result in unequal crime rates per capita among districts, because disruptive social forces, aggravated by poverty, are stronger in one than in another. It is this cause of difference in crime rates per capita that will be the subject of the following analysis, which abstracts from differences in population among districts by assuming equal population in all districts.

In this analysis, a city is divided into two residential districts, P and R. P is a district of poor households; R, of rich. P and R are equal in population and area. Initially, crime in the city as a whole is minimized, but the crime rate is higher in the poor district than in the rich.

In both districts, prevention of crime is an increasing-cost industry. As crime is reduced, it becomes more difficult to prevent one more crime. The level of difficulty is measured by the marginal cost of crime prevention. If the police force is so distributed that this level is the same in Districts P and R, so that crime is minimized, it will be only a coincidence if the rates of crime remaining in P and R are the same.

Figure 13-1 illustrates this generalization. The x-axis of the diagram measures the crime rate: the number of crimes occurring in the district in question during a given period of time.[1] The y-axis measures the marginal cost of crime prevention: this is the cost of preventing one more crime in that district during that period of time. The curve, R_0R_1, shows the cost of preventing one more crime for any given level of existing crime, in District R. Only a segment of the curve is shown. We do not know the total of crime prevented, so there is no point in trying to extend the curve out to the right where it would intersect the x-axis. The intersection would indicate the rate of crime that would be occurring if there were no police force at all. Such a question is scarcely answerable, and certainly is of no practical import. Nor is the curve extended to the left where it could cut the y-axis, indicating the marginal cost when all crime was prevented. Attainment of such a goal is quite impossible, if only because some crimes are the result of many and unforeseeable forces that happen to combine at a given time and place.

In Figure 13-1, if transfer of a policeman, being paid $5,000 a year, from the rich district to the poor district would prevent two

1. In Figures 13-1 and 13-2, absolute number of crimes in the two districts are compared, since it comes to the same as crime rate per capita under the assumption of equal populations.

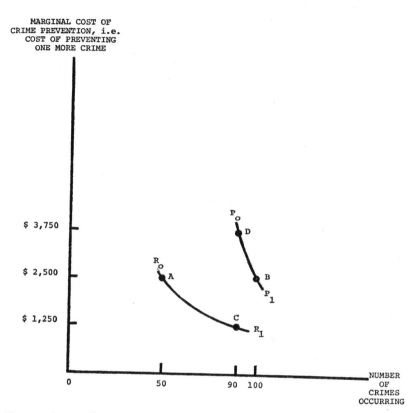

Figure 13-1. Differing marginal costs of crime prevention in rich and poor areas of equal population. P_0P_1: Marginal cost curve for rich area. R_0R_1: Marginal cost curve for rich area.

more crimes a year in the poor district and allow two more crimes a year to occur in the rich district, the marginal cost of crime prevention is the same in both districts, and is $2,500. Crime is minimized. At the same time, we assume, the number of crimes occuring is 50 a year in the rich district and 100 in the poor district. This state of affairs is reflected by Points A and B in Figure 13-1.

If, now, several policemen were transferred from the rich district to the poor district, crime would no longer be minimized. If so many policemen were transferred from District R to District P that the crime rate rose in R from 50 to 90, the crime rate in P would decline only from 100 to 90. The implied assumption of this kind of rate of transformation will be expressly stipulated in Figure 13-2. At these levels, as indicated by points C and D in Figure 13-1, the cost of preventing one more crime in R would be only $1,250; in P, $3,750. Evidently, a small reverse transfer of police service from P to R would now reduce crime in R at the rate of three per $3,750 of expenditure increase while unleashing crime in P at a rate of only one per $3,750 of expenditure reduction. There would be a net gain of two crimes prevented. Yet there is this to be said for points C and D: with this distribution of the police force, the rate of crime is equal in the two districts, at 90 per year. A resident of R now faces the same probability of being victimized by crime as does a resident of P.

One might be tempted to say that, by moving from points A and B to points C and D, equity could be achieved at the cost of economic efficiency. But this would be an incorrect assertion, for two reasons.

First, the C-D combination, equal crime rates and unequal marginal costs, is not demonstrably inefficient economically in the sense that by a reallocation of resources some individuals could be made better off without others being made worse off. Any reallocation of the police force from C-D that benefited residents of R would harm residents of P, and vice versa.

Second, equality of crime rate in Districts R and P is not necessarily the best test of equity even on a rough, common-sense basis. Perhaps the residents of P are more careless than those of R, or more interested in other goals than suppression of crime; the more law-abiding residents of R may then argue that it would be unjust to them, to aim at equalizing crime rates in the two districts. The R residents may further argue that, even if the higher crime rate (at equal marginal costs) in P is due to causes beyond control of the residents of P, more crimes in total may be being prevented in P than in R, even though the remaining crime is at a higher level in P than R. There are, say, many more policemen assigned to P than to R, even at points A-B, where marginal costs are equal but the crime rate in R is only 50 against 100 in P. This assumption that a greater total of crimes is being prevented in one district than in another is a dubious one, since we can never know what total of crimes would occur in a district if no police force at all were allocated to it. But the fact that total input is demonstrably greater—more policemen in P than in R— carries a strong, if irrational, weight in the argument. When comparison of total outputs is impossible, the desire to get an answer of some sort leads easily to a comparison of total inputs.

In the face of these conflicting interests of the different consuming groups, we can only suggest how the issue is in fact determined, by presenting the problem as one of rates of transformation and indifference patterns. Figure 13-2 serves this purpose. On the x-axis is measured the number of crimes occurring in District P; on the y-axis, the number occurring in District R. Each crime

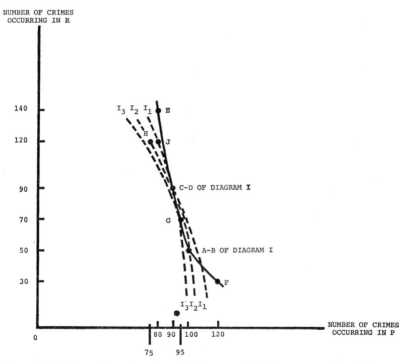

Figure 13-2. Transformation (production-possibility) curve and indifference curves for distribution of a fixed total amount of police protection between districts P and R (of equal population).

is still assumed to be equally noxious. The two districts have the same population.

The given police force may be so distributed between Districts P and R that there are 90 crimes occurring in each. This is point C-D on the curve EF; it represents points C and D on Figure 13-1, the equal-protection distribution of police. Alternatively, the police force may be so distributed that 100 crimes are occurring in P but only 50 in R. This is shown by point A-B, which reflects points A and B in Figure 13-1. The line joining A-B and C-D in Figure 13-2 is the production-possibility curve for the two products, prevention of crime in P and prevention of crime in R, with a given total police force. In Figure 13-2 this line has been extended a little in both directions, to points E and F (these points are not reflected in Fig. 13-1), to emphasize the increasing cost of preventing crime in P, or in R, or in both. This production-possibility curve is convex to the origin rather than concave, as in the usual production-possibility diagram, because the axes measure undesirable things, "anti-goods," rather than desirable ones. The object is to minimize the number of crimes occurring, not explicitly to maximize the number of crimes prevented (recall that we can never ascertain the latter).

When 100 crimes are occurring in P and 50 in R, a reallocation of police that reduces crime in P from 100 to 90, that is, prevents 10 crimes, leads to an increase of 40 crimes in R, where the rate rises from 50 to 90. A further transfer of policemen to P that prevents another 10 crimes, reducing the crime rate there from 90 to 80, gives rise to 50 more crimes in R, where the rate rises from 90 to 140.

On this same diagram there may be plotted a system of indifference curves. They may be community indifference curves, or just police department indifference curves; at any rate, whoever decides these matters has some implicit system of preferences and indifferences.

We assume that the decision maker becomes more and more concerned over an incremental crime in one district, the higher is the crime rate there compared with the other district. Consider indifference curve I_1, which passes through points J and C-D.

It says, for instance, that if the crime rate were 120 in R and 80 in P (point J) an equally attractive (or unattractive!) combination would be attained by reducing crime in R by 30 and permitting an increase of crime in P by only 10, so that the rates would be 90 and 90 (point C-D).

The indifference curve is concave to the origin, rather than convex, as in the usual indifference curve diagram, since the axes measure anti-goods rather than goods. An indifference curve closer to the origin represents a preferred position. Thus, curve I_2, which passes through points H and A-B, yields a smaller total of crime in either one of the districts for a given amount of crime in the other district. If 120 crimes are occurring in R, 75 will be occurring in P on indifference curve I_2 (point H) and 80 on indifference curve I_1 (point J).

The best possible combination will be achieved at that point where the closest-in indifference curve is tangent to the crime-prevention-possibility curve. In Figure 13-2 this point is assumed to be at G, that is, neither at C-D (equal crime rates) nor at A-B (equal marginal costs). At point G, 95 crimes are occurring in P and 70 in R. Figure 13-2 has been constructed deliberately to cause the optimum point to fall at G, to illustrate the fact that there is nothing in the nature of the case that requires the optimum to be at C-D or A-B.

Equal population has been assumed up to this point for Districts P (Poor) and R (Rich). Let us suppose, instead, that although the districts cover equal areas P contains three times as many people as R, and that a distribution of police that equates crime rates per capita will not equate the number of crimes prevented by a marginal policeman. Starting from this position, i.e. equal crime rates per capita, transfer of one policeman from R to P would, let us assume, prevent three more crimes in P while allowing one more crime in R. This transfer would, of course, result in a crime rate per capita higher in R than in P. It might now appear that the goal of minimization had become an ambiguous one. Transfer of one policeman from R to P does indeed reduce the total absolute number of crimes in the city as a whole. But the service that residents of P desire is reduction of crime in

P per resident of P; and R's residents desire reduction of crime in R per resident of R. The transfer of one policeman from R to P would increase the former service only by just as many percentage points as it would reduce the latter service (three less crimes in an area three times as populous, against one more crime in the other area). From this concept of product, if everyone counts for one, no gain in total product is achieved by the transfer.

In fact, however, this apparent conflict between two concepts of minimization is nothing but the conflict between "equity" and "efficiency" encountered above when population was assumed the same in the two districts, but with the roles of the districts reversed. When enough policemen have been transferred from R to P to minimize total crime, the crime rate per capita will be higher in R than in P. It will be so, because the residents of R live in a more sparsely populated area than the residents of P. This fact is analogous to the supposition made earlier (though with the reverse result) that the inhabitants of P were more crime-ridden, owing to poverty, than those of R.

Every crime has counted for one, in the analysis thus far. In fact, some types of crime are regarded as more serious than others, and some types of crime (not necessarily the same ones) are more difficult to reduce. These refinements can be incorporated into the analysis by postulating a production-possibility curve for a given police force in a given district that shows by how much one kind of crime can be reduced at the expense of allowing more of the other crime to occur, and by a system of indifference curves that show what combinations of amounts of the two crimes are regarded with equal appreciation or equal dismay, and what combinations are viewed as preferable or inferior to other combinations.

The city may be able to afford so much police service that crime is reduced in both R and P, not quite to the point where crime is zero, but to the point where crime is so random, with respect to location, that no one can foresee whether the transfer of a policeman from one district to another would result in an increase or a decrease in total crime. The test for the existence of this state of affairs, assuming a small absolute number of crimes, would be the occurrence of crimes in the several districts of a city within, say, a year, in a series that approximated the Poisson distribution, much as did the famous series of death by horse-kicks in Prussian army-corps-years. Let the city consist of, say, ten districts, and let crimes be counted in each district for each of, say, three years. If the average number of crimes per district per year is given by z, and if the frequency distribution of crimes per district per year turns out to approximate the following distribution:

Number of crimes in a district in a year

	0	1	2	3	4
Frequency	$\dfrac{z^0 e^{-z}}{0!}$	$\dfrac{z^1 e^{-z}}{1!}$	$\dfrac{z^2 e^{-z}}{2!}$	$\dfrac{z^3 e^{-z}}{3!}$	$\dfrac{z^4 e^{-z}}{4!}$

$$\ldots \text{and so on,} = e^{-z} = z e^{-z}$$

we may then conclude that causes in terms of location cannot be assigned to the crimes that do continue to exist,[2] and that the foregoing analysis in terms of equating costs and benefits at the margin cannot be applied.

---

2. In other words, the probability of any number of crimes in any given district-year, where y is the given number of crimes and z is the average number of crimes observed per district-year, is

$$P(y) = \frac{z^y e^{-z}}{y!}$$

A crime is here an isolated event in a continuum of space-time; we count the number of times crime did occur but cannot count (so vast is the number) the number of times it did *not* occur.

CHAPTER 14

THE ALLOCATION OF POLICE PROTECTION BY INCOME CLASS

John C. Weicher

> Almost a decade ago Aaron Director proposed a law of public expenditures: Public expenditures are made for the primary benefit of the middle classes, and financed with taxes which are borne in considerable part by the poor and the rich. . . . Fire and police activities, for example, are clearly middle-income oriented to the extent that they protect property, and it would be interesting to investigate the extent to which such activities are provided more liberally in middle than in lower income areas of cities.
>
> —George J. Stigler 1970.

THIS PAPER EXAMINES the directions and the extent of the income redistribution that is generated by municipal expenditures on police patrol activities, and the taxes levied to finance these expenditures. Police protection is provided by the "allocation branch" of government; it is undertaken by government because it cannot be provided efficiently by private enterprise (Buchanan, 1970). However, the allocation of resources by a police department may redistribute income as a side-effect. Economists have generally devoted little attention to these redistributive side-effects, although a few studies have investigated the redistribution generated by local government fiscal activities, including police protection. These studies have generally assumed, with little or no attempt at empirical verification, that police protection is provided on the basis of property or income; when this assumed pattern of expeditures is combined with estimates of the incidence of the major elements of the local government tax structure, it appears that income is redistributed from the poor to the

Reprinted, with permission from *Urban Studies*, October 1971, pp. 207-220.

rich and middle-class residents of a city.[1] The present study investigates both the assumption and the pattern of income redistribution derived from it, and finds both to be incorrect.

To avoid confusion, it is important to define "income" before beginning to estimate "income redistribution." The income families receive from police patrol is measured in this study as the amount spent in providing police patrol to them. This is also the definition used in the studies previously cited.

There are substantial shortcomings in this definition. In particular, families may not feel that their economic well-being is increased by the amount spent in providing police patrol to them; they may place a greater or lesser value on the services provided. Virtually nothing is known about the value to the recipients of the benefits conferred by police patrol.

Two kinds of services are typically provided by patrolmen: (1) they answer calls for service for noncriminal matters, such as taking sick or injured persons to hospitals in emergencies; (2) they patrol areas in an attempt to prevent crime. It is relatively easy to measure, at least conceptually, the value of the services provided by the police in responding to calls for service. These services could be valued at the price of providing them privately; the price of using an ambulance would then measure the value of the services provided by patrolmen in taking someone to a hospital. Unfortunately, the data used to estimate the distribution of police patrol expenditures by income class do not contain any information on the extent to which patrolmen are used to answer such demands for service.

More difficult measurement problems arise in estimating the value of expenditures made in attempting to prevent crime. Very little is known about the extent to which police patrolmen actually succeed in preventing crime;[2] even less is known about the

---

1. Adler (1951); Musgrave and Daicoff (1958); Gillespie (1965); Brownlee (1960); Tax Foundation (1967). Adler and Gillespie assert that expenditures are incurred on behalf of property; Musgrave and Daicoff make three alternative allocations on the basis of property, income and *per capita;* Brownlee makes alternative allocations on the basis of property, *per capita,* and half on each basis; the Tax Foundation study uses each of the latter two assumptions.

2. Press (1969) finds that increases in patrol manpower tend to reduce several categories of property crimes and misdemeanours.

value which families place on such prevention. Indeed, it can be argued that some families place a zero or negative value on these services; poor families, particularly, may view the police as enemies. However, this extreme valuation seems unlikely in view of the evidence that the poor are disproportionately the victims of crime, although it may be true that poor persons place a relatively low subjective value on the services they receive from the police department (President's Commission, 1968). At the opposite extreme, some families may derive great satisfaction from police patrol, placing a subjective value on patrol activities far in excess of the amount actually spent in serving them.

Unfortunately, there appears to be no empirical evidence on the validity of these conjectures, or any way of measuring the subjective value to the recipients of the services provided by the police. The empirical work presented in this paper casts some light on the plausibility of these conjectures, but does not directly confirm or refute them.

Despite its shortcomings, the definition of income used in this paper has the merit of being an objective concept: the amount actually spent in providing police patrol services to a family in an income class.[3] Moreover, this definition permits comparison with the previous literature, since the same definition has been employed in these studies.

Since the income received by a family is measured as the amount spent in providing services to that family, income redistribution is correspondingly measured in terms of the fiscal residuum when both expenditures and taxes are considered. Income is said to be redistributed to a family if more is spent in providing police patrol services to it than it pays in taxes for the services; and income is redistributed from a family in the opposite situation.

It should be stressed that this paper does not attempt to build a model to explain the allocation of police patrolmen. Rather, it takes the allocation decisions as given, and investigates their redistributive consequences. It is quite possible that some or all of the variables used to investigate redistribution should be included

---

3. The reader is, of course, free to assign whatever subjective dollar valuation seems appropriate to him to the expenditure estimates by income class calculated in this paper, and to modify the conclusions accordingly.

in a model of resource allocation; however, building such a model is beyond the scope of the present paper.

POLICE PROTECTION AS A PUBLIC GOOD

In contrast to the explicit studies of the income redistribution generated by local government expenditures and taxation, the standard texts on public finance generally treat law enforcement as a public good (Buchanan, 1970; Due, 1968; Sharp and Sliger, 1970). If police protection is indeed a public good, then the benefits accrue equally to all residents of the city; each resident receives more in benefits than he pays in taxes, and there is no income redistribution in the usual sense. However, this assumption is not correct when applied to the services typically provided by police patrolmen.

As mentioned previously, patrolmen provide two types of services. Neither is appropriately classified as a public good. In answering calls for service, the police patrolmen provide services of direct benefit to the recipients, and probably to no other person.

The other service performed is crime prevention. In providing this service, patrolmen are assigned to "beats" in particular neighbourhoods, and provide protection only within that neighbourhood. Even within a neighbourhood, moreover, crime prevention is not a public good. There is no *a priori* basis for asserting that crime prevention can be provided at zero marginal cost. It would seem more reasonable to expect that the amount of protection per person or per family by a given number of policemen would vary inversely with the number of persons or families to be served. If an additional family moves into a neighbourhood, then some additional amount of time must be spent by the police in patrolling the area in which that family lives. This additional time might be extremely brief, but it is not zero; even if the protection merely consists of driving a patrol car past the house in which the family lives, the time spent in front of that house cannot be spent elsewhere. Neighbourhood effects almost surely exist, since a policeman in front of one house is also providing protection to adjacent houses. In addition, the policeman can reach houses a block or two away more quickly than those two or three miles away; standard police theory holds that more protection is therefore provided to the nearer houses, since the probability of arrest is greater, the more rapidly the police can get to the scene of a crime (Wilson, 1950). But these externalities are not sufficient to justify considering police protection a public good, at least outside an extremely limited area which changes as the policeman moves around his beat.

Nor is it necessarily true that the individual policeman provides protection uniformly throughout his beat. The above discussion indicates that an individual patrolman may provide service unequally within his beat (which may include 3,000 to 5,000 persons), by spending more time in certain areas, or in front of individual residences or businesses. The patrolman can easily vary the amount of protection he provides to the individual families within his beat. Further, the more he protects one family or one block, the less he can protect another,[4] although very little is known about the precise nature of the tradeoff (Griffin, 1958; Joseph, 1970).

In this study, it will be assumed that police protection is subject to the exclusion principle. While such an assumption ignores the neighbourhood effects, it is more nearly applicable than the opposite assumption that police protection is a public good. In addition, this assumption, like the definitions of "income" and "income redistribution," is consistent with the assumptions made in the previous studies.

THE INTRACITY DISTRIBUTION OF POLICE PATROLMEN

While there is virtually no data on the amount of protection provided within individual beats, data do exist on the number of policemen allocated to various police districts within a city; these data can be used to relate the amount spent in providing protection to the income of the residents of the district.[5] This study analyses police protection expenditures and manpower allocation

---

4. Buchanan (1970) mentions the limited geographic range of police and fire protection, but does not attempt to specify the range in which either service may be regarded as a public good.

5. We are ignoring the services provided by city-wide police branches charged with particular functions, such as the detective bureau, homicide squad, etc. These will be discussed briefly later.

by district in Chicago in 1959, as a function of income and of the number of entities to be served.[6]

While the data are not recent, they appear to be the best available at this time, for several reasons. Chicago in 1959 was divided into 38 police districts, providing enough observations for statistical analysis; only the largest cities meet this requirement.[7] Manpower allocation data for 1960 are unavailable, in the wake of the police-burglary scandal of that year, and in 1961 the department was reorganised and the number of districts reduced to 21. Also, 1959 is the latest year for which detailed intracity income statistics are available from the U.S. Census. Data for the 1970 Census, when available, will permit a similar analysis for 1969, although the statistical problems generated by the reduction in the number of districts would complicate the analysis.

It is possible that more recent data, or data for other cities, would show a substantially different manpower allocation pattern. The Chicago Police Department was not regarded as one of the better or more modern departments at that time (*Fortune*, 1958), and police organisation in general has been improved in the last decade. Investigation for other cities, and for more recent periods, would be useful as a check on the general validity of the pattern reported in this paper.

Protection is provided to the same individual in several different places, of which the most important probably are his residence, his place of employment, and the stores in which he shops. In determining the amount spent in providing protection to him, therefore, it is necessary to take account of the amount spent in each of these locations. Data are available which permit estimation of the amount spent in two of these places, but not the third. Data by census tract are available for the income of the resident population in the 1960 Census; data on retail sales by census tract are available from a special tabulation of the 1958 Census of Business (Berry and Tennant, 1963). These data have been aggregated across census tracts into police districts, to put them on

---

6. Data are taken from *Statistical Report for (First, Second, Third, Fourth) Quarter, 1959* (Chicago: Chicago Police Department Records and Communications Section, 1959-1960).

7. Cincinnati, for example, has only seven police districts.

the same basis as the data on the number of policemen. Unfortunately, the available data on the location of employment within the city are inadequate, and therefore no estimate of the protection provided on this basis is included.[8] However, since the Loop, that is, the Central Business police district is omitted from the analysis, it seems likely that the failure to measure protection provided at the place of employment does not greatly affect the results.[9]

In Table 14-I police protection *per capita* is regressed against several measures of income, retail sales *per capita*, and the population of the district.[10] The results directly contradict the com-

---

8. The only available data are for employment in "large" manufacturing establishments (those with 50 or more employees) in 1958 (*Locational Patterns of Major Manufacturing Industries in the City of Chicago,* Research Division, Department of City Planning, City of Chicago, 1960). Data for smaller establishments were not presented. Moreover, the "data" for the large plants consist of dots on a rather small map of the city. In an attempt to use the data, these dots were assigned to police districts by comparing the map to a map of police district boundaries. Results for regressions using this manufacturing employment variable were very similar to those reported in Table 14-I, with the manufacturing variable insignificant.

9. Three districts are omitted from the statistical analysis: the Loop, the Central Business District, where protection is not provided to any significant extent to district residents; a small district on the Near West Side, centering on Skid Row, where protection is provided primarily to unrelated individuals whose incomes are not available in the data; and a district on the Far Southeast Side, where a significant but indeterminable number of policemen were assigned as a "racial detail," to prevent trouble in the racially integrated Trumbull Park public housing project. Omission of these districts, particularly the Loop, reduces the probable statistical importance of employment and retailing as explanatory variables. However, it is more convenient to make adjustments for the Loop separately after calculating expenditures by income class in the more residential districts. In the absence of employment data for the other districts, there is no way to estimate expenditures on people in their capacity as workers, by income class. However, in part, this will be measured by retail sales, since employment in retailing is probably distributed roughly proportionally to sales outside the Loop. Other types of employment (finance and real estate, for example) should also be distributed in a similar way.

10. Population is included since each district station has about the same number of supervisory personnel assigned to it, regardless of the size of the district. The number of captains, lieutenants, and sergeants ranges from 13 to 17, while the population of the districts ranges from 41,000 to 219,000. Therefore, larger districts would be expected to have lower ratios of police to population, *ceteris paribus.*

TABLE 14-I

REGRESSION ANALYSIS OF POLICE PROTECTION, CHICAGO
POLICE DISTRICTS, 1959

Equation	Constant	P	R/P	Y_m	Y_m-Y_n	Y_r	R^2
(1) ..	4.883	−0.00648	0.370	−0.406	—	—	0.832
	(0.325)	(0.00144)	(0.115)	(0.046)	—	—	—
(2) ..	5.085	−0.00583	0.415	−0.454	0.154	—	0.843
	(0.349)	(0.00149)	(0.117)	(0.057)	(0.107)	—	—
(3) ..	4.895	−0.00531	0.241	−0.545	0.218	0.192	0.880
	(0.317)	(0.00133)	(0.119)	(0.059)	(0.098)	(0.064)	—

Variables:

P = Population of the police district, 1960 (in thousands of persons).

R/P = Ratio of retail sales in 1958 to population in 1960 (in thousands of dollars *per capita*).

Y_m = Median family income within the police district in 1959 (in thousands of dollars).

Y_m-Y_n = Difference between median family income within the district and median family income of all census tracts surrounding the district and lying within one mile of the district boundaries, 1959 (in thousands of dollars).

Y_r = Interquartile range of income within the police district, 1959 (in thousands of dollars).

The dependent variable is the number of policemen in 1959 per 1,000 population in 1960.

mon assumption that protection is provided on the basis of income or property.[11] Equation (1) shows that the number of policemen in a district falls markedly as the median family income of the district rises. Richer districts get far fewer policemen than poorer ones.

It can be argued that the result in equation (1) does not prove that patrol expenditures are made primarily to provide service to poor persons, at least in so far as those expenditures which are incurred in attempting to prevent crime are concerned. Policemen may be assigned to an area either to protect the persons there from crime, or to attempt to deter potential criminals residing in the area from committing crimes, either in the area or elsewhere, by functioning as visible reminders to the potential criminals of the probability of apprehension and punishment. In the former case, policemen provide protection in the districts to which

11. Since we are primarily interested in the income variables, discussion of the results for retail sales will be deferred to the end of this section.

they are assigned, and the coefficient of income in equation (1) implies that more is spent in providing protection and other services to poor persons. In the latter, policemen are concentrated in poorer districts because potential criminals tend to live in such districts; the concentration of policemen serves to deter potential criminals from committing crimes anywhere in the city. On this hypothesis, protection is provided to rich residents by concentrating manpower in poor neighbourhoods, and the negative coefficients of the income variables have no implications about the distribution of expenditures on protection by income class.

It may be worth pointing out that standard police administration theory is based on the former hypothesis, and rejects the latter. O. W. Wilson, for example, makes the point forcefully: "Crime and misconduct of any type under police control result from the coexistence of the desire to commit the misdeed and the belief that the opportunity to do so exists. If either factor is absent, criminal acts will not be committed. . . . The elimination of the actual opportunity, or the belief in the opportunity, for successful misconduct is the basic purpose of patrol. A thief's desire to steal is not diminished by the presence of a patrolman, but the opportunity for successful theft is."[12]

Such assertions of course are not proof that expenditures are made to serve the residents of the area patrolled; nor are they refutations of the alternative hypothesis, although they may be suggestive. Instead, specific tests of the competing hypotheses are needed.

One possible test may be constructed along the following lines: if the police protect persons in an area from crime by patrolling in that area, then the number of policemen in the area should be positively related to the crime rate; areas with high crime rates would require greater expenditures. On the other hand, if protection is provided by patrolling areas inhabited by potential criminals, then the number of policemen in the area should be

12. Wilson (1950). Wilson also argues that the number of patrolmen in an area should be proportional to the need, where need is defined as the crime rate. He explicitly rejects any attempt to allocate patrolmen on the basis of the residence of felons.

positively related to the number of criminals and potential criminals living there.

Such a test, however, is not feasible for two reasons. First, data on the residence of criminals in Chicago is not available. Second, even if it were, it appears that criminals and victims both tend to be poor (President's Commission, pp. 135-159). It is likely, therefore, that statistical tests of the two hypotheses, using such data, would be inconclusive.

A more clear-cut test of the competing hypotheses can be formulated indirectly. This test makes use of the concept of the "victim area," an area of relatively high income surrounded by much poorer areas (Rossi and Dentler, 1961). Such areas, as the name implies, are particularly likely to have high crime rates. If protection is provided by patrolling the area in which crime is likely to occur, more should be spent in such areas than in areas of similar incomes which are surrounded by equally rich areas. If, on the other hand, protection is provided by patrolling areas likely to be inhabited by criminals, then the number of policemen in an area should rise as an area becomes *poorer* relative to surrounding areas, in order to inhibit the residents from becoming criminals.

The concept of the victim area is introduced into equation (2) as the variable $Y_m - Y_n$, the difference between the median family income within the district, and the median family income of the area surrounding the district and lying within one mile of the district boundaries.

While the coefficient is not significant in the usual sense, the t-ratio of $1 \cdot 4$ indicates that the probability that the true coefficient is negative is slightly less than $0 \cdot 10$. The results suggest that expenditures within a district increase as the district becomes richer relative to surrounding districts. The coefficient tends to support the hypothesis that protection is provided to residents of an area by assigning policemen to that area, rather than by assigning them to areas likely to produce criminals; it further suggests that the larger number of policemen assigned to poorer areas are providing protection and other services to residents of those areas. Therefore, expenditures in a district should be regarded as expenditures made for the residents of that district, that is, as income for the residents.

Equation (2) suggests a further hypothesis about the relationship between income and police protection expenditures. The significant coefficient of $Y_m - Y_n$ implies that the expenditures in a neighbourhood depend not only on the absolute level of income within the neighbourhood, but also on the level of income within the neighbourhood relative to that of other neighbourhoods in the vicinity. There is no reason why this "neighbourhood effect" should exist only between districts; more policemen should be assigned to a rich enclave in a generally poor district than to equally rich areas in richer districts, since the enclave has a high income relative to surrounding areas. That is, expenditures within a police district should depend both on the level and the distribution of income within the district.

Equation (3), incorporating a measure of the income distribution within the district (Y_r, or $Y_{q3} - Y_{q1}$, the interquartile range), supports this hypothesis. The coefficient of Y_r is significant and positive. Moreover, in equation (3) the coefficient of $Y_m - Y_n$ is also significant and positive. These results imply that the number of policemen assigned to an area depends not only on the general level of income in the area, but on the distribution of income within the area, and on the level of income in the area relative to adjacent areas. The results further imply that the relationship between the income of a family and the amount spent in protecting it is more complicated than has been assumed in the literature; the amount spent on families in the same income class will vary, being greater if the family is rich relative to its neighbours, and less if the family is relatively poor. It is therefore incorrect to allocate expenditures on police protection to individuals merely on the basis of their income, as has been done in the literature.

The results for R/P indicate that a significant minor fraction of the policemen in a district were utilised to provide services to people where they shop, rather than where they live. The mean district had retail sales of $1,150,000 in 1958. The coefficient of R/P in equation (3) implies that protection would have been reduced by 0·28 policemen per 1,000 population, if the mean district had had no retail activity. This would represent a reduction of 14 percent in the number of policemen in the district. The amount spent in providing these services may be allocated in proportion to consumption, or roughly in proportion to income, assuming that the protection is provided primarily to property (the merchandise and fixtures of the store), and that the benefits of the protection (such as smaller losses from theft, and perhaps lower insurance rates) are passed on by storeowners to customers. Thus, we may conclude that about 14 percent of the patrol expenditures can be assigned to individuals in proportion to their income; excluding supervisory personnel, the remainder was spent disproportionately on the poorer residents of the city.

EXPENDITURES ON INDIVIDUAL FAMILIES BY INCOME CLASS

The results in Table 14-I can be utilised to estimate expenditures by the income class of the recipient. In doing so, however, it is necessary to take account of the fact that the amount spent on families in a given income class will vary from district to district, depending on the income of the other residents of the district and of surrounding areas. Therefore, the procedure followed is to calculate the amount spent on a family in each income class in each district, and to average these amounts across districts to estimate the average expenditures on families in each income class. Families are used as the units to which patrol is provided since income data is available only for families.

The results of equation (3) in Table 14-I are used in order to estimate the amount spent in providing police patrol to any family. This equation measures the way in which the number of policemen varies between districts as the income of families varies. We assume that the results also apply within a district when a family in any income class moves into (or out of) that district, and then calculate the way in which the number of policemen in the district changes as we add (or subtract) a single family in any income class. We assume that the change in the number of policemen as a single family moves in or out is the number of policemen who provide patrol services to that family. Since families are differentiated only by income class and district of residence, the same number of policemen are provided to each family of a given income class in a given district.

Mathematically, we calculate $\frac{\partial PP_i}{\partial F_j}$ for all i and j, where the symbols are defined as follows:

PP = number of policemen
F　= number of families
i　 = police districts ($i = 1, \ldots, 35$)
j　 = income class of a family; classes are those used in the 1960 Census, ranging from "Under \$1,000" to "\$25,000 and over," ($j = 1, \ldots, 13$).

These partial derivatives can be calculated by taking the partial of equation (3) with respect to F_j, and rearranging terms:

$$\frac{\partial\left(\frac{PP}{P}\right)_i}{\partial F_j} = -0\cdot545\,\frac{\partial Y_{mi}}{\partial F_j} + 0\cdot218\frac{\partial Y_{mi}}{\partial F_j}$$

$$+ \ 0\cdot192\,\frac{\partial Y_{ri}}{\partial F_j} + 0\cdot241\,\frac{\partial\left(\frac{R}{P}\right)_i}{\partial F_j} \qquad (5)$$

$$\frac{P_i\,\frac{\partial PP_i}{\partial F_j} - PP_i\,\frac{\partial P_i}{\partial F_j}}{P_i{}^2} = -0\cdot327\frac{\partial Y_{mi}}{\partial F_j}$$

$$+ \ 0\cdot192\left[\frac{\partial X_{q3i}}{\partial F_j} - \frac{\partial Y_{q1i}}{\partial F_j}\right]$$

$$+ \ 0\cdot241\left[\frac{P_i\,\frac{\partial R_i}{\partial F_j} - R_i\,\frac{\partial P_i}{\partial F_j}}{P_i{}^2}\right] \qquad (6)$$

$$\frac{\partial PP_i}{\partial F_j} = P_i\left[-0\cdot327\,\frac{\partial Y_{mi}}{\partial F_j} + 0\cdot192\left(\frac{\partial Y_{q3i}}{\partial F_j} - \frac{\partial Y_{a1i}}{\partial F_j}\right)\right.$$

$$\left. + \ 0\cdot241\left(\frac{1}{P_i}\right)\left[\frac{\partial R_i}{\partial F_j} - \left(\frac{R}{P}\right)_i\left(\frac{\partial P_i}{\partial F_j}\right)\right]\right] + \left(\frac{PP}{P}\right)_i\frac{\partial P_i}{\partial F_j} \qquad (7)$$

Convenient approximations for the terms $\frac{\partial P_i}{\partial F_j}$ and $\frac{\partial R_i}{\partial F_j}$ are employed.[13] The change in population when an additional family moves into the district is assumed to be four persons. The change in retail sales is assumed to be equal to the income of the family (measured as the midpoint of the income class, and using $50,000 for the top class). This procedure is followed both for purposes of convenience and because police protection is provided to establishments in which people save, such as banks and savings and loan associations, as well as to those in which they spend. Financial institutions are not included in the retail sales data; the assumption is made that the coefficient of R/P in equation (3) is applicable to financial institutions as well, in lieu of attempting to measure the amount of financial activity in each police district.[14]

With these approximations, equation (7) becomes:

$$\frac{\partial PP_i}{\partial F_j} = P_i \left[-0 \cdot 327 \frac{\partial Y_{mi}}{\partial F_j} + 0.192 \left(\frac{\partial Y_{q3i}}{\partial F_j} - \frac{\partial Y_{q1i}}{\partial F_j} \right) \right.$$
$$\left. + 0 \cdot 241 \left(\frac{Y_j - 4 \left(\frac{R}{P} \right)_i}{P_i} \right) \right] + 4 \left(\frac{PP}{P} \right)_i \quad (8)$$

The partials of the income measures with respect to F_j may be easily calculated. The median may be written as

$$Y_m = L_m + \left[\frac{\frac{1}{2} \sum_{j=1}^{13} F_j - \sum_{j=1}^{m-1} F_j}{F_m} \right] C_m \quad (9)$$

---

13. We are explicitly ignoring the effect of an increase in the number of families in an income class on the median income of the surrounding area; an increase of one family in the "Over $25,000" category will raise Y_n for surrounding police districts, as well as raising Y_m in the district into which the family moves. Since Y_n is calculated for the area within one mile of a given police district, it would be necessary to make some assumptions about the location of the new family within the district, in regard to how close it is to each bordering district. We also ignore the reduction in expenditures per family generated because the number of supervisory personnel is unchanged. This is the same in all income classes in all districts, and is negligible; the results would be essentially the same if it were included.

14. The possibilities of shopping in other districts, or in the Loop, can be ignored, since protection must be provided to individuals wherever they shop. The assumption that all additional shopping is done in the district of residence is convenient and does not alter the results.

where F_m is the number of families in the income class in which the median lies, L_m is the lower bound of the income class, and C_m is the class interval. Since the relevant income classes each have an interval of \$1,000, and the income variables have been measured in thousands of dollars, C_m is unity. It can easily be seen that

$$\frac{\partial Y_{mi}}{\partial F_j} = -\frac{1}{2F_m}, \; j = 1, \; .., \; m - 1 \tag{9a}$$

$$\frac{\partial Y_{mi}}{\partial F_m} = \frac{\sum\limits_{j=1}^{m-1} F_j - \sum\limits_{j=m+1}^{13} F_j}{2F_m{}^2} \tag{9b}$$

$$\frac{\partial Y_{mi}}{\partial F_j} = \frac{1}{2F_m}, \; j = m + 1, \; .., \; 13. \tag{9c}$$

Similarly, the first quartile may be written as

$$Y_{q1} = L_{q1} + \left[\frac{\frac{1}{4} \sum\limits_{j=1}^{13} F_j - \sum\limits_{j=1}^{q1-1} F_j}{F_{q1}} \right] C_{q1} \tag{10}$$

where F_{q1} is the number of families in the income class in which the first quartile lies. The partial derivatives are

$$\frac{\partial Y_{q1}}{\partial F_j} = -\frac{3}{4F_{q1}}, \; j = 1, \; .., \; q1 - 1 \tag{10a}$$

$$\frac{\partial Y_{q1}}{\partial F_{q1}} = \frac{3 \sum\limits_{j=1}^{q1-1} F_j - \sum\limits_{j=q1+1}^{13} F_j}{4F_{q1}{}^2} \tag{10b}$$

$$\frac{\partial Y_{q1}}{\partial F_j} = \frac{1}{4F_{q1}}, \; j = q1 + 1, \; .., \; 13. \tag{10c}$$

The calculations for the third quartile are similar, except that for 12 districts, the third quartile lies in the \$10,000 to \$15,000 income bracket, so that the term C_{q3} must be included explicitly:

$$Y_{q3} = L_{q3} + \left[\frac{\frac{3}{4} \sum\limits_{j=1}^{13} F_j - \sum\limits_{j=1}^{q3-1} F_j}{F_{q3}} \right] C_{q3} \tag{11}$$

$$\frac{\partial Y_{q3}}{\partial F_j} = \left(-\frac{1}{4F_{q3}} \right) C_{q3}, \; j = 1, \; .., \; q3 - 1 \tag{11a}$$

$$\frac{\partial Y_{q3}}{\partial F_{q3}} = \left(\frac{\sum\limits_{j=1}^{q3-1} F_j - 3 \sum\limits_{j=q3+1}^{13} F_j}{4F_{q3}{}^2} \right) C_{q3} \qquad (11b)$$

$$\frac{\partial Y_{q3}}{\partial F_j} = \left(\frac{3}{4F_{q3}} \right) C_{q3}, \, j = q3 + 1, \, .., \, 13. \qquad (11c)$$

The partial derivatives from equations (9)-(11) are calculated for all i and j and substituted into equation (8). The resulting partial derivatives $\frac{\partial PP_i}{\partial F_j}$ are then averaged over all districts i for each income class, weighing the partials by F_{ij}, the number of families in that income class in each district, to estimate the average number of police patrolmen per family in each income class.

These averages are shown in Column (1) of Table 14-II.[15] (Each has been multiplied by \$5,400, the salary of a patrolman on the Chicago police force in 1959, to convert them to dollar estimates.) They show a strong negative relationship between the average expenditures on police protection and income up to

---

15. Fifty-two of the 455 $\frac{\partial PP_i}{\partial F_j}$ were negative, implying that police protection is reduced as an additional family in income class j moves into district i. These generally occur in the third quarter of the income distribution, where $\frac{\partial Y_{m\,i}}{\partial F_i}$ and $\frac{\partial Y_{q3i}}{\partial F_j}$ are both negative, and $\frac{\partial Y_{q1i}}{\partial F_j}$ is positive. All occur in the brackets between \$5,000 and \$10,000 with the majority in the \$7,000-\$8,000 and \$8,000-\$9,000 brackets. These have been treated as zeroes in calculating Table 14-II, since it is highly unlikely that police protection is actually reduced in any area when an additional family of any income bracket is added. If the relevant entries in Column (1) of Table 14-II are calculated only on the basis of those values of $\frac{\partial PP_i}{\partial F_j}$ which are positive, ignoring the negative values completely, the table would read:

Income Class	(1)
\$	\$
5,000-6,000	44.58
6,000-7,000	30.53
7,000-8,000	25.89
8,000-9,000	40.03
9,000-10,000	43.04

The argument in the text would not be substantially modified if these values were inserted in lieu of those in the text.

TABLE 14-II

POLICE PATROL EXPENDITURES AND TAXES BY INCOME CLASS

Income Class	(1) Average Expenditures per Family	(2) Taxes per Family (Larson)	(3) Taxes per Family (Tax Foundation)	(4) Net Gain (Larson)	(5) Net Gain (Tax Foundation)
Under $1,000	$ 97.76	$ 11.11	$ 4.43	$ 86.65	$ 93.33
$ 1,000-2,000	96.37	33.33	13.30	63.04	83.07
2,000-3,000	88.85	38.57	18.78	50.28	70.07
3,000-4,000	76.33	34.13	25.56	42.20	50.77
4,000-5,000	61.01	38.99	31.31	22.02	29.70
5,000-6,000	44.28	37.65	37.25	6.63	7.03
6,000-7,000	25.82	39.37	41.22	–13.55	– 15.40
7,000-8,000	13.84	46.45	46.18	–32.61	– 32.34
8,000-9,000	13.32	53.79	50.80	–40.47	– 37.48
9,000-10,000	22.25	60.12	56.74	–37.87	– 34.49
10,000-15,000	58.20	68.24	70.04	–10.04	– 11.84
15,000-25,000	84.24	58.67	103.44	25.57	– 19.20
Over 25,000	143.99	146.67	258.61	– 2.68	–114.62

the $8,000 to $9,000 income class; above this level, a strong positive relationship exists. Much the largest amount per family is spent on the handful of families (less than 1% of the total) earning more than $25,000. These families tend to be concentrated on the North Side of the city, along Lake Michigan, adjacent to rather low-income neighbourhoods inland; the police districts in which they live are small, with particularly unequal income distribution, and are heavily patrolled.

In general, the results in Column (1) indicate that police patrol expenditures are made primarily to serve the rich and the poor; very little goes to that half of the city composed of middle-income families, earning between $5,000 and $10,000. Far from being provided in a way which is "clearly middle-income oriented," as Stigler hypothesised, police protection appears to be provided at a disproportionately low rate to the middle-income classes.

INCOME REDISTRIBUTION GENERATED BY POLICE PATROL

The foregoing results are not adequate for determining the directions of income redistribution generated by police protection expenditures; it is necessary also to investigate the burden of the taxes used to finance these expenditures.

There appear to be no published estimates of the incidence of the Chicago tax structure by income class, or indeed of any purely local government tax structure. However, there have been several studies of the incidence of the overall state and local tax structure, which usually include separate estimates for the most important taxes. There are also studies of the overall state and local tax incidence pattern for specific areas, including Cook County, which contains Chicago. Detailed studies of the incidence pattern of particular taxes also exist.

The results of all of these studies can be applied to the Chicago data in order to generate estimates of the incidence of the taxes levied to finance police patrol expenditures. Two approaches are taken in this paper. The simplest uses the published estimates of incidence by income class of the overall state and local tax burden, making no attempt to refine these in light of the Chicago tax structure. A somewhat more complicated approach relies on the estimates of the incidence of those taxes which provide the bulk of the revenue in Chicago. The city in 1959 received 43 percent of its general revenue from property taxes, 17 percent from general and selective sales taxes, 12 percent from other taxes, including licenses, and the remainder from other governments, charges and special assessments (U.S. Bureau of Census, 1961). To estimate the incidence pattern in Chicago, we construct a weighted average of the incidence patterns of the property and sales taxes, since these were the most important sources of revenue to Chicago, and since more detailed estimates of the incidence patterns of these taxes have been published in other studies.

These incidence patterns are then compared to expenditures by income class to estimate the directions and extent of income redistribution. The estimated expenditures per family in Column (1) of Table 14-II are multiplied by the number of families in each class; these figures sum to approximately $42,800,000. This sum is then apportioned among income classes in accordance with a particular incidence pattern.

Several sets of incidence patterns were investigated. Columns (2) and (3) present two of these. Column (2) is derived from a study of Arlyn J. Larson of the incidence of the Illinois state and local tax structure (1964). His estimates of the incidence of property and sales taxes within Cook County are weighted by the relative importance of these taxes to Chicago. Column (3) contains the Tax Foundation's estimates of the incidence of the overall state and local tax structure on a national basis (1967). In general, these are the most and least regressive patterns, respectively, among all patterns estimated.[16]

Despite the different tax incidence patterns, the patterns of income redistribution shown in Columns (4) and (5) are quite similar. Income is redistributed to the poor (those earning less than $5,000) and from the middle-income classes (those earning between $5,000 and $10,000). The position of the rich is ambiguous, except for the very richest class.[17] (Unfortunately, the top two classes are combined in all of the studies of tax incidence; it is possible that separation of these brackets might alter the results somewhat.) However, the pattern for the poor and middle-income classes is clear: under a wide variety of assumptions about the incidence of state and local taxes, and utilising any of several empirical estimates of incidence, income is redistributed from the middle-income families to the poor.

---

16. Estimates were also made on the basis of the incidence patterns of several other studies. These were: the overall state and local pattern estimated by Gillespie; and weighted averages of the property and sales tax patterns estimated by Gillespie, by Musgrave and Daicoff, and by the Tax Foundation. Preliminary investigation of other patterns, including but not limited to those studies cited in note 1, suggested that patterns would be similar to those estimated.

17. The other estimated patterns were essentially the same as the two included in Table 14-II with the following exceptions. Both patterns based on Gillespie show income being redistributed to families in the $10,000-$15,000 bracket and from families in the $5,000-$6,000 bracket. In the $15,000-$25,000, the Musgrave-Daicoff estimate is very similar to that in column (3); all the others show income being redistributed to families in this bracket.

These results cast doubt on the notion that the poor residents place a zero or negative value on the services of the police. If this notion were accurate, it would imply that almost half of police patrol expenditures were wasted. These expenditures could have been made for the other residents of the city, who would value them, and who would not have to pay any additional taxes to receive the additional services. The police department would then be in the position of ignoring the desires of the majority of citizens in order to provide unwanted services to a minority. Politically, such a position would be virtually impossible for the department to sustain. Moreover, unless the middle-income classes place an inordinately high subjective value on the services they receive, the results would imply that almost everyone in the city would be made worse off by the combined expenditure and tax pattern. This seems unlikely even though it remains possible that the subjective valuations of the expenditures do differ substantially by income class.

CONCLUSION

Contrary to the common assumption, expenditures on police protection, in so far as they can be allocated to income classes, are not made primarily to serve rich and middle-income families and do not involve income redistribution in favour of these groups; rather, expenditures are made primarily in poor districts, to serve poor families, who are subsidised by the middle-income classes. The position of the rich is ambiguous; they may be subsidised by the middle-income classes, or they may join those classes in subsidising the poor. In either case, their position is very different from that commonly assumed.

The foregoing conclusions are based on police patrol expenditures for only thirty-five Chicago police districts. Two of the three omitted districts deserve special mention. In the Loop, expenditures are almost entirely designed to serve people where they work and shop, since virtually nobody lives in the district. The distribution of these expenditures by income class has not been attempted. However, even if these expenditures were allocated entirely to the rich and middle-income families, the results in Table 14-II would not be appreciably affected; perhaps the richest residents might show an overall net gain as a result, for the most regressive tax patterns.

Counterbalancing the Loop is the Skid Row district on the near West Side, where substantial expenditures are made on a relative handful of the very poorest residents of the city. The inclusion of these two districts is therefore unlikely to affect the overall results.

Police patrol expenditures amounted to about 54 percent of the total police budget in 1959; the balance was largely devoted to special squads assigned to investigate particular classes of crimes, such as homicide, arson and vice. It is not clear how expenditures for these squads should be allocated. If expenditures for each squad are allocated proportionally to the number of crimes under the jurisdiction of the squad, then the overwhelming share of these expenditures should be allocated to the poor districts, since these are the areas in which the crimes are committed. The results shown in Table 14-II would be generally valid for these expenditures also.

Alternatively, it is possible that these squads devote proportionately more attention to the relatively few crimes committed in the richer districts. However, the clearance data by district do not support such a hypothesis. There is no tendency for clearance rates for any Part I crime to vary with any of the income variables used in this study.[18] If clearance rates can be used as a proxy for manpower assigned to investigate crime (and therefore for expenditures), these results imply that expenditures per family are about the same in all income classes. Combined with any estimated tax incidence patterns the results further imply that income is redistributed to the poor from middle-income families, and clearly in this instance from the rich as well.

Extension of the analysis to other services would be useful. Fire protection has commonly been assumed to be related to property, but the *a priori* case is no more plausible for one than for the other. If firemen are allocated where fires occur, then fire protection might also involve redistribution to the poor (Laing 1970, p.

18. The regressions supporting this statement have been omitted from this paper; specific results are available from the author. "Part I" crimes are murder, rape, aggravated assault, burglary, larceny, robbery, and auto theft.

1). Sanitation expenditures may be provided primarily on the basis of income; garbage is probably a positive function of income, but the income-elasticity of demand for private sanitation services (such as disposal units) is probably also high. The benefits of highway expenditures are perhaps more closely related to income than those for any other service.

These four services accounted for over 53 percent of total general expenditures (excluding education and welfare) by cities having at least 50,000 population in 1960 (U.S. Bureau of Census, 1961); the extent of redistribution generated by other services, individually, therefore, is likely to be relatively small.

The results may help to explain the flight to suburbia. It seems clear that a middle-income family can improve its financial position by leaving Chicago, and purchasing similar housing in some suburb. Even if it pays the same taxes for police protection in the suburb, the family will gain since it will receive the benefits of the expenditures made by the suburb on police protection. There will be little if any income redistribution in favour of the poor, since there will be few if any poor families living in the suburb. The dollar amounts are small, although marginally they may be important. In this connection, it is interesting to note that Muth has found that the growth of low-income population in a central city tends to increase the size of the suburban population. He suggests that this phenomenon may occur because central city expenditure for health and welfare would rise as the number of poor residents increase; richer families may move to the suburbs in order to avoid paying taxes to support these services (Muth, 1969). The present study suggests that expenditures for other local government services may be producing the same result.

REFERENCES

Adler, J. H.: The fiscal system, the distribution of income and public welfare. In Poole, Kenyon E. (Ed.): *Fiscal Policies and the American Economy.* New York; Prentice-Hall, 1951, pp. 385-386.

Berry, B. J. L., and Tennant, R. J.: *Chicago Commercial Reference Handbook.* Chicago, Department of Geography, University of Chicago, 1963.

Brownlee, O. H.: *Estimated Distribution of Minnesota Taxes and Public Expenditure Benefits.* Minneapolis, University of Minnesota, 1960, pp. 33-34.

Buchanan, J. M.: *The Public Finances,* 3rd ed. Homewood, Richard D. Irwin, 1970, pp. 26, 356.

Chicago Police Department (1959-60). *Statistical Report for (First, Second, Third, Fourth) Quarter, 1959.*

Due, J. F.: *Government Finance: Economics of the Public Sector,* 4th ed. Homewood, Richard D. Irwin, 1968, p. 109.

Fortune, The Editors of: *The Exploding Metropolis.* Garden City, Doubleday, 1958, pp. 70-75.

Gillespie, W. I.: The effect of public expenditures on the distribution of income: an empirical investigation. In Musgrave, R. A. (Ed.): *Essays in Fiscal Federalism.* Washington, The Brookings Institution, 1965, pp. 156-157.

Griffin, J. I.: *Statistics Essential for Police Efficiency.* Springfield, Thomas, 1958, pp. 14-15.

Joseph, R. A.: Selling security: crime busting pays off for private concerns that offer protection. *Wall Street Journal,* 14 August, 1970.

Laing, J. R.: Arson in the ghetto: suspicious fires rise rapidly in black slums, worrying authorities. *Wall Street Journal,* 9 April, 1970.

Larson, A. J.: Estimated burden of state and local taxes in Illinois. *Illinois Government,* No. 22, 1964.

Musgrave, R. A., and Daicoff, D. W.: Who pays the Michigan taxes?, In *Michigan Tax Study Staff Papers.* Lansing, pp. 154-155, 1958.

Muth, R. F.: *Cities and Housing.* Chicago, University of Chicago, 1967.

President's Commission on Law Enforcement and Administration of Justice: *The Challenge of Crime in a Free Society.* New York, Avon, 1968.

Press, S. J.: A case study of some effects of an increase in police manpower on crime. *Urban Economics Report* 28. Chicago, Department of Economics, University of Chicago, 1969.

Rossi, P. H., and Dentler, R. A.: *The Politics of Urban Renewal.* New York, The Free Press of Glencoe, 1961, p. 31.

Sharp, A. M., and Sliger, B. F.: *Public Finance,* rev. ed. Austin, Business Publications, Inc., 1970, p. 16.

Stigler, G. J.: Director's law of public income redistribution. *Journal of Law and Economics,* Vol. XIII, pp. 1-10, 1970.

Tax Foundation Inc.: *Tax Burdens and Benefits of Government Expenditure by Income Class, 1961 and 1965.* New York, Tax Foundation Inc., 1967, pp. 28-31.

U.S. Bureau of the Census: *Compendium of City Government Finances in 1960.* Washington, U.S. Government Printing Office, 1961.

————: Censuses of Population and Housing: 1960, Final Report PHC (1)-26, Census Tracts: Chicago. Washington, U.S. Government Printing Office, 1962.

Wilson, O. W.: *Police Administration,* 1st ed. New York, McGraw-Hill, 1950, p. 116.

CHAPTER 15

ECONOMIES OF SCALE AND MUNICIPAL POLICE SERVICES: THE ILLINOIS EXPERIENCE

NORMAN WALZER

EMPIRICAL ANALYSES in the private sector have disclosed significant economies of scale (e.g. Adams, 1967 and Johnston, 1960). Interest naturally turned to an examination of the possibilities for scale economies in the public sector. This issue is particularly important as local governments encounter greater difficulties in financing the services demanded by their residents.[1] The increased financial pressures arise from a larger number of residents demanding services of a better quality as well as the limited ability of fragmented governmental units to raise revenue.

Likewise, inflation has taken a heavy toll on municipal budgets (Walzer, 1971). Municipal services are largely of a personal nature and significant increases in productivity may not be easily achieved (Baumol, 1967). This is especially important in police protection where wages and salaries account for almost 90 percent of total expenditures.

The labor-intensiveness of police services has led researchers to doubt the presence of significant scale economies. The claim has been made that extra costs of maintaining substations and precinct headquarters will offset cost reductions from mass purchases, etc.[2] However, a large police department can concentrate more

Reprinted, with permission of the Harvard University Press, from *Review of Economics and Statistics,* November 1972, pp. 431-438.

1. A summary of the research on costs of urban services is available in Hirsch (1968). This research should be distinguished from expenditure studies which are discussed in Wilensky (1970).

2. The major issues involved with horizontally-integrated functions appear in Hirsch (1959).

313

resources on a particular neighborhood during critical periods such as during expected criminal activity. Also, neighborhoods can be sealed off after a crime has been committed and research has suggested that immediate investigation by police officers substantially increases the likelihood of apprehending the offender (*Challenge of Crime*, 1967). Since lengthy investigations are time-consuming and thus very expensive, large police departments should have a decided cost advantage. Larger departments are also able to employ computerized data storage-retrieval systems and specialized personnel to a greater extent. On an a priori basis, one might expect specialized investigators to solve cases more quickly than would relatively inexperienced officers.

This paper reviews some of the earlier findings on scale economies in police protection, suggests a new measure of scale, and reports the results of an empirical investigation on a sample of Illinois cities. Finally, an expenditure per capita and population analysis is conducted on the same sample to determine whether the observed declining average cost curve results from sample differences or variations in measurement techniques.

PRIOR RESEARCH FINDINGS

Early research on economies of scale in the public sector has employed regression analysis to study the statistical association between city population size and expenditures per capita on police protection. Additional variables thought to be important determinants of the quality of service were included to adjust for variations in service among the observations.[3] A statistically significant negative relationship between population (size of plant) and expenditures per capita (average cost) was necessary to accept the hypothesis of scale economies. The analysis reported here differs somewhat in that it pays more attention to the services

3. Concern has been expressed (and correctly so) that not enough emphasis has been placed on obtaining clearer definitions of service levels. In addition, there has been a tendency to include both demand and supply factors in the expenditure function. See Musgrave (1968, pp. 572-574), Richardson (1969, p. 198). Recent attempts at quantifying service levels for housing, local health services, and highways can be found in S. P. Gupta and J. P. Hutton, "Economies of Scale in Local Government Services," Royal Commission on Local Government in England, Research Studies 3 (London: H. M. S. O., 1968).

performed by police officers rather than relying on population as a proxy for scale.

Per Capita Expenditures and Population

Hirsch (1959) presented one of the earliest studies using per capita expenditures and population. The following regression equation was estimated using a sample of sixty-four police departments in cities ranging from 200 to 865,000 residents in the St. Louis area.

$$X_1 = a + bX_2 + cX_2^2 + dX_3 + eX_4 + fX_5 \\ + gX_6 + hX_7 + iX_8 + jX_9 + kX_{10}$$

when,

X_1 = per capita total expenditures for police protection. X_2 = night-time population. X_3 = total miles of streets. X_4 = night-time population density per square mile. X_5 = percent of nonwhite population. X_6 = percent of night-time population under 25 years of age. X_7 = combined receipts of wholesale, retail and service establishments. X_8 = number of wholesale, retail and service establishments. X_9 = index of scope and quality of police protection. X_{10} = average per capita assessed valuation of real property.

Hirsch presented the following results:

$$b = 0.0000103$$
$$r12.2^2345678910 = -.180$$
$$c = +0.00000000000351$$
$$r12^2.2345678910 = +0.0589$$
$$R^2 = .90$$

From these results the author concluded that economies of scale were not indicated. As size of population increased, expenditures per capita did not vary significantly, other factors considered.

Studies involving per capita expenditures and population have several limitations. First, economies of scale in the private sector refer to declining long-run average cost as *scale* increases. The precise relationship between population and scale of police operations has yet to be determined. Second, since administrators are as frustrated as researchers in the area of quality measurement, they frequently employ measures such as police officers per capita as indices of manpower needs. If a city grows by 3,000 residents, police administrators may request two additional police officers so that a 1.5 officer to 1,000 population ratio can be maintained.[4] Since labor accounts for a large proportion of total police expenditures, a nearly constant ratio of expenditures to population is likely.[5]

Studies of expenditures per capita and population size may be more appropriate in planning for growth than in a "cost" sense. Two issues should be identified. The first concerns the declining cost curve (economies of scale). The second involves spreading total expenditures over a larger number of residents. These two concepts are conceptually different and an attempt should be made to distinguish between them.

With respect to the first issue, several important findings were reported by Schmandt and Stephens (1960) in a study of local governments in Milwaukee county. The authors used the number of activities performed by police departments as a measure of output. In this analysis, the number of activity categories was correlated with each of the following variables: (a) total population; (b) per capita current expenditures; (c) total current budget (debt service and capital outlay excluded); (d) population density per square mile; (e) age of municipality; (f) area in square miles; (g) equalized per capita property valuation; (h) percent of land area developed.

Although population was *not* significantly related to per capita expenditures, a positive correlation was found between the index of service and population. The highest correlation between the service index and population (.91) was found in the area of police protection. From these results the authors concluded that economies of scale were possible.

These findings are undoubtedly influenced by the organizational structure of the various police departments. For example, a similar service may be provided by two departments but one divides the operation into two distinct subfunctions. This analysis does

---

4. This point was suggested in a letter to the author, dated October 28, 1969, from an official of a state association of police administrators. Ratios as guides were subsequently reinforced in conversations with police officers in Illinois cities.

5. For a detailed listing of the composition of police expenditures, see Walzer (1971).

have the advantage, though, of explicitly considering service provided.

Average Cost and Technical Requirements

Another innovative approach to this area of investigation was reported by Robert E. Will. He determined the per capita cost of meeting technical standards for fire equipment and personnel provided by professional agencies. After regressing this per capita cost on city population, the author concluded ". . . there are significant economies of scale associated with the provision of municipal fire protection services, at standard levels of service, for central cities ranging from 50,000 to nearly one million in population" (1965, p. 60). As was pointed out, this approach relies heavily on standards suggested by the National Board of Fire Underwriters, etc. and these standards may have economies of scale already built into them (Will, 1965, p. 59).

METHODOLOGY

Police protection is a public service which is very difficult to measure. The exact relationship between police services (operations performed) and protection is not completely understood. At best it would seem that apprehension and resulting punishment is intended to serve as a deterrent to future crimes. Police protection, then, might be viewed in light of the tasks performed by police officers in their attempt to deter future offenses. The same general efforts are likely to be made in most cities, i.e. offenses and traffic accidents will be investigated, traffic flows will be regulated, preventive night patrols will be made, etc. This, of course, is not to say that police protection is of the same quality in all cities. In some cities, for example, a very low percentage of the reported offenses are cleared by arrest.

It seems reasonable, then, to study output or service provided by police departments through an analysis of the tasks which they perform. Using this approach one might assume that the solution of the same type of offense in two cities will provide essentially the same deterrent to future criminal acts in both cities. With data on the types of services performed by police officers one can study the unit cost as size of operations increases. Police departments are in reality multiproduct firms since there is more than one type of service provided.[6] A way must be found to combine the various activities so that a scale measure can be constructed.

The "index of service" used in this study is a composite of the number of offenses cleared, number of accidents investigated, and miles traveled by police vehicles.[7] Data on offenses cleared for nine major groups, on the number of traffic accidents investigated, and on the number of miles traveled by police vehicles were available for a sample of thirty-one Illinois cities with populations ranging from 22,000 to 143,000.[8] The miles traveled was used as a proxy for general police service.

Since offenses cleared, accidents investigated, and miles traveled are not comparable activities, a weighting system was needed. The number of occurrences of each component in the index was weighted by the amount of time spent by a police officer on an "average" task of each variety. Estimates of time spent were obtained from a study of the Berkeley police department (Benson and Lund, 1969). Comparable data for Illinois cities would have improved the analysis but were not available within the resources of this study.

The time spent on each type of activity was converted to twenty-minute units. For example, if an "average traffic accident" took 80 minutes of a police officer's time, it was given a weight of 4. Twenty traffic accidents investigated would count as 80 units in the index of service. In the case of miles traveled, an estimate of the average speed for a squad car on patrol was obtained from

6. See Johnston (1960, p. 94) for a discussion concerning the use of an index to quantify output for a multiproduct firm.

7. An index of this general variety has been used previously to study the impact of inflation on service levels. See John C. Bollens and Stanley Scott, *Effect of Inflation on City Costs and Services: Case Study of Berkeley, California* (Berkeley, Bureau of Public Administration, 1949). A preliminary study using an index of more limited scope is presented in Walzer (1972).

8. The categories include murder and non-negligent manslaughter, manslaughter by negligence, forcible rape, robbery, aggravated assault, burglary—breaking and entering, larceny—$50 and over, larceny—under $50, and auto theft. These specific classifications were used for collection purposes since they are the groupings employed by the Federal Bureau of Investigation.

the police records of an Illinois city with approximately 50,000 population. Miles traveled by police vehicles were then incorporated into the index.[9]

The activities index serves as our measure of scale. The cost of solving *particular types* of offenses in the different cities would have been useful, but the central interest in this study focuses on variations in average cost as the index of service increases.

Obviously, an index of this variety does not provide a cardinal measure of police service. A particular limitation of this technique is the indirect relationship with policy variables since a unit increase in the index of service may result from an increase in any of its components.

REGRESSION ANALYSIS

The following linear regression equation was used:

$$AC = a + b\,S + c\,S^2 + d\,Pd + e\,Pc + f\,CR + g\,W + h\,A$$

when

AC = average cost. S = scale of operations (index of service). Pd = population density. Pc = ratio of police officers to population. CR = ratio of offenses cleared by arrest to offenses reported. W = average wage paid to recruits. A = land area of the city in 1960.

a. *Average Cost:* Municipal police expenditures were divided by the index of service.

b. *Scale:* The economies of scale hypothesis will be accepted if a negative relationship, significantly different from zero, is found between the scale measure and cost. This variable has been

---

9. A question may arise with respect to the case of a very effective police force which, through efficient manpower allocation, reduces offenses to a minimum. This may be reflected in a high average cost figure. The service index includes miles traveled as a measure of general protction. To the extent that more patrols contribute to the reduction in offenses, this should be indicated as a larger service. The problem of inaccurate reporting has not been solved, however. In recent years better reporting procedures have been developed. More accurate reporting may cause an increase in the service measure. It was not possible to test for the accuracy in reporting in this sample, therefore it was assumed that differences among the cities did not significantly bias the results. One might expect any bias to be more serious with time series data than with cross-section data.

included in both first order and squared terms to test for a U-shaped average cost curve.

c. *Population Density:* The only available data on land area in these cities were from the 1960 Census. Consequently, the population figures for both 1958 and 1960 were divided by the 1960 estimate of land area to obtain a measure of population density. The rationale for including this variable is that it is more difficult to apprehend offenders in densely populated cities. These areas may include minority groups having close ties which make it easier for suspects to disappear. This situation will increase the cost of police protection as it is measured here.

d. *Ratio of Police Officers to Population:* The ratio of police officers to population is one proxy for the availability of police protection. A larger number of police officers per capita should afford a greater potential for service. This obviously measures input not output. Because miles traveled is a large component in the service index, the number of police officers per capita may be indicating differences between one- or two-man patrols. A municipality employing two-man patrols will exhibit a higher cost. This is not to say that two-man patrols are not more effective; it simply suggests that with the measure of police service in this study the added expense will raise the average cost.

On the other hand, the more officers available, the more opportunity there will be for residents to report offenses. Increasing the size of the force, then, may cause an increase in the number of offenses reported.[10] This would suggest a negative relationship between police per capita and "average cost."

e. *Percentage of Known Offenses Cleared by Arrest:* In a cost study attention must be paid to quality of service but as is well known, quality measures are very difficult to obtain.[11] The number of offenses cleared by arrest calculated as a percentage of total reported offenses was used in this study. The ratio was derived by constructing an index of the offenses cleared by arrest using

10. See Schur, E., *Crimes Without Victims* (Englewood Cliffs, Prentice-Hall, 1965).

11. For a detailed discussion of attempts to correct for quality, see Hirsch (1963).

the weights described above and dividing it by a similar index composed of the total reported offenses.

f. *Average Wage:* The average wage of patrolmen was included in the equation figuring that higher wages will attract recruits with greater potential. This, of course, requires sufficient mobility so that higher wages will attract better applicants for police training. If these conditions hold, one would expect a negative correlation between wages and average cost. This relationship may not be found for several reasons, however. First, because of the personal nature of police service, major productivity differences may not be discovered. Second, police officers may be productive in ways not reflected in the service index. Given these conditions, higher wages may show up as higher average costs.

g. *Area:* The land area of the municipality has been included to adjust for differences in physical size of the cities. Because the number of miles traveled by police constitutes a significant part of the service index, an adjustment must be made for the number of miles to be patrolled. For example, 25,000 miles traveled in a city with 25 miles of streets suggests that "an average mile" was traveled almost three times a day. In a city containing 100 miles of streets, the same total implies that an average mile was traveled only about once every day and a half.

Each of the variables has been discussed along with its rationale for being in the equation. The hypothesized relationships have also been indicated. It now remains to discuss the findings of the analysis.

EMPIRICAL RESULTS

The results of the regression analysis for 1958 and 1960 are shown in Table 15-I.[12] These years were chosen because they are contemporary with the studies discussed earlier. Later in the paper a model using per capita expenditures and population will be tested on this sample of Illinois cities. If economies of scale are found using the index, one wonders whether the economies

---

12. In line with the earlier discussion concerning the difficulties of measuring scale, Hirsch's notation "Quasi Long-Run Average Cost" has been adopted in Table 15-I.

TABLE 15-I

QUASI LONG-RUN AVERAGE COST CURVE

	Scale	[Scale]^a	Population Density	Police per Capita	Clearance Ratio	Wage	Area	
1958								
Coefficients	-.00008^b	.24E—08^a	.00052^b	3398.16^b	.386	.00038	.296^b	R^2 = .85
t-ratios	3.94^b	1.69	5.81^b	5.40^b	.52	1.88	5.65^b	SEE = .58
1960								
Coefficients	-.00010^b	.27E—08^b	.00077^b	2246.97^b	.563	.00018	.060^b	R^2 = .90
t-ratios	5.60^b	2.72^b	8.20^b	4.56^b	2.01	1.62	6.31^b	SEE = .53

[a] Numbers smaller than five digits to the right of the decimal are shown in computer notation.
[b] Significant at 5 percent level (two-tail test).

result from sample differences or from the way in which scale is being measured. If the latter is the case, then results consistent with earlier findings should be obtained when population and per capita expenditures are used.

The regression results in Table 15-I clearly support the economies of scale hypothesis since a significant negative relationship between scale and cost is indicated in both 1958 and 1960. However, the coefficients of the scale variables are quite small. In 1960 a significant positive relationship was indicated between average cost and the squared term suggesting some upward-bending of the cost curve.

A positive relationship exists between population density and average cost as was hypothesized. Increased population density suggests a higher average cost of police protection. This most likely results from closer social ties, as described earlier, and from increased traffic congestion which impedes police vehicles and slows down response time.

The number of police officers per capita is positively related to the cost measure. The relationship was significant at the 5 percent level in both years. This is to be expected since police expenditures consist largely of wages and salaries. A higher ratio of police officers to population shifts the cost curve upward.

The percentage of reported offenses which had been cleared by arrest was not significantly related to cost, but in both cases did exhibit the expected sign. Part of the difficulty with this variable is measurement error since the available data do not indicate when these offenses took place. An offense cleared by arrest in 1960, for example, might have taken place in 1958. This variable could have been markedly improved with a measure of the time which had elapsed between occurrence and arrest. The conviction ratio would also have been meaningful but it was not available for all cities.

In neither year was the average wage of patrolmen a significant explanatory variable. Several reasons may account for this behavior. First, higher wages may have attracted police officers with better attitudes when working with local residents but these traits were not revealed in the index. Second, mobility of labor may not have been sufficient so that higher wages, in reality, attract more qualified recruits. At any rate, in both years, the signs of the coefficient were positive and the coefficients were relatively stable—of the same order of magnitude.

The last variable used in the analysis, land area in the city, was significant at the 5 percent level in both years suggesting that the average cost was higher in those cities spread out over larger areas. It seems reasonable that patrol cars take longer to arrive at the scene of an offense in more dispersed cities. In addition, the number of substations is partially determined by the land area in the city since current police thinking seeks to reduce the time involved in transporting prisoners to the lockup.[13] Additional substations and administrative staff will raise the average cost of providing service.

As indicated in Table 15-I, these independent variables account for approximately 85 percent of the variation in the dependent variable. The standard error of estimate is about 50 cents with a mean average cost of approximately 5.17 dollars.

POLICE PER CAPITA AS A MEASURE OF SERVICE

Earlier, a discussion centering around the use of the number of police officers per capita as an indication of staff requirements was presented. One might question the appropriateness of this measure. If the clearance ratio used in the earlier analysis is a meaningful measure of police effectiveness, one would expect a significant correlation between number of police officers per capita and the clearance ratio. In neither 1958 nor 1960 was the simple correlation coefficient between police per capita and the clearance ratio significant at the 5 percent level. For 1958, the value was 0.061; and for 1960, it was 0.079. Several reasons could explain these results. First, a higher ratio of police officers may cause more offenses to be reported. The confidence of the citizens may be reinforced by the greater availability of police officers. This may tend to reduce the *percentage* which is cleared by arrest. Second, arresting one offender may cause another offense

---

13. This view is reflected in Wilson (1965). This source suggests that land area rather than population size is the major determinant of the number of substations. One would expect a significant positive correlation between land area and size of population, though.

to occur. Research suggests that placing one suspect in jail, in certain cases, leads to an illegal act by an associate to raise bail money.[14]

To summarize, in this sample of municipal police departments a significant correlation was not found between police officers per capita and the clearance ratio. This has interesting implications for per capita expenditure analyses. If the number of police officers per capita plays a significant role in determining necessary staff numbers, and if the ratio is fairly constant or increases with city size, expenditures per capita will remain nearly constant or increase.

POPULATION AND PER CAPITA EXPENDITURES

Since the findings from this statistical analysis differ considerably from those reported in earlier studies, an analysis was undertaken on this sample with per capita expenditures as a measure of cost and population as a measure of scale. The regression equations for 1958 and 1960 are shown in Table 15-II. Not all of the variables used in earlier studies were available for this sample, thus the results of the various studies are not completely comparable.

As is shown in Table 15-II, a significant relationship between per capita expenditures and population was found in neither year. The size of the coefficients is quite small in both instances and a negative relationship is indicated. These results are compatible with those reported by Hirsch, for example, in this same general period. The coefficient of the squared term was not significant in 1958 or 1960. This coefficient also changed sign.

The coefficient of population density was not significant in the first year but was significant in 1960. This may be explained partially by measurement error since the 1958 value had to be estimated while the figure in the second year was obtained from census data.

Police per capita and percentage of reported offenses cleared by arrest were included in the analysis as indices of quality. In all cases significant positive coefficients were found. Again, police

14. For further discussion of this point, see President's Commission (1967), p. 26.

TABLE 15-II

EXPENDITURE PER CAPITA FUNCTION

	Population	(Population)²	Population Density	Police per Capita	Percent Solved	Wage	Land Area	
1958								
Coefficients	-.0004	-.26E—13ᵃ	.00009	4437.17	1.14	.0008ᵇ	-.92	$R^2 = .90$
t-ratios	1.20	1.02	.48	9.58ᵃ	2.12	5.50ᵇ	.75	SEE = .46
1960								
Coefficients	-.0005	.20E—12ᵃ	.00049	2512.36	1.65	.0007ᵇ	.17	$R^2 = .90$
t-ratios	1.35	1.11	2.58ᵇ	5.50ᵇ	3.40ᵇ	4.86ᵇ	1.27	SEE = .47

ᵃ Numbers smaller than five digits to the right of the decimal are shown in computer notation.
ᵇ Significant at 5 percent level (two-tail test).

per capita may be measuring whether a department uses one- or two-man patrols. Expenditures per capita and police per capita are highly correlated because of the composition of police expenditures. The ratio of police officers to population might also be correlated with average wage. Police administrators have to choose between larger salaries for existing personnel and a larger police force.[15]

The findings of this analysis are compatible with earlier studies using population and per capita expenditures. This similarity leads one to believe that the conflicting findings between this analysis and that reported earlier using a scale index, result from differences in measures of scale and cost rather than variations between the samples.

The question which must be raised, then, involves the appropriateness of an index of scale vis-à-vis population. If the former is accepted, more research is clearly needed on the effectiveness of consolidating police departments in reducing costs.

Population as a measure of plant size does not consider police department activities unless one can measure how well police departments are meeting the demands of the population. On the other hand, our index of scale, with its measurement problems, does not encompass all activities performed by a police department. If nothing else, these findings should encourage further research to obtain better measures of police service and scale.

SUGGESTIONS FOR FURTHER RESEARCH

In police services one might expect that certain functions will be more likely to have declining costs than others. Record keeping, for example, would seem to be a likely candidate for cost-savings while general patrolling activities would not. As more refined and sophisticated measures are developed, these various activities might be separated. Certain activities could be consolidated while others remain decentralized. For example, allowing "hometown" police officers to patrol streets may give residents of smaller communities a feeling of security.

One approach with some potential is to study the cost of per-

15. The simple correlation coefficient between wages and police per capita was −.41 in 1958 and −.24 in 1960.

forming *a specific service* as the scale of operations increases. The various services of police departments would be studied individually. In other words, further disaggregate the services rendered by police.

CONCLUSIONS

In this paper we have constructed an index of service for police departments based on activities performed. This scale measure was then used to study average cost as size of operations increased. In 1958 and 1960, a significant negative relationship was found between average cost and scale. Because these findings differed markedly from those reported by other researchers with per capita expenditures and population, this analysis was performed on the sample of Illinois cities. The findings were compatible with those reported in earlier studies—no significant relationship between per capita expenditures and population.

The main conclusion of this paper is that because the scale variable plays such a crucial role in accepting or rejecting the economies of scale hypothesis, much more research is needed before we can dismiss consolidation as a possibility for cost-reductions in the provision of municipal police protection.

REFERENCES

Adams, W. F.: *The Structure of American Industry*. New York, The Macmillan Company, 1967.

Baumol, W. J.: Macroeconomics of unbalanced growth: the anatomy of urban crises. *American Economic Review*, LVII:414-426, 1967.

Benson, C. S., and Lund, P. B.: *Neighborhood Distribution of Local Public Services*. Berkeley, Institute of Governmental Services, 1969.

Heflebower, R.: Full costs, cost changes, and prices. *Business Concentration and Price Policy*. New York, National Bureau of Economic Research, 1955.

Hirsch, W. Z.: The supply of urban public services. In Perloff and Wingo (Ed.): *Issues in Urban Economics*. Baltimore, The Johns Hopkins Press, 1968, 477-526.

————: Quality of government services. In Schaller, H. G. (Ed.): *Public Expenditure Decisions in the Urban Community*. Washington, Resources for the Future, 1963, 163-180.

————: Expenditure implications of metropolitan growth and consolidation, *Rev Econ Statist*, XLI:232-241, 1959.

Johnston, J.: *Statistical Cost Analysis*. New York, McGraw-Hill, 1960.

Musgrave, R. A.: Discussion of part III. In Perloff and Wingo (Ed.): *Issues in Urban Economics.* Baltimore, The Johns Hopkins Press, 1968, 567-574.

President's Commission on Law Enforcement and Administration of Justice: *Challenge of Crime in a Free Society.* Washington, U.S. Government Printing Office, 1967.

President's Commission on Law Enforcement and Administration of Justice: *Task Force Report: The Police.* Washington, U.S. Government Printing Office, 1967.

Richardson, H. W.: *Regional Economics.* New York, Praeger Publishers, Inc., 1969.

Schmandt, H. J., and Stephens, G. R.: Measuring municipal output. *National Tax Journal, XIII:*369-375, 1960.

Scott, S., and Feder, E. L.: *Factors Associated with Variations in Municipal Expenditure Levels.* Berkeley, Bureau of Public Administration, University of California, 1957.

Walzer, N.: A price index for police inputs. *Journal of Criminal Law, Criminology, and Police Science,* Vol. 62, No. 2:270-75.

————: Cost of police protection and size of city: A note. *Economic and Business Bulletin,* Spring, 1972.

Wilensky, G.: Determinants of local government expenditures. In Crecine, John P. (Ed.): *Financing the Metropolis: Public Policy in Urban Economies.* Beverly Hills, Sage Publications, 1970, 197-218.

Will, R. E.: Scalar economies and urban services requirements. *Yale Economic Essays, V:* 3-60, 1965.

Wilson, O. W.: *Police Administration.* New York, McGraw-Hill, 1965.

Chapter 16

THE INTERDEPENDENCE OF MUNICIPAL AND COUNTY POLICE FORCES: AN ECONOMIC ANALYSIS

Julius A. Gylys

ABSTRACT—In our politically fragmented urban areas, sheriff's police services, like all municipal services, are distributed free of any direct charge. This study attempts to determine the optimal quantities of county police activity each political district should receive as well as their matching tax bills. The outcome of the analysis is pronouncedly influenced by the peculiar nature of externalities that occur in the provision of urban law enforcement services. Achievement of optimality conditions indicates an inverse relationship between sheriff's per capita expenditures and per capita tax base values of the participating political units.

T HE MOST RECENT CENSUS DATA have indicated that during the last decade a sizeable centrifugal population movement was taking place in the United States from the central cities. Assuming that per capita incomes continue to increase, the likelihood is great that the country's suburban population will continue to increase in the seventies.

The mounting outmigration is being met by increased demands for municipal police services. Metropolitan areas are experiencing a crime pandemic and already the rate of crime rise in the suburbs is exceeding that of central cities. Even though tax bases of some

Reprinted with permission from *The American Journal of Economics and Sociology,* Vol. 33, No. 1, January, 1974, pp. 75-88.

This article, which stems partly from the author's Ph.D. thesis, is also based on a paper presented in May 1972 to the National Urban Conference at Wayne State University, Detroit, Michigan. I gratefully acknowledge the financial assistance of Resources for the Future, Inc., which greatly eased the burden of this project.

suburban political units in per capita terms approach those of the central cities, many outlying areas do not possess a tax base big enough to support an adequate police department. This is particularly true for the unincorporated areas which share a common characteristic, that of low population density, one that makes adequate patrol activities extremely expensive. On the other hand, the incorporated areas during the last few decades evolved into microcosms of central cities. Emerging shopping plazas equipped with bank branch offices are becoming attractive new targets for the urban criminal world.

It is very likely that a large proportion of the outlying urban population will be turning to the county governments for the acutely needed protection services, through the sheriff's office or some equivalent form of county police. A question arises as to how the county sheriff's office should react to these new demands. It will be argued that if Samuelsonian efficiency considerations for allocation of public services are to be adhered to[1] the distribution of sheriff's services should be inversely proportional to the amounts of contributed county tax revenues by individual political units. The outcome of the analysis will be heavily influenced by the peculiar nature[2] of externalities that occur in the provision of law enforcement services.

CLASSIFICATION OF POLICE-GENERATED EXTERNALITIES

Municipal police department service, which is composed of numerous activities, possesses certain "indivisibility" characteristics attributable to public goods. Presence of the latter property gives rise to externalities in the provision of this public service. However, externalities do not arise from technical considerations

1. For a public good that is equally available for consumption by all, the necessary condition for its optimal production states that the sum of marginal rates of substitution for all persons consuming that good must equal the marginal cost of its production. For more details see Samuelson (1955).

2. According to Mishan (1971) this genre of externalities arises whenever one encounters what economists call a shared good. If a group of individuals purchase a service for its own consumption and if the service is simultaneously consumed by some other group without any diminution of benefits to the original group, the service is then classifiable as a shared good. For more details see F. J. Mishan, *Journal of Economic Literature,* March 1971.

in connection with the actual provision or production of law enforcement. A rather convincing argument for their presence could be found if one were permitted to examine municipal police activities from the consumption point of view. The concept of "indivisibility" implies inability to exclude noncontributing individuals from consumption of the service when it is provided by a political jurisdiction for the protection of its tax-paying residents. The resultant spillovers of benefits can be categorized into two separate divisions. The first category of externalities will be classified as intra-jurisdictional in nature and stem from direct consumption of police services. The second category will be referred to as an inter-jurisdictional set of externalities which tend to originate from indirect consumption of the law enforcement activity.

Once a political unit establishes a certain level of police activity for its residents, services become equally available to all persons present within the unit's jurisdictional boundaries.[3] This includes not only the residents of the political area who actually support the department's activities with their tax contributions, but also noncontributing individuals who reside in neighboring municipalities. The influx of "outsiders" varies rather predictably throughout a 24 hour workday cycle and is largely determined by the volume of commercial activity and the centrality of the political area under consideration. The visitors by their mere presence in a foreign political area become direct consumers of the area's police service. Since they receive the benefits of the local service just like the indigenous taxpayers, such spillovers will be classified as externalities of intra-jurisdictional nature.

Inter-jurisdictional externalities in the consumption of police services occur when the recipients of the benefits are not present within the producing area's political boundaries. Let us say that residents of the latter area are enjoying a certain level of police patrol activity. An arrest of a drunk driver by the area's police

---

3. In reality it is very likely that different parts of a city may be receiving different levels of police service, even if all of them are property tax contributors in support of this service. However, this does not detract from the following analysis. For a more detailed analysis of police input distribution within political area see Weicher (1971).

will confer benefits to many other political areas, assuming the driver was planning to drive through these areas. This means that residents of numerous neighboring political areas are directly consuming the benefits of the patrol services. Several criminological studies provide more concrete evidence of discrepancies between where offenders reside and where the corresponding crimes occur.[4] Crimes like forcible rape and miscellaneous robbery occurrences are apparently randomly distributed among the urban social areas. Target and offender areas are usually disassociated without presenting any distinguishable pattern of behavior. But the high occurrence rates for homicide, assault, and residential burglary in high-offender neighborhoods suggest that the assailants and victims are most likely to be local residents. Familiarity between offenders and their victims is strongly influential not only in crimes against persons but it also tends to precipitate illegitimate entry for purposes of theft. Knowing when the premises are occupied and unoccupied, how to get in and out of buildings without deception, when the watchmen make their rounds—all this information is more readily obtained in the criminal's own neighborhood than in other areas.

Yet when it comes down to business robbery, nonresidential day and night burglary, auto theft, and grand larceny, the association between ocurrence rates and the urbanization index[5] is rather strong, but quite low with the offenders' residences. Attraction of higher valued targets in neighborhoods other than the offenders' is influential for the criminal's inter-area activities. Then it is very likely that an arrest of a criminal from the latter category by a given area's police department will confer positive interjurisdictional externalities to the neighboring political units. This implies that residents of the adjacent areas are indirectly con-

4. This is the conclusion reached in the studies of intra-city distributions of crime occurrence. The most recent of these are: Sarah Boggs (1965), Calvin F. Schmid (1960a and 1960b). Prior to this are three very early studies: Clyde R. White (1932), Calvin Schmid (1937), and Stuart Lottier (1939). Also in Fulton County, adjacent to Toledo SMSA, 25 percent of the criminals arrested in 1970 resided in the central city county.

5. The urbanization index is based on the fertility ratio, proportion of single-family dwelling units, and proportion of women in the labor force. Sarah Boggs (1965), p. 905.

suming the benefits of the patrol service, as evidenced by a lower probability of becoming future victims of this mode of criminal behavior.[6] But a more comprehensive lesson to be learned from our two kinds of externalities is that where urban police services are provided by many separate departments, populations receive benefits not only from the police department which they finance with their own tax contributions but also from neighboring law enforcement organizations which they do not support in any possible fashion.

The argument for the generation of benefits could be seriously challenged if a spillout of criminal activity from the central city into adjacent political areas were to take place whenever a central city police department increased its input levels.[7] One recent study credits a police contention that a 40 percent increase in police manpower within a New York police precinct resulted in a decrease of 23.68 felonies per week.[8] However, in adjacent Central Park, felonies rose by 7.13 during the same period. Less dramatic increases took place in other neighboring precincts. Basically, the study asserted that in the more diligently patrolled precinct certain types of crime decreased, some were essentially unaffected, while others were partially displaced to adjacent precincts.

Presence of intra-city spillout of criminal activity under the above circumstances is not surprising. With only marginal geo-

6. Since the study's primary concern lies with efficient allocation of police inputs within overlapping urban police jurisdictions, it will not address itself to the more controversial discussion of how increased police inputs may affect urban crime rates. For that see President's Commission on Law Enforcement and Administration of Justice (1967).

In order to satisfy the study's objective, police output is defined in terms of probability for a resident of a given area to become a victim of crime per given unit of time. This means that relatively larger police outputs will be reflected in falling probabilities of becoming a victim of crime. For more details see Carl Shoup (1964).

7. As of September 1971, an introduction of a selective enforcement unit in Toledo's high crime districts resulted in no noticeable crime uprise in the suburban areas, according to chiefs of police of several larger suburban areas.

8. See S. J. Press. Professor Press used 20th Precinct's data. Readers should be warned that the validity of local police data is subject to question. Local departments are notorious for their lack of exactitude in the compilation of local crime information. Most frequently lack of complete accordance with fact is due either to carelessness or political expediency.

graphic moves, the degree of familiarity between offenders and their new targets is hardly affected. The expected cost for committing a crime through increased probability of getting arrested in an adjacent intra-city area rather than in a more distant inter-political area, hardly changes. With the higher police activity in a subpart of the indigenous area, a criminal by transplanting his activity to another neighborhood is simply trying to minimize the expected costs of operation. Surely, if central city police inputs were to increase by an unprecedentedly high amount, some crimes would spill out into the outlying areas. But a criminal's unfamiliarity with the neighborhood's physical layout and the residents' behavior pattern would make the ratio of crimes transplanted into suburban areas to crimes eliminated in the central city considerably lower than in the New York experiment. Furthermore, since our present metropolitan areas are marked by a high degree of fragmentization, the value of the above ratio of any particular suburban political unit would decline even to a substantially lower level than under less fragmented conditions. Suburban units with the lowest police inputs, *ceteris paribus,* would be the recipients of the greatest shares of the displaced activity. Thus even if some minuscule amounts of negative spillouts were to become realities, it is being maintained here that the overall net effect from both the direct and indirect consumption for any particular political unit would not be negative.

A similar argument is applicable to the subsequent analysis of sheriff's services. While the whole county stands to gain from the sheriff's police services, those political units which receive a greater percentage of the service have more to gain than the more neglected units. Nevertheless, the latter political units, either through direct or indirect consumption, are receiving a sizeable amount of benefits which spill over from the more favored areas.

OPTIMALITY CONDITIONS FOR LOCAL POLICE SERVICE LEVELS

The analysis is conducted within the framework of a one county metropolitan community which is composed of many political subareas. For any subarea, subsequently referred to as a community in contrast to county-community, police externalities can be specified with a community utility function depicting consumption of a collection of private goods, a set of police services provided in neighboring municipalities, and police activities enforced within its own jurisdictional boundaries. Then a utility function for political unit j can be defined in the following manner:

$$U^j = U^j (X_{1j}, X_{2j}, \ldots, X_{mj}, Y_1, Y_2, \ldots, Y_j, \ldots, Y_n)$$

In j's utility function, $X_{1j}, \ldots, X_{mj}$ denotes m separate private goods, and $Y_1, \ldots, Y_j, \ldots Y_n$ stands for police services in n communities, where Y_j represents police services provided within the jth political area. Our utility function includes police services performed within the jurisdictions of other municipalities because j residents, either by direct or indirect consumption, derive benefits from their provision. This means that residents of each political area have a positive marginal rate of substitution between another area's consumption of police services and the goods that it consumes itself. The optimality conditions[9] for any specific political subarea can be established by equating the sum of all such marginal rates of substitution to the marginal rate of transformation. For the provision of police services in the jth community the optimality condition can be stated as

$$\sum_{i=1}^{n} MU^i_{yj}/MU^i_r = C_{yj}/C_r$$

The term on the lefthand side of the equality represents the summation, including all n political units in the metropolitan area, of each community's marginal utility from police service Y_j to the marginal utility from some numeraire private good r. The ratio on the righthand side stands for the marginal cost of providing police protection in j community which is expressed in terms of the same numeraire good. The marginal rates of substitution between Y_j and the numeraire good summed over all political units in the county area must equal the marginal rate of transformation; or, summed marginal evaluations of Y_j service must equal the marginal cost in its provision.

---

9. For the approach in setting up the above optimality conditions I owe a great intellectual debt to Mark V. Pauly (1967).

When police services are being provided within a political area its residents are bound to receive the largest proportion of the benefits generated by that service. The immediate members of the community will experience a higher marginal evaluation for this service than the remaining county-community inhabitants, *i.e.* the marginal rate of substitution between the police service and the numeraire good will be lower for the latter groups. Nevertheless, these lower marginal rates of substitution express a positive marginal evaluation for the provided service. Presence of positive marginal evaluation for a neighboring political area's police services indicates that if provision of the service were left solely up to that area alone, external benefits to neighboring areas will be rendered.

At first glance, conceptual determination of optimum amount of police service for any municipality seems rather simple. Let us say that within area j a certain level of police activity is being enforced. If the remaining political units are evaluating positively an additional increment of this service, then all the remaining political areas should provide additional revenue for j's police budget, in addition to what j's residents already have contributed. Such subsidy would be provided until optimality condition is satisfied.

However, some complications may arise preventing the establishment of the optimality condition. These difficulties stem from the peculiar nature of reciprocal externalities[10] which occur in the provision of some public services. The extra amount of benefit from an additional amount of police protection that political unit j provides to the county-community depends on the level of police activity that j is consuming within its boundaries. But, on the other hand, the decision by j residents whether to maintain a given level of police services is greatly influenced by the existing enforcement levels in the remaining communities. Presence of reciprocal externalities creates the possibility that equilibrium will never be reached. The final outcome will be determined by the ability of the various political units to hide their real preferences or on their bargaining skills.

---

10. See Buchanan and Tullock (1965).

RELATIONSHIPS BETWEEN LOCAL AND COUNTY
POLICE ACTIVITIES

To examine the interrelation between maintaining of one's own local police and county police, it is desirable to go through the subsequent exercise. Assume, initially, that the county is not providing any sheriff services and all political units are charged with the responsibility to procure their own police. Then each political area will allocate its budget among police expenditures and private goods so that their respective utility functions will be maximized. This means that area j will behave so that $MU^i_{yj}/MU^i_r = C_{yj}/C_r$ is satisfied.

Professor Sacks's study suggests that per capita police expenditures have a tendency to vary directly with the per capita size of the tax base.[11] Political areas with higher tax bases are spending relatively larger per capita amounts than their counterparts which have lesser fiscal endowments. But if the local per capita police expenditures are extremely low for any particular area, it is very likely that the marginal benefits to the rest of the county from the additional sheriff's expenditures will be quite large.[12] Incorporated units, where relatively higher per capita tax bases are more typical, are spending relatively higher per capita amounts on local police services and already possess good quality police services. Consequently, for the latter areas, our county-community evaluates additional police services to be close to or at zero. Here high per capita police expenditures in the incorporated areas are providing benefits to the rest of the county in an inframarginal manner.[13] But for the unincorporated areas, which have low per capita tax bases and do not have any local police services or only very poor services provided by part-time police officers, the county-community evaluates additional services highly. Accordingly, the unincorporated areas should receive large supplements

11. Seymour Sacks and William F. Hellmuth, Jr. (1961).

12. Benefits to the county are interpreted as summed marginal evaluations of all political units except of the one that is receiving the additional services.

13. Let us say that a certain municipality already has a superior police department. But if that particular community still decides to increase its police budget and use this money to replace all the tires on the patrol cars with white sidewall tires, then the benefits that would accrue to the neighboring communities will be of inframarginal nature.

of sheriff's services. In this case the externalities are marginal, not inframarginal, and the county-community stands to gain high marginal benefits. Thus provision of sheriff's services should vary inversely with the size of the community's per capita tax base and should continue until the county-community evaluates the additional service increments to be of zero value.

An equilibrium relationship, marking Pareto optimal conditions, will take place only if all the political areas continue to spend the same amount of money on their local police services before any sheriff's services were provided to them. This is highly unlikely because of the inherent reciprocality in the generated externalities. Quite surely, some county police will be substituted for the local police, lending to a deviation from the equilibrium relationship. A lengthy process of expenditure adjustment and readjustment will be taking place and an equilibrium relationship defined by the equality of marginal evaluation summation to the MC of providing the service will be obtained only if some additional behavioral assumption for the political units are introduced.[14]

Let us continue the exercise but this time introduce an assumption that individual political units are not providing any local police services. Then the county will provide sheriff's services commensurably to the received county tax revenues. But if some subareas decide to augment the level of law enforcement within their own political boundaries by introduction of local police activities, such actions will be Pareto optimal. Expenditure contributions were made only by those areas which wanted to improve the services within their own jurisdictions. Political areas behaving this way will have increased their expenditures up to that point where their own marginal evaluation for an additional unit of police expenditure equals the marginal cost.[15]

But even if individual political units of the county are providing

---

14. Without any further behavioral assumptions it is impossible to specify the optimal expenditures that either party should make in order to satisfy the above equilibrium condition. This will be done in the following pages when community choice functions are established.

15. *I.e.* condition $U^1_{y_j}/U^1_r = C_{y_j}/C_r$ holds for all political areas behaving this way. The additional expenditures go for the subcontracted services from the sheriff's police department.

their own services in addition to that of the sheriff's, it is quite possible that some given evaluation of additional service still may be greater than the marginal cost, *i.e.*

$$\sum_{i=1}^{n} ME > MC.$$

In the above situation the county-community's marginal evaluation, even though lower now than it was before when subareas' local expenditures were zero, could very well still be positive. Then the latter inequality must still hold, indicating existence of nonoptimality. Since the county-community's evaluation for an additional unit of police service has a tendency to decrease the more a particular political unit is spending on its own, the sheriff, reacting to the county-community evaluation, will reduce his level of services.

When it was assumed that only local police expenditures and no county police expenditures were being made, removal of the latter restriction led to a decrease of local spending with accompanying increases of sheriff's expenditures. Similarly, when only county police outlays and no local expenditures were permitted, removal of this latter assumption caused a reduction of county funds with accompanying increases in local spending. One may conclude in our one county metropolitan area that a simple removal of sheriff's services or of local police services will not lead to any Pareto optimum but will most likely produce all kinds of adjustments and readjustments.

DETERMINATION OF OPTIMUM EXPENDITURE LEVELS

In order to determine optimal expenditure configurations for individual political areas, one must not only be enlightened on how each area will react when additional sheriff's services are offered to bolster local police forces, but he also must be able to define sheriff's reactions to given levels of local outlays. Such behavioral characteristics can be expressed with the help of choice functions—one for the county-community and one for each participating political unit—located in a plane defined by per capita sheriff and local police expenditures. Since there is substantial substitutability between local and county police services, all choice functions will have a negative slope.

But a county-community choice function, in contrast to the other ones, has several important characteristics of its own. Basically it intends to depict the sheriff's behavior who, in turn, is responding to the county-community's preferences. A sheriff is elected by the voters residing within the political area of the county. Desiring to retain and perpetuate his position, the sheriff, it is assumed, will act in such a way that preferences of the county's residents are reflected in his official actions. The inhabitants of the county, who are direct or indirect consumers of each other's political services, must have some preconceived notion what the minimum level of per capita police expenditures should be in every political unit. This amounts to assuming that the demand curve for overall police protection within the county's jurisdictional limits is perfectly inelastic in the relevant range and that the income effect on the metropolitan county-community choice function from various levels of police services with local political jurisdiction is zero.

Function NM is our metropolitan county-community choice function. According to the above assumption that residents of our one county-community area have certain predetermined notions what the "standard" level of police protection in any political areas should be, the absolute slope of the function will be equal to unity. Figure 16-1 shows that the lowest possible per capita expenditures that the community "standard" will allow is ON, where ON = OM. Consequently a political area without any local police force will receive sheriff's services which will amount to ON level. But if it has a local department and is already spending OM amount or more, it will not receive any services from the sheriff's department at all.

Before we can determine expenditure levels for political areas using both police services, characteristics of choice functions pertaining to individual political units must be examined. They can be either linear or curvalinear and have a slope that is greater than unity. This is so because police service possesses the proper-

ACHIEVEMENT OF UTILITY MAXIMIZING EXPENDITURE LEVELS

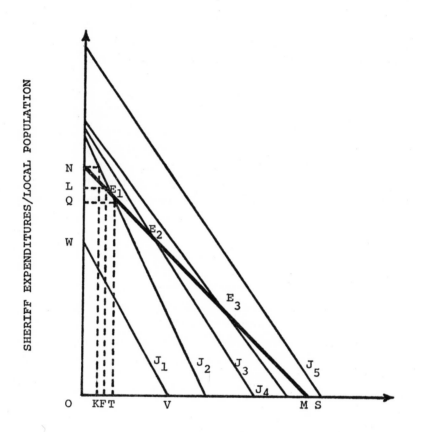

LOCAL POLICE EXPENDITURES/LOCAL POPULATION

Figure 16-1

ties of a normal good[16] and each political unit will want more of a police service for which it does not have to pay than of the local police force for which it must pay the full marginal cost. The po-

16. Police service is called a normal good because political units have a tendency to increase per capita police expenditures with corresponding increases in the assumed evaluation of the tax base. See Seymour Sacks and William Hellmuth, Jr. (1961).

sition of a political area's choice function is basically determined by its fiscal strength. According to Figure 16-1, political area with choice functions J_5 is capable of spending more than the minimum required standard of ON, while its counterpart with functions J_1 can afford only OV. Since the per capita size of a tax base is a predominant influence in determining the level of per capita police expenditures, then the above arrangement of functions J_1, J_2, J_3, J_4, J_5 must be in an ascending order of county equalized property evaluation. Choice functions closest to the origin must represent political units characterized by low tax bases, *e.g.* unincorporated areas and villages, while the ones further out and beyond the metropolitan choice function must belong to incorporated areas which have relatively higher fiscal bases.

Presently we are ready to determine how any particular area, after receiving a given level of sheriff's services evaluated at certain lump sums of money, will start readjusting its own police expenditures. Diagrammatically such adjustments can be demonstrated by movements along the political unit's choice function until the utility maximizing local expenditure level is reached. Let us use J_2 political area's choice function to illustrate in greater detail the mechanics of attaining a utility maximizing equilibrium. As it is shown in the illustration, J_2 residents are enjoying police protection services rendered by both departments. If for some reason J_2 decides to cease the provision of local service, it will receive the "standard" ON level of service from the sheriff's department. But J_2 area's choice function is such that if ON is provided by the sheriff, it will be willing to procure OK level of local services on its own. Willingness of J_2 to provide local services decreases the community's marginal evaluation for additional service and, consequently, the sheriff's department will decrease its expenditures to the OL level. This process of adjustment and readjustment will continue but, in the meantime, we will be drifting toward an equilibrium situation E_1. Equilibrium is defined as the point where metropolitan and J_2 choice functions intersect each other. Here per capita police expenditures by local authorities and by the sheriff's department are OT and OQ, respectively. Marginal evaluation of the metropolitan county-community for additional police protection is zero and that of J_2 community equals its marginal cost. If J_2 area were to receive any higher level of police services than indicated by E_1 equilibrium, the community's marginal evaluation of such additional expenditures would be zero and that of political area J_2 would be less than the marginal cost. In order to reach the optimal situation, a reduction in police services would be required. On the other hand, if J_2 is enjoying police services designated by some amount less than the equilibrium calls for, the metropolitan community would evaluate additional police service positively. Also J_2 area's marginal evaluation would exceed the marginal cost, indicating a need for expansion of services in order to recapture the optimality conditions.

Equilibrium per capita expenditures for the next two political areas and the respectively corresponding sheriff's contributions are similarly established by the intersection of their choice lines with the metropolitan community choice function at E_2 and E_3. For a low per capita tax base area like J_1, which does not want to or can afford to provide only OV local police activities, the sheriff's department will be the sole provider of police services which will be generated at the minimally acceptable ON level. On the other hand, for a high per capita tax base community like J_5 whose choice function does not intersect the metropolitan community's choice function, no sheriff's services will be provided. Such a relatively wealthy community will be willing to spend OS amount on its local residents.

In order to satisfy Pareto efficiency conditions, there is a call for sheriff's expenditures to be allocated in inverse proportions to the per capita tax bases of the participating political units. For political areas with relatively large enough bases to provide themselves the "standard" level of services, the sheriff should optimally provide none. At the other extreme, for units which have such small tax bases that they cannot provide any local services at all or only services below the county's desired standard, the optimal sheriff's expenditures should be equivalent to the minimal standard level. Lastly, for political units which are in between the above extremes, the sheriff's contributions, in order to establish the optimum relationship, should vary inversely with the amount provided locally.

Even though no fine data are presently available to back up the results of our analysis, some empirical information in support of the basic theoretical implications was located in Wayne County, Michigan.[17] With the cooperation of the county sheriff's department, it was possible to determine how this organization allocated its patrol and detective investigative services among the incorporated and unincorporated political units.[18] A thorough analysis was made of the road patrol and detective investigative records listing responses to requests for service during the period of January to November, 1962. The contents of these records revealed the nature of the service supplied and whether the incident took place in an incorporated or an unincorporated political unit. The incorporated areas, with an average per capita tax base of $6,407, received 7 percent of motorized road patrol and 10 percent of the detective services, while the unincorporated units, with an average per capita tax base of $4,272, obtained 93 percent and 90 percent of each service respectively.[19] Even though the unincorporated areas were the recipients of the substantially more generous share of the services, they financed only 9 percent of these activities through their county tax contributions.

CONCLUSION

In order to maximize the benefits in the consumption of urban police services in our fragmented metropolitan areas, it is imperative that the fiscally deprived political units start receiving more adequate county police services. In 1971 crime increased fastest—11 percent—in suburban areas, compared with 10 percent in rural areas and 5 percent in cities with more than 25,000 population.[20] Communities with more sumptuous tax bases should be charged with the bill of these services. Our urban areas al-

17. Detroit, Michigan is located in Wayne County.

18. In Michigan all cities and villages are classified as incorporated and townships as unincorporated areas.

19. For the same period the average county equalized valuations of incorporated and unincorporated areas were $234,840,000 and $17,279,000 respectively. All the final information was obtained from Wayne County Auditors, 400 Woodward Avenue, Detroit 26, Michigan.

20. This was announced March 30 by the then Acting Attorney General Richard G. Kleindienst on the basis of preliminary figures in the Uniform Crime Reports of the Federal Bureau of Investigation for 1971.

ready have the administrative machinery to execute such policies. In order to achieve Pareto optimality the county sheriffs will have to start acting more like modern day Robin Hoods—take the money collected in fiscally superior political areas and spend it in the relatively more deprived ones. Only this kind of behavior by county's law enforcement organizations will enable our metropolitan communities to reap the highest marginal benefits from extra dollars spent.

REFERENCES

Boggs, Sarah: Urban crime patterns. *American Sociological Review*, 30:899-908, 1965.

Buchanan, J. M., and Tullock, Gordon: Public and private interaction under reciprocal externalities. In Margolis, J. (Ed.): *The Public Economy of Urban Communities*. Washington, Resources for the Future, 1965, pp. 52-73.

Lottier, Stuart: Distribution of criminal offenses in metropolitan regions. *Journal of Criminal Law and Criminology*, 29:37-50, 1939.

Mishan, F. J.: The postwar literature on externalities: an interpretive essay. *Journal of Economic Literature*, March, 1971.

Pauly, Mark V.: Mixed public and private financing of education: efficiency and feasibility. *American Economic Review*, March 1967, p. 120.

President's Commission on Law Enforcement and Administration of Justice: *The Challenge of Crime in a Free Society*. Washington, U.S. Government Printing Office, 1967, p. 98.

Press, S. J.: Some Effects of an Increase in Police Manpower in the 20th Precinct of New York City, The University of Chicago, an unpublished study.

Sacks, Seymour, and Hellmuth, William F., Jr.: *Financing Government in a Metropolitan Area*. New York, Free Pr, 1961, p. 131.

Samuelson, Paul: Diagrammatic exposition of a theory of public expenditures. *Review of Economics and Statistics*, November 1955, p. 35.

Schmid, Calvin: *Social Saga of Two Cities*. Minneapolis, Minneapolis Council of Social Agencies, 1937, pp. 334-41.

———: Urban crime areas: part I. *American Sociological Review*, 25:527-542, 1960a.

———: Urban crime areas: part II. *American Sociological Review*, 25:655-678, 1960b.

Shoup, Carl: Standards for distributing a free government service: crime prevention. *Public Finance*, No. 4, 1964, p. 383.

Weicher, John: The allocation of police protection by income class. *Urban Studies*, November, 1971, p. 207.

White, Clyde R.: The relation of felonies to environmental factors in Indianapolis. *Social Forces*, 10:498-509, 1932.

Chapter 17

EVALUATING EVERYDAY POLICIES: POLICE ACTIVITY AND CRIME INCIDENCE

E. TERRENCE JONES

DONALD T. CAMPBELL's (1969) seminal essay on policy evaluation has rightfully received much attention among policy-oriented social scientists. It has reminded us all how our methodologies, especially quasi-experimental designs, can be used to discover whether governmental actions are achieving their avowed purposes. Hitherto, however, this type of analysis has been applied to major shifts in policy (Weiss, 1972, pp. 357-361). Campbell and Ross (1968), for example, have studied the 1955 Connecticut crackdown on automobile speeding; another major analysis (Caporaso and Pelowski, 1971) examined the impact of the European Economic Community on economic and political integration.

Since sharp policy changes provide strong independent variables whose effect(s) should be, in principle, easily detected, this concentration is quite understandable. Mankind is continually testing the proposition that it can purposively deal with the social world, that, in Deutsch's (1963) terms, it can assume the helmsman role of cybernetic theory. In evaluating man's capability to achieve "the active society" (Etzioni, 1968), it makes some sense to examine nonincremental changes first.

Most governmental actions, however, are incremental adjustments, not dramatic changes. Within this set of small shifts, the most common and regular governmental actions are changes in expenditure and manpower levels. At constant intervals—usually

Reprinted, with permission of Sage Publications, from *Urban Affairs Quarterly*, Volume 8, No. 3, March 1973, pp. 267-279.

annually—governments must decide whether to increase, hold constant, or decrease expenditures and personnel for a wide set of agencies. Many of these activities (e.g. police and fire protection) have relatively clear goals (e.g. minimize crime and fire damage). Thus, we can view many of these budgetary and personnel decisions as quasi-experiments, as adjustments made in a treatment variable in order to bring about a desired change in one or more dependent variables. In order that the quasi-experimental approach have the widest possible applicability to constructing more effective public policies, it should be extended to as many of the everyday incremental changes as possible.

Unfortunately, taking the incremental adjustments one by one, a quasi-experimental approach is not that fruitful, since, for any single case, the impact of small changes in the independent or treatment variable could be overwhelmed by other events. Say, for example, Boston increased the number of uniformed policemen by 10 percent between 1966 and 1967 and the number of auto thefts went down 15 percent whereas, in the same period, Cleveland's uniformed police manpower remained constant and its auto thefts increased slightly. Although one can infer from this test that an increase in police manpower caused a decrease in auto thefts, there are several other plausible rival hypotheses; for example, some other factor (e.g. a theft prevention advertising campaign) was present in Boston and absent in Cleveland, and that factor is the primary cause.

Moreover, the three time-series designs (interrupted time series, multiple time series, regression discontinuity analysis; Campbell and Stanley, 1966, pp. 37-43, 55-57, 61-64) used to evaluate major policy changes are not that appropriate in the incremental context. All these designs work best when there are three or four time-series observations both before and after the reform. One then examines the difference between the prereform and postreform trends of the data points, both alone and, where possible, compared with control group trends, in order to arrive at a conclusion concerning policy impact. For the incremental changes, however, the reforms occur too frequently to generate a lengthy time series. Using Campbell and Stanley's symbols—0's for dependent variable measurements and X's for occurrences of the independent variable, with 0 subscripts indicating time and X subscripts representing different levels of the independent variable—the interrupted time-series representation is:

$$O_1 \; O_2 \; O_3 \; X \; O_4 \; O_5 \; O_6$$

whereas the incremental change situation is:

$$O_1 \; X_3 \; O_2 \; X_1 \; O_3 \; X_2 \; O_4$$

Clearly, we cannot use the time-series model to evaluate the impact of incremental changes; inter alia, there are simply not enough dependent variable observations before and after the occurrence(s) of the independent variable. Nor, since the policy change is typically not that substantial, can we confidently make conclusions based on one or two instances. What we can do instead is to take a large number of budgetary and manpower changes having a reasonable amount of variability and test whether, for the entire set, changes in the avowed goal (e.g. auto thefts) tend to be associated with changes in the independent variable (e.g. uniformed police manpower).

In a sense, what is being suggested is a variant of the widely used nonequivalent control group design. That design, in its pure form,

> involves an experimental group and a control group both given a pretest and a posttest, but in which the control group and the experimental group do not have pre-experimental sampling equivalence. Rather, the groups constitute naturally assembled collectives such as classrooms, as similar as availability permits but yet not so similar that one can dispense with the pretest. The assignment of X to one group or the other is assumed to be random and under the experimenter's control [Campbell and Stanley, 1966, 47].

Since, in most instances, we cannot randomly assign X (the treatment or independent variable), we must compensate for this deficiency and attempt to recapture in part the virtues of randomization by examining impact for a large number of roughly similar groups (e.g. large cities). In addition, in dealing with expenditure and personnel changes, the treatment variable is not simply present or absent, but instead assumes a wide range of values.

Using the same symbols, we can represent this adjusted design as

$$
\begin{array}{ccc}
O_1 & X_2 & O_2 \\
O_1 & X_1 & O_2 \\
O_1 & X_0 & O_2 \\
O_1 & X_{-1} & O_2 \\
O_1 & X_{-2} & O_2
\end{array}
$$

The above design also bears some similarity to the equivalent time-samples design (Campbell and Stanley, 1966, pp. 43-46).

This adapted design is, of course, far from foolproof. For example, because the treatment variables' values are not randomly assigned, there is no assurance that some uncontrolled and unmeasured factor is not contaminating the results. Nonetheless, this approach's major assumption—if expenditure or personnel changes for an agency or program are having an impact on some goal, then, for a large number of cases, there should be a noticeable relationship between changes in expenditures or personnel and changes in some measurement(s) of the goal—seems viable.

In this paper, this mode of analysis is applied to the impact that year-to-year changes in police protection expenditures, uniformed police manpower, and civilian police manpower have on year-to-year changes in the rates for eight types of crime (murder, forcible rape, aggravated assault, robbery, burglary, grand larceny, petty larceny, and auto theft) in the 155 American cities with a 1968 population greater than 100,000. These impacts will be examined for the one-year changes between 1958 and 1970 for the manpower factors and between 1959 and 1969 for the expenditure variable. Although city officials frequently act as if increasing police expenditures and personnel will decrease crime incidence (or at least lessen the rate of crime increase), this proposition has yet to receive a systematic test based on a large number of cases.

The most serious obstacle confronting any attempt to assess the impact of changes in police activity on changes in crime incidence involves the process by which crime has been measured in the United States. The standard source of crime data— the Federal Bureau of Investigation's annual *Uniform Crime Reports* (UCR)—has been the subject of several criticisms (Biderman and Reiss, 1967; Ostrom, 1971; President's Commission on Law Enforcement and Administration of Justice, 1967). The three most relevant defects of the FBI's measurement procedures for this study are the unknown relationship between the number of reported crimes (i.e. the number given in UCR) and the number of true crimes (i.e. the number actually committed) for any type of crime; the degree of unreliability caused by allowing each jurisdiction to be the principal data collector; and the use of population as a base for all types of crime.

Since, in the short run, there is no way of knowing the precise relationship between changes in reported and true crime rates, we must assume here that there is a positive relationship between the two: the greater the increase (decrease) in the reported rate for each city, the greater the increase (decrease) in the true rate. In order to lessen the possible pitfalls of making this assumption, the crime rate changes will be treated as ordinal variables with moderately broad categories: decrease ($< -25\%$), small decrease (-25% to -0%), small increase ($+0\%$ to $+10\%$), moderate increase ($+11\%$ to $+50\%$), and large increase ($> +50\%$).

Despite the FBI's efforts to standardize reporting practices, differences in data collection procedures undoubtedly exist among cities. In this analysis, however, the focus will be on within-city changes; there will be no direct comparison of crime rates between cities, thereby lessening the reliability problem. Reliability lapses still remain, however, since there have been some changes in reporting practices within cities from one year to the next; fortunately, these instances are far outnumbered by cases where the same reporting practices prevailed.

In computing the rate for any type of crime the most common base employed is the number of inhabitants in a particular jurisdiction. Although this denominator might be the best for certain crimes (e.g. murder), other bases are more appropriate for other indicators (Boggs, 1965); examples include number of females for forcible rapes and number of automobiles for auto thefts. Unfortunately, the individual investigator has no capability of collecting these data on a longitudinal basis for a large number of cities. Hence, we must assume that the year-to-year changes in the number of inhabitants are directly proportional to annual changes in the more appropriate populations-at-risk.[1] The dangers of making this assumption for this study are lessened somewhat by only dealing with one-year changes. In a one-year period, substantial changes in any base (e.g. number of automobiles) are the exception and not the rule.

The manpower figures are also from the UCR, while the expenditure data are from the U.S. Bureau of the Census' *City Government Finances*. As is the case with the crime data, any unreliability effects caused by any differences in cities' reporting practices are lessened by only using these data to calculate within-city changes. All three variables are per capita, the expenditure data are expressed in constant dollars, and changes in manpower and expenditure levels are treated as five-category ordinal variables. For the two manpower variables, the intervals are less than −2.5%, −2.5% to −0.0%, +0.0% to +2.5%, +2.6% to +7.5%, and greater than +7.5%; for the expenditure variable, the five categories are less than −5.0%, −5.0% to −0.0%, +0.0% to +5.0%, +5.1% to +10.0%, and greater than +10.0%.

Since personnel changes almost invariably mean expenditure changes, these three factors are not viewed as three independent dimensions but rather as three interrelated measurements of a single concept: police activity. Using multiple measurements increases confidence that the larger concept—police activity—is being tapped; if changes in police activity are related to changes in rates for a certain crime, then at least one of the measures of police activity should reveal that relationship.

Having specified indicators for police activity and crime incidence, the two now need to be linked temporally. Given a change in police activity and assuming police activity influences crime incidence, how much of a lag will there be between the occurrence of the cause (e.g. a 5% increase in uniformed policemen per capita) and the occurrence of the effect (e.g. a 10% decrease in auto thefts per capita)? Our choices as to lags which can be tested are limited by society's record-keeping practices. Both ex-

---

1. A city's population for years between decennial censuses is estimated by a linear interpolation from the census figures.

penditures and crimes for cities are aggregated for one-year periods although, as will be discussed below, the periods do not always coincide. Manpower data, on the other hand, are given for a certain day (e.g. December 31) at one-year intervals. Hence, the effective lag time alternatives tend to reduce to one-year units: the effects are primarily felt in the same year the causal change occurs, in the next year, in the next year plus one, and so on. Since it is both desirable and plausible that police activity changes should influence crime incidence within a relatively short time after the activity changes occur, a lag interval of less than one year is examined here; we will, for example, test the impact of an increase in police expenditures between 1/1/64 to 12/31/64 and 1/1/65 to 12/31/65 by seeing whether the various 1965 crime indices are lower than the comparable 1964 indices.

As mentioned above, the expenditure, manpower, and crime data are not always temporally comparable in their original format. First, the expenditure data are for fiscal years, the dates of which differ from city to city; the crime data, conversely, are reported by calendar years. When a city uses the calendar year for its fiscal accounting—as a majority of cities in this study do—comparability exists. When a city's fiscal year differs from the calendar year, the expenditure and crime data must be brought into a common line. If the fiscal year is, for example, 7/1/64 to 6/30/65, then a crime figure for this same period is calculated by averaging the 1964 and 1965 per capita rates, weighting each rate equally since there are the same number (six) of months from each calendar year; if the fiscal year is 9/1/64 to 8/31/65, the 1965 crime figures are weighted twice as much as the 1964 data since the fiscal year has two times more months in 1965 than in 1964.

Second, unlike the expenditure and crime data, the manpower figures are not aggregated for an entire year but instead are given as of a certain date: April 30 in 1958 and 1959 and December 31 for 1960 through 1970. It is assumed that the April 30 figures are satisfactory estimates for typical 1958 and 1959 manpower levels; the estimates for typical 1960 to 1970 manpower levels are computed by averaging the year-end figures for the current and preceding years (e.g. the 1962 estimate is the arithmetic mean of the 12/31/61 and the 12/31/62 figures), with the 4/30/59 figures considered as the preceding year-end data for the 1960 estimates.

FINDINGS

The twelve one-year changes in uniformed and civilian manpower levels (1958-1959 to 1969-1970) for the 155 cities can generate 1,860 (12 × 155) separate tests for each of the eight categories of crime; the ten one-year changes in expenditure levels (1959-1960 to 1968-1969) can produce 1,550 individual tests for each type of crime. Treating the variables more generically—three police activity indicators and eight crime measures—there are potentially 42,160 separate instances where the impact of changes in police activity on changes in crime incidence can be examined. Missing data reduce this total by about 15 percent (i.e. to approximately 36,000), but this remains a substantial data base.

What, then, do these slightly more than 36,000 quasi-experiments reveal about the influence of police activity changes on crime incidence? Uniformly, they indicate that year-to-year changes in expenditures, uniformed police manpower, and civilian police manpower have virtually no relationship with year-to-year changes in murder, forcible rape, aggravated assault, robbery, burglary, grand larceny, petty larceny, and auto theft rates. To the very minimal extent that a relationship sometimes exists, that association is positive; for example, as can be seen in Table 17-I, there is a slight tendency for annual increases in manpower levels to be accompanied by annual increases in robbery rates. This relationship, it must be added, is the strongest (i.e. highest absolute correlation) of all 24 combinations of the three police activity indicators and the 8 crime measures.

We cannot unambiguously interpret these results as meaning that changes in police activity have little or no impact on changes in crime incidence. In order to make that conclusion a safer one, there should be no instances where an increase in police activity is accompanied by a decrease in crime incidence; but, as Table 17-I indicates, such situations exist. Are these instances simply

TABLE 17-I

UNIFORMED POLICE MANPOWER AND ROBBERY CHANGES IN
AMERICAN CITIES, 1958-1959 TO 1960-1970[a]

Manpower		Annual Percentage Change Robberies					
	<-25	-25 to -0	$+0$ to $+10$	$+11$ to $+50$	$>+50$	Total	n
<-2.5	32	15	7	15	30	99[b]	369
-2.5 to -0.0	7	32	13	34	14	100	256
$+0.0$ to $+2.5$	9	20	17	41	13	100	431
$+2.6$ to $+7.5$	5	26	13	39	18	101	403
$>+7.5$	19	15	8	21	37	100	253

[a] See text for variable and case definitions.
[b] Because of rounding, totals do not always equal 100%.

the product of chance (i.e. if both police activity and crime incidence indicators go up and down, a solely chance-based distribution would include some police activity up, crime incidence down cases) or are there certain condition(s) which, when present, encourage successful (i.e. police activity up, crime incidence down) outcomes and, when absent, inhibit successful impacts? Since the set of possible conditions is effectively infinite, the definitive test cannot be performed. Nevertheless, we can probably make a better decision by specifying certain conditions likely to affect the distribution of successful and unsuccessful outcomes and seeing how the values of these conditional variables relate to these distributions.

The four city-level indicators chosen for the conditional analysis are 1960 population (less than 250,000, 250,000-500,000, greater than 500,000); 1959 median family income (less than $5,500, $5,501-6,200, greater than $6,200); percentage of population change between 1960 and 1970 (less than −10%, −10% to +10%, greater than +10%), and the Clark Index of Governmental Reformism (Clark, 1971: 300). The last indicator credits a city with one point for each of the three reform governmental structures (professional city manager, at-large constituencies, nonpartisan elections) which it possesses; hence, it ranges from zero (highly unreformed) to three (highly reformed). As before, these vari-

ables—even though they could be viewed as interval measures—
are treated ordinally because our modest purpose is to see whether, within broad categories of these conditional variables, the
success-failure ratio of outcomes differs. Finally, these four factors were selected not so much because, a priori, one might expect particular scores on each to encourage successful outcomes,
but more because they tap four important elements of a city's
environment: size, economic resources, speed of change, and
governing structure. If conditional factors exist, then the likelihood is high that they are aspects of one or more of these broad
concepts.

To ascertain the relevance of each conditional factor, the distribution of successful (uniformed police manpower up, crime
incidence down) and unsuccessful (uniformed police manpower
up, crime incidence up) outcomes was determined for each category of the conditional variable.[2] If the conditional variable matters, then the bivariate relationship between the conditional variable and the success-nonsuccess distribution should depart from
statistical independence. A difference of 10 percent or more in the
proportion of successes between any two categories is regarded
as worth noting. (For those preferring significance tests, even
though these cases do not constitute a probability sample, a 10
percent difference corresponds quite closely with a chi-square
significant at the .05 level.)

The only differences exceeding 10 percent involved the population size and population change variables. Increases in uniformed manpower are accompanied by decreases in murder,
forcible rape, aggravated assault, and robbery more frequently
in smaller (i.e. less than 250,000) than in the largest (i.e. greater
than 500,000) cities; for these four types of crime, the smaller
city success rate is anywhere from eleven to nineteen percentage
points higher than the 500,000-plus cities' rate and six to nine
points higher than the intermediate (250,000-500,000) cities'

2. Cases where police activity decreased are set aside for this portion of the
analysis. Since the purpose here is exploratory, since all three police activity
variables are positively correlated, and since uniformed manpower shifts are
probably the most frequently suggested anti-crime police activity, only the uniformed manpower increases are reported here.

rate, with the smaller cities' success rates ranging from 35 percent (robbery) to 48 percent (murder).

Uniformed manpower increases are associated with murder, robbery, and auto theft decreases more frequently in growing (i.e. 1960-1970 population increase greater than 10%) than in constant (i.e. 1960-1970 population change between plus-or-minus 10%) or declining (i.e. 1960-1970 decrease less than minus 10%) cities. The success rate differences between growing and declining cities range from eleven to fourteen percentage points, the gap between growing and constant cities goes from four to ten percentage points, and the success rate for growing cities is around 40 percent for all three types of crime.

Since there is a relatively high negative correlation between cities' 1960 population and their percentage of population change between 1960 and 1970, it is difficult to disentangle the relative importance of each factor. Examination of the differences in the bivariate correlations and analyses controlling, respectively, for each factor suggest, however, that population size is probably the more important condition.

Even though increases in uniformed police manpower are somewhat more likely to decrease most types of personal crime in smaller cities, the major conclusion to be drawn from the conditional analysis is that the conditions are irrelevant in most instances and that, even where success rate differences occur, distinctions are not that large. Thus, it becomes more credible that the original lack of an overall relationship between police activity changes and crime incidence shifts is more the result of a chance distribution of truly unrelated factors than the product of two or more offsetting conditional relationships.

CONCLUSION

Broadly speaking, there are at least two conclusions which are compatible with these results. One can conclude, first, that these findings accurately describe the real world and that changes in police activity have virtually no impact on changes in the incidence of the eight types of crime considered here. Conversely, one can reason that the more-police-activity-equals-less-crime theory has yet to receive an adequate test, primarily because of the crime measurement problems outlined earlier. It could be, for example, that two things tend to happen when police activity increases: more crimes are reported because there are more resources (e.g. more policemen) to report them, and more crimes are prevented because there are more resources to prevent them. Taken together, these two tendencies might cancel each other, thereby yielding a net zero relationship between police activity and crime incidence. Indeed, one might use precisely this line of reasoning to argue that this study's results, which tended to show a very slight positive relationship between changes in police activity and shifts in crime incidence, actually indicate that, once an unknown over-reporting factor is removed, police activity changes are negatively associated with crime incidence shifts.

Since, however, the thousands upon thousands of quasi-experiments which large American cities have conducted in the recent past fail to reveal any systematic impact, the burden of proof now rests even more with those who claim that changing police activity levels is the best way to cope with crime. The first conclusion, after all, is a finding based on the best available evidence; the second remains a possibility which has some a priori persuasiveness but has yet to be put to the test. In any event, since the active society requires both theories which can predict the consequences (e.g. change in crime incidence) of policies (e.g. change in uniformed police manpower) and measurements which permit quick and accurate feedback about the impact of policies, neither conclusion speaks well of the current society's capability of controlling its affairs.

REFERENCES

Biderman, A. D. and Reiss, A. J., Jr.: On exploring the "dark figure" of crime. *Annals, 374:*1-15, 1967.

Boggs, S. L.: Urban crime patterns. *Am Soc Rev, 30:*899-908, 1965.

Campbell, D. T.: Reforms as experiments. *Am Psychologist, 24:*409-429, 1969.

——, and Ross, H. L.: The Connecticut crackdown on speeding: time-series data in quasi-experimental design. *Law and Society Rev, 3:*33-53, 1968.

Campbell, D. T., and Stanley, J. C.: *Experimental and Quasi-Experimental Designs for Research.* Chicago, Rand McNally, 1966.

Caporaso, J. A., and Pelowski, A. L.: Economic and political integration in Europe: a time-series quasi-experimental analysis. *Am Pol Sci Rev, 65:* 418-433, 1971.

Clark, T. N.: Community structure, decision-making, budget expenditures, and urban renewal in 51 American communities. In Bonjean, C. M., *et al.* (Eds.): *Community Politics.* New York, Free Pr, 1971, pp. 293-313.

Deutsch, K. W.: *The Nerves of Government.* New York, Free Press, 1963.

Etzioni, A.: *The Active Society.* New York, Free Press, 1968.

Ostrom, E.: Institutional arrangements and the measurement of policy consequences: applications to evaluating police performance. *Urban Affairs Q, 6:*447-476, 1971.

President's Commission on Law Enforcement and Administration of Justice: *Crime and Its Impact—An Assessment.* Washington, Government Printing Office, 1967.

Weiss, C. H. [Ed.]: *Evaluating Action Programs.* Boston, Allyn & Bacon, 1972.

Chapter 18

CRIME RATES AND PUBLIC EXPENDITURES FOR POLICE PROTECTION: THEIR INTERACTION

MICHAEL J. GREENWOOD AND WALTER J. WADYCKI

FOR A NUMBER OF YEARS crime rates have been alarmingly high, and their continued rise has evoked pleas for additional police protection. The cost to society of devoting additional resources to police protection is the value of foregone alternatives to which those resources could have been put. Channeling additional resources into police protection, however, produces an anomalous result. In the analysis that follows we suggest that given the distribution of total crime between reported and unreported, and given the efficiency of additional police personnel in detecting relative to preventing crime, additional policemen result in an increase rather than a decrease in measured crime rates. The rise in measured crime rates may in turn induce new demands for increased police protection.

The plan of the study is as follows. In the next section we formulate and discuss a simultaneous-equations model that links expenditures on police to measured crime rates. We argue that several factors determine the sign of this relationship, and we present a simple but realistic numeric example to illustrate a situation in which an increase in police is followed by an increase in the reported crime rate. The results of estimating the model are discussed in section two. These results show the anomalous situation of increased police protection causing increased measured crime. The concluding section summarizes our results and

Reprinted, with permission of the Association for Social Economics, from *Review of Social Economy*, October 1973, pp. 138-151.

provides an explanation for the paradox found in our estimated model.

SPECIFICATION OF THE MODEL

Several earlier studies have attempted to relate state or local government expenditures in general, or expenditures for particular categories of public goods, to a number of relevant factors.[1] We relate expenditures for police protection to measured crime rates and other factors. In our model the expenditures that society chooses to make on police protection determine the quantity of police protection that society gets. The model is completed by taking the output (as measured by the crime rate) of the law-enforcement sector to be a function of the quantity of input (the number of police).

The Federal Bureau of Investigation published 1960 crime-rate data for 199 of the 212 Standard Metropolitan Statistical Areas (SMSA's) in the United States (in 1960). These 199 SMSA's constitute the sample employed in the study. The model we employ is described by the following system of simultaneous equations, where all variables except D are expressed in logarithms:

Output equations:

$$C_1 = f_1 \text{ (POL, POV, DEN, BLK, D, VAL, } e_1) \text{ and} \quad (1)$$
$$C_2 = f_2 \text{ (POL, POV, DEN, BLK, D, } e_2), \quad (2)$$

Expenditure equation:

$$\text{EXP} = f_3 \text{ (} C_1, C_2, \text{INC, TAX, } e_3) \quad (3)$$

Input equation:

$$\text{POL} = f_4 \text{ (EXP, } e_4), \quad (4)$$

where variables are defined as follows:

Endogenous variables

C_1 = per capita crimes against property, 1960, where crimes against property include burglary, larceny, and auto theft;

C_2 = per capita crimes against persons, 1960, where crimes against persons include murder or non-negligent man-

---

1. See, for example, Bahl and Saunders, Bishop, Fisher, Gabler and Brest, Henderson, Horowitz, Sacks and Harris, and many others.

slaughter, forcible rape, robbery, and aggravated assault;

EXP = per capita local government expenditures for police protection, 1962;

POL = per capita full-time equivalent employment in police protection, 1962;

Exogenous variables

POV = percentage of families with 1959 family income below $3,000, 1960;

DEN = population per square mile, 1960;

BLK = percentage of population that is black, 1960;

VAL = median value of owner-occupied housing units, 1960;

D = South-North dummy variable, where all observations south of a line drawn across the country at the northern border of North Carolina, Tennessee, Oklahoma, etc. take a value of one and all observations north of such a line take a value of zero;

TAX = per capita property taxes, 1962;

INC = median 1959 income of families residing in the SMSA in 1960;[2]

e_i = random errors, where $i = 1, \ldots, 4$.

Since the crime indices C_1 and C_2 are restricted to so-called "serious crimes," the FBI crime data are less than ideal. Some examples of crimes that are not "serious" include prostitution, arson, narcotics violations, tax and insurance fraud, kidnapping, forgery, and embezzlement. Therefore, the crime indices exclude many types of crime that the law and the public may regard as more serious than the crimes actually included in the indices. In addition, each crime index is a simple sum of its components. For example one robbery increases C_2 by as much as one murder. A weighted sum would seem appropriate if the difficult problem

---

2. Data sources are as follows: (1) C_1, C_2: U.S. Department of Justice, Table 4; (2) EXP, POL: U.S. Bureau of the Census (1964), Tables 12 and 8, respectively; (3) POV, INC, BLK, VAL, TAX: U.S. Bureau of the Census (1967), Table 3.

of a choice of weights could be solved. The use of the FBI data over time tends to present a false picture of increasing lawlessness.[3] Our study, however, is cross-sectional in nature and hence is not affected by this limitation of the data. Furthermore, the FBI data do have the advantage of uniformity of definition and administrative application across our sample of SMSA's. Finally, these data are the only readily available source for a study of this kind. Let us next turn to a discussion of the variables and their interrelationships.

It is appropriate to use a simultaneous-equations model to explain the level of expenditures provided for, and the level of service provided by, the law-enforcement segment of the public sector, since the level of service, as measured by prevailing crime rates, is a function of the expenditures that society chooses to make for police protection, and the expenditures are themselves dependent upon the level of service. The model that has been specified above is circular in the sense that crime rates are viewed as determining the amount of expenditures that society chooses to devote to police protection. Given the cost of police protection, the amount of expenditures decided upon by society determines the quantity of police protection that can be employed. The quantity of police protection is in turn a determinant of crime rates.

Note that two different crime rates have been employed in this study, one relating to crimes against property (C_1) and the other to crimes against persons (C_2). The use of two crime-rate variables is preferable to the use of a single variable relating to aggregate crimes. There is no reason to suppose that the magnitudes in which certain "determinants" of crime exert themselves are the same for all types of crime. Moreover, there is no reason to suppose a priori that police protection is equally effective in either preventing or detecting all types of crimes. Finally, it is unlikely that society is equally sensitive to various types of crime, and hence it is unlikely that society's reaction with regard to expendi-

---

3. For a further discussion of some of the problems associated with interpreting the FBI crime-rate data, see Biderman, especially pp. 111-129.

tures on crime protection will be the same regardless of the type of crime. Let us next turn to a more detailed discussion of each of the equations of the simultaneous-equations system.

The direction of the relationship between the quantity of police personnel (POL) and the crime rates cannot be specified a priori. The reason for our being unable to specify this relationship is that police perform two major functions—crime prevention and crime detection. The magnitude and direction of the relationship are critically dependent upon two factors: (1) the percentage of total crime reported relative to the percentage unreported, and (2) the efficiency of additional police personnel in detecting relative to preventing crime.

For a given locality let R represent reported crime, U unreported crime, and T total crime. Then $R + U \equiv T$. Dividing both sides of this identity by T, we get $R/T + U/T \equiv 1$, or the fraction of crime reported plus the fraction unreported must account for 100 percent of the crimes committed in the locality. Since neither the value of U nor that of T is known, it is not possible to assign a value to either R/T or U/T. However, for the sake of example, let us assume that 50 percent of all crimes are reported; i.e. that $R/T = 0.5$ and $U/T = 0.5$.[4] Now let us further assume that an additional policeman is added to the locality's police force, and that this policeman is equally efficient in detecting and in deterring crime. Suppose his presence on the police force results in the prevention of four crimes and in the detection of four crimes that would otherwise go undetected. If we assume that the crimes prevented are distributed over reported and unreported in the same proportions as all crimes, then both reported and unreported crimes will fall by two. However, since the presence of the additional policeman also results in the detection of four crimes, unreported crimes fall by four more, or by a total of six, while reported crimes rise by four, with a resulting net increase of two. Measured crime thus rises.

It is apparent, then, that given the values of R/T and U/T, the

---

4. Available evidence suggests that these proportions are not unrealistic. A survey of 10,000 households taken for the President's Commission on Law Enforcement and Administration of Justice indicates that about half of actual crime goes unreported. For details of this survey, see Ennis.

greater is the efficiency of additional police resources in detecting relative to deterring crime, the higher will be the resulting measured crime rate, while the greater is efficiency in preventing relative to detecting crime, the lower will be the resulting measured crime rate. Unfortunately, no evidence is known to us that suggests police to be more efficient in one of their functions than in the other. Moreover, given such relative efficiencies, the higher (lower) is the value of R/T, the smaller (larger) will be the resulting measured crime rate. It is thus plausible that in the crime-rate equations the coefficients of POL be negative, positive, or even equal to zero.

Becker and others have suggested that, rather than being an activity in which only moral deviates engage, crime is an activity that persons enter on the basis of rational judgments regarding the benefits and costs associated with engaging in an illegal activity as compared to the benefits and costs associated with other occupations. Thus, lawbreakers are regarded as individuals who perceive benefits and costs differently, and not as individuals whose basic motivation differs from normal. Becker's approach has many advantages and is utilized in our discussion of the (exogenous) determinants of crime rates.

One factor that is expected to exert an important influence on the costs of committing crimes, and hence on crime rates, is income. The lower an individual's level of income, the lower is his opportunity cost of engaging in an illegal activity, and thus, *ceteris paribus*, the higher is his expected benefit-cost ratio associated with the activity. To reflect such costs we have chosen to employ a measure of the locality's degree of poverty. Thus, the greater the percentage of families with income below $3,000 (POV), the higher the expected crime rate.

Population density (DEN) is another variable that is generally expected to be an important determinant of crime. The more densely populated a given locality, the greater the likelihood that anonymity will be preserved by a lawbreaker, and hence the smaller the probability of his being apprehended. Since under such circumstances the expected cost of crime tends to be lower, crime rates should be higher in more densely populated localities. Moreover, particularly with respect to crimes against persons, the greater the population density the greater the number of potential "targets" of crime in any area, and hence the higher the expected crime rate.

The percentage of population that is black (BLK) is also expected to exert a positive influence on the crime rate. A number of economic and social characteristics of the black population are relevant to our argument here. Blacks have generally lower income levels and higher unemployment rates than whites. Moreover, it is apparent that blacks find it somewhat more difficult to be "absorbed" in society than do whites. Consider, for example, the following information. For the 100 SMSA's (not including Honolulu) that had a 1960 population in excess of 250,000, the average (1960) unemployment rate among whites was 5.0 percent, while that among nonwhites was 9.6 percent. However, while the average unemployment rate among white (1955-1960) in-migrants to these SMSA's was 5.1 percent (in 1960), that among nonwhite in-migrants was 12.7 percent.[5] This information is particularly relevant given the substantial migration of black persons that occurred during the decade of the 1950's. Another point of relevance is that it appears that many black persons regard the law as an instrument that has historically been used to suppress them, and thus they feel alienated from the law.[6] Such factors as these tend to make the economic and social costs of crime lower as perceived by blacks.

We have employed a South-North dummy variable to account for systematic differences in crime due to demographic and social differences between the regions as well as to capture the effect of climate. If crimes are higher in the South than in the North, *ceteris paribus*, the dummy variable (D) should have a positive sign.

---

5. U.S. Bureau of the Census (1963).

6. Support for this contention is found in the *Report of the National Advisory Commission on Civil Disorders:* "There is a widening gulf in communications between local government and the residents of the erupting ghettos of the city. As a result, many Negro citizens develop a profound sense of isolation and alienation from the processes and programs of government. . . . Further, as a result of the long history of racial discrimination, grievances experienced by Negroes often take on personal and symbolic significance transcending the immediate consequences of the event." [p. 148]

The factors that we have previously discussed generally relate to the characteristics of the population from which lawbreakers are drawn, and as such reflect the costs of committing crime. It is also necessary to discuss the benefits of crime. The median value of owner-occupied housing (VAL) has been employed as a proxy for the benefits associated with committing crimes against property. The greater is the value of owner-occupied housing, the greater the expected crime rate.

We have chosen not to employ a variable that reflects the benefits of such crimes in the equation for crimes against persons. It appears that in many crimes against persons the lawbreaker has no definite knowledge of the economic status of his target, and for some crimes, such as rape, economic status is irrelevant. Note, however, that the population density variable may pick up certain effects associated with the benefits of committing crimes against persons.

In the equation for expenditures for police protection, both crime-rate variables are expected to have positive signs, since increased crime rates are likely to result in a decision by society to increase the resources it devotes to police protection. Expenditures for police protection are assumed to be drawn in part from revenues provided by property taxes. Hence higher per capita property taxes (TAX) allow higher per capita expenditures for police protection. It is probable that those who pay higher property taxes expect more (publicly provided) police protection for the property on which they pay (the higher) taxes, as well as for themselves. Communities with higher income levels tend to make greater expenditures for public goods of various sorts, including police protection, and a positive sign is expected for the income variable (INC). Moreover, since potential losses from crime are positively correlated with the income-level of potential victims of crime, we would expect high-income persons to demand more police protection.

Finally, in the equation for police per capita, per capita expenditures (EXP) for police protection is expected to have a positive sign, since society's decision to increase its expenditures on police protection is likely to reflect a desire to hire more policemen. Let us next turn to a discussion of the empirical results.

THE ESTIMATION OF THE MODEL

The simultaneous-equations system presented in the previous sections was estimated by three-stage least squares.[7] Since the variables of the model are expressed as logarithms, their coefficients may be interpreted as elasticities.

Table 18-I contains the coefficients and corresponding t-ratios associated with the variables employed in the model.[8] As an indication of the explanatory power of the four equations of the system, the coefficients of multiple determination (R^2's) associated with the ordinary least squares estimates of each equation are also included in Table 18-I. In general, the variables do not have unexpected signs, and the coefficients are significant. Four variables fail significance at 10 percent, namely, DEN and BLK in the equation for crimes against property and DEN and D in the equation for crimes against persons. All other variables are significant at better than the 2.5 percent level, except VAL in the equation for crimes against property. The R^2's associated with the ordinary least squares estimates of the equations of the model are reasonably high—0.34 on the C_1 equation, 0.54 on C_2 0.49 on EXP, and 0.83 on POL. We next turn to a more detailed discussion of the estimates of each of the structural equations of the model.

In both crime-rate equations the per capita police variable is positive and highly significant. The coefficients suggest that a 1 percent increase in the number of police per capita results in a 1.30 percent increase in per capita crimes against property and a 1.68 percent increase in per capita crimes against persons. We infer from these findings that it is likely that additional police are more efficient in detecting than in deterring crime, and that a relatively small percentage of all crimes are reported, with the con-

---

7. Ordinary least squares (OLS) is an inappropriate estimating technique for a simultaneous system such as ours. Three stage least squares (3SLS) yields the consistency property (which OLS lacks). Furthermore, 3SLS is preferable to other simultaneous estimators such as two stage least squares since each of our equations is over-identified and it is likely that the equation disturbances have a nondiagonal covariance matrix. In such circumstances 3SLS has greater asymptotic efficiency than 2SLS (For further details see Christ, pp. 592-626).

8. In a simultaneous-equations model, the ratios of the estimated coefficients to their standard errors are approximately normal, and large values give a rough indication of statistical significance (See Christ, p. 598).

TABLE 18-I

SIMULTANEOUS-EQUATIONS MODEL OF CRIME RATES AND PUBLIC
EXPENDITURES FOR POLICE PROTECTION: THREE STAGE LEAST
SQUARES ESTIMATES (β) AND t-RATIOS (t)

Independent Variables	C_1	C_2	Equation for EXP	POL
C_1	β: —	—	0.29	—
	t: —	—	(2.23)	—
C_2	—	—	0.13	—
	—	—	(2.31)	—
EXP	—	—	—	0.68
	—	—	—	(19.74)
POL	1.30	1.68	—	—
	(5.04)	(4.82)	—	—
POV	0.23	0.54	—	—
	(1.97)	(3.06)	—	—
DEN	−0.03	−0.02	—	—
	(−1.27)	(−0.50)	—	—
BLK	0.001	0.29	—	—
	(0.04)	(6.86)	—	—
D	0.22	0.14	—	—
	(2.81)	(1.10)	—	—
VAL	0.24	—	—	—
	(1.61)	—	—	—
INC	—	—	0.85	—
	—	—	(5.49)	—
TAX	—	—	0.18	—
	—	—	(3.86)	—
INTERCEPT	2.06	1.95	−10.65	−3.33
	(0.92)	(0.88)	(−7.42)	(−20.16)
OLS R^2	0.34	0.54	0.49	0.83

sequence that a rise in the number of police per capita results in
an increase rather than a decrease in measured crime rates. Note
that the elasticity associated with POL is higher in the equation
for crimes against persons than in the equation for crimes against
property. This finding is an indication that either police efficiency
in detecting relative to preventing crimes against persons is
greater than police efficiency in detecting relative to preventing
crimes against property, or that relatively more crimes against
property are reported.

The poverty variable is positive and highly significant in both
crime-rate equations, which suggests that the cost of crime is
indeed lower for low-income persons than for high-income per-

sons, and hence an increase in the percentage of low-income families results in an increase in both crimes against property and crimes against persons. Note, however, that the coefficient on POV is considerably higher in the equation for crimes against persons than in the equation for crimes against property (0.54 as compared to 0.23).[9] This is an interesting result for it suggests that for low-income persons the benefit-cost ratio associated with crimes against persons is higher than the benefit-cost ratio associated with crimes against property. This result may be somewhat surprising since the crimes against persons typically carry more severe punishment than do those against property.

"Benefits" associated with crimes against property are unlikely to be particularly high in areas characterized by high percentages of low-income families. Moreover, it is likely that to a considerable extent our POV variable reflects the incidence of slums within the SMSA's that serve as our data base. It has been demonstrated that slums tend to create serious personality and social adjustment problems for their inhabitants, and for these and other reasons (similar to those cost-related factors previously discussed) slums tend to breed crime. It is probable that, as compared to non-slum areas, relatively much of the crime that is committed against property goes unreported. Much of the crime may not even involve objects of sufficient value to be counted by the police in their crime reports.

In both crime-rate equations the population density variable has a negative sign, but in neither instance is the variable significant. The negative coefficient is consistent with our view that anonymity is associated with high density. That is, the percent of crime that is unreported or undetected increases as anonymity increases. It appears that this percent is sufficiently high so that the reported crime rate falls with increased density. Since the density coefficients are not highly significant, perhaps little should

9. The coefficient of POV (as well as of the other exogenous variables) indicates a shift in the particular equation. The resulting change in the equilibrium values of the endogenous variables is best seen from the derived reduced form which takes into account interactions implied by a simultaneous model. Since the magnitudes of the reduced form coefficients are similar to the structural estimates, the discussion in the text is confined to the latter.

be made of this variable. However, the failure of DEN to be highly significant is of interest in itself since some sociologists and criminologists have long believed that high population density tends to breed crime.[10] Our results suggest that there are more "basic" determinants of crime than density.

While the percentage of the population that is black is positive in both crime-rate equations, it is basically significant only in the equation for crimes against persons. That BLK is significant only in the equation for crimes against persons is not totally surprising for the same reasons that POV has a higher elasticity in the crimes-against-persons equation than in the crimes-against-property equation.

The value of owner-occupied housing exerts a significant positive influence on crimes against property. We have argued that VAL is a variable that reflects the benefits to the lawbreaker of committing crimes against property. Hence, our results here suggest that, given the potential lawbreaker's expected costs of committing such crimes, the greater are the potential benefits, the greater will be the incidence of these types of crimes. This finding is also consistent with Becker's hypothesis that the criminal, rather than being a moral deviate, considers the benefits and costs associated with his illegal activities.

The South-North dummy variable is positive in both crime-rate equations, and while it is highly significant in the equation for crimes against property, it is significant at the 13 percent level in the equation for crimes against persons. The southern "social climate" seems more conducive to crime and our results are also consistent with other findings that temperate weather is conducive to higher crime rates.

In the expenditures equation both crime-rate variables are positive and highly significant. A 1 percent increase in crimes against property induces a 0.29 percent increase in percapita expenditures for police protection, while a 1 percent increase in crimes against persons induces a 0.13 percent increase in such expenditures. Presumably, the level of society's authorized expenditures

10. It is worth noting that reestimating the model without density results in no appreciable changes in the parameter estimates of the other variables.

for police protection bears a close relationship to the amount that society is willing to pay to avoid losses due to crime. For the SMSA's in our sample the mean number of crimes against property exceeds the mean number of crimes against persons by a factor of 6.6. It is thus likely that society's perceived losses from crimes against property are considerably higher than the perceived losses from crimes against persons.

The positive and significant coefficient on the per capita property tax variable in the expenditures equation suggests that a 1 percent increase in per capita property taxes results in a 0.18 percent increase in per capita expenditures for police protection. Moreover, the income elasticity associated with expenditures for police protection is also positive and significant. A 1 percent increase in median family income results in a 0.85 percent increase in per capita expenditures for police protection. Potential losses due to crime are positively correlated with the income level of the potential victim of the crime. Thus higher income persons are willing to pay a greater amount to avoid (the greater possible) losses due to crime.

Finally, the positive and highly significant coefficient on the expenditures variable in the per capita police equation indicates that a 1 percent increase in per capita expenditures for police protection results in a 0.69 percent increase in the number of police per capita. It is obvious that expenditures for policemen are not the only important expenditures made for police protection. Society also makes expenditures for a number of other inputs, such as patrol cars. However, since data on such other inputs are not available for SMSA's, we have not included such factors in our model. It should also be recognized that certain expenditures made specifically to reduce crime rates are not included in our measure of expenditures for police protection. An example of such an expenditure is the installation of high-intensity street lights in heavy crime areas.

SUMMARY AND CONCLUSIONS

We have argued that it is appropriate to study that segment of the public sector that provides police protection by means of a simultaneous-equations model, since not only are measured crime rates a function of the number of police employed, but the number of police employed are a function of measured crime rates, via the impact that crime rates have on the expenditures that society chooses to make for police protection. We have seen that an increase in crime rates induces an increase in per capita expenditures for police protection, with an increase in the crimes-against-property rate inducing a larger increase in per capita expenditures than does an increase in the crimes-against-persons rates. The increased per capita expenditures for police protection in turn result in an increase in the number of policemen employed per capita. Since police perform a dual role, crime deterrence and crime detection, it is not possible a priori to specify the direction of the change in the measured crime rate that results from the additional policemen. The direction and magnitude of this change depend both upon the relative efficiency of the additional police personnel in their two major functions and upon the percentage of all crimes that are reported. The results of this study suggest that the additional police (per capita) are more efficient in detecting than in deterring crime and/or a relatively small fraction of all crimes is recorded, with the consequence that an increase in the number of police per capita results in an increase in measured crime rates.

The conclusions we have drawn from our model should not be construed as a condemnation of all increases in expenditures on police protection. Our model is mute on the question of the extent by which actual crime, as distinct from measured crime, declines with an increase in the quantity of resources devoted to police protection. It is also appropriate to recall our earlier discussion of the limitations of the FBI crime data and especially that crimes such as forgery or tax fraud are excluded from our measures of crime. If the primary objective of placing additional resources in police protection is to prevent crime, then an increase in measured crime rates may simply mask the achievement, or partial achievement, of this objective.[11] It should also be pointed

---

11. Biderman and others argue that the FBI crime-rate data have a secular upward bias. If this is true, and it probably is, then this factor may lead over time to further increases in measured crime rates, in addition to the increases that result from hiring more policemen. (Note that since our study employs cross-sectional data, this data shortcoming does not lead to bias in our results.)

out that crime prevention is not independent of crime detection. An increase during the current time period in detection coupled with apprehension and conviction may result in crime prevention in future periods.

Finally, let us briefly compare the results of the present study with the findings of a recent study by Pressman and Carol. Pressman and Carol find a significant positive correlation between police per capita and crime rates. They argue that "this (significant positive correlation) is most probably explained by the hypothesis that in an area with high crime rates, more police are employed" [p. 229, parentheses ours]. Clearly, Pressman and Carol recognize the simultaneous nature of the relationship between police per capita and crime rates. However, the model they specify takes no account of this simultaneous relationship. In our model we have attempted to account for the interaction between police and crime by specifying a simultaneous-equation system. Since the positive correlation between police and crime persists even in an appropriately specified and estimated model, we conclude that the observed relationship is a function of police efficiency in detecting relative to deterring crime.

On a number of points our results corroborate the findings of Pressman and Carol, but on several points the two studies are in some contrast. In both studies population density fails to be a significant deterrent of crime. Both studies suggest that the percentage of the population that is black exerts a positive influence on crimes against persons. However, while Pressman and Carol uncover a positive relationship between percentage black and crimes against property, we find no significant relationship between these variables. Contrary to (our) expectations, Pressman and Carol find a negative relationship between a measure of poverty and crimes against property. In both of our crime-rate equations, our poverty variable is positive and highly significant.

REFERENCES

Bahl, R. W., Jr., and Saunders, R. J.: Determinants of changes in state and local government expenditures. *Nat Tax J, 18*:50-57, 1965.

Becker, G. S.: Crime and punishment: an economic approach. *J Polit Econ, 76*:169-217, 1968.

Biderman, A. D.: Social indicators and goals. In Bauer, R. A. (Ed.): *Social Indicators*. Cambridge, 1966, 68-153.

Bishop, G. A.: Stimulative versus substitutive effects of state school aid in New England. *Nat Tax J, 16*:133-143, 1964.

Christ, C. F.: *Econometric Models and Methods*. New York, 1966.

Ennis, P. H.: Criminal victimization in the United States: a report of a national survey. *Field Surveys II, President's Commission on Law Enforcement and Administration of Justice*, Washington, 1967.

Fisher, G. W.: Interstate variation in state and local government expenditure. *Nat Tax J, 17*:57-74, 1964.

Gabler, L. R. and Brest, J. I.: Interstate variations in per capita highway expenditures. *Nat Tax J, 20*:78-85, 1967.

Henderson, J. M.: Local government expenditures: a social welfare approach. *Rev Econ Statist, 50*:156-163, 1968.

Horowitz, A. R.: A simultaneous-equation approach to the problem of explaining interstate differences in state and local government expenditures. *Southern Econ J, 34*:459-476, 1968.

Pressman, I. and Carol, A.: Crime as a diseconomy of scale. *Rev Social Econ, 19*:227-236, 1971.

Report of the National Advisory Commission on Civil Disorders, Washington, 1968.

Sacks, S., and Harris, R.: The determinants of state and local government expenditures and intergovernmental flows of funds. *Nat Tax J, 17*:75-85, 1964.

U.S. Bureau of the Census: *Census of Governments: 1962: Local Government in Metropolitan Areas*, Washington, D.C., 1964.

———: *County and City Data Book, 1967*, Washington, D.C., 1967.

———: *U.S. Census of Population: 1960*, Subject Report, *Mobility for Metropolitan Areas*, Washington, D.C., 1963.

U.S. Department of Justice, Federal Bureau of Investigation: *Uniform Crime Reports for the United States: 1960*, Washington, D.C., 1961.

Chapter 19

LAW ENFORCEMENT EXPENDITURES AND URBAN CRIME

LEE R. MCPHETERS AND WILLIAM B. STRONGE

INTRODUCTION

THE DRAMATIC INCREASE in reported crime over the past decade has sparked considerable research dealing with the efficiency of the criminal justice system. The bulk of the research undertaken has focused on two major problem areas. One area of study has to do with attempts to explain the causes of crime. The second line of research has dealt with examination and analysis of the determinants of expenditures for police services. Below, the results of our investigation suggest that these two areas of study are, in fact, closely related and are best analyzed in the context of a simultaneous model. We show that criminal activity is an important determinant of the level of police expenditures, and police expenditures in turn have a significant impact on the level of criminal activity.

CRIME AND POLICE EXPENDITURES

A number of recent studies have explored the analysis of crime as an economic activity with rational participants. The most notable theoretical contribution to date has been that of Becker (1968), who developed a formal model of the crime decision. Here, a prospective criminal enters into criminal activity on the basis of his assessment of the probability and cost of punishment. A number of extensions, principally those of Harris (1970), Stigler (1970), and Tullock (1969), have followed. Since the probability of arrest due to police activity is a major determinant of the criminal's perceived costs of undertaking a crime, the influence

Reprinted with permission from *The National Tax Journal,* December, 1974.

of police expenditures enters at least implicitly into most of these theoretical models.

While the theoretical relation between the level of police expenditures and criminal activity is negative in sign, empirical studies have found a perverse positive relation between police expenditures and crime. Pressman and Carol (1971), analyzing SMSA data for 1965, interpreted this positive result as "suggestive that more police may not be the answer to higher crime rates and that larger expenditures on police protection are not cost effective in combating crime" (p. 229).

In a subsequent study, examining 1960 data for cities in the Chicago area, Allison (1972) found no evidence of a significant negative influence of police expenditures on reported crime. He attributed this result to declining marginal efficiency of police protection in the face of rising population (p. 195), which is somewhat of a variant of the unbalanced growth model of William Baumol (1967). As population increases, crime increases by a greater proportion. Thus, reasons Allison, successively larger increments of police expenditures are required for public protection.

Similar results are reported by Pogue (1973), Kakalik and Wildhorn (1971), and in a recent study by Jones (1973). This surprising but persistent positive empirical relation between crime and police expenditures is shown in our analysis below to be the result of an identification problem. Previous studies with single equation models which have failed to consider the interrelation of crime and police expenditures have generated results which may have misleading policy implications, since, in these previous studies, increased police expenditures are shown to have no deterrent effect on crime, either in the long or short run. Before we turn to our alternative simultaneous equation model, we briefly discuss some earlier findings with respect to police expenditures.

Police expenditure models have essentially been treated as one class of public expenditure function. The literature on such expenditure functions for government has grown substantially since the early work of Fabricant (1952). Within this literature, police expenditure functions are of particular interest because they are a horizontally integrated type of service, analysis of which may potentially lead to insights concerning a number of similar municipal functions.

An early police expenditure study by Hirsch (1959) developed the police expenditure framework, and a number of others have since extended his basic approach. In the Hirsch study, expenditures on police services were seen to be determined by population, population density, miles of street in the jurisdiction, and a number of other variables reflecting service condition and quality of service. In the ensuing years, numerous other studies, particularly those of Adams (1967), Brazer (1959), Bahl (1968), Pidot (1969), and Weicher (1970) have attempted to explain variations in police expenditures, utilizing various and ever-increasing numbers of explanatory variables.

Typical of these subsequent studies is the recent paper by Weicher (1970). Weicher hypothesizes that police expenditures may be explained by a large number of variables measuring city size, revenue and fiscal capacity, political fragmentation, tastes, and service conditions. Using central city data for 1960, Weicher thus employs least squares regression analysis to examine the influence on police expenditures of such variables as income, unemployment, percentage of the population nonwhite and population density, as well as a number of others. In all, twenty-two variables appear as independent or explanatory variables in the police expenditure equation. Although the principal objective of police agencies and thus, police expenditures, is to deter and respond to crime, a crime measure does not appear as an independent variable in this or any of the other models mentioned above.

The absence of a crime measure in previous police expenditure functions is puzzling, since much of the literature on police administration has been concerned with the allocation of police services in accordance with "proportionate need" ever since the pioneering work of O. W. Wilson (1972). The need for police services in a particular area or locality typically calls forth four major police activities: routine patrol, response to calls for assistance, investigation of crime, and rendering of incidental services to the community. Responses to calls reporting serious crimes are usually given top priority within police assignment schemes. Furthermore, public concern over crime may lead to larger police budgets and larger police expenditures. It is for these reasons that we believe crime to be an important determinant of the level of police expenditures.

The introduction of crime as an independent variable in the equation for police expenditures introduces simultaneity into the model, however. This is because police expenditures can be expected to deter crime to the extent that they raise the cost of crime to the rational criminal. Thus, higher levels of police expenditures are likely to reduce the number of criminal events, other things being equal. Once it is recognized that police expenditures and crime are jointly determined, in a simultaneous system, much of the previous empirical literature on the explanation of these variables loses validity, and a completely new approach is called for.

Recognition of the simultaneity of the relationship between crime and police expenditures has been forthcoming in a recent paper by Greenwood and Wadycki (1973). Here, crime is seen as a function of police per capita and a number of variables such as population density, median family income, etc., thought to be determinants of crime; police per capita is determined by per capita expenditures for police protection; and per capita expenditures for police protection is in turn determined by the level of crime, median family income, and per capita property taxes.

Although this model is conceptually superior to earlier single equation models of police expenditures, it does not provide us with satisfactory empirical results. While the influence of crime on police expenditures is positive, as expected, the influence of police activity (police per capita) on crime is seen also to be positive. Further, the influence of other explanatory variables in the crime functions are much weaker than the positive influence of police activity. All this leads to the perverse policy conclusion that an increased police force will increase reported crime.

Greenwood and Wadycki (1973, pp. 145-146) support this latter conclusion by stating: "it is likely that additional police are more efficient in detecting than in deterring crime, and that a relatively small percentage of all crimes are reported, with the consequence that a rise in the number of police per capita results in an increase rather than a decrease in crime."

While it is possibly indeed true that increased police may record and report more crime, it is doubtful that this influence would be so potent as Greenwood and Wadycki suggest. It is probably the case that most crime reports originate with victims or witnesses (President's Commission, 1967c, p. 29), not with police. The possibility of police discovering even a solitary criminal event in progress may, in fact, be quite remote. One study suggests that, in a city with the general characteristics of Los Angeles, a police officer would expect to detect a robbery only once every 14 years (President's Commission, 1967c, p. 12).

Since most crime apparently is committed out of the sight of the police (Eliot, 1973), increased police numbers could not be expected to increase the level of reported crimes by a very large amount. A more likely explanation for the findings of Greenwood and Wadycki lies in the specification of their model, particularly the crime function.

It is our argument that previous studies of crime and law enforcement expenditures have been deficient in specification of the model to be tested. In the next section, we attempt to extend and improve upon previous studies of both crime and law enforcement expenditures. Bearing in mind Hirsch's observation that most expenditures studies have serious shortcomings (1968, p. 500), "the single most important one being the absence of a rigorous, logical underlying theory," we develop in this paper a simultaneous model of urban police expenditures, relying upon traditional tools of economic theory to provide us with our analytical approach.

THE MODEL

Expenditures on police services (PE) depend on the level of criminal activity (TC), the municipal budget constraint facing policy makers (R), and a portmanteau variable (Z) reflecting the community's taste for police expenditures other than those induced by crime:

$$PE = f(TC, R, Z) \qquad (1)$$

Assuming the municipal budget constraint and the taste variable fixed at some known values, the relationship between police expenditures and crime can be graphed as shown in Figure 19-1. Measuring crime along the vertical axis and police expenditures along the horizontal axis, the police expenditure function can be represented by the curve P. At zero level of criminal events,

CRIME AND POLICE EXPENDITURES

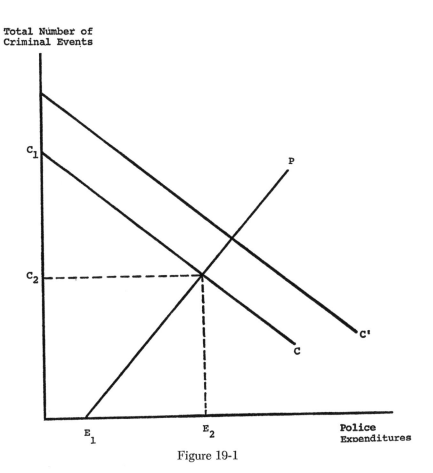

Figure 19-1

the provision of police services is restricted to such incidental services as handling domestic disputes, crowd control, and monitoring of traffic. This point is shown as E_1. As crime increases, additional expenditures on police services are required and we move up the P curve.

The crime reaction function can in turn be represented by

$$TC = g(PE, K_1, \ldots K_n, W) \tag{2}$$

where the variable W is a taste variable, reflecting social proclivity to criminal behavior, and the K_i are members of a family or vector of environmental variables which are "causes" of crime. Fixing W and the K_i variables at certain known levels, the relationship between crime and police expenditures can also be graphed. This is represented by the curve C in Figure 19-1, which slopes downward and to the right from an intercept upon the vertical axis, at C_1. This point of origin corresponds to a low level of expenditures on police services, where the deterrent capability of police is severely limited. At higher levels of police expenditures, or points further out the horizontal axis, criminal events requiring service tend to decrease. An equilibrium exists at C_2 and E_2.

The equilibrium point is the simultaneous solution to (1) and (2). It represents a level of police expenditures (E_2) which is consistent with a level of crime (C_2) that would induce that level of police expenditures, for given levels of W, R, Z, and $K_1, \ldots, K_n$.

The relationships (1) and (2) are assumed to be relatively invariant across space and over time (ignoring the problem of lags, for the moment). Thus, the variation in number of crimes or levels of police expenditures observed among cities, for example, is regarded as solely attributable to variations in R, Z, W, and $K_1, \ldots, K_n$. Different levels of the parameters of the police expenditure function, such as the municipal budget, and different mixes of the causes of crime lead to different levels of police expenditures and crime rates among cities.

The comparative statics of the model are straightforward. An increase in the causes of crime shifts C to the right (C'), which leads to an increase in the number of crimes committed and in the level of expenditures for police services, and *vice versa*.

An increase in the budget constraint of a local government shifts the P function to the right and leads to fewer crimes and greater police expenditures.

If one gathers data on crime and police expenditures for different cities, what is being observed is a series of equilibrium points. A positive correlation would therefore not be surprising, but would have no meaning unless the curve was invariant throughout the sample; that is, unless all cities had the same values of the R and Z variables.

One comment concerning our specification of the police expenditure function is in order at this point. Drawing from previous studies, some observers might suggest that variables such as population density, percentage of black population, or age of housing should appear in the police expenditure function. We would argue that such variables are important determinants of police expenditures *only to the extent that they are causes of crime*. Their influence is thus captured in a proper specification of the crime function.

THE EMPIRICAL ANALYSIS

This section presents our estimated version of the model. The data employed throughout are observations on the forty-three largest United States central cities, for the year 1970.

Before estimation, a decision had to be made as to the components of the vector of environmental variables, $K_1, \ldots, K_n$, which are to represent the causes of crime. Rather than select a small and possibly incomplete number of environmental variables to avoid problems of multicollinearity, we chose to use instead a large number of environmental variables measuring important economic and demographic characteristics of central cities. We reduce the information contained in this larger data matrix through application of principal component analysis, thus obtaining a smaller number of uncorrelated index variables which are descriptive of certain basic characteristics of central city areas (for a discussion, see Dhrymes, 1970, pp. 53-65).

Such methods are applicable in situations where (a) there is a large number of interrelated variables whose effects cannot be separated and included explicitly in the analysis or (b) in large econometric models where the number of exogenous variables often exceeds the numbers of observations, implying singularity of moment matrices (Mitchell, 1970).

The principal components are derived from the variables shown in Table 19-I. It may be seen that this data set includes measures of economic conditions (income, unemployment), housing conditions, and population characteristics, as well as income fragmentation (ratio of SMSA median family income to central city median family income). Many of these variables have appeared independently as explanatory variables in previous models of crime or law enforcement expenditures.

TABLE 19-I

ORIGINAL INPUT VARIABLES TO PRINCIPAL COMPONENT ANALYSIS
(43 Largest United States Central Cities)

Variable Name	*Definition*
V1	percent change in White population, 1960-70
V2	percent change in Black population, 1960-70
V3	population per square mile
V4	housing units per square mile
V5	per capita recreation expenditures
V6	per capita education expenditures
V7	median family income
V8	percent families receiving welfare assistance
V9	percent families with income < $3,000 per year
V10	percent labor force unemployed
V11	percent population college graduates
V12	percent housing with > 1.5 persons per room
V13	percent housing substandard
V14	per capita assessed property value
V15	percent change in total population, 1960-70
V16	percent housing built before 1940
V17	percent population with < 1 year high school
V18	per capita health expenditures
V19	percent population Black
V20	ratio of SMSA median family income to central city median family income
V21	percent population between 15-24 years of age

Source: Variables V1, V2, V3, V4, V15, V19 and V21 are from the United States Department of Commerce, 1972b; variables V7-V11, V17 and V20 are from the United States Department of Commerce, 1972a; V12, V13 and V16 are obtained from the United States Department of Commerce, 1972c; variables V5, V6 and V8 are from the United States Department of Commerce, 1972d; variable V14 is from the United States Department of Commerce, 1968.

TABLE 19-II

LOADINGS USED TO CONSTRUCT PRINCIPAL COMPONENT INDICES

Original Variables	K1	K2	K3	K4	K5	K6
V1	−.8100	.2064	.4937	.0363	−.0137	−.0389
V2	−.4201	.2704	.6012	.2337	−.1799	.0356
V3	.7414	.4725	.0213	.1164	−.1051	.1771
V4	.7729	.4663	.0275	.1006	−.1249	.1668
V5	.2419	.3967	−.1384	.0087	.0687	−.2353
V6	.4684	.7103	.0231	−.0426	.0557	.2072
V7	−.5654	.7408	−.1644	.0228	−.0831	−.1226
V8	.6766	.1234	.5097	.0299	−.0329	.2724
V9	.5637	−.6963	.2372	.1719	.0437	.2089
V10	.0967	.3580	.4622	−.2289	.3334	.2869
V11	−.6005	.1413	−.2074	.5259	.2353	.1794
V12	.2992	−.5324	.4623	.3882	.4124	−.1971
V13	.3806	−.0735	.1581	−.3801	.6223	−.0518
V14	.6539	.4589	.0109	.2872	−.2554	−.3899
V15	−.7456	.2086	.3414	.1831	−.1152	.1001
V16	.6883	.2361	.2446	−.1624	.5781	.0712
V17	.7840	−.3311	.2574	−.4408	−.1534	−.1116
V18	.3312	.4070	−.2979	.2131	.1216	−.0432
V19	.5872	−.2047	.6484	.3074	.1445	.0444
V20	.8149	.0416	.2378	.2366	.0196	−.0307
V21	−.3644	−.3041	.3202	.1339	.0544	.6517
Cumulative proportion of variance	.3519	.5212	.6262	.7067	.7739	.8236

Extracting principal components until the resulting eigen-value fell below 1.0, we derived six orthogonal components which accounted for 82 percent of the variance in the original large data matrix. The loadings shown in Table 19-II measure the correlation between the original variables and each of the respective components. Through the use of these simple correlations, each of the components can be associated with characteristics of central city areas.[1]

---

1. The principal components are orthogonal and explain a maximum amount of the variance of the original data matrix. We made no use of factor rotation methods which result in loadings which are either very large or very small. While rotation may facilitate interpretation of each component, such transformations may affect orthogonality and the maximum variance property, which are of prime concern in the present study.

The first component (K1) is interpreted as a measure of central city decay. This component is highly correlated with a decline in both white population and total population, high housing density, and the income fragmentation variable. The second component (K2) is associated with central city affluence, since it is most highly correlated with median family income, and strongly negatively correlated with the percentage of families in poverty.

The third component (K3) is interpreted as a measure of minority presence, highly correlated with percentage of black population, percentage of families on welfare and inmigration of new families. The fourth component (K4) is quite likely a measure of education, since it is highly positively correlated with percentage of college graduates, but negatively correlated with the percentage of the population with less than one year of high school.

The next component (K5) is an inverse measure of housing quality, positively correlated with percentage of housing substandard and the overcrowding variable: percentage of housing with greater than 1.5 persons per room. The final component (K6) is a measure of youth presence, correlated most highly with percentage of the population between the ages of fifteen to twenty-four. This component is also quite strongly but negatively correlated with property value per capita.

Constructed principal component indices were then combined with a specific variable, police expenditures (PE) as explanatory variables in our crime function. The crime function was estimated also with the lagged value of crime on the right hand side. This approach was followed because it is our belief that crime depends on a distributed lag of past and present determinants, rather than only on their current level. The distributed lag of past and present expenditures, for example, is justified by the argument that crime is deterred not by actual police expenditures but by *perceived* police expenditures, and the perceived level is a distributed lag function of the actual levels. Similarly, a distributed lag of crime causes allows for gradual adjustment of crime levels to their causes.

Assuming that these distributed lag functions have weights which follow a declining geometric progression, an adjustment due to Koyck (1954) may be applied to replace the distributed lags with the lagged dependent variable. This approach is widely used in econometric work, when it is assumed that the independent variables are within a structure having a series of geometrically declining weights; the transformation of an equation

$$Y_t = a \sum_{i=0}^{\infty} \lambda^i X_{t-1}$$

to the form

$$Y_t = aX_t + \lambda Y_{t-1}$$

has become known as the Koyck transformation.

Crime data for 1970 are expressed in total crime rates per 1,000 persons, obtained from various tables in the Uniform Crime Reports for the United States, 1970 (United States Department of Justice, 1971). The police expenditure variable employed is per capita police expenditures for 1970, obtained from The United States Department of Justice (1972). We thus estimated the following equation (t-values are in parentheses under coefficients):

$$\begin{aligned}
TC = \ &20.37 + 4.86 \ (K1) + 2.92 \ (K2) - .05 \ (K3) \qquad (3) \\
&(4.93) \ \ (3.20) \qquad \quad (2.44) \qquad \quad (-.06) \\
&+ \ 2.40 \ (K4) + .57 \ (K5) + .85 \ (K6) \\
&\ \ (2.96) \qquad \ \ (1.54) \qquad \ \ (1.92) \\
&\qquad + .88 \ (TC_{t-1}) - .39 \ (PE) \\
&\qquad \ \ (14.32) \qquad \quad (-2.88) \\
R^2 = \ &.935 \qquad F = 65.97 \qquad S = 4.40
\end{aligned}$$

The overall fit of this equation is quite satisfactory, as seen by the coefficient of determination, adjusted for degrees of freedom. The constructed principal component indices for urban decay (K1), affluence (K2), education (K4) and youth presence (K6) are positive and significant at the 5 percent level.

The positive influence of the urban decay measure is as expected, since population shifts and resulting employment shifts (following, for example, Kain, 1968) no doubt reduce the set of legitimate employment opportunities available to potential criminals. The positive and highly significant values of the coefficients for our indices of affluence and education would seem at first inspection to be of the wrong sign. We interpret these components as in some sense measuring the potential gains to criminals; that is, areas with high incomes and well educated persons will necessarily return higher gains to criminals. The use of an income measure as a proxy for gains from crime has been employed in previous studies, with good results (see Ehrlich, 1973), and this interpretation is apparently applicable here.

Our constructed measure of youth presence also has a positive influence on total crime rates. This finding is in accord with FBI data which show that over half of arrests for crime involve persons under the age of twenty-four (United States Department of Justice, 1971). Assuming some proportionality between arrests and crime, variation in youth presence is apparently responsible for a significant portion of the intercity variation in total crime rates.

Constructed measures of minority presence (K3) and housing quality (K5) are not significant at the 5 percent level, although housing quality is significant at the 10 percent level. While it may be a tenet of conventional wisdom that minority presence is responsible for a great deal of crime, our results show that this variable is not a strong determinant of intercity variation in crime rates, when other factors, such as urban decay, are accounted for.[2] This finding supports an earlier position of the Task Force on Assessment, of the President's Commission on Law Enforcement and Administration of Justice (1967a, p. 78). They concluded that, *with all other factors held equal,* the differential criminal participation rate between blacks and whites is virtually zero.

Results for the housing quality component, an inverse housing quality measure, suggest that as housing quality declines, crime increases. Again, this result is not unexpected, in light of previous studies. This influence on criminality has long been suggested as one undesirable side effect of the conditions of slum living (see in particular, Rothenberg, 1967, ch. 10).

The coefficient of the lagged crime variable (TC_{t-1}) is large,

---

2. One reader has suggested that since the primary determinants of minority presence (percent black and change in black population) appear in each and every component, the overall influence of minority presence is understated in our results for variable K3. Inspection of Table 19-II shows that these variables do not load dominantly on any component other than K3. Thus, their influence is by no means pervasive over components.

but less than unity, and hence the system is stable. Importantly, the significance of this coefficient suggests that variation in police expenditures and the causes of crime do, indeed, impact upon reported crime rates in a lagged fashion. The coefficient for police expenditures (PE) is seen to be negative, indicating the existence of the hypothesized deterrent effect of police expenditures on crime. The significance of this result is that when a sufficient number of basic causal variables appear in the crime function, the true deterrent influence of police expenditures on criminality becomes evident.[3]

Having estimated the crime function, we then estimated the police expenditure function. The budget data employed were per capita municipal revenues for 1970, obtained from the United States Department of Commerce (1972d). The results of least squares regression analysis are:

$$PE = 3.45 + .26 \ (TC) + .04 \ (R)$$
$$(.7874)(2.76) \qquad (5.87)$$
$$R^2 = .6476 \qquad F = 36.75 \qquad S = 8.81$$

$$(4)$$

Per capita police expenditures are positively and significantly related to the perceived need for such service (crime rate) and the budget constraint facing policy makers. While this equation does not have the high coefficient of determination we found for our crime functions, the statistical fit is better than that found by Brazer (1959, p. 25) (.260) and Greenwood and Wadycki (1973, p. 146) (.49), is similar to that found by Bahl (1968, ch. 3) (.643), and approaches that found by Weicher (1970, p. 85) (.727), who used many more variables, not including crime.

While these results indicate the strong influence of crime in explaining police expenditures, the interrelated nature of the system may best be examined by analysis of the short and long run multipliers implied by the estimated coefficients of 3 and 4. To derive the multipliers, first write the equations in matrix form:

$$AY_t = BY_{t\text{-}1} + CX_t \qquad (5)$$

---

3. In preliminary tests excluding the lagged crime term, the sign of the police expenditure coefficient in the crime function was consistently positive. This result confirms the importance of the role played by lagged crime determinants in clarifying the deterrent role of police expenditures in the present period.

where Y_t is the vector of endogenous variables

$$Y_t = \begin{bmatrix} TC_t \\ PE_t \end{bmatrix} \tag{6}$$

Y_{t-1} is its lagged value and X_t is the vector of exogenous variables and intercepts

$$X_t = \begin{bmatrix} 20.3758 \\ 3.4554 \\ K_{1t} \\ K_{2t} \\ K_{3t} \\ K_{4t} \\ K_{5t} \\ K_{6t} \\ R_t \end{bmatrix} \tag{7}$$

where the first two elements are the intercepts, the next six are the environmental components and R_t is the municipal budget. The matrices are

$$A = \begin{bmatrix} 1 & .3946 \\ -.2640 & 1 \end{bmatrix} \tag{8}$$

$$B = \begin{bmatrix} .8765 & 0 \\ 0 & 0 \end{bmatrix} \tag{9}$$

$$C = \begin{bmatrix} 1 & 0 & 4.8567 & 2.9196 & -.0461 & 2.4021 & .5701 & .8504 & 0 \\ 0 & 1 & 0 & 0 & 0 & 0 & 0 & 0 & .04045 \end{bmatrix} \tag{10}$$

The reduced form system is

$$Y_t = A^{-1}BY_{t-1} + A^{-1}CX_t \tag{11}$$

so that the matrix of short run multipliers is $A^{-1}C$. These are presented in Table 19-III. The long run multipliers are given by $(I-A^{-1}B)^{-1}A^{-1}C$ and are also presented in Table 19-III.

The intercepts can be interpreted as taste variables. Thus, an increase in the crime function, through a shifting of intercept 1, can be interpreted as an increase in society's tolerance for crime. Such a change in taste or tolerance possibly occurred in the early part of the decade of the sixties. Between 1960 and 1970 the total number of reported crimes increased by over 175 percent, while before this period crime had been increasing at a much more gradual rate (United States Department of Justice, 1971, p. 21).

TABLE 19-III

MULTIPLIERS FOR CRIME AND LAW ENFORCEMENT EXPENDITURES

Variables	Crime		Law Enforcement Expenditures	
	Short Run	Long Run	Short Run	Long Run
Intercept 1	.9057	4.3922	.2391	1.1596
Intercept 2	− .3587	− 1.7332	.9057	.5424
K_1	4.3985	21.3318	1.1612	5.6316
K_2	2.6441	12.8236	.6981	3.3854
K_3	− .0418	− .2025	− .0110	− .0535
K_4	2.1755	10.5506	.5743	2.7854
K_5	.5163	2.5040	.1363	.6611
K_6	.7702	3.7352	.2033	.9861
R	− .0145	− .0701	.0366	.0219

An increase in the taste for crime, at given levels of environmental variables and lagged crime, causing an increase of one crime per thousand persons, would actually result in an increase of only .9057 crimes per thousand in the short run. This is because the rise in crime would induce a rise in law enforcement expenditures of (1) × (.2640). This rise in law enforcement expenditures would reduce crime by (.2640) × (.3946) = .10417 crimes per thousand persons. The reduction in crime would induce a reduction in law enforcement expenditures of (.10417) × (.2640) which in turn would cause crime to increase. The magnitude of the spillover effects from crime to law enforcement expenditures and *vice versa* diminishes at each "round." At the end of the process, crime would have increased by .9057 crimes per thousand and law enforcement expenditures would be up by .2391 dollars per person.

A similar analysis for the intercept of the expenditure function could be undertaken. This intercept might be interpreted as a taste variable reflecting society's taste for law enforcement or police services, apart from the perceived need for those services to specifically combat crime. A change in this intercept cannot be induced by crime, because such effect is captured by the crime variable in equation 2. It could, however, be induced by an increased public view of police as social servants, and this trend has, in fact, been rather important in recent years: most police time (70 to 80%) is now taken up with providing to the community a host of noncrime related services (see Clapp, Doering, Steinberger and Strumpler, 1972; Misner, 1967; and Wilson, 1968).

For whatever reason, a shift in the law enforcement expenditure function causing expenditures to increase by one dollar per capita would result in a rise in expenditures of only .9057 dollars after the spillover effects are taken into account.

Note that the municipal budget has a relatively weak impact on both crime and police expenditures, having the smallest multiplier for each variable. This reflects the importance of crime as an explanation for law enforcement expenditures and the relatively small size of the deterrent effect of law enforcement expenditures on crime. These results suggest that, historically, law enforcement expenditures have tended to *respond to crime* rather than *vice versa*. Indeed, under this interpretation, it might be more accurate to regard law enforcement expenditures as expenditures to "clean up" after crime rather than specifically to deter future crime. It is this relationship here which has undoubtedly been picked up by previous studies finding a positive relationship between crime and police expenditures and which has led to the incorrect conclusions concerning police deterrence which have thus followed.

The major determinants of crime are clearly the environmental variables, particularly urban decay (K1) and the affluence measure (K2). These two variables represent two important aspects of the criminal decision. Individuals will apparently enter into criminal activity if legitimate opportunities are diminished, as is the case under urban decay, and also if the potential gains through attack on more affluent sectors of society are relatively large. The third aspect of the crime decision, of course, deals with the probability of arrest as perceived by the prospective criminal. Our results indicate that increases in police expenditures apparently act to increase the criminal's perceived probability of arrest.

Turning to the long run multipliers, it is evident that crime responds to changes in its causes very slowly. Thus, the long run multipliers for crime are almost five times the size of the short run multipliers. This reflects the large size of the coefficient of lagged crime in the crime equation (.8765). Because the effects of the exogenous variables on crime are large in the long run, the variables which directly affect crime but only indirectly affect law enforcement expenditures (intercept 1, K1, K2, K3, K4, K5, K6) have larger long run mulitipliers for law enforcement expenditures. Variables which directly affect law enforcement expenditures, on the other hand, have smaller long run multipliers. This reflects the reduction in crime induced by law enforcement expenditures which is larger in the long run than in the impact period. The large long run reduction in crime negates part of the increase in law enforcement expenditures resulting from an increased budget or shifts in intercept 2.

CONCLUSIONS

Most previous studies of police expenditure functions have neglected to include crime as a determinant of such expenditures. Further, while theoretical analyses of the relation between law enforcement activity and crime suggest that increased police expenditures will have a deterrent effect on crime, empirical treatments of this proposition have found a perverse positive relation between these two variables. This paper corrects these shortcomings of earlier studies by analyzing crime and police expenditures within the framework of a simultaneous system.

A crime function is estimated, utilizing as explanatory variables constructed indices of certain central city characteristics, a lagged crime variable to allow for a gradual impact of the causes of crime on changes in crimes rates, and per capita police expenditures. The results confirm what economic theories of crime have suggested: increases in police expenditures have a deterrent effect on crime. Additionally, an estimated police expenditure equation indicates that these expenditures are related to crime, a budget constraint variable, and the community's taste for law enforcement services.

Analysis of the implied multipliers shows that law enforcement expenditures are essentially undertaken to correct or respond to past increases in criminal activity, which no doubt helps to explain the perverse positive relation between crime and police expenditures found in earlier studies.

This result, coupled with the rather potent influence of the constructed indices of central city environmental characteristics, suggests that society must mount a two-pronged attack upon crime. It is essential that we move, on the one hand, to correct the social and economic conditions which contribute to criminal behavior. Such change must come through broad based social programs for, as noted by the President's Commission on Law Enforcement and Administration of Justice (1967b, p. 2), police agencies cannot be expected to change the conditions which cause crime. On the other hand, our results seem to indicate that increased police expenditures do have a definite deterrent impact upon criminal activity. Resources for crime control should thus be apportioned among both social and law enforcement allocations in order to maximize national welfare.

REFERENCES

Adams, R. F.: On the variation in the consumption of public services. In Brazer, H. F. (Ed.): *Essays in State and Local Finance.* University of Michigan, 1967.

Allison, John P.: Economic factors and the rate of crime. *Land Economics,* May, 1972, pp. 193-196.

Bahl, R. W.: *Metropolitan City Expenditures.* University of Kentucky, 1968.

Baumol, W. J.: Macroeconomics of unbalanced growth: the anatomy of urban crisis. *American Economic Review,* June, 1967, pp. 415-426.

Becker, Gary: Crime and punishment: an economic approach. *Journal of Political Economy,* March/April, 1968, pp. 169-217.

Brazer, H. E.: *City Expenditures in the United States.* New York, National Bureau of Economic Research, 1959.

Clapp, D. E., Doering, R. D., Steinberger, E. A., and Strumpler, K. R.: Engineering management methodology applied to police department operations. *Police,* June, 1972.

Dhrymes, P. J.: *Econometrics: Statistical Foundations and Applications.* New York, Harper and Row, 1970.

Ehrlich, I.: Participation in illegitimate activity: a theoretical and empirical investigation. *Journal of Political Economy,* May/June, 1973, pp. 521-564.

Elliot, J. F.: *Interception Patrol.* Springfield, Thomas, 1973.

Fabricant, Solomon: *The Trend of Government Activity in the United States.* New York, National Bureau of Economic Research, 1952.

Greenwood, Michael J., and Wadycki, Walter J.: Crime rates and public expenditures for police protection: their interaction. *Review of Social Economy*, October, 1973, pp. 138-151.

Harris, J. R.: On the economics of law and order. *Journal of Political Economy*, January/February, 1970, pp. 165-174.

Hirsch, Werner: Expenditure implications of metropolitan growth and consolidation. *Review of Economics and Statistics*, August, 1959, pp. 232-241.

Hirsch, Werner: The supply of urban public services. In Perloff, Harvey S. and Wingo, Lowdon (Eds.). *Issues in Urban Economics*, Resources for the Future. Baltimore, The Johns Hopkins Press, 1968.

Jones, E. Terrence: Evaluating everyday policies: police activity and crime incidence. *Urban Affairs Quarterly*, March, 1973, pp. 267-279.

Kakalik, James S., and Wildhorn, Sorrell: *Aids to Decision Making in Police Patrol*. The Rand Corporation, 1971.

Kain, John F.: The distribution and movement of jobs and industry. In Wilson, James Q. (Ed.): *The Metropolitan Enigma*. Cambridge, Harvard University Press, 1968.

Koyck, L. M.: *Distributed Lags and Investment Analysis*. Amsterdam, North Holland, 1954.

Misner, Gordon: The urban police mission. *Issues in Criminology*, Vol. 3, 1967.

Mitchell, Bridger. *Estimation of Large Econometric Models by Principal Component and Instrumental Variable Methods*. Stanford University, March, 1970.

Pidot, George: A principal components analysis of the determinants of local government fiscal patterns. *Review of Economics and Statistics*, May, 1969, pp. 176-188.

Pogue, Thomas F.: Intercity-difference in crime rates: the roles of law enforcement activities and economic conditions, paper presented at the annual meetings of the Southern Regional Science Association, New Orleans, 1973.

President's Commission on Law Enforcement and Administration of Justice, Task Force on Assessment: *Task Force Report: Crime and Its Impact—An Assessment*. Washington, U. S. Government Printing Office, 1967a.

President's Commission on Law Enforcement and Administration of Justice, Task Force on Police: *Task Force Report: The Police*. Washington, U. S. Government Printing Office, 1967b.

President's Commission on Law Enforcement and Administration of Justice, Institute for Defense Analyses; *Task Force Report: Science and Technology*. Washington, U. S. Government Printing Office, 1967c.

Pressman, I., and Carol, A.: Crime as a diseconomy of scale. *Review of Social Economy*, March, 1971, pp. 227-236.

Rothenberg, Jerome: *Economic Evaluation of Urban Renewal.* Washington, Brookings Institution, 1967.

Stigler, George J.: The optimum enforcement of laws. *Journal of Political Economy,* May/June, 1970, pp. 526-536.

Tullock, Gordon: An economic approach to crime. *Social Science Quarterly,* 50:59-71, 1969.

United States Department of Commerce, Bureau of the Census: *1970 Census of Population and Housing, General Demographich Trends for Metropolitan Areas, 1960 to 1970.* Washington, U. S. Government Printing Office, 1972.

United States Department of Commerce, Bureau of the Census: *1970 Census of Housing, Housing Characteristics for States, Cities and Counties.* Washington, U. S. Government Printing Office, 1972.

United States Department of Commerce, Bureau of the Census: *City Government Finances in 1970-71.* Washington, U. S. Government Printing Office, 1972.

United States Department of Commerce, Bureau of the Census: *Assessed Valuations for General Property Taxation,* CG-P4. Washington, United States Government Printing Office, 1968.

United States Department of Justice, Federal Bureau of Investigation: *Uniform Crime Reports for the United States, 1970.* Washington, U. S. Government Printing Office, 1971.

United States Department of Justice, Law Enforcement Assistance Administration: *Expenditure and Employment Data for the Criminal Justice System, 1969-70.* Washington, U. S. Government Printing Office, 1972.

Weicher, John C.: Determinants of central city expenditures: some overlooked factors and problems. *National Tax Journal,* December, 1970, pp. 379-396.

Wilson, O. W.: *Police Administration,* 3rd ed. New York, McGraw-Hill, 1972.

Wilson, James Q.: *Varieties of Police Behavior.* Cambridge, Harvard University Press, 1968.

Section IV

ECONOMIC ANALYSIS AND OPERATIONS RESEARCH IN CRIMINAL JUSTICE

Chapter 20

AN ECONOMIC ANALYSIS OF THE DETERRENT EFFECT OF LAW ENFORCEMENT ON CRIMINAL ACTIVITY

Llad Phillips and Harold L. Votey, Jr.

INTRODUCTION

Economics has been referred to as "the dismal science," an appellation which probably stems from Thomas Malthus' 18th century essay on population,[1] in which he predicted dire consequences for the world's people as a consequence of rapid rates of population growth. While the immediate conclusions from some of our research on the economics of crime may seem to contribute to a dismal outlook, we would prefer to argue that a problem is dismal only if we cannot see a clear path to a solution and thus run out of hope.

A recent headline in the *Los Angeles Times*[2] read "L.A. Crime Rate Could Collapse Justice System, Computer Says." Allowing for the tendency of the press to attribute occult powers to computers, we find that a research team from the University of Southern California has predicted a possible collapse of the system of

Reprinted, with permission of the Northwestern University School of Law, from *Journal of Criminal Law, Criminology, and Police Science*, September 1972, pp. 330-342.

The authors wish to acknowledge the support of the National Institute of Law Enforcement and Criminal Justice, United States Department of Justice, under whose auspices the original research for this paper was conducted. Continuing research on these topics is presently being supported by the California Council on Criminal Justice—Task Force on Science and Technology.

1. The reference was "to respectable professors of the dismal science." Carlysle (1850).

2. Drummond (1970). This story was based upon McEachern (1970).

criminal justice in Los Angeles as a consequence of an overload on facilities at all levels. However, from an examination of the formal documentation of the work performed by the USC group, it appears that their analysis was based on a "simplistic" inertial model in which crime generation and crime countermeasures were treated as inertial forces. Although this very extensive study has produced projections that will be invaluable in alerting policy-makers to the very real consequences of allowing present trends to go unchecked, it does little to provide an understanding of how the criminal justice system will respond to continuing rates of change. This is because simplistic inertial models are not designed to analyze underlying processes, and consequently do not yield an understanding of how a system works, nor do they provide clues to action necessary for controlling the various forces within a system.

The dire predictions about the consequences of continually rising crime rates raise a number of questions. Where do we break into this system to bring crime levels within reasonable limits? Are there alternative approaches or solutions to the problem? What will happen to law enforcement effectiveness and crime rates if we continue with present expenditure policies? How much would it cost to keep law enforcement effectiveness from deteriorating? Can we afford to hold constant or reduce the current level of offenses?

In this study we have utilized the techniques of economics for evaluating and controlling economic systems in an analysis of crime control. Using the most recently available data including that from the Uniform Crime Reporting Section of the FBI and the California Bureau of Criminal Statistics, our study analyzes the processes generating crime, the productivity of law enforcement agencies, and welds these two processes together in a model that permits an analysis of underlying causes and the various appropriate responses to the crime problem.

ECONOMIC MODEL OF CRIMINAL JUSTICE

This study is based on a model which incorporates interaction between the process that generates crime and the system of law enforcement. We postulate that law enforcement not only responds to crime for the purpose of meting out punishment, but more importantly that it creates a deterrent effect which tempers the process of crime generation. In this more sophisticated model, one of the potential theoretical outcomes will still be the collapse of the criminal justice system. More important for our purposes, however, is the use of such a model to critically examine the processes of crime generation and crime control.

Our study deals primarily with the major felonies which may be classified as economic crimes: crimes for which there is a clear-cut economic motive. Many of the results, however, are more general in nature and will apply to noneconomic crimes as well. Our analysis conveniently breaks down into three parts. We will deal separately with the process of crime generation and with the analysis of law enforcement viewed as a service industry, finally synthesizing these results to create an interacting system. This system is illustrated schematically in Figure 20-1. The logic of this schematic is as follows: Law enforcement is viewed as acting on offenses and clearing them by arrest. The effectiveness of law enforcement is determined by technology and expenditures on law enforcement. The effectiveness of law enforcement is, in turn, presumed to affect the behavior of offenders. In addition to law enforcement, attitudes and economic conditions are postulated to determine offense rates. The inclusion of the impact of the judicial and correctional systems on offense rates is illustrated by broken lines to indicate that these systems have not been analyzed in the present study, but could readily be incorporated within this conceptual framework.

In our empirical analysis of crime generation we included larceny, burglary, auto theft, and robbery as defined and reported in the Uniform Crime Reports of the Federal Bureau of Investigation. Our study breaks the population down into subsets classified by age, sex, and race. There are sound reasons for this. For example, the evidence shows rather emphatically that these crimes are largely a youthful phenomenon. We find that both the distribution of crimes by age and the rates of increase of crimes by age are greater for the ages under twenty. Consequently, we selected 18 to 19 year olds as an appropriate group to study. We found further that for these crimes, except for larceny, 94 percent or

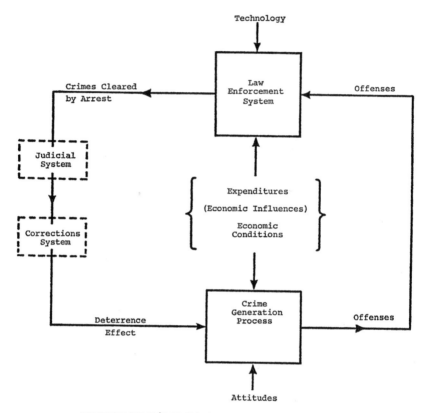

SCHEMATIC DIAGRAM OF THE CRIMINAL JUSTICE SYSTEM

Figure 20-1

more are committed by males in the 18 to 19 year old group. For larceny the figure is 75 percent. We also observed that arrest patterns vary by race for reasons which became apparent as the study progressed.

CRIME GENERATION

For several centuries criminologists have been suggesting economic motives as one of the possible causes of property crimes. Illegal gains are an alternative to income earned honestly. The critical question is how does one choose between socially acceptable and illegal alternatives for earning income. Here economic theory can make an important contribution. Theory tells us that a rational individual will, implicitly at least, consider all

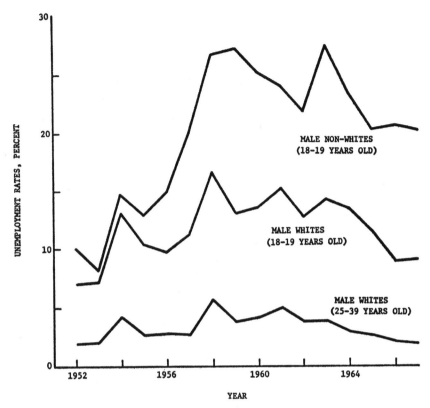

Figure 20-2. Male unemployment rates by race, selected age groups. (Based on data from Dept. of Labor, Manpower Report of the President [1970].)

of the alternatives open to him in terms of a benefit-cost analysis. From normal employment, the benefit is a stream of wage payments. The associated costs include the every-day costs of acquiring and maintaining a job. In the case of a crime, the benefits are any returns from its commission. The costs include the direct costs associated with the actual commission of a crime; advance research, transportation, the transactions' costs of disposing of illegally obtained goods.[3] In addition, there may be the costs associated with being apprehended, including the cost of having an arrest on one's record, the cost for legal defense, the loss of in-

---

3. The benefit (value) the criminal receives from illegal goods may be considerably less than the market price.

come from being incarcerated, and the psychic cost of being branded a criminal. The expected cost of these latter possibilities will be the cost associated with the event multiplied by the probability that the event (arrest, trial, imprisonment) takes place. When our rational individual considers this whole array of possibilities he will quite naturally choose that activity which yields him the greatest net material and psychic benefits. Should some elements of this choice set be eliminated for any reason, the individual would, of course, choose from those alternatives remaining.

The next step is to see how this theory of choice relates to economic realities for the 18 to 19 year old group. What do we know about their set of alternatives? If we look at the data for the period 1952 through 1967 (Fig. 20-2) we find that unemployment rates for white males go from a low of 7.0 percent in 1952 to a high of 16.5 percent in 1958, then decline erratically to 9.0 percent in 1967. Over the same period, unemployment rates for nonwhites go from a low of 10.0 percent in 1952 to a high of 27.2 percent in 1959, then decline to 20.1 percent in 1967. By contrast, average unemployment rates for the total labor force never rise above 6.8 percent over this entire period.

Another measure of the economic well-being of a population subset is the group's labor force participation rate. This is a measure of the proportion of the group who are either employed or actively seeking work. A decline in participation rates for youths generally comes about for one of two reasons. An individual may be attending school, or he may be so despondent about the possibility of obtaining work that he leaves the labor force. Referring to Figure 20-3, we observe that in terms of their participation rates, 18 to 19 year olds are worse off than the population as a whole, and nonwhites are again relatively disadvantaged.

The impact of school enrollment on this process is also important. Going to school represents an investment in greater future earning power for the individual. A rational individual will look at the lifetime possibilities associated with greater schooling as compared to immediate full time employment. The array of opportunities facing an 18-19 year old thus has a time dimension and includes schooling as one of the legal activities from which

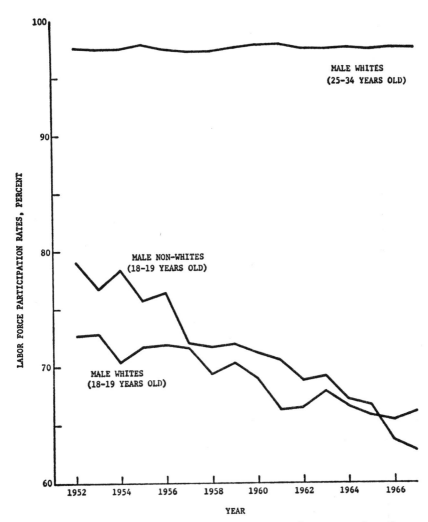

Figure 20-3. Male labor force participation rates by race, selected age groups. (Based on data from Dept. of Labor, Manpower Report of the President [1970].)

he can choose. However, the choice of further education may also depend on immediate employment opportunities, since schooling requires an immediate investment for a return that may commence years hence. Consequently, lacking either savings or a job, the opportunity to attend school may be eliminated from an individual's alternatives for reasons beyond his control. Referring to Figure 20-4, which depicts statistics for school enrollment, we find that in 1952, 38.1 percent of 18 to 19 year old white males were enrolled in school. This may be contrasted with 34.6 percent for nonwhite males of the same age. By 1967 these figures had risen to 61.5 percent and 53.5 percent respectively. Once more we see that nonwhites have become relatively disadvantaged.

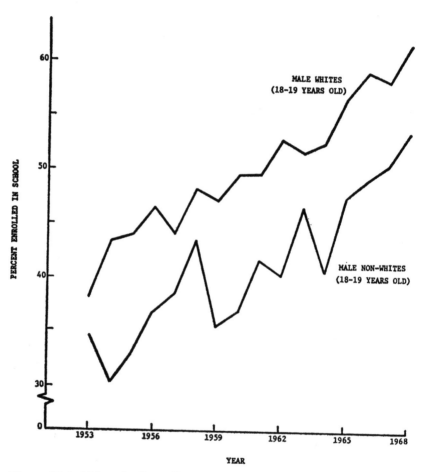

Figure 20-4. Male school enrollment ratios by race. (Based on data from Dept. of Commerce, bureau of the census, current population reports, Series, P-20, selected issues.)

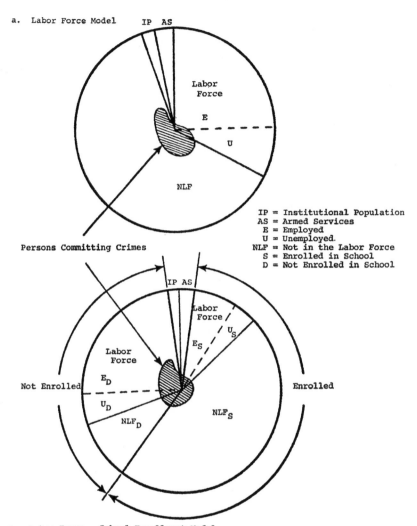

Figure 20-5. Venn diagrams of population categories used in models of crime generation. The ratio of shaded area to total area, which may be measured by age specific arrest rates for any given age population, represents the probability of arrest.

To study the impact of economic opportunity for youth on their criminal activity one can formulate a probability model of behavior based on a population breakdown by labor force characteristics. Figure 20-5 is a Venn diagram of such a breakdown. It is obvious that crimes committed by this age group must involve individuals in one of the subsets of the total eighteen to nineteen-year-old population. The shaded area in the center represents those who have committed crimes in a given year. If we believe that employment status and school enrollment status affect the individual's inclination to commit a crime, then we would expect the probability of arrest to vary according to the subset of the population in which an individual is found. As noted above, we know that the number of individuals in each of these categories varies over time and have data on this variation. We also have data on how arrest rates for eighteen to nineteen-year-olds vary over the same period. If we use arrest rates as a measure of the probability of arrest and the data on school enrollment and labor force status to represent the probability of being in one of these population groups, we can estimate the impact of changing school enrollment and job opportunities on arrest rates. We find that we can "explain" 98 percent of the variation in arrest rates for eighteen and nineteen-year-olds by changes in their economic opportunities.[4]

This suggests that an improvement in economic opportunities for youth in terms of some form of education or immediate employment will have an ameliorating effect on youthful crime rates. This in itself is hardly a new idea. Although sociologists have been asserting this for some time, the important thing here is that solid statistical verification of this relationship is provided within a formally specified analytical framework.[5]

The policy implication from our result is that there is a trade-off between policies which control crime and those which affect the generation of crime. An important aspect of the latter policy is a cumulative one. The evidence on recidivism is discouraging. Once an individual commences on a pathway of crime as the

---

4. See Votey and Phillips (1969).

5. For the development of our analytical framework and a discussion of earlier studies by others, *see* Phillips, Votey and Maxwell (1972).

source of economic sustenance, it is difficult to reroute him toward socially acceptable earning activities for a number of reasons. Thus, any measures which tend to remove the incentive for crime generation may have both an important immediate effect on crime rates and a more important long-run effect on the level of crime.

LAW ENFORCEMENT PRODUCTION FUNCTION

So far we have analyzed crime generation on the assumption that the impact of law enforcement on the process is constant. Since we cannot be sure this is true it is equally important to analyze the process of law enforcement from an economic point of view. To an economist, a law enforcement agency may be viewed in essentially the same manner as a firm in a service industry. A firm will maximize profits, given the prices it can charge for its services and the cost of inputs. Similarly, a law enforcement agency will maximize its output, given the annual budget determined by some external public body.

To acquire a conceptual understanding of the analysis of such an agency from an economic point of view, refer to Figure 20-6. The activity of the agency (police department) may be regarded

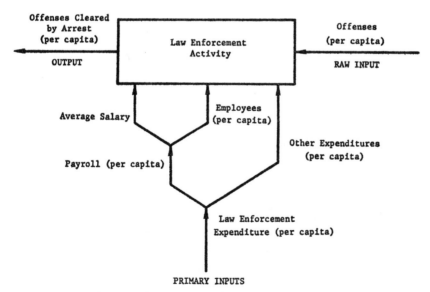

Figure 20-6. Schematic diagram of a law enforcement production process.

as a process into which flows an array of reported offenses. Police personnel operate on these offenses utilizing their time and capital equipment consisting of patrol cars, communication equipment, laboratories, etc., and produce a list of crimes cleared by arrest. For our analysis, we do not concern ourselves with the disposition of those arrested, but only assume the process works beyond the point of arrest.

The production function approach to law enforcement serves to emphasize a very important point. If offense rates are increasing, expenditures on law enforcement must be increased fast enough, or police effectiveness will fall. The necessary rate of increase in expenditures can be determined. If the offense rate increases and there is no increase in expenditures on law enforcement and no improvement in law enforcement technology, offenses cleared by arrest will increase but at a diminishing rate, as police resources are stretched more thinly. Beyond some point police will be unable to clear further crimes without being allotted additional resources. Consequently, police effectiveness as measured by the clearance ratio (the ratio of offenses cleared by arrest to offenses) will fall. (Refer to Fig. 20-7.) Conversely, if the offense rate is not changing and there are increases in expenditures or improvements in technology, police effectiveness will increase. If both offense rates and expenditures are increasing, the nature of the relationship between inputs and outputs will determine the impact on police effectiveness.

The important thing is that it is possible to estimate statistically the parameters of this production relationship. Based on national experience we can determine what percentage of increase in clearances one might expect with a 1 percent increase in police manpower or from a 1 percent increase in capital equipment. This information is of importance in making general estimates of how to allocate resources for the control of a particular crime, given that we wish to obtain a particular outcome in terms of the level of clearances for that crime. These "elasticities," *i.e.* percentage changes in output for a given 1 percent change in one of the inputs, are shown in Table 20-I.

One would expect a relatively larger coefficient on Other Ex-

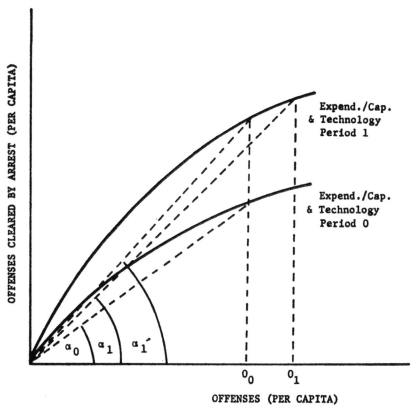

Figure 20-7. Diagram of the production function for law enforcement with alternative levels of expenditures/capita and technology.

penditures on Law Enforcement for crimes which require a more intensive use of capital in their solution. The crimes which we find to be more capital intensive by this reasoning are robbery and auto theft. These results seem to be consistent with a casual inspection of law enforcement experience. Robbery appears to be a crime whose solution depends upon a high degree of mobility of the police force and on communications since typical robberies are committed in areas in which continued surveillance is virtually impossible. Clearances for auto theft also seem to depend upon the mobility of the police force and more recently on computerized tracing techniques, all highly capital intensive. Thus it should

TABLE 20-I

EFFECTIVENESS OF INPUTS INTO THE LAW ENFORCEMENT SYSTEM

| Crime | Offenses | *Percentage Change in the Crimes Cleared by Arrest for a One Percent Change in* | |
		Police Personnel	Other Expenditures on Law Enforcement
Larceny	.628	.405	.143
Burglary	.186	.722	.303
Auto Theft	.546	*	.287
Robbery	.529	*	.131

* Police personnel did not have a statistically significant impact on crimes cleared by arrest for auto theft and robbery.

Source: Votey and Phillips, *Police Effectiveness: The Law Enforcement Production Function*, 1 J. LEGAL STUDIES, 423 (1972).

not be surprising that Other Expenditures appears more important in these estimated relationships. On the other hand, burglary solutions seem to depend more upon analytical techniques of a detective force and upon surveillance. Here we find that Police Personnel is a more important input in terms of the relative size of the coefficients. The solution of larceny (theft) depends almost entirely on surveillance and once more the variable Police Personnel is relatively more important than Other Expenditures on Law Enforcement.

The policy implications of these results are illustrated for the case of robbery in Figure 20-8. The solid line represents the actual experience of police in clearing crimes over the period studied. Over this is superimposed the predicted values based on our production function.

Our estimated production function fits the actual experience quite well. We see that whereas expenditures for law enforcement (police personnel and other expenditures on law enforcement) were rising fairly steadily over the entire period, offenses, which remained fairly steady through 1960, were rising much more rapidly from that year on. The consequence of this was that police effectiveness deteriorated rapidly in the latter period following a moderate rise from 1952 to 1957. If there had been a

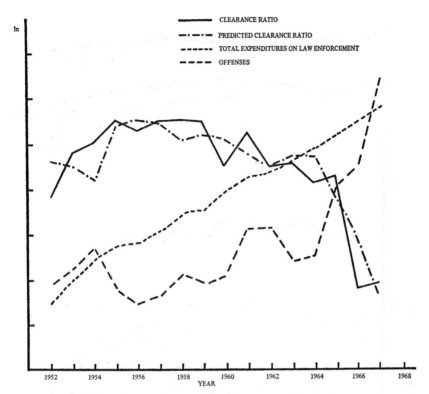

Figure 20-8. The time pattern of (the logarithms of) the clearance ratio, predicted clearance ratio, total expenditures on law enforcement and offenses. (Data from the Uniform Crime Reports of the Federal Bureau of Investigation and Dept. of Commerce, Governmental finance, selected issues.)

properly balanced increase in police personnel and other expenditures on law enforcement from 1960 onward to offset the rise in offenses, law enforcement agencies would have been able to maintain the level of police effectiveness.

SIMULTANEOUS SYSTEM OF CRIME GENERATION AND CONTROL

At this point, we have two relationships which comprise a simplified model of crime generation and control. Referring to Figure 20-1, we recall that deterrence is the link between crime control

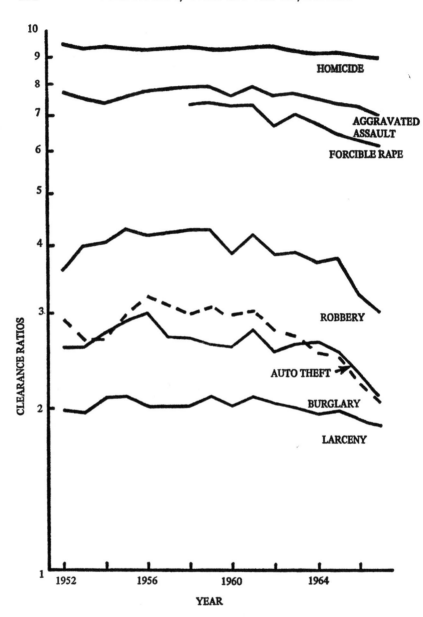

POLICE EFFECTIVENESS FOR THE FBI INDEX CRIMES

Figure 20-9

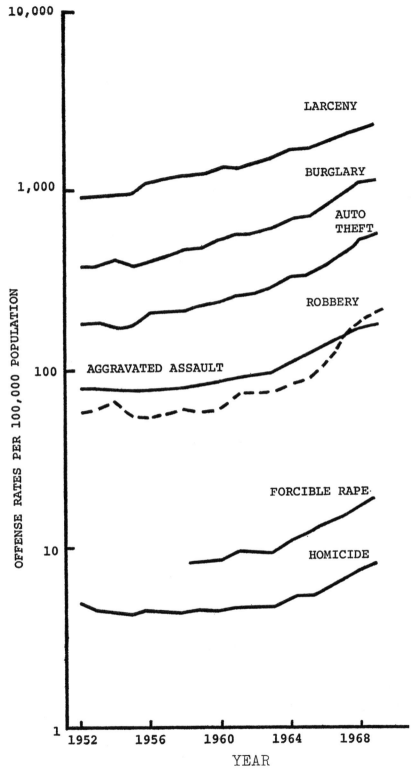

Figure 20-10. Offense rates for the FBI index crimes. (Based on data from Uniform Crime Reports, Federal Bureau of Investigation.)

and crime generation. Figure 20-9 shows clearance ratios for the index crimes from 1952 to 1967 for the cities covered by the Uniform Crime Reports of the FBI. The clearance ratio is both an index of police effectiveness in apprehending criminals and a measure of the probability of a criminal being arrested for a single offense. This probability should enter the potential criminal's cost calculations when he is choosing between economic alternatives. As the clearance ratio falls with no change in other variables in the system we would expect more criminal activity since the probability of arrest has fallen. This is in fact what we have observed. Figure 20-10 shows the alarming rise in offenses over the same time period.

The interaction of rising offenses with an insufficient rise in expenditures for law enforcement has resulted in the clearance ratio tracing a pattern resembling an inverted U as illustrated in Figures 20-8 and 20-9. The two relationships we have derived are illustrated in Figure 20-11a in such a manner as to reveal the

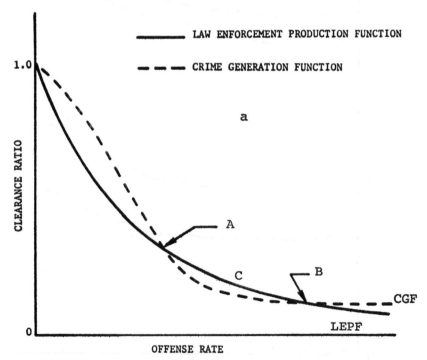

Figure 20-11

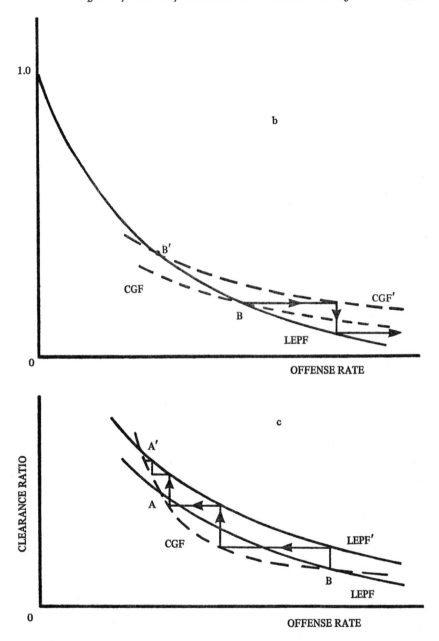

THE INTERACTION OF CRIME GENERATION AND CRIME CONTROL

Figure 20-11

interaction between them. The clearance ratio is plotted on the vertical axis. If law enforcement activity were completely successful the clearance ratio would be 1.0, *i.e.* clearances would equal offenses. The lower limit to the ratio is zero. For a given level of police technology and law enforcement expenditures, we would expect the clearance ratio to fall as offenses rise. Law enforcement personnel will be spread thinner and thinner in terms of the job they face, until only a small proportion of crimes is effectively dealt with. This relationship is illustrated by the solid line. Simultaneously, we must consider the crime generation function, which indicates how the offense rate will vary with the probability of arrest, given a particular state of affairs as determined by economic opportunities and social attitudes. That relationship is illustrated by the broken line. The two relationships will lead to an equilibrium solution with all forces in balance at point A. If the relationship is as we have drawn it, we will have a stable equilibrium.

Note that Figure 20-11a illustrates the determination of the clearance ratio and the offense rate (point A) for a given level of expenditures and state of technology for law enforcement and a given state of economic conditions for crime generation. As law enforcement expenditures rise or the state of technology improves, the crime-control curve will rotate upward and to the right. (The endpoint on the vertical axis representing a clearance ratio of one will remain fixed.) As economic conditions or social attitudes worsen the crime generation function will also tend to rotate in this same manner. If economic conditions worsen or social attitudes deteriorate, expenditures will have to increase in order to maintain the effectiveness of law enforcement. However, even in this case the offense rate will rise. If the equilibrium had been at some point C to the right of A and there had been a change in socioeconomic conditions (*e.g.* a decline in unemployment rates) to shift the crime generation function such that the new equilibrium would be at A, we would find that the level of the clearance ratio, as indicated by C on the crime control function, produces a greater probability of arrest than that anticipated by criminals. In successive moves a lower level of offenses will prevail until we reach the equilibrium point of A. Should offenses have been below A, a similar but opposite situation would exist such that we would find a lower clearance ratio than anticipated and crimes would rise until the system is once more in balance. This stable equilibrium represents the situation which we believe prevails in the United States at this time.

An example is the case of auto theft,[6] in which we note that the equilibrium is stable. A decline of 0.75 percent in the clearance ratio will induce a 1 percent increase in the offense rate, which in turn only causes a decline of 0.66 percent in the clearance ratio. Thus we see that changes precipitated by shifts in crime generation (or shifts in crime control caused by changes in law enforcement expenditures) will damp out and for auto theft the system will approach a point like A. Consequently, the system remains subject to control.

Using the results of simultaneously estimated relationships such as those we estimated independently for the crime generation function and law enforcement production function, it is possible to calculate some of the alternative rates of change for the clearance ratio and offense rates for auto theft which would have been possible to achieve by varying law enforcement expenditures.[7] These are presented in Table 20-II. We observe that during this period the per capita offense rate for auto theft was growing at 6.1

---

6. It should not be surprising that auto theft, which of the seven major felonies had one of the lowest average clearance ratios (26%) over the period 1952-1967, had one of the highest average offense rates (264 auto thefts per 100,000 population), suggesting that a low level of deterrence is directly linked to a high level of offenses.

7. The estimated functional relationships are:

$$\ln CR_t = \ln k + \lambda t + (a - 1)\ln O_t + \beta \ln E_t$$
$$\ln O_t = \ln j + \theta t + \gamma \ln CR_t + \delta \ln(\mu\rho)_t,$$

where CR, O, t, and $\mu\rho$ are defined as the clearance ratio, offense rate, time, and the product of the unemployment rate and participation rate, respectively. Time is included in the crime control function to measure changes in productivity due to technological change and in the crime generation function to measure systematic changes in social attitudes. The estimates for auto theft are:

a	β	γ	δ	λ	θ
0.339	0.222	–1.330	–0.193	0.022	0.045

A detailed explanation of the calculations for Table 20-II can be found in Votey and Phillips (1969), App. C, at 5.

TABLE 20-II

POSSIBLE CHANGES IN ANNUAL MEASURES FOR AUTO THEFT
GIVEN CRIME GENERATION FORCES AND ALTERNATIVE RATES OF
GROWTH OF EXPENDITURES ON LAW ENFORCEMENT

Growth of Expenditures on Law Enforcement	Consequent Changes of Clearance Ratio	Resultant Increase in Offense Rates
2.9%	−1.3%	6.1%
3.6%	0.0%	4.5%
5.4%	3.3%	0.0%

percent per year, and the rate of offenses cleared by arrest per capita was growing at 4.8 percent per year. Consequently, the clearance ratio was falling at the average rate of 1.3 percent per year. Implementation of the estimated relationships yields the results that per capita expenditures on law enforcement should have increased at the rate of 3.6 percent per year to keep the clearance ratio from falling. In fact, law enforcement expenditures were growing at only 2.9 percent per year. Even if expenditures on law enforcement had grown at 3.6 percent per year, the per capita offense rate for auto theft would have risen at 4.5 percent per year. It would have been necessary to increase per capita expenditures on law enforcement at the rate of 5.4 percent per year to maintain the auto theft offense rate at a constant level during this period. Referring to Table 20-II we see that if there had been no decrease in law enforcement effectiveness (0% rate of growth of the clearance ratio) offenses would have grown by 4.5 percent compared to the actual rate of increase of 6.1 percent. We conclude that approximately 75 percent of the observed rise in offense rates is attributable to changes in crime generation forces and only 25 percent to the failure to maintain law enforcement effectiveness.

The finding of stability over this period gives no grounds for complacency, however, for we can envision another altogether different situation. It is conceivable that police effectiveness could fall so low that we approach another equilibrium point as shown at B. Here we have an unstable equilibrium such that a shock to the system moving us in either direction from B will find no correcting force to bring about a return.

Should the law enforcement production function shift upward from LEPF to LEPF', as illustrated in Figure 20-11c, as a consequence of a rise in expenditures on law enforcement, starting from B we would find an increased probability of arrest leading to a decrease in offenses. We would reach a new stable equilibrium at A'.

Suppose, however, that instead unemployment rates increase so that the crime generation function shifts from CGF to CGF' as illustrated in Figure 20-11b. In this case the clearance ratio (and the probability of arrest expected by criminals) will be lower than anticipated and crimes will increase unchecked with the system out of control. This is the analogue in the sophisticated model to the collapse predicted by the simplistic inertial model.

There is another dynamic and presently unevaluated aspect of this system. It is conceivable that there may be an indirect and possibly inverse relationship between expenditures on law enforcement and the shape of the crime generation function. A heavy emphasis on law enforcement to the neglect of economic conditions could have the effect of worsening social attitudes in the form of a resentment of law enforcement and a general attitude of antagonism between levels of society.

SUMMARY

The value of the sophisticated model is that the outcome results from a number of plausible causes. Policy makers at one level may simply not be providing sufficient resources to combat crime, while policy makers at another level may not be taking sufficient action to maintain economic opportunities for an important segment of the population. In addition, social attitudes may be changing as a consequence of what leaders on all levels do or fail to do in attempting to cope with serious social problems. The solution to the problem is largely one of society's being willing to pay both the costs of law and order and the costs of maintaining healthy economic conditions and social attitudes. In the past we simply have not kept abreast of the problem.

What then is the appropriate policy for the nation or the state to follow to control crime? It is clear to us that law enforcement should be bolstered substantially. We are also convinced that such measures alone may be insufficient. We must control crime generation for two reasons. First, this is the only way to guarantee that we have control of both processes and thus can maintain social stability and, second, because the social cost of crime through recidivism is certain to be lower if we remove the incentives for the first offense. Our model serves to emphasize a point made by ex-Attorney General of the United States, Ramsey Clark, who said, "Law enforcement can only deal with the symptoms of crime. It's like bailing out the basement without turning off the water." We are in favor both of turning off the water and bailing out the basement.

REFERENCES

Carlysle, T.: Latter Day Pamphlets, No. 1, 1850.

Drummond, L. A.: *Crime Rate Could Collapse Justice System, Computer Says.* Los Angeles Times, Sept. 13, 1970.

McEachern, *et al.:* Criminal Justice Simulation Study: Some Preliminary Projections, Public Systems Research Institute, U.S.C., June 30, 1970.

Phillips, Votey, and Maxwell: Crime, youth, and the labor market. *J Pol Econ, 80:*491, 1972.

Votey, H., and Phillips, L.: Economic Crimes: Their Generation, Deterrence and Control 41, 23a, 27a. National Technical Information Service PB 194 984, 1969.

Chapter 21

AN ECONOMIC ANALYSIS OF CRIMINAL CORRECTIONS: THE CANADIAN CASE

KENNETH L. AVIO

INTRODUCTION

FOUR YEARS AGO, the Canadian Committee on Corrections issued an extensive report (*Ouimet Report*, 1969) on the state of correctional procedures and institutions in Canada, the third such study since 1938. It is interesting that there was not a single economist on the five-member Committee nor on the thirty-member Panel of Consultants to the Committee, although specialists in other areas of the social sciences were included (*Ouimet Report*, 1969, pp. 1-4). This oversight is rather surprising when one considers that economists have recently been devoting a considerable amount of attention to the "economics of crime,"[1] and have long been interested in the theory and administration of nonprofit organizations in general. In this paper a model is presented which draws on aspects of these two literatures to examine current correctional procedures in Canada.

The provision of protection services to society is the primary

Reprinted, with permission of the University of Toronto Press, from *Canadian Journal of Economics*, Volume VI, No. 2, May 1973, pp. 164-178.

1. See, for example, Becker (1968, pp. 169-217); Tullock (1969, pp. 59-71); and Stigler (1970, pp. 526-36). The basic assumption in these papers is that a prospective offender's supply of criminal offences depends upon his rational evaluation of the expected returns (including psychic income) from criminal activities vis-à-vis his returns from legitimate activities.

An opposing viewpoint can be found in Gordon (1971, pp. 51-75). Gordon questions the methodological underpinnings of the conventional economic approach.

function[2] of the Criminal Justice System (CJS), which is composed of the police force, the courts, and the various correctional programs. To place this study in proper perspective, the basic policy issues concerning the CJS should be noted. They are: (1) How many of society's scarce resources should be devoted to the CJS? (2) How should the resources devoted to the CJS be allocated among its member branches? (3) How should a particular branch of the CJS use its budgeted resources to provide the maximum in protection services to society?

This paper concentrates on question 3 for the correctional branch of the CJS. An economic model of a correctional institution is presented, with attention focused on the trade-offs among alternative uses of resources. The model is essentially an application of the standard theory of the nonprofit, multi-product firm. It is argued that correctional officials, as producers of these products, are in a better position to choose an efficient product mix than the courts. Reasons why the currently constituted Canadian judiciary would not be expected to choose efficient sentence lengths are listed. A parole program may, in part, redress the misallocation of resources occasioned by the courts; if sentence lengths are excessive, parole acts to make correctional institutions more efficient, with the result that the entire CJS moves closer to a position of optimality.[3] However, it will be argued that parole is a desirable part of any correctional system which features pre-incarceration sentencing, regardless of the abilities of sentencing authorities. A proposal to increase the incentive to obtain an early release through parole is discussed.

---

2. It will be assumed here that the provision of protection services is the *sole* output of the CJS. Police activities such as transporting pregnant women to hospitals, sponsoring youth groups, etc., may be rationalized as *indirect* crime prevention techniques. The police are more effiective in providing protection services if they gain the trust and co-operation of the community.

3. In this paper, "efficiency" of a correction program refers to the idealized solution of a *constrained* maximization problem, where the constraint is in terms of a budget. Whether or not society is operating in an "optimal" manner as regards over-all policies toward crime and criminals depends upon the idealized solution of an *unconstrained* optimization problem, such as that specified by Becker (1968, p. 181), and necessarily involves answering questions 1 and 2 above. For an attempt to answer these questions in a framework stressing the investment in human capital aspect of rehabilitative training, see Avio (1972, pp. 69-84).

THE PRISON AS AN ECONOMIC ENTITY

As noted above, the CJS may be defined as the set of institutions which provides protection services to society. Theoretically, the volume of such services may be measured by the number of crimes prevented (weighted by the severity of each crime) as a result of the existence and/or the implementation of procedures adopted by the CJS.

Correctional institutions, as an integral part of the CJS, may be viewed as nonprofit firms which produce two services intermediate to protection services: (1) incarceration services, and (2) training services. The former category of services affects the level of criminal activity in two ways. First, while incarcerated, an offender cannot commit crimes against "legitimate" members of society (the "removal" effect), and second, the mere existence of incarceration services provides a deterrent to prospective offenders (the "deterrent" effect). Thus, if incarceration services were the only output of correctional institutions, then the removal and deterrent effects would ensure that an increase in the average incarceration length for each offence category would raise the level of protection of society.

However, prisons also produce training services for society, services which may be viewed as investments in human capital. Such training services encompass a wide variety of programs, including formal education, vocational training, and on-the-job training.[4] They are intermediate to protection services in that if

4. The form of rehabilitative training may be less important than the length of the training period. For evidence, see Glaser (1964, ch. 11). Glaser notes that: (1) regular work during incarceration would be the longest continuous employment that most prisoners have ever had; (2) regularity of prior employment is statistically a better indicator of post-release success than is type of work previously performed, and (3) the major contributions of work in prison to inmates rehabilitation are the positive influence of work supervisors on inmates, *and* habituation of inmates to regularity in employment. In the terminology of Becker (1962, pp. 9-49), it is "general" and not "specific" training that is the major rehabilitative influence of prison employment. This is significant because in the noninstitutional part of the economy, general training must be paid for the labourer (p. 13). This suggests that one characteristic common to offenders is that they refuse to pay the cost of general training when given the choice. (Another possibility is that offenders are willing to pay the cost of general training,

they raise the expected legitimate income of an incarcerated prisoner, then the number of offences committed after release will be less than otherwise.[5] Unfortunately, training may be "negative" in the sense that a prisoner may spend his time increasing his productivity as a criminal. This occurs via a "technological diffusion" effect and a "production complements" effect. The former effect includes productivity increases due to increased knowledge of criminal production processes, and the latter effect (probably much more important) includes productivity increases due to an increased pool of complementary inputs (i.e. other criminals) from which to draw upon after release from prison. Hence, "negative" training acts to increase the expected return to criminal activity.

While in custody, it is likely that a prisoner will experience both "positive" and "negative" training. Therefore, whether the correctional institution is providing *training* services which increase or decrease the level of protection of society depends upon the balance of the two types of training services. To formalize the relationship between positive and negative training, a technological relationship of the form

$$t^- = n(t), \; n'(t) < 0 \tag{1}$$

will be assumed for each and every prisoner. In equation 1, t is an index ranking quantity and quality combinations of rehabilita-

---

but are unable to obtain jobs which would allow them the opportunity to purchase such training. This would suggest that the general training received while in prison might act as an inducement to some individuals to commit crime! However, there is no evidence that this effect is strong, and it will be ignored in the subsequent discussion.)

5. It is widely believed that there is discrimination against ex-convicts in the job market, with the result that a greater amount of "positive" training is needed to raise the expected wage of ex-convicts than is needed to raise the expected wage of non-convicts by the same amount, other things equal. Hence, for any amount of training accorded to incarcerated offenders, a reduction in discrimination will raise their expected legitimate wage and reduce the number of repeat offences. This reduction in discrimination could be partially effected by a government sponsored "hire ex-cons" campaign similar to those conducted for physically handicapped workers. In addition, the government could reduce its own discrimination against released offenders. (For a discussion of the legal disabilities placed upon offenders in Canada by Federal and Provincial legislation, see McGrath, 1969, pp. 240-54.)

tive training accorded *per day* per prisoner, and t^- is an index ranking quantity and quality combinations of negative training accorded per day per prisoner. Each of the two indices provides a complete ordering of all bundles of its own type (positive or negative) of training quantities and qualities. For example, the index t might be constructed by adding the number of hours per day a prisoner devotes to educational, vocational, and on-the-job training, each weighted by a factor representing the quality of the training.

The restriction $n'(t) < 0$ implies that positive and negative training compete for the available time and mental effort that a prisoner can expend. An increase in the quantity and/or quality of positive training should reduce the resources (time and/or effort) that a prisoner has available to devote to negative training. For example, substituting high quality professional instruction for low quality instruction provided by inmate instructors should reduce the amount of effort expended on negative training, even though the *quantity* of positive training might be held constant. This assumption of competition among the two types of training may not be justified in all cases (consider the psychedelic drug manufacturer who attains a chemistry degree while incarcerated), but for most cases it appears reasonable.

A production function for protection services supplied by correctional institutions may now be postulated. This function is written

$$PC = g(t, t^-, f; d), \qquad (2)$$

where PC is the level of protection services supplied by correctional institutions,[6] t and t^- are defined above, f represents sentence length,[7] and d is a parameter representing all other

6. Implicit in the preceding discussion is that the *current* values of t and t^- affect only the level of *future* crimes, whereas the "deterrent" and "removal" effects of the *current* value of f affect the number of *curent* offences. This makes the concrete interpretation of PC a bit difficult, as crimes prevented in different time periods are involved. However, a satisfactory theoretical solution is to measure all crimes prevented by a monetary denominator and then discount back to the present.

7. Rather than viewing f as an unidimensional variable it may be preferable to interpret it as a vector of sentence lengths, with each component of the vector pertaining to a specific category of crime.

factors which affect the level of criminal activity and are not provided or controlled by correction officials, including the size and technology of the police force, quality of the courts, degree of legal protection of suspects, private expenditures on crime prevention, the unemployment rate, etc.

In view of the technological relationships posited in equation 1, the production function equation 2 may be rewritten as

$$PC = s(t, f; d). \qquad (3)$$

"Isoquants" for equation 3 are represented in Figure 21-1 in a (t, f) space; it is understood that the level of d is held constant throughout the space. The curves are assumed to be negatively-

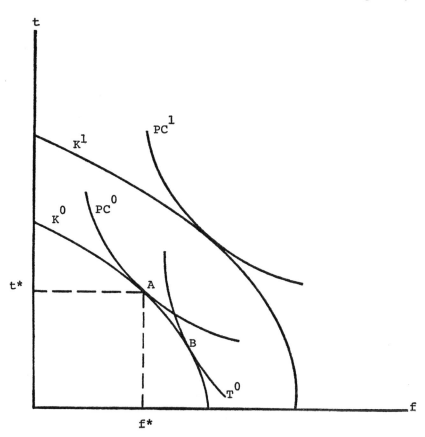

Figure 21-1. The allocation of resources by correctional institutions.

sloped and convex to the origin; i.e. the deterrent effect of longer sentences is assumed capable of compensating for reductions in positive training, but the increments in f needed to substitute for reductions in t must increase to offset the effects of increased "negative" training. In addition, for any given vector of sentence lengths, an increase in the level of rehabilitative training increases the amount of protection services supplied to society, i.e. in Figure 21-1, $PC^1 > PC^0$.[8]

The financial constraint under which correctional institutions operate in providing their services over the budget period may be written as

$$K = j(t, f), \tag{4}$$

where K is the annual budget provided by the legislature and j is the "service transformation" function indicating the bundles (t, f) that exhaust the budget. Insight into the form of the function j can be gained by examining the effects of changes in t and f on three categories of prison expenditures: security, training, and general living expenditures. First consider an increase in rehabilitative training, holding f constant. To generate such an increase, either higher quality instruction must be provided and/or the quantity of training activities provided to each inmate per day must be increased. In either case, expenditures for training prisoners would increase substantially. This increase in costs may be offset partially by the effects of an increase in t on living expenses, security expenses, and prison industry income,[9] but these

---

8. Of course, the *PC* map as depicted in Figure 21-1 is not the only possibility. If the deterrent effect were extremely weak, then it may be that for values of t below some critical level t^c, negative training becomes so overwhelming that *increases* in sentence lengths (for a constant t) *reduce* the level of protection. This implies a discontinuity in the map of protection isoquants; for values of $t < t^c$, the curves are positively-sloped and higher levels of protection are obtained by moving toward the t-axis.

9. To examine each of these possibilities in turn, first note that in so far as the increased training pertains to prison maintenance tasks (e.g. on-the-job training as a plumber), a reduction in prison costs might be forthcoming. Second, an increase in training may allow for a small reduction in security expenditures, as a quantitative increase in training per day reduces the "leisure" time of inmates, affording less chance for disorder and disturbances. Finally, if the increased training results in an increase in the output of prison industries, prison income may increase.

offsets are probably of a second-order nature when compared with the requisite increase in training expenses. Next consider an increase in sentence lengths, holding t constant. For all offenders subjected to correctional procedures, such a change implies a direct increase in all three categories of expenditure due to the increased number of days that each prisoner must be secured, trained, and provided with necessities. In addition, longer sentences probably increase the number of prison escape attempts,[10] thus requiring additional security expenses. These increased costs may be offset partially by the effects of an increase in f on the *number* of offenders incarcerated (via the "deterrent" effect), but on balance, it seems reasonable to assume that f and K are positively related.

The preceding discussion implies that the marginal costs of training and sentence lengths for correctional institutions are positive (i.e. $j_t > 0$ and $j_f > 0$). In addition, t and f exhibit "non-neutrality" in production, in the sense that an increase in one service output results in a change in the marginal cost of the other service output.[11] As depicted in Figure 21-1, the product transformation curves may be concave to the origin,[12] with $K^0 < K^1$.

From Figure 21-1 it can be seen that the bundle (t^*, f^*) represented by the point A is an efficient bundle, given the resource constraint K^0. This bundle possesses the property that the ratio of marginal benefits to marginal costs is the same for training services and incarceration services [i.e. $(s_t/j_t) = (s_f/j_f)$]. The locus of all points possessing such a property is represented as

---

10. If a prisoner knows he is going to be released in a short while, the benefits of a successful escape may not justify an attempt. However, if he has fifty years to serve, the benefits of a successful escape may outweigh the expected cost.

11. For example, an increase in training reduces the incremental amount of security expenditures required for an extra day's incarceration, due to the beneficial effects of rehabilitative training on prisoners' attitudes.

12. The second derivative of the product transformation curve $K^0 = j(t, f)$ is:

$$(d^2t/df^2)_{K=K^0} = -(1/j_t{}^2)[j_t j_{ff} - 2j_f j_{tf} + (j_f{}^2/j_t)j_{tt}],$$

so that increasing marginal costs ($j_{tt} > 0$, $j_{ff} > 0$) and technical complementarity ($j_{tf} < 0$) are sufficient conditions for concave to the origin product transformation curves.

$$e(t^*, f^*; d) = 0, \qquad (5)$$

the correctional institution's efficient expansion locus.

The above model of protection services provided through correctional procedures has an interesting and important policy implication. In Canada, the budgeting, training and incarceration length decisions are not made by one central authority, but are each primarily controlled by separate authorities. The legislature determines the maximum limits on incarceration in its prescription of the Criminal Code. In addition, the legislature determines the size of the Solicitor General's budget, which finances the RCMP, the Department of Penitentiaries, and the National Parole Board. The judicial branch of the CJS determines maximum lengths of incarceration for individual offenders within the prescription of the Code. The prison authorities oversee the actual incarceration of offenders, and as such, choose the quality and quantity (per day) of training. Finally, parole officials determine whether the offender will be required to serve his entire sentence in a correctional institution, or will be paroled back into society.

The implication of the model presented here is that under present Canadian institutional arrangements, such decentralized decision-making likely results in an inefficient bundle of training services and sentence lengths supplied by correctional institutions. The budget authorities determine the efficient pair (t^*, f^*) in their budget allocation to the Department of Penitentiaries. Given the disposition of government agencies to spend all funds allotted to them, correctional officials will choose a level of training services that is on the resource frontier, but since training services are largely a "residual" (in the sense that correctional institutions must give priority to the provision of the required amount of incarceration services), the level of training services will be efficient only if the courts choose sentence lengths[13] that are efficient in accordance with the prescribed resource constraint.

There appear to be three reasons why, under the existing Canadian institutional framework, an efficient bundle may not be chosen. First, the sentencing authority may possess sufficient

---

13. A discussion of parole is deferred to the next section.

knowledge to choose an efficient bundle, but such a choice may be inconsistent with the authority's own private maximization calculus. Such a possibility is easy to visualize under the current system. Consider a judge attempting to maximize his "tenure," T,[14] which depends to an extent upon public acceptance of his choice of sentence length. Then if both "retribution" (i.e. revenge upon the criminal), R, and protection services, PC, are desired by the public, the judge would choose values of f (and indirectly, t) to maximize

$$T = T[R(f), PC(t, f)], \tag{6}$$

where $T_R > 0$, $R_f > 0$ and $T_{PC} > 0$, and T is maximized subject to the product transformation curve of correctional institutions and to the sentence length prescriptions of the Criminal Code. The marginal rate of substitution along an "equal tenure" curve (such as T^0 in Fig. 21-1) is $(T_R R_f + T_{PC} s_f)/T_{PC} s_t$, which (for any particular bundle) is greater than s_f/s_t, the marginal rate of substitution along an "equal protection" curve. Hence, as illustrated in Figure 21-1, the chosen bundle B would provide an excess of incarceration services (and a shortage of training services) over the amount required for efficiency; "retribution" is purchased at the cost of a reduction in protection services. The policy implication is that any change in sentencing administration which dilutes the importance of the revenge factor leads to a more efficient system.

The second and third reasons for probable inefficiencies do not depend upon the motivation of the sentencing authorities but rather upon their abilities as resource allocators. The probability of a member of the currently constituted judiciary correctly perceiving the relationship between training services, sentence lengths, and protection services (i.e. the map of protection "isoquants" in Fig. 21-1) is small. In Canada, approximately 95 percent of all indictable offences are handled in magistrates' (i.e. provincial) courts (*Ouimet Report*, 1969, p. 166). However, most Canadian magistrates have not received formal training in cor-

---

14. The "tenure" of a judge may be explicated as the present discounted value of his expected income stream as payment for his services as a judge. As such, T depends both upon his years on the bench and on his upward mobility within the judicial system.

rectional philosophy.[15] Furthermore, it appears that appointments to such courts are sometimes more dependent upon political considerations than upon the inherent abilities of the appointees.[16] Under these conditions it would be most fortuitous if the sentencing authorities would be able to perceive accurately the role of rehabilitative training in providing protection services to society.

Even if the sentencing authorities did possess accurate knowledge of the protection service "isoquant" map, knowledge of the "service transformation curve" of correctional institutions is also necessary for choosing the efficient level of sentence lengths. This implies that the sentencing authority possess an intimate knowledge of prison programs. A strong case may be made that Canadian magistrates lack such knowledge. Young adult offenders, for example, are sometimes sentenced with the suggestion that they learn a certain trade while incarcerated; but due to lack of resources, it may be the case that no such trade program exists in the correctional institution, or if it is available, the particular training program may be incompatible with the sentence length handed down by the court.[17] Unfortunately, nothing can be done retroactively about such sentences under the present legal framework, as the courts lose their jurisdiction over an offender upon the imposition of sentence. Unless the sentence is appealed for some reason unrelated to the provision of training services, the original sentence will not be changed.

The *Ouimet Report* suggests that deficiencies in sentencing procedures would be overcome if all magistrates were required to have legal and correctional training (1969, pp. 166-67, pp. 212-15),

15. Indeed, many are not even trained in the law! The proportion of magistrates that possess legal training is below 50 percent in all provinces except Ontario according to Hogarth (1967, p. 126). In Ontario, over 70 percent of magistrates are qualified lawyers, but a recent Ontario Royal Commission felt that there were enough exceptions to recommend that the selection of magistrates be limited to include only qualified lawyers as candidates (*Ontario Royal Commission Inquiry into Civil Rights* vol. II, 1968, p. 544).

Arguments in favour of the present appointment system and the lack of need for specialized training by magistrates are found in Falzetta (1967, pp. 137-46).

16. The *Ontario Royal Commission Inquiry into Civil Rights* (vol. II, 1968, 539) strongly condemned the appointment of magistrates on a political basis.

17. On this and other anomalies in current sentencing procedures, see Gingeroff (1968, pp. 12-24).

and if a sort of "handbook" of criminal institutions were periodically issued to, and utilized by, all sentencing authorities in order that they might familiarize themselves with the various correctional programs available (p. 209). However, given the traditional bias of the courts in regarding the determination of guilt or innocence as their primary function, the question arises as to whether it would be more efficient to adopt an alternative sentencing scheme than to attempt to train in the courts.

It would appear that one very reasonable alternative to the current system would be to place the sentencing authority in the hands of specialists in the correctional field (with consideration given to suggestions for sentencing made by the court).[18] Criminologists and penologists, trained in the causes of crime and familiar with the day-to-day functioning of Canadian correctional institutions, would be expected to be better resource allocators than magistrates. Whether these specialists would be less responsive to the public's demand for retribution depends upon job survival criteria, and hence cannot be determined indepenent of the criteria. However, removal of the sentencing authority from the relatively "public" atmosphere of the courtroom—with the attendant sensationalism of the trial—should reduce the public's interest in sentence disposition, and therefore act to reduce the importance of the retribution factor as a source of inefficiency.

It should be noted that the predicted inefficiency of the model presented above is not in accordance with most models of firms producing multiple products subject to a resource constraint.[19] The primary difference between the standard model and the correctional institutions model is that correctional authorities do not have control over the mix of products which they are required to supply. It might justifiably be argued that it is not decentraliza-

18. The *Ouimet Report* contains a rejection of this alternative system in any form, although the grounds for rejection are not clear. It appears that the investigation of alternative sentencing schemes by the Committee was not very complete (1969, pp. 216-17).

19. The classic case of air defence presented in Hitch and McKean (1960, pp. 110-14), is an excellent example. Subject to a budget, the authorities must choose an efficient mix of a strategic bombing force and an air defence force to provide maximum "military worth."

tion *per se* that is the source of inefficiency, but rather the faulty sentencing procedures of the currently constituted judiciary; centralized decision-making will lead to an efficient allocation of resources only if the centralized decision-maker has a superior knowledge of the relationship between incarceration length and rehabilitative training. However, since these two service outputs are the result of a single joint-production process, the "firm" that produces them should have a major advantage in selecting a superior product mix.

Furthermore, the above argument implies that it is not necessarily the nonprofit nature of correctional institutions that is responsible for inefficient correction programs. For instance, consider an alternative system: a program of incentive contracting in which the government lets bids to private firms to rehabilitate prisoners, and rewards these firms financially according to their rehabilitation records.[20] Now unless society is willing to accord the incarceration length decision to these private firms, they would face the same difficulty in providing a *socially* efficient product mix as does the Penitentiary Service under existing institutional arrangements. To see this, first recall the previously established result that for each level of expenditures on correction procedures, there exists a unique pair (t^*, f^*) that is efficient. The profit maximizing prison, constrained to provide a given value of f for each prisoner, would choose a value of t such that the marginal cost of training equals the firm's marginal benefit. But the prison's revenue function (i.e. the schedule relating rehabilitation success with monetary rewards) is chosen by government authorities. Hence, unless the authorities choose the particular revenue function which ensures that the profit maximizing value of t is on the prison's efficient expansion locus (given the court-determined value of f), the adopted pair (t, f) will not be socially efficient. If the authorities are not able to choose the proper revenue function, then the only possibility for an efficient privately operated correction system is for the government to relinquish control of the sen-

---

20. I am grateful to Morgan Reynolds for suggesting an investigation of this alternative system.

tence length decision to private firms. From a pragmatic standpoint, such a system may not be palatable to the public.

AN ECONOMIC RATIONALE FOR PAROLE

Parliament has empowered the National Parole Board to determine, within certain limits[21] and in accordance with the welfare of society, the portion of offenders' sentences served within correctional institutions and the portion served under supervised parole in the community. The analysis of the preceding section immediately suggests one possible rationale for parole—faulty decision-making at the sentencing stage of the correction process may be rectified by parole if sentence lengths are excessive. Indeed, it might be argued that extensive use of parole is *prima facie* evidence that the courts are choosing inefficient sentence lengths. However, the arguments discussed below suggest that a parole program is warranted on its own merits, independent of the abilities of the sentencing authorities.

It was stated previously that the map of "equal protection" curves visualized by a court is partially based upon beliefs concerning the effects on offenders of actually serving a prison sentence. It will be assumed here for simplification that these beliefs are contained in the court's *ex ante* estimates that offenders will be recidivists[22] upon release. Whether the objective (i.e. "true") probability of recidivism changes as an individual prisoner serves his sentence depends upon changes in the values of the variables that influenced the decision to commit the crime for which the offender was originally incarcerated. In turn, changes in these variables depend upon training intensity, length of stay in prison and a vector of variables which affect the "psychic income" from criminal activity.

These considerations may be formalized by writing $r_i = r_i$ $(t_i, f_i, u_i; r_i^0)$, where r_i is the objective probability that the ith

21. In Canada, current regulations on parole state that for definite sentences of a duration less than the offender's life, parole may be granted after serving one-third of the sentence or four years, whichever is less. If parole is not granted upon the first such consideration, the Board must reconsider the case at least once every two years.

22. Here "recidivist" refers to a criminal who commits a crime after release from prison, whether or not he is apprehended and convicted for the repeat offence.

offender will be a recidivist if released after serving f_i days in custody, t_i is the level of "positive" training received each day, u_i is a vector of factors that influence "tastes" for criminal activity, and r_i^0 is the probability that the offender would commit a further crime if not subjected to correctional procedures for committing the original crime. Further, define $\bar{t}_i$ as the level of positive training that affects the expected returns to legitimate and criminal activity in such a way as to generate a constant probability of recidivism. That is (dropping subscripts), $\partial r / \partial f \lesseqqgtr 0$ as $t \gtreqqless \bar{t}$. This may be explained with reference to Figure 21-2, where the training intensities t^1 and t^2 are ranked $t^1 > \bar{t} > t^2$. The probability of recidivism falls as the sentence is served when the training in-

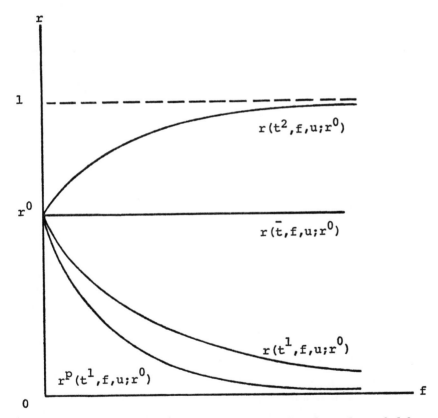

Figure 21-2. The effect of training and sentence length on the probability of recidivism.

tensity is t^1, and rises when the training intensity is t^2. In the latter case, the level of "negative" training is sufficiently strong to adversely affect the variables which determine criminal activity.[23]

The effects of the introduction of parole into a criminal justice system may now be considered. If the granting of parole is contingent upon the parole board's evaluation of a prisoner's probability of recidivism, and if an early release is deemed desirable by prisoners, then parole provides an incentive to behave in a manner consistent with rehabilitation, e.g. better performance in training programs, the establishment of positive relationships with other inmates and supervisory personnel, etc. If such behaviour is realized, then any pair (t, f) becomes more effective in the sense that a new set of "probability-of-recidivism" paths is generated; for any value of t, the new path lies below the corresponding path in the system without parole (compare the paths $r(t^1, f, u; r^0)$ and $r^p(t^1, f, u; r^0)$ in Fig. 21-2, where the latter path admits the possibility of parole). Furthermore, the stronger are the incentives for an early release, the greater is the divergence of the probability paths in the two systems.[24]

----

23. Figure 21-2 has implications for the current public furore over parole administration in Canada. Critics of the current program are arguing that parole is being granted too soon, as evidenced by the number of crimes committed by offenders who are on parole. However, the "optimal" parole may not be attained by simply adjusting length of incarceration alone; if prisoners are currently accorded a value of t that yields positively sloped "probability-of-recidivism" paths, then reducing the length of parole *decreases* the level of protection of society, *ceteris paribus*. Hopefully the response of the Solicitor General to the public outcry will be to re-examine *all* correction procedures, not just those pertaining to the National Parole Board.

24. This rationale for parole may be interpreted in terms of the production function for protection services discussed earlier. The introduction of an effective parole program increases the amount of *expected* protection services generated by any (t, f) bundle due to the decrease in r. If the *realized* level of protection services increases, then the introduction of parole may be said to have effected a technological change upon the production function for protection services.

This suggests, incidentally, that the cost of using parole to rectify certain types of sentencing errors may be the loss of the incentive effect. For example, suppose that the courts have perfect foresight with respect to the effect of any (t, f) bundle on offenders, but due to the retribution factor, choose sentences which are uniformly 10 percent too long. If it is observed by prisoners that parole is being used to rectify the sentencing error, then the incentive effect would be lost. Hence, parole should not be viewed as a substitute for efficient decision-making at the sentencing stage of the correctional process.

One possibility for change in the current Canadian system which would increase the incentive effect of parole is the elimination of remissions. The *Penitentiaries Act* automatically awards statutory remission of one quarter of sentence length to all fixed-term prisoners.[25] In addition three days' remission for each month of incarceration may be "earned."[26] Many offenders obtain early release not by parole, but through these remissions.[27] The difficulties are that (1) some offenders feel that their chances of obtaining parole, as the program is currently administered, are virtually nonexistent, and (2) some offenders may be in a situation where obtaining an early release through parole is deemed not worth the effort, since an early release will be obtained through remissions.[28] In effect, such prisoners place a zero marginal return on any effort above the minimum necessary to achieve and maintain remissions. The incentive to behave in a manner consistent with rehabilitation would increase if parole were the only way to obtain an early release. For such a change to be effective, the flexibility of the parole program would have to be increased to ensure that all fixed-term prisoners perceive the possibility of attaining parole.

---

25. Section 22(1). Statutory remission is automatically revoked if parole is violated, and may also be revoked by correctional authorities for disciplinary reasons, although such instances are relatively infrequent.

26. *Penitentiaries Act*, section 24(1). According to this section, the prisoner must have ". . . applied himself industriously . . ." during the month to obtain such a remission. However, offenders typically perceive this "good time" as a right to which they are entitled for *lack of misconduct* rather than a reward for industrious application to training programs. Furthermore, earned remissions cannot be revoked for any reason. Making earned remissions revocable would increase the incentive to perform continuously in a manner consistent with rehabilitation.

27. In 1970, 2,674 male prisoners were released from Canadian penitentiaries on parole, and 1,627 were released due to expiration of sentence (DBS, 1970, 28). (There is no breakdown of the latter figure into releasees with remissions and those without, but one would be hard-pressed to find a releasee who has not obtained some "good time.")

28. The time differential between a parole at first opportunity and a release with maximum remissions is approximately one-third of sentence length. This differential is reduced as parole is denied on successive applications. Hence, the nearer an offender is to being released due to remissions, the weaker are the incentives to behave in a manner consistent with post-release success. The elimination of remissions would not change the nature of the problem, but it would increase the maximum benefits of a paroled release to two-thirds of sentence length.

The second rationale for parole arises due to the necessity (under the current set of Canadian correctional procedures) of imposing sentence prior to observing the effects of incarceration upon individual offenders. It is doubtful that, in the short time an offender appears before the court, sufficient information is obtained to estimate correctly the probability-of-recidivism path taken by the offender.[29] Parole allows for a review of the incarceration length decision; if an offender's response to rehabilitation efforts is better than anticipated by the court, the offender may be granted an early release. The existence of a parole program, then, allows the utilization of additional information in determining the actual length of incarceration.[30]

It should be noted, as a final remark, that a radical alternative to fixed-term sentences (with parole and remission possibilities) exists under Canadian law. Federal legislation provides for the use of indeterminate sentences for offenders classified as "habitual" or "dangerous sexual."[31] In such cases, the offender is not released until he has demonstrated his rehabilitation. The advantage of such a sentencing scheme is that it jointly maximizes the amount of information obtained prior to determining sentence length and the incentive to behave in a manner consistent with rehabilitation. Whether the application of indeterminate sentences should be extended to other classes of offenders or withdrawn completely is subject to debate.[32] One obvious factor is that considerable resources may have to be expended to prevent misuse of the sentencing power. Furthermore, indeterminate sentences cannot

---

29. The *Ouimet Report* (1969, p. 210), recognizing this problem, recommended mandatory predisposition reports on all offenders subsequently sentenced to at least six months in custody.

30. Again, the interpretation of this rationale for parole in terms of Figure 21-1 is straightforward. Additional information may lead to the visualization of a different map of expected *PC* curves, and hence, to the choice of a different (t, f) bundle. Parole allows the attaining of this new bundle (assuming, of course, that the offender's response to incarceration is better than anticipated).

31. Criminal Code of Canada, part XXI. British Columbia and Ontario also permit indeterminate sentences of two years to be added to definite sentences of less than two years.

32. The *Ouimet Report* (1969, pp. 241-71, p. 283) advocated the abolition of all indeterminate sentences except for a proposed new category of "dangerous" offenders.

be evaluated independent of the level of t accorded to prisoners. If training is provided in such limited amounts that offenders attain only positively-sloped probability-of-recidivism paths, then indeterminate sentences, in effect, would be sentences of life imprisonment.

SUMMARY AND CONCLUDING COMMENTS

In this paper an economic model of a correctional institution was presented. The prison was viewed as a nonprofit, multi-product firm producing incarceration services and training services for society. It was noted that current Canadian correctional procedures probably lead to a misallocation of resources by correctional institutions. A system of centralized decision-making was suggested, wherein the sentencing authority would be taken out of the hands of the courts and yielded to correctional officials. The supposition is that a decision-maker familiar with a firm's joint-production process is capable of choosing a better (i.e. more efficient) product mix than a relatively uninformed decision-maker. It might be argued that proper training of the courts would provide an equally satisfactory solution, but such training is unnecessary (and hence, inefficient) if the requisite knowledge is already possessed by the correctional branch of the Criminal Justice System. Furthermore, diverting the attention of the courts from legal issues to training in correctional programs and philosophies may prove to be of such practical difficulty as to ensure that only lip service would be paid to such an attempt.

The behavioural assumption of choosing correction policies to maximize the single variable "protection services" has implications which may not be widely accepted. One implication is that offenders committing similar crimes may be accorded substantially different sentence lengths. A second implication is that an offender, once convicted, is sentenced without consideration of his own welfare. In effect, the commission of an offence acts to remove the offender's utility index from the social welfare function. It should be noted, however, that maximizing the welfare of "legitimate" society may be consistent with maximizing the welfare of individual offenders, particularly if differences in *ex ante* and *ex post* utilities are taken into consideration. (That is, offenders

would choose not to enter prison if given the choice, but if rehabilitation is effected by incarceration, offenders might feel in retro-
spect that incarceration provided substantial benefits.) Nevertheless, these simple examples illustrate the types of difficulties
encountered in admitting only efficiency criteria in the design of
correction policies. The relationship between efficiency and equity
in this context certainly deserves further exploration.

The emphasis of this paper on the rehabilitation of criminals
should not be construed as minimizing the importance of adopt-
ing policies that prevent the launching of criminal careers. Many
members of the current generation of criminologists believe that
the distribution of intelligence among offenders is not significantly
different from that of the population at large. However, it is well
known that educational achievements and job-skill levels are much
lower for the prison population. This suggests that anti-dropout
and vocational training programs should be given high priority
and administered at an early age.

It is hoped that this paper will stimulate the interest of Canadian economists in the problems of prisons and rehabilitation.
Empirical work is needed to determine how close current Canadian policies are to optimal policies, and to make specific recommendations for changes in all aspects of the Canadian CJS. It is
rather puzzling that so little economic work has been done in the
area of correctional institutions, when so much work has been
done on other nonprofit organizations (e.g. hospitals and the
postal service).[33] Cost-benefit analyses of temporary leave and
parole programs, evaluations of different prison training programs
(including both vocational and formal education) and a review
of the laws regulating the types of products produced by prison
industries are only a small sampling of work awaiting economic
analysis.[34]

---

33. Of course, the feasibility of empirical work on any branch of the Canadian
CJS depends upon the availability of data. Published statistics on Canadian correctional institutions, for example, are exceedingly sparse. The co-operation of
the Solicitor General in gathering and providing data appears to be a necessary
condition for significant research in the area.

34. On the latter points, one could visualize a flexible job-training program in

It may seem unusual for economists to be delving into areas traditionally reserved for specialists in "deviant" behaviour but it should be noted that choosing proper correction policies is primary an efficiency problem (subject to the considerations discussed above), and economists are, after all, familiar with efficiency problems. Indeed, in light of the Kingston riots of April, 1971, it is tempting to speculate that an effort by the government to seek the counsel of economists on correction policies would at least not retard the development and implementation of imaginative correction programs.

REFERENCES

Avio, K. L.: *Two Topics in Applied Microeconomics: Criminal Correction Policies and Statutory Interest Rate Ceilings on Consumer Loans*, Unpublished Ph.D. dissertation, Purdue University, 1972.

Becker, G.: Crime and punishment: an economic approach. *Journal of Political Economy*, 76:169-217, 1968.

————: Investment in human capital: a theoretical analysis. *Journal of Political Economy*, 70:9-49, 1962.

Canadian Committee on Corrections: *Toward Unity: Criminal Justice and Corrections (Ouimet Report)*. R. Ouimet, chairman, Ottawa, 1969.

Dominion Bureau of Statistics: *Correctional Institution Statistics, 1970*, Ottawa.

Falzetta, A.: The appointment of magistrates. *Canadian Journal of Corrections*, 9:137-46, 1967.

Gingeroff, A. K.: Crime, criminal law and the concept of treatment. *Canadian Journal of Corrections*, 10:12-24, 1968.

Glaser, D.: *The Effectiveness of a Prison and Parole System*. Indianapolis, 1964.

Gordon, D.: Class and the economics of crime. *Review of Radical Political Economy* 3:51-75, 1971.

Hitch, C. J., and McKean, R. N.: *The Economics of Defense in the Nuclear Age*. Cambridge, 1960.

Hogarth, J.: Towards the improvement of sentencing in Canada. *Canadian Journal of Corrections*, 9:122-36, 1967.

---

which conditions in the Canadian labour market dictate the particular skills offered to offenders. Under the present set of prison industry regulations almost the opposite is the case. Prisoners produce goods which are not sold in the marketplace; thus the specific skills they learn may not help them find jobs after release from prison.

McGrath, W. T.: Formal recognition of rehabilitation: legal and social issues. *Canadian Journal of Corrections, 11*:240-54, 1969.

Ontario Royal Commission Inquiry into Civil Rights. J. C. McRuer, chairman, Toronto, 1968.

Roy, R.: An outline for research in penology. *Operations Research, 12*:1-12, 1964.

Stigler, G.: The optimum enforcement of laws. *Journal of Political Economy,* 78:526-36, 1970.

Tullock, G.: An economic approach to crime. *Social Science Quarterly, 50:* 59-71, 1969.

Chapter 22

A CLIMATOLOGICAL MODEL FOR FORECASTING THE DEMAND FOR POLICE SERVICE

NELSON B. HELLER AND ROBERT E. MARKLAND

CRIME CONTROL, particularly in large urban areas, is undoubtedly one of our country's most formidable social problems. In 1966, President Johnson reported that the annual cost of crime in the United States had reached $27 billion. It was estimated that expenditures that year by all public agencies of criminal justice totaled $4.3 billion, of which about 61 percent went to police activities (U.S. Department of Justice, 1967). In New York City alone, the 1967 to 1968 executive budget allocated $502 million to law enforcement, of which $361 million was earmarked for police services (King, 1967).

The efficient utilization of police resources in large metropolitan areas is a particularly acute problem. Here the concentration of population, the unusually dynamic and competitive economic and social circumstances, and the concentration of valuable property, make greater demands on police service than anywhere else in the country. The provision for and management of police services in the cities becomes progressively more difficult and costly with each passing year.

Crime prevention and control, and adequate response to calls-for-service are largely dependent on the effective allocation of tactical resources. The allocation of these resources represents the general problem to which this study is addressed. More specifically, this paper suggests a simple procedure for forecasting called-

Reprinted, with permission of the National Council on Crime and Delinquency, from *Journal of Research in Crime and Delinquency*, July 1970, pp. 167-176.

for-service workloads which appears useful in dealing with those allocation problems related to manpower scheduling.

The proper allocation of their manpower has long been of interest to police agencies. Attempts to schedule patrols in accordance with the anticipated geographical demands for police service, known as proportional distribution, date back at least to 1909 when Police Chief August Vollmer assigned the Berkeley, California, patrol force to beats laid out in accordance with the number of calls anticipated in each part of the city (President's Commission, 1967).

Early attempts at proportional distribution were seriously handicapped by their lack of current data and of data processing facilities. Today, a growing number of police agencies have overcome both handicaps. This has brought proportional distribution into the realm of feasibility, and it has been given serious attention by several cities (Smith, 1961). One of the most advanced proportional distribution systems now in operation is the Resource Allocation System of the St. Louis Metropolitan Police Department (St. Louis Police Department, 1968; Data Processing; Pauly, *et al.*, 1967).

The research presented in this paper differs from previous research in that it deals with *all* calls-for-service (of which crime represents only about 20%), and with city-wide aggregate statistics rather than for smaller regions, such as census tracts, within the city. Analysis of called-for-service activity in St. Louis indicates that for smaller regions, or for more refined categories of calls-for-service (e.g. assaults), the seasonal variation is less clear and the reliability of forecasts drops significantly.

STATEMENT OF THE RESEARCH PROBLEM

In police terminology, a "call-for-service" represents a request from a citizen for assistance. Called-for-service patrols are radio-equipped patrol car units whose responsibility it is to respond to calls for assistance by accepting assignments from their radio dispatcher. The servicing of a call involves traveling to the scene of the incident, investigating the incident and taking the appropriate correctional measures, completing the necessary reports, and, finally, checking back with the dispatcher to report availability for further calls.

The number of calls-for-service per week is typically higher than average in the warmer months and lower in the colder months. For example, in St. Louis, calls per week averaged roughly 11,000 in January, 1968 as compared to 15,000 in July, 1968. A preliminary analysis of St. Louis Police Department data indicated that this cyclical behavior repeated from year to year, motivating the present, more comprehensive study, and the inclusion of data from Chicago and Detroit.

The cyclical variation in called-for-services during the year has important implications for the scheduling and deployment of the patrol force. It appears that fewer vacations should be scheduled in the summer than in the winter, and that the number of cars utilized during the different working "watches" of the day ought to be varied by season of the year.[1] These and other similar seasonally dependent allocation problems suggested the need for development of reliable forecasts of the seasonal demand for called-for-services.

METHODOLOGY OF THE STUDY

Two generic approaches to forecasting the number of calls-for-service have dominated previous studies. They are:

1. Statistical regression analysis, and
2. Exponential smoothing.

The Franklin Institute Research Laboratories have studied the use of a statistical regression model to predict the occurrence of crimes as a function of meteorological and demographic factors (weather, age distribution of district residents, unemployment, school enrollment, etc.). Hour-by-hour and district-by-district estimates of the probabilities of different types of crime were derived from the regression model. This model was tested on crime data for Philadelphia; it appears to be cumbersome and lacks reliability (Stein, 1967).

Exponential smoothing is the basis of the forecasting model

---

1. For an interesting discussion of these types of allocation problems, see Heller (1969).

used by the St. Louis Resource Allocation Program. Forecasts are separately computed for each of eight categories of called-for-services, with the resultant forecasts being summed to arrive at a total figure. The forecasting procedure corrects for cyclic variation by hour of the week and week of the year (Crowther, 1964).

The methodology of the present research is a form of statistical regression analysis. In essence, it is hypothesized that the number of service calls per week (dependent variable) is related to two weather variables and to a simple linear trend variable (independent variables). The two weather variables are:

1. The average daily temperature and
2. The average number of minutes from dawn to sunset (possible sunlight) per day.

Data Used in the Study

Called-for-service and weather data from three cities were employed in the study:

1. Chicago, Illinois
2. Detroit, Michigan
3. St. Louis, Missouri

Weather data for the respective cities were obtained from their weather bureaus. The data included daily normal temperatures, and daily sunrise and sunset tables, for each of the cities. Calls-for-service data, in weekly totals, were provided by the police departments of each of the cities. The amount of calls-for-service data available varied by city as follows (dates are given as *day of year/year*):

1. Chicago—140 weeks of data—14/66 to 255/68
2. Detroit—156 weeks of data—7/66 to 364/68
3. St. Louis—112 weeks of data—161/66 to 210/68

THE FORECASTING MODEL

The forecasting model developed is a moving multiple regression model of the form:

$$c(j) = a_1 + a_2 (j\text{-}26.5) + a_3 [t(j) - t] + a_4 [s(j) - s] + e(j) \quad 1 < j < 52, \text{ integer}$$

where:

$c(j)$ = is the number of calls during the *jth* week of the 52 weeks of data used to estimate the coefficients;

a_1 = the average number of calls per week;

a_2 = the rate of increase (or decrease) in calls per week each week (e.g. a value of ten implies an increase of 520 calls per week over a year). The constant 26.5 is subtracted from j so that the independent variable $(j - 26.5)$ will sum to zero over a full year;

a_3 = the coefficient relating calls per week to temperature;

$t(j)$ = the *normal* average temperature for week j, in F degree;

t = the annual average temperature, in F degrees;

a_4 = the coefficient relating calls per week to possible sunlight;

$s(j)$ = the *average* number of minutes from dawn to sunset each day for week j (i.e. possible minutes of sunlight each day);

s = the average, computed over a full year, of the number of minutes from dawn to sunset each day;

$e(j)$ = the residual, or error term, for week j.

Forecasts are made by estimating the coefficients a_1 through a_4 from the most recent set of fifty-two weeks of calls per week data available, and substituting these into the forecasting model. Thus, if the forecast for week $J + W$ is desired, the present week being week J, and the year of calls data terminates with the calls for week J:

$$c'(J + W) = a_1 + a_2 (26.5 + W)$$
$$+ a_3[t(J + W) - t] + a_4 [s(J + W) - s]$$

where:

$c'(J + W)$ = forecasted number of calls-for-service during week $J + W$;

W = number of weeks into the future for which a forecast is desired (i.e. the leadtime for the forecast). Leadtimes of one to eight weeks were tested in the study.

Note that $t(J + W)$ and $s(J + W)$ refer to the normal weather conditions for week $J + W$. If the weather data is stored by week of year in the input data arrays, with j being 1 for the first week of the year, then it is necessary to convert the week index $J + W$ to the week of the year.

While carrying out the multiple regression analysis to estimate the coefficients, it is possible to test, statistically, the hypotheses that either the linear trend, the temperature, or the possible sunlight are *not* useful in explaining the variation in calls per week over the year. The corresponding statistical hypotheses are $a_2 = 0$, $a_3 = 0$, and $a_4 = 0$; the appropriate test procedure may be found in any of several statistics texts.[2]

TEST RESULTS

The forecasting model was programmed in FORTRAN IV, utilizing card input for the test data. The programs were run on IBM 7040 equipment at the St. Louis Metropolitan Police Department.

Output from the programs is summarized in tabular and graphical form below.

The forecasted weekly calls-for-service and the average weekly weather data (normal temperatures and normal available sunlight) are plotted against time, by city, in Figures 22-1, 22-2, and 22-3. The forecasts shown are for a four-week leadtime.

A graphical comparison of the forecasted weekly calls-for-service and the actual weekly calls-for-service is presented, by city, in Figures 22-4, 22-5, and 22-6. Again, the forecasts shown are for a four week leadtime.

A summary of statistics reflecting the accuracy of the forecasts is presented in Table 22-I, by city, for leadtimes of from one to eight weeks. Each figure represents the average or standard deviation (as indicated) of the identified statistics over the set of $N - 52 - W$ forecasts which could be computed and compared with actuals from the available data, where:

$N =$ the total number of weeks of called-for-service data;

$W =$ the forecast leadtime in weeks.

For example, for Chicago, 140 weeks of data were available. For a leadtime of four weeks it was possible to compute and de-

---

2. See, for example Graybill 1961.

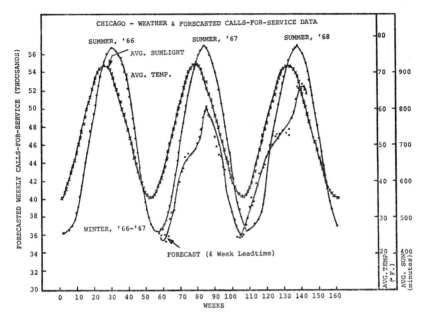

Figure 22-1

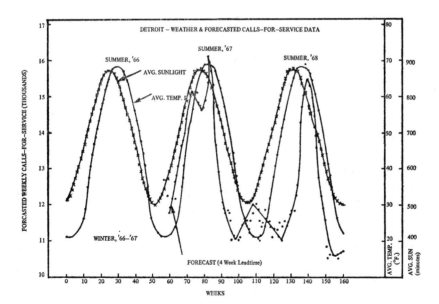

Figure 22-2

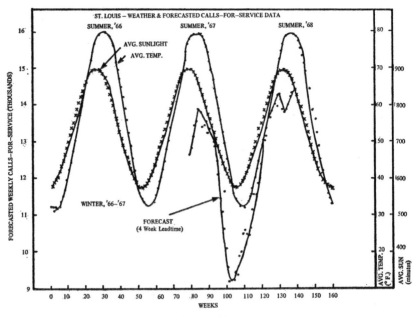

Figure 22-3

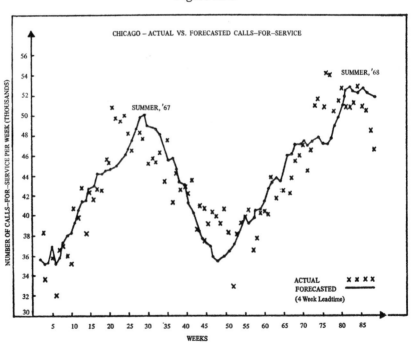

Figure 22-4

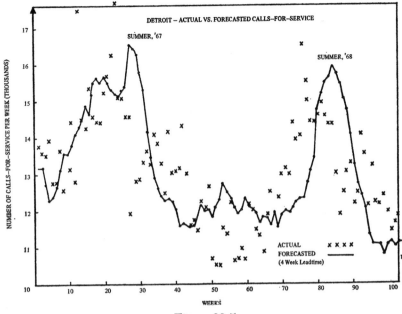

Figure 22-5

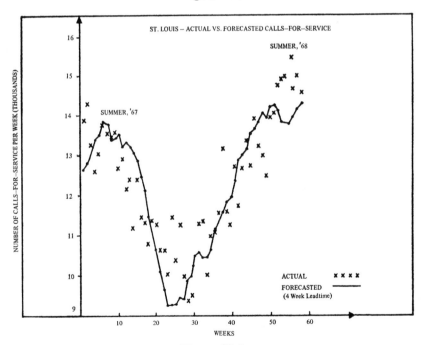

Figure 22-6

TABLE 22-1

SUMMARY OF FORECASTING ACCURACY STATISTICS

City	Leadtime (Weeks)							
	1	2	3	4	5	6	7	8
CHICAGO	140 weeks of data from 12-66 to 225-68							
	min. no. of forecasts = 81							
Sigma/c	4.91	4.93	4.94	4.95	4.96	4.97	4.98	5.00
F test ($n_1 = 4$, $n_2 = 48$)	79.6	79.0	78.4	77.8	77.3	76.8	76.3	75.9
% Error	0.66	0.63	0.59	0.70	0.34	0.22	0.25	0.16
Std. Dev'n. (% error)	6.46	6.57	6.74	6.99	6.64	6.69	6.87	6.90
Abs. % Error	4.69	4.98	5.27	5.49	5.46	5.57	5.88	5.95
Std. Dev'n. (abs. % error)	4.46	4.30	4.21	4.34	3.75	3.67	3.50	3.43
DETROIT	156 weeks of data from 7-66 to 364-68							
	min. no. of forecasts = 97							
Sigma/c	6.98	6.98	6.99	7.00	7.01	7.01	7.02	7.02
F test ($n_1 = 4$, $n_2 = 48$)	23.9	23.8	23.7	23.6	23.5	23.5	23.4	23.3
% Error	0.27	0.20	0.09	-0.03	0.02	0.03	0.08	0.13
Std. Dev'n. (% error)	8.59	9.49	10.24	10.98	11.74	12.25	12.90	13.34
Abs. % Error	6.90	7.60	8.00	8.58	9.19	9.79	10.44	10.79
Std. Dev'n. (abs. % error)	5.06	5.64	6.34	6.80	7.25	7.29	7.50	7.78
ST. LOUIS	112 weeks of data from 161-66 to 210-68							
	min. no. of forecasts = 53							
Sigma/c	4.92	4.92	4.92	4.92	4.92	4.92	4.92	4.93
F test ($n_1 = 4$, $n_2 = 48$)	75.2	74.8	74.5	74.2	74.1	74.1	74.0	74.0
% Error	-0.46	-0.53	-0.56	-0.64	-0.67	-0.63	-0.67	-0.79
Std. Dev'n. (% error)	6.27	6.79	7.08	7.28	7.56	7.86	8.33	8.57
Abs. % Error	5.19	5.57	5.63	5.90	6.05	6.04	6.44	6.65
Std. Dev'n. (abs. % error)	3.48	3.84	4.27	4.23	4.52	4.98	5.25	5.40

Definitions:

Sigma/c = (standard deviation/average cells per week) for model.

F test = F statistic for zero dependence of calls/week on input variables

% Error = average forecast error, expressed as a percent.

Std. Dev'n. (% error) = standard deviation of % error over set of forecast, in %.

Abs. % Error = average absolute forecast error, expressed as a percent.

Std. Dev'n. (abs. % error) = standard deviation of the absolute error (in %) over the set of forecasts.

Note: Critical level—$F_{(4, 48)}$ (5%) = 2.56

termine the accuracy of $140 - 52 - 4 = 84$ forecasts. Thus, the figure 0.70 shown for "percent error" for a four-week leadtime for Chicago is the average over 84 forecasts.

The final set of output data presented are the average F-test statistics (over the set of $N - 52 - W$ forecasts) for the significance of each of the three independent variables. This summary is presented in Table 22-II, by city for leadtimes of from one to eight weeks.

DISCUSSION OF TEST RESULTS

A number of interesting observations can be made from examination of the test results. First, it can be observed that the climatological model fits the data of all three cities extremely well. Referring to Table 22-I, note that the F statistic for the significance of the four variable model is very high for all three cities *(Critical level—$F_{4, 48}$ (5%) = 2.56);* for example, the lowest average statistic computed for any of the cities was 23.3.

Second, it appears that the normal weekly average temperature is the more important of the two weather variables in explaining calls per week (i.e. more important than sunlight). This can readily be seen by referring to the F-statistics summarized in Table 22-II *(Critical level—$F_{1, 48}$ (5%) = 4.04)*. The lowest temperature statistic computed was 9.8; the lowest sunlight statistic was 4.2. Note also that the linear trend effect is important in all three cities, and hence should be included in the model. Chicago and St. Louis exhibited an increase in the number of calls per week, while Detroit's calls per week declined over the test period.

Third, the accuracy of the model generally deteriorates slightly with increasing leadtime, for leadtimes of one to eight weeks. The behavior of forecasting accuracy is most clearly reflected in the error standard deviation estimates. For example, for St. Louis, this figure increased from 6.27 percentage points for a leadtime of one week to 8.57 for a leadtime of eight weeks. In addition, the forecasts are quite unbiased, with the average forecasting error being very close to zero, and relatively unaffected by increases in leadtime. Note further that the average *absolute* forecasting errors are also very small, and are similarly unaffected by increases in leadtimes.

TABLE 22-II

SUMMARY OF F-TEST STATISTICS

City	Leadtime (Weeks)							
	1	2	3	4	5	6	7	8
CHICAGO ($n_1 = 1$, $n_2 = 48$)								
Linear trend	6.2	6.1	6.9	5.8	5.6	5.4	5.2	5.0
Temperature	23.1	22.1	22.7	22.5	22.3	22.2	22.1	22.9
Sunlight	4.7	4.8	4.8	4.9	4.9	5.0	5.1	5.1
DETROIT ($n_1 = 1$, $n_2 = 48$)								
Linear trend	5.2	5.3	5.3	5.4	5.4	5.5	5.5	5.6
Temperature	9.8	9.9	9.9	9.9	9.9	9.9	9.9	9.8
Sunlight	4.2	4.2	4.3	4.3	4.3	4.4	4.4	4.4
ST. LOUIS ($n_1 = 1$, $n_2 = 48$)								
Linear trend	5.3	5.3	5.2	5.1	5.1	5.2	5.3	5.4
Temperature	17.2	17.4	17.6	17.7	18.0	18.3	18.6	18.9
Sunlight	8.7	8.7	8.8	8.9	8.9	8.8	8.6	8.3

Note: Critical level—$F_{1, 48}$ (5%) = 4.04.

CONCLUSION

The results of the study indicate that the seasonal variation in the number of calls-for-service per week is sufficiently large in each of the cities tested to motivate attempts to schedule vacations and other activities affecting manpower availability by season. Furthermore, the results of applying the moving regression model appear encouraging, as very accurate forecasts were obtained for each of the three cities. A logical extension of the present study is to develop vacation schedules and patrol deployments responsive to the seasonal workload cycles indicated by the regression model.

REFERENCES

Crowther, R. F.: *The Use of a Computer for Police Manpower Allocation in St. Louis, Missouri.* Bloomington, Indiana University, Department of Police Administration, June, 1964.

Data Processing Division, International Business Machines Corporation: *Resource Allocation at the St. Louis Metropolitan Police Department.* IBM Application Brief, White Plains, IBM Data Processing Division.

Graybill, F. A.: *An Introduction to Linear Statistical Models, I.* New York, McGraw-Hill, 1961, pp. 128-148.

Heller, N. B.: Proportional Rotating Schedules, unpublished doctorate dissertation, University of Pennsylvania, August, 1969.

King, S. F.: *Twelve Percent Rise Proposed in City Spending Without New Tax.* New York Times, April 16, 1967, p. 1.

Pauly, G. A., McEwen, J. T., and Finch, S. J.: Computer mapping—a new technique in crime analysis. *Law Enforcement Science and Technology.* Washington, Thompson, 1967, pp. 739-748.

President's Commission on Law Enforcement and Administration of Justice: *Task Force Report: The Police.* Washington, U.S. Government Printing Office, 1967, p. 52.

Smith, R. D.: *Computer Applications in Police Manpower Distribution.* Washington, Field Services Division, International Association of Chiefs of Police, February, 1961.

Stein, J. P., *et al.*: The prediction of crime in a metropolitan area. *Law Enforcement Science and Technology.* Washington, Thompson, 1967, pp. 749-753.

St. Louis Metropolitan Police Department: *Allocation of Patrol Manpower Resources in the Saint Louis Police Department,* Vol I and II. St. Louis, Metropolitan Police Department, 1968.

U.S. Department of Justice: *Second Annual Report to President and the Congress on Activities Under the Law Enforcement and Assistance Act of 1965.* Report No. 16-175, April 1, 1967.

Chapter 23

INCREASES IN CRIME: THE UTILITY OF ALTERNATIVE MEASURES

ROLAND J. CHILTON AND ADELE SPIELBERGER

REPORTED INCREASES in offenses known to the police in the United States for the years since 1958 suggest that the United States crime rate has increased dramatically in recent years, with the rate for 1967 being double that reported for 1958.[1] Interpretation of this sharp rise in the crime rate is complicated by a number of factors, but primarily by the sparseness of national data with which the trend may be compared. More complete and more comparable arrest data, for example, would provide an additional series with which "offense-known" trends could be compared. Periodic victim surveys might also provide independent confirmation of the trends reported by the FBI, as might systematic and reasonably complete records from the juvenile and adult courts in the United States. But for all practical purposes only offense-known data is available.

The use of offenses known to the police as an official government index of crime in the United States began in 1930 when legislation was enacted permitting the Division of Identification and Information in the Department of Justice (later the FBI) to adopt a program developed by the International Association of Chiefs of Police. In the decade preceding that development, other measures of crime were considered. And for some time after 1930, an attempt was made to collect uniform judicial and prisoner

Reprinted, with permission of the Northwestern University School of Law, from *Journal of Criminal Law, Criminology, and Police Science*, March 1972, pp. 68-74.

1. The crime rates presented in this report are drawn from the Federal Bureau of Investigation's annual reports, *Crime in the United States, Uniform Crime Reports*. Information was available for Florida and six Standard Metropolitan Statistical Areas for most years from 1958 through 1967.

statistics.[2] However, only the FBI's program succeeded in gaining widespread acceptance as an index of crime and for this reason is presently the only available, national indicator of crime in the United States.

Criticism of this use of offenses known to the police has been voiced since 1930, including major critiques by Cressey (1957), Beattie (1960), and Robinson (1966). Although some of the most often questioned features of the program, such as the use of population estimates based on the preceding decennial census and the inclusion of petty larceny in the index, were changed in 1959, the basic procedure developed by the International Association of Chiefs of Police in 1928 and 1929 is still in use. Moreover, not all academic criminologists have been critical of the offense-known index. Some have used it in their analyses of crime and its distribution, sometimes in connection with other criminal justice indices (Schuessler, 1962; Tittle, 1969). The same index was also used extensively by the assessment staff of the President's Commission on Law Enforcement and Administration of Justice although the staff did not ignore possibilities for the development of other crime indicators.

Interest in the development of alternative measures persists and finds expression from time to time in proposals such as those put forward by the President's Commission. Nevertheless, no alternative national measures of crime in the United States are currently available for comparison with the trends suggested by offenses known to the police.[3] Consequently, the analysis and discussion which follows is limited almost entirely to crime and delinquency data for Florida. Geographically limited as such data are, they illustrate the utility of additional indicators of trends in crime by permitting a comparison of juvenile delinquency referral rates with rates of offenses known to the police for the state of Florida and six metropolitan areas in the state. The additional indicator of criminal activity employed in this analysis is a product of

2. For examples of the debate which preceded and followed the adoption of offenses known to the police as an official measure of crime see Davies (1931); Mead (1929); Moley (1928); Sellin (1931); Warner (1931).

3. Arrest information is gathered and published by the FBI; but it is not presented in a form which permits comparison with information about offenses known to the police.

Florida's uniform juvenile court statistical reporting program which has been in operation since 1956.[4]

THE STATEWIDE TREND

When percentage increases in the rates of crimes known to the police for Florida and the United States are compared with percentage increases in the Florida juvenile delinquency referral rate for 1958 through 1967, an interesting divergence appears (see Fig. 23-1). From 1962 to 1967, the percentage change in the crime rate for Florida roughly approximates that for the United States, but the percentage increase in the delinquency referral rate is much smaller at the end of this period than the increase in both crime rates.

There is no way to know why the delinquency referral trend diverges so sharply from the offense-known trend. But arrest data for the United States and delinquency data for Florida provide support for an explanation which has been put forward by a number of criminologists (Robison, 1966; Sellin, 1951; President's Commission, 1967). This explanation, which recognizes the relation of changes in the age composition of a population to changes in its crime rates, suggests that total population is not the most appropriate base for the computation of a crime rate, and that its use may produce a distorted indication of trends in crime.

An examination of percentage increases in the number of children in selected age categories and the results obtained when these figures are used to compute rates illustrates the importance of using the population base to compute crime rates for a state with a rapidly changing age structure. The number of children in Florida in grades 7 through 12 (approximate ages, 12-17) increased 76 percent from 1958 to 1967, while the state experienced only a 33 percent growth in total population.[5] Since most children referred to the juvenile and county courts of the state are between

---

4. Uniform statistical reports on all children referred to the 67 juvenile courts of Florida were submitted by the courts to the Florida Department of Public Welfare from 1956 through July, 1968. We are indebted to the department and the Florida Division of Youth Services, the agency presently charged with the responsibility for collecting and compiling the information, for making these data available to us.

5. School enrollment data for the state and its 67 school districts (one per county) were provided by the Florida Department of Education. This information

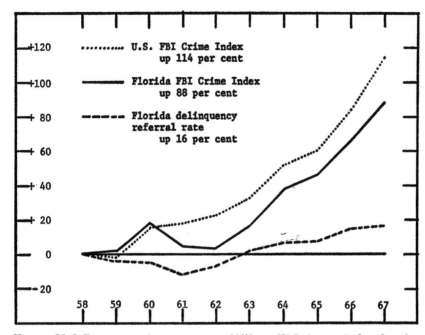

Figure 23-1 Percentage increases over 1958 in FBI Crime Index for the U. S. and Florida and percentage increases over 1958 in delinquency referrals to juvenile courts of Florida.

thirteen and sixteen years of age, it would obviously be inappropriate to use estimates of the total population in the computation of delinquency rates. A more meaningful population base, but one which would still produce misleading results, is the number of children enrolled in grades one through twelve of Florida's public schools.[6] It is a reasonable indication only of the number of chil-

under-represents the number of school-age children because it does not reflect private school enrollment. For this analysis, we have assumed that the proportion of children missed in this way would not greatly alter the trend lines presented. An examination of private school enrollments for the period suggests that 3 percent of the school-age children in the state were enrolled in private schools in 1958 and 7 percent in 1967.

6. Recognizing that a number of children stop attending school when they reach 16 and that some children are either over or under the age expected for a particular grade, we have assumed that the proportions of children were roughly the same in 1958 and 1967. The loss of 17 and 18 year old young people is not as important a problem as their inclusion in the base because almost all children referred to juvenile court in Florida are 16 or younger.

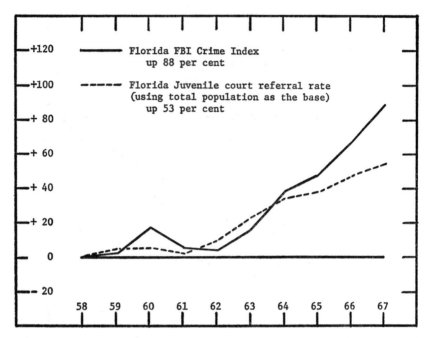

Figure 23-2. Percentage increases in Florida's crime rate compared with increases in the delinquency rate when total population is used as a base, 1958 to 1967.

dren in the state who are six through seventeen years old. However, limiting the population base to children enrolled in grades seven through twelve more closely reflects the number of children in the area who are twelve through seventeen years old, the age group in which most children referred to juvenile courts are found.[7]

When total school enrollment figures are used to compute delinquency referral rates, there is a noticeable effect on Florida's delinquency trend. The increase in the delinquency rate for 1967 over the 1958 rate would have been 34 percent if the number of all school age children were used to compute the rate and 53 percent if estimates of the state's total population were used, but only

---

7. Our analysis of this information is somewhat less accurate than an age-specific analysis would be if single years of age were used. However, our age-specific analysis produced substantially similar results. *See* Chilton and Spielberger (1971).

16 percent when the base is limited to children between the ages of twelve and 17. Figure 23-2 illustrates the effect of the use of a total population base on the delinquency trend relative to the crime trend. Increases in the delinquency rate would still lag behind those in the crime rate, but the results suggest much more similarity in the two trends than is suggested by the data presented in Figure 23-1.

Figures 23-1, 23-2, and 23-3 present another problem in the interpretation of Florida's crime and delinquency trends. Population estimates increased rather evenly during the period selected for these comparisons. But, as shown in Figure 23-3, the rate of increase was greater for the first half of the period than it was for the last half. However, changes in the state's crime and delinquency rates present a reverse trend. The slope of the crime index (Fig. 23-1), although irregular, shows little increase during the first five

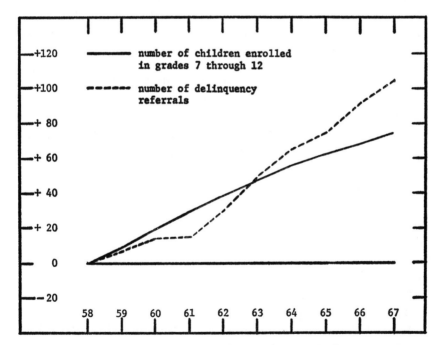

Figure 23-3. Percentage increases in the number of children in grades 7 through 12 in Florida compared with percentage increases in the number of delinquency referrals.

years but increased sharply during the last five, while the delinquency referral rate decreased during the first three years of
the period and increased thereafter. The net effect of these
trends is the suggestion that crime and delinquency may have
been under-reported for the first three or four years of the period
and over-reported for the last five years.

One plausible explanation of this lag is the time it takes municipal governments in a rapidly growing urban area to respond
to an increase in population. With a sizable influx of population
and a relatively stable set of facilities for responding to law
violation, the lag suggested by Florida's crime data may simply
reflect the failure of police agencies to grow with the population.
If, as Erikson (1966) and others suggest, there is a constancy of
deviance in that the machinery of criminal justice can respond to
only so much rule violation, the lag in Figure 23-3 may reflect a
short term failure of several municipal governments to recognize
the need for additional police services and to adjust police budgets accordingly. In such a situation, the rates would be expected
to rise sharply after the expansion of these forces.[8]

METROPOLITAN AREA COMPARISONS

In an attempt to examine in greater detail the questions raised
by the statewide data, comparisons of crime and delinquency
trends similar to those made for the state were undertaken for
each of six Standard Metropolitan Statistical Areas in Florida for
which these data were available. Examination of Figure 23-4 suggests that the delinquency referral rates for 1967 differed very
little from those reported in 1958 for the Orlando, West Palm
Beach, and Tampa-St. Petersburg areas and that this rate was
almost 25 percent lower for Miami at the end of the ten year
period. Only the Jacksonville and Pensacola courts reported appreciably higher rates in 1967 than in 1958. Jacksonville's 1967
rate had increased 37 percent over the 1958 rate, and Pensacola's
had increased by 69 percent.

Four of the metropolitan areas show the same divergence be-

8. The rapid increase in rates for the second half of the period may also be
related to changes in reporting practices recommended by the IACP for Jacksonville in 1964 and Miami in 1962.

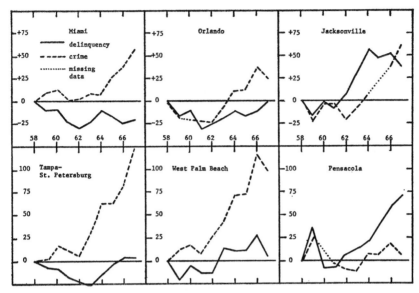

Figure 23-4. Percentage increases in crime and delinquency rates for six standard metropolitan statistical areas in Florida from 1958 through 1967.

tween the crime and delinquency trends as that observed for the state. But the trends are reversed for Pensacola, with increases in the delinquency referral rate outstripping increases in the crime rate. The crime rate for Jacksonville suggests a continuous rise from 1962 to 1967, as contrasted with the delinquency referral rate which levels off after 1964.

An examination of Figures 23-4 and 23-5 suggests that increases in delinquency referrals fluctuate but generally follow increases in the number of children between the ages of twelve and seventeen for four of the six metropolitan areas, with Jacksonville and Pensacola being the exceptions. Delinquency referral rates in all six areas appear to decrease or remain constant until 1961 or 1962 and then to rise sharply for two, three, or four years in succession, presenting a turning point which is roughly similar to the trend observed in the statewide crime and delinquency rates.

DISCUSSION

The information presented in Figure 23-4 suggests that crime rates for these metropolitan areas remained relatively stable from

1958 to 1962 and increased sharply during the following five-year period. There is no way to know the extent to which this reflects actual changes in the amount of criminal activity in these areas as opposed to a tendency to under-report during the earlier period of time. But if under-reporting did occur, it would suggest that some portion of the subsequent increase in crime rates for these areas must be attributed to improved reporting practices.

Since the delinquency rates for this period also decline or remain constant, it is conceivable that increases in the number of criminal events in the state were actually exceeded by increases in the number of inhabitants. But this contingency seems extremely unlikely in view of Florida's urban growth and the crime trends in urban areas outside of Florida. It is more plausible to assume that the delay in governmental response which is discussed above is responsible for these trends. In any event, when the initial lag is examined in connection with the sharp increases in crime rates which begin after 1962 for Miami, Jacksonville,

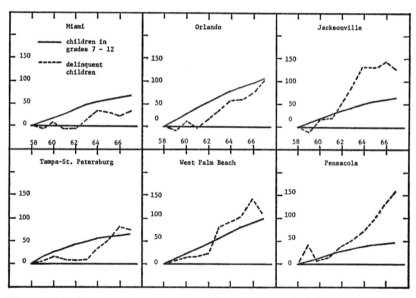

Figure 23-5. Percentage increases in the number of children enrolled in Grades 7 through 12 and in the number of children referred to juvenile court for six metropolitan areas in Florida, 1958 through 1967.

Tampa-St. Petersburg, and Orlando, it suggests that factors other than the occurrence of criminal events have influenced the ten-year trends.

Similar questions are raised by the delinquency trends. It is possible but unlikely that the children in the Jacksonville metropolitan area are more delinquent than the children in the Miami or Tampa-St. Petersburg metropolitan area.[9] It is even less likely that the children in the Jacksonville area in 1967 were more delinquent than the children in the Jacksonville area in 1958 to 1962, especially since no similar change occurred in any other major metropolitan area of the state. Of the six metropolitan areas examined, only the trends for Jacksonville and Pensacola suggest that increases in the number of delinquent acts increased more rapidly than the number of children available for the commission of delinquent acts.

A more reasonable explanation is that the changes in the delinquency referral rates in Duval County (Jacksonville) reflect changes in the operation of the police departments of the county, possibly combined with changes in the philosophy or the record keeping procedures of the juvenile court. In brief, the most compelling indications that crime and delinquency trends in Florida reflect reporting variations rather than changes in the rate of occurrence of criminal acts in the state are (1) the divergence of crime and delinquency trends for the urban counties of the state, (2) the divergence of delinquency trends from school enrollment in Jacksonville and Pensacola, and (3) the fact that increases in national crime and delinquency trends have been more or less constant for the period from 1958 through 1962.

One explanation for the divergence of the lines representing percentage increases in the state and standard metropolitan statistical area crime rates and those representing percentage increases in the delinquency referral rates for Florida is that the

---

9. The rates reported for Jacksonville in 1958 suggested that 62 children per 1,000 enrolled in grades seven through twelve were referred to the court. The figure for the same year was 64 for Tampa-St. Petersburg and 56 for Miami. By 1967 Jacksonville's rate rose to 85, whereas Tampa-St. Petersburg was 66 and Miami's 44.

total population is not only an inappropriate base for the computation of a delinquency referral rate, but also an inappropriate base for the computation of a crime rate which is to be used in a time series analysis. Unfortunately, there is no way to know, at this time, what the most relevant age category for the computation of such a crime rate would be. Arrest data suggest that the highest proportion of persons arrested for robbery, auto theft, and burglary are eighteen, sixteen, and fifteen years old respectively.[10] Given the weight of these offenses on the crime index, the number of persons twelve through twenty years of age would probably be more relevant than the total population. But this question will probably be satisfactorily resolved only after suitable alternative measures of crime are developed.

CONCLUSION

In this use of juvenile court data, we have examined one alternative to the use of offenses known to the police as a measure of crime. Other alternative measures would be provided by victim surveys, uniform arrest reports, and judicial statistics for adult courts. Of these, the victim survey seems to be the most promising, although it is also the most expensive alternative to current methods used in the generation of criminal statistics. Experimentation with this procedure by the National Crime Commission produced results which indicated that there is a good deal of unreported crime occurring in the United States (President's Commission, 1967). Their findings clearly suggest that increased police activity and effectiveness could result in still larger increases in the number of crimes known to the police without any increase in the actual number of criminal events per year.

However, any single measure of crime will have serious disadvantages if it is used alone. Neither periodic victim surveys nor uniform arrest reports nor judicial statistics can be accurately viewed as a replacement for offenses known to the police as a measure of crime. Such techniques are suggested here only as supplementary, alternative measures which will provide more information and greater reliability than can be obtained from

---

10. Crime in the United States, Uniform Crime Reports 121, 1968.

police figures alone. The utility of such additional indicators lies, of course, in the possibilities they provide for more rational interpretations of the amount and kinds of crime occurring in specific areas during selected periods of time. Moreover, alternative measures would contribute to more accurate and more useful descriptions of the nature and extent of crime and would, in this way, make possible more detailed analysis of factors believed to be related to changes in amounts and kinds of crime.

Since the emphasis in our analysis has been on the importance of age composition for crime trends, our results illustrate the potential value of mandatory, uniform arrest reports more clearly than they indicate the utility of victim surveys. If a uniform booking report form were developed and all police agencies in a state were required to submit reports for all persons cited or taken into custody, such information could provide an additional indication of the trends in crime in the state. Such a system would have a number of limitations, but it would provide more detailed and more complete information about crime than is currently being provided by reports of the number of offenses known to the police. In particular, it would provide the information on age needed for computation of age-specific rates. Assuming a more or less consistent ratio between offenses and arrests in specific geographical areas, an assumption which could be tested in areas with periodic victim surveys, such data would permit more accurate discussion of trends in crime for specific cities and states.

Although debated by sociologists as recently as 1968, academic criminologists generally recognize the futility of reliance on, or a search for, *the* best index of crime. Clearly a number of indicators are needed and a number of measures are currently feasible.[11] What appear to be required are more detailed examinations of the obstacles to, and pressure against, changes in the mea-

11. One alternative which is capable of producing useful results was developed by Sellin and Wolfgang in 1964. Their technique attempts to take into account the serious of offenses known to the police in the construction of a crime index. Despite its obvious utility, little use has been made of their procedure. Perhaps nothing less than a full-scale experiment with the procedure by the FBI or a state bureau of criminal statistics would be sufficient to overcome the inertia in federal crime statistics.

surement and interpretation of crime in the United States. This is most clearly indicated by the continuing and growing influence of the FBI's crime index, despite its serious limitations. This is a phenomenon worthy of study in its own right.

REFERENCES

Beattie: Criminal statistics in the United States—1960. *J Crim L C & P S, 51:*49, 1960.

Chilton and Spielberger: Is delinquency increasing? Age structure and the crime rate. *Social Forces, 49:*487, 1971.

Cressey: The state of criminal statistics. *Nat'l Probation & Parole Assoc J,* 3:230, 1957.

Davies: Criminal statistics and the national commission's report. *J Crim L C & P S, 22:*347, 1931.

Erikson, K.: *Wayward Puritans,* 1966.

Mead: Police statistics. *Annals, 146:*74, 1929.

Moley: The collection of criminal statistics in the United States. *Mich L Rev,* 26:747, 1928.

President's Commission on Law Enforcement and the Administration of Justice: *Crime and Its Impact—An Assessment,* 1967.

Robison: A critical view of the uniform crime reports. *Mich L Rev, 64:*1031, 1966.

Schuessler: Components of variations in crime rates. *Social Problems, 9:*314, 1962.

Sellin: The basis of a crime index. *J Crim L C, 22:*335, 1931.

Sellin: The significance of records of crime. *L Q Rev, 67:*489, 1951.

Tittle: Crime rates and legal sanctions. *Social Problems, 16:*409, 1969.

Warner: Crimes known to the police—an index of crime? *Harv L Rev,* 65:307, 1931.

Chapter 24

MODELS OF A TOTAL CRIMINAL JUSTICE SYSTEM

ALFRED BLUMSTEIN AND RICHARD LARSON

THE CRIMINAL justice system (CJS), comprising the agencies of police, prosecution, courts, and corrections, has remained remarkably unchanged through the significant social, technological, and managerial changes of recent decades. This stability results partly from the insularity of these institutions, and their relative freedom from external examination and influence; but it also results from the independence of the individual components of the system, each of which operates within a set of prescribed rules to approach its own suboptimized objective. Nowhere is there a single manager of a CJS with control over all the constituent parts.[1]

In the past few years, there has been an increasing trend toward examining the interactions among the parts of the CJS. The report of the President's Commission on Law Enforcement and Administration of Justice (1967a) urged much closer relations among the parts of the system. The Omnibus Safe Streets and Crime Control Act of 1968 provides Federal funds to State planning agencies to develop "a comprehensive statewide plan for the improvement of law enforcement throughout the State" (Section 203(6)(1). Federal subsidy grants are to be provided on the basis of these plans.

Reprinted, with permission of the Operations Research Society of America, from *Operations Research*, 1969, pp. 199-232.

1. The closest to which the existence of a single manager is approached is in the Federal CJS, in which the police (Federal Bureau of Investigation), prosecutors (U.S. Attorneys), and corrections (Federal Bureau of Prisons) all report to the Attorney General. The courts, however, are completely independent. We do not suggest that a single manager would be desirable: there are strong checks-and-balances reasons for retaining the institutional independence.

471

Thus, there is developing an especially strong need for models permitting one to study a total CJS. Such models are needed only partly for reasons of resource allocation; perhaps even more importantly, they can provide tools for examining the effects on crime of actions taken by the CJS, for most crimes are committed by people who have previously been arrested. Thus, an examination of the feedback process is central to an improvement in the system's performance. In the present state of extensive ignorance on the cause-and-effect relations, the model of this paper will at least identify the data needs and the research questions that will permit analyses of the crime consequences of the actions taken.

DESCRIPTION OF CRIMINAL JUSTICE SYSTEM

The CJS comprises the public agencies concerned with apprehending and dealing with the persons, both adult and juvenile, who violate the criminal law. The basic structure of the CJS is depicted in Figure 24-1; this outline is, of course, a highly simplified version of a very complicated procedure (for a more detailed description, *see* McIntyre, 1967; or for a more condensed version, Hazard, 1966).

Society, comprising former offenders (recidivists) and those not previously so identified, gives rise to criminal acts. Of all crimes which are detected (and many like shoplifting go largely undetected) and reported to the police (and many go unreported)[2] only a fraction lead to the arrest of a suspect.

An arrested person may simply be admonished at the police station and returned home, or he may be referred to some social-service agency outside the CJS. An arrested adult is usually brought before a magistrate, who may dismiss the case or formally accuse the suspect of the original or a lesser charge and set his bail.

The district attorney, who is responsible for prosecution of an accused adult, may dismiss the complaint against the defendant at any time prior to the trial. Those defendants who are not dismissed may plead guilty or stand trial either by a jury or a

---

2. A Crime Commission survey in three Washington, D.C., precincts found a victimization rate 3 to 10 times (depending on type of crime) that reported to the police (President's Commission, 1967b).

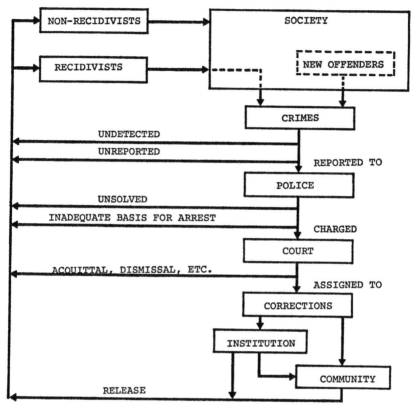

The criminal justice system.

Figure 24-1

judge. Those who are not acquitted can receive a sentence by a judge that can be of various forms, but usually one of the following:

1. A monetary fine.
2. Probation, usually with a suspended sentence.
3. Probation, following a fairly short jail term.
4. Assignment to a state youth authority.
5. A jail term (usually of less than one year).
6. A prison term (usually of no less than one year at a state institution).
7. Civil commitment for some specified treatment.

In addition to newly sentenced offenders from court, prisons can also receive probation and parole violators. Release from prison is usually under parole supervision. Parole violators, if returned to prison, may subsequently be released either on another period of parole, or unconditionally if their sentence has been served.

The processing of juveniles is similar to that of adults, but it is far less formal, with far more freedom of choice exercised by the juvenile authorities.

This processing by the CJS typically involves a series of stages, with the alternatives at most of these stages being either return to the community or further penetration into the CJS. Since virtually all offenders return to society eventually, they are afforded repeated opportunities to return to the CJS by a subsequent arrest, followed by a recycling through the system.

This cursory description suggests two approaches to modeling the CJS. First, there is the simple production process, in which the principal concern is the flow through the system, and the accumulation of costs flowing from a single arrest. Such a linear model provides an opportunity (1) to examine at each stage the workload, the personnel requirements that result, and the associated costs, (2) to attribute these to types of crimes, and (3) to project all of these planning variables as functions of future arrest rates (Roy, 1964, has discussed such models in a preliminary way).

The second is a feedback model, which considers the recidivism probability associated with each released defendant, and his subsequent processing for future arrests after he has once been released by the CJS. Such a feedback model building on the work of the Space-General Corporation (1965) permits estimating the costs of a total criminal career (considering the succession of re-arrests of an individual) and the consequences of alternative actions within the CJS to lower recidivism probabilities.

Some preliminary results with these two models on aggregated U.S. data have been reported previously (Blumstein, et al., 1967). This paper provides some of the details on the form of these models, and presents some results for California, the single state that comes closest to having an adequate data base.[3] Hopefully, as the use of such models increases, more complete data will begin to become available and the results will increase in reliability and usefulness.

THE LINEAR MODEL

A steady-state, linear model is used to compute the costs and workloads at the various processing stages and to establish manpower requirements to meet the anticipated workloads. The *workload* is the annual demand for service at the various processing stages (e.g. courtroom hours, detective man-hours); the *manpower requirement* is derived from the workload by dividing by the annual working time per man (or other resource); total operating *costs* are allocated to offenders by standard cost-accounting procedures (these allocated costs are then assumed to be variable costs).

The flow of persons through each processing stage is described by a vector whose ith component represents the yearly flow associated with characteristic type i ($i = 1, \ldots, I$). These characteristics can be any attribute associated with individual offenders, their crimes, or their previous processing by the CJS. In most of our studies, there have been seven characteristics (i.e. $I = 7$), corresponding to the seven *index* crimes (the seven types of crimes which the FBI annually tabulates *[Crime in the United States]* to get an "index" of crime in the United States are willful homicide, forcible rape, aggravated assault, robbery, burglary, larceny of $50 or over, and auto theft).

The independent flow vector to the model, which must be specified as input, is the number of crimes reported to police during one year (hereafter, unless stated otherwise, all computed variables and data are considered as seven-component vectors; the flow variables represent annual flow rates). The outputs are the computed flows, costs, and manpower requirements that would result if the input and the system were in steady state.

---

3. A complete description of the models, the input data, and the results is available in the appendixes to the version of this paper published by the Institute for Defense Analyses.

Each processing stage is characterized by vector cost rates (per unit flow) and branching probabilities (or branching ratios). The input flow at each processing stage is partitioned into the appropriate output flows by element-by-element vector multiplication of the input flow and the branching probability (e.g. $F_{i, n} = F_{i, m} P_{i, mn}$), where

$F_{i, m}$ = number of offenders associated with crime-type i entering processing stage m during one year,

$F_{i, n}$ = number of offenders associated with crime-type i following route n out of processing stage m, and

$P_{i, mn}$ = probability that an offender associated with crime-type i input at stage m will exit through route n ($\Sigma_n P_{i, mn} = 1$).

A simple processing stage, representing the verdict of a jury trial, is depicted in Figure 24-2. The input N_{t_1} is the number of defendants who receive a jury trial. The outputs N_{tg_1} and $N_{\overline{tg}_1}$ are the numbers found guilty and not found guilty, respectively. The branching probability P_{tg_1} is the probability that a jury trial de-

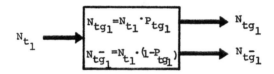

DEFINITIONS:

N_{t_1} = NUMBER OF DEFENDANTS WHO RECEIVE JURY TRIALS

N_{tg_1} = NUMBER OF JURY TRIAL DEFENDANTS FOUND GUILTY

$N_{\overline{tg}_1}$ = NUMBER OF JURY TRIAL DEFENDANTS NOT FOUND GUILTY

P_{tg_1} = PROBABILITY THAT A JURY TRIAL DEFENDANT IS FOUND GUILTY

The jury-trial stage.

Figure 24-2

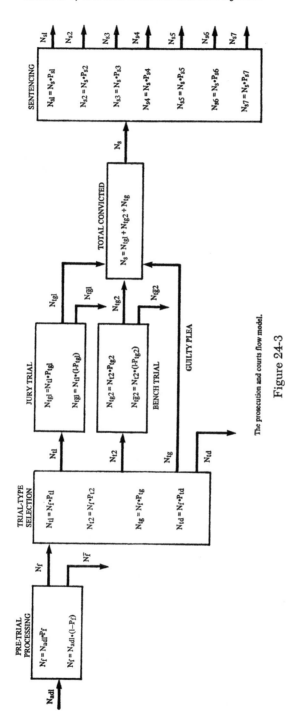

The prosecution and courts flow model.

Figure 24-3

fendant will be found guilty. With seven crime types, the seven components of P_{tg_1} are required as input data for this stage.[4]

Describing the entire model in detail is not warranted here. To illustrate the details, however, we briefly discuss the prosecution and courts submodel. The flow diagram is given in Figure 24-3. The input to this part of the model is the vector, N_{ad_1}, the number of adult arrestees who are formally charged with index crimes. This submodel produces seven output vectors corresponding to the seven sentence types. These provide the inputs to the subsequent processing stages. In addition, there are four intermediate output vectors characterizing defendants who never reach the sentencing stage, namely:

1. N_f^- = number of adults formally charged who do not reach trial stage.
2. N_{td} = number of defendants whose cases are dismissed or placed off calendar at the trial stage.
3. $N_{tg_1}^-$ = number of jury-trial defendants not found guilty.
4. $N_{tg_2}^-$ = number of bench- and transcript-trial defendants not found guilty.

Clearly, any other intermediate flows can also be calculated, if desired.

This submodel calls for four classes of branching probabilities. These refer to:

1. Whether or not the defendant reaches the trial stage.
2. The type of trial (or whether dismissed at trial stage).
3. The trial verdict.
4. The sentencing decision.

The definitions of all the flow-and-branching probability variables of Figure 24-3 are given in Table 24-I.

Having determined the flow through each processing stage,

---

4. A more general model would define each branching probability as a function of an offender's prior path through the system and other information which had become known since arrest. The branching probabilities describing the sentencing decision, for instance, would depend on whether the defendant had pleaded guilty, had a jury trial, or a bench or transcript trial. In effect, the possible number of characteristics that could be associated with a flow variable could grow exponentially with the depth of system penetration; the demands for data, of course, grow comparably.

TABLE 24-I
DEFINITIONS OF FLOW AND BRANCHING PROBABILITIES IN
THE PROSECUTION AND COURT SUBMODEL
(Output flows and corresponding branching probabilities are given as matched
pairs. Only the definition of the flow is stated.)

N_{ad_1}	The number of adult arrests who are formally charged by the magistrate.
(N_f, P_f)	The number of adults formally charged who receive a Superior Court felony disposition.
$(N_f^-, 1 - P_f)$	The number of adults formally charged who do not receive a Superior Court felony disposition.
(N_{t1}, P_{t1})	Number of defendants who reach trial stage and who receive *jury trials.*
(N_{t2}, P_{t2})	Number of defendants who reach trial stage and who receive *bench* or *transcript trials.*
(N_{tg}, P_{tg})	Number of defendants who reach trial stage and who plead guilty.
(N_{td}, P_{td})	Number of defendants who reach trial stage and who are dismissed or placed off calendar.
(N_{tg1}, P_{tg1})	Number of defendants who receive jury trials who are found guilty.
$(N_{tg1}^-, 1 - P_{tg1})$	Number of defendants who receive jury trials who are not found guilty.
(N_{tg2}, P_{tg2})	Number of defendants who receive bench or transcript trials who are found guilty.
$(N_{tg2}^-, 1 - P_{tg2})$	Number of defendants who receive bench or transcript trials who are not found guilty.
N_s	The number of defendants who are sentenced.
(N_{sj}, P_{sj})	The number of sentenced defendants who receive sentence type j $(j = 1, 2, \ldots, 7)$.

we can determine the total costs simply as the product of the unit costs and the flow rates. Costs are separated into pre-trial and trial costs, and for each, court and prosecutor's costs.[5] In addition, there is a cost of pre-trial detention.

The flows through the appropriate processing stages permit calculating annual workloads in terms of total trial-days for jury-and-bench (i.e. judge) trials and man-days for pre-trial detention in jail. The annual manpower requirements (e.g. the required number of prosecutors, judges, and jurors) are then calculated on the basis of unit productivity (e.g. annual trial days available per prosecutor).

5. Much of the court-cost data was estimated from other jurisdictions, particularly Washington, D.C., and the Federal Court System.

Some illustrative results were developed based on data principally from California (State of California, Department of Justice). In some cases, where California data were unavailable, data from other jurisdictions were invoked. The input data are presented in Table 24-II.

It is interesting to note, for instance, that P_{t_1}, the probability that a defendant will receive a jury trial, increases with the severity of the offense, but never exceeds 0.25 [the numerical estimate of P_{t_1} is formed by computing the ratio (number of jury-trial defendants/total number of defendants) for a given year]. Regardless of crime type, a majority of those who reach trial plead guilty. Probabilities of being found guilty in a trial are roughly three-quarters.

Table 24-II also shows time and cost data. The average jury-trial length, T_1, ranges between 4.6 and 1.6 days (a trial day is typically five hours long), depending on the type of crime. The average cost per day of jury trial was computed by first allocating the total court costs to "judgeships," and then dividing the judgeship annual cost by the annual number of judge working days spent in trial. (There are additional court costs to the prosecutor and to police investigators, attributed before and during trial.) This obviously simplified cost-allocation procedure clearly needs

TABLE 24-II

CALIFORNIA INPUT DATA TO THE PROSECUTION AND
COURTS MODEL

	Homicide	Robbery	Assault	Burglary	Larceny	Auto Theft	Rape
P_{t1}	0.25	0.18	0.12	0.07	0.06	0.03	0.11
P_{t2}	0.18	0.13	0.25	0.17	0.20	0.16	0.21
P_{tg}	0.50	0.61	0.52	0.67	0.66	0.75	0.58
P_{tg1}	0.81	0.81	0.75	0.78	0.68	0.83	0.54
P_{tg2}	0.68	0.71	0.77	0.71	0.89	0.75	0.61
T_1	4.6	3.1	2.3	2.2	3.0	1.6	2.9
C_J	3680	2480	1840	1760	2400	1280	2320
T_2	1.1	1.1	1.0	1.0	1.1	1.0	0.8
C_b	620	620	560	560	620	560	450

T_1, T_2 = Average number of jury (T_1) and bench trial (T_2) days per case.
C_J, C_b = Average jury (C_J) and bench trial (C_b) cost per trial, including prosecution and court costs.

much more refinement when the necessary cost data become available.

Limitations of the Model

However complex this model may appear, it is still a gross simplification of reality. Each processing stage represents a number of detailed processing stages in the real system; the description could have been made more detailed, but the finer data were not available, and little but complexity would have been gained.

The unit costs at each processing stage have been calculated simply by dividing current total yearly cost by current yearly work-load. This implied linear relation between flow and cost (i.e. all costs are variable) ignores the fact that many costs are fixed and independent of flow (e.g. the cost of courthouses). However, this simplification also avoids the problem of having to identify which costs are fixed and which are variable, since many costs that are fixed over a slight variation in flow become variable if there is a large variation in flow. By this costing procedure, certain facilities that may currently be operating well below capacity (e.g. rural courts) would show an excessively high unit cost.

The variables in the model are assumed to be constant over time (a steady-state assumption) and independent of each other or of exogenous variables. There undoubtedly are interactions that limit the validity of this simplification. Certain service times (e.g. detention times) and branching ratios (e.g. probability of prison sentence) are probably functions of the magnitudes of demands. Such interactions need further examination.

Despite these limitations, the model does permit a reasonable first estimate of costs, workloads, and flows, and allocation of these to crime type and processing stage. Furthermore, these planning variables can be projected into the future if the crime or arrest rate can be projected, and if the branching probabilities are either constant or can be projected.

SENSITIVITY ANALYSES

An important phase of the analysis is to determine the effects of changes in one subsystem on the workload, costs, and manpower requirements of another subsystem; for instance, if there were indications that an improved fingerprint-detection system would increase the burglary arrest rate (i.e. arrests per burglary), it would be necessary to plan for the increased cost-and-workload effect on the subsequent court and corrections subsystems. In addition, the allocation of costs to various subfunctions is of interest in considering possible reallocation of resources. A sensitivity analysis permits an examination of this distribution.

Given any two system flows, C_i and $N_i (i = 1, 2, \ldots, I)$ we find it useful to define the following two quantities:

$\partial C_i/\partial N_i$ = incremental change in C_i per unit change in N_i (first partial derivative of C_i with respect to N_i);

$(\partial C_i/\partial N_i)/(C_i/N_i)$ = incremental fractional change in C_i per unit fractional change in N_i ("elasticity" of C_i with respect to N_i); a "unit fractional change" could be, for instance, a 1 percent change.

To indicate the interpretation of these two quantities, suppose C_i represents the cost at stage 12 associated with processing individuals charged with crime i. Consider that N_i represents the flow of persons into stage 6. In terms of N_i, suppose C_i is linearly related to N_i, i.e. it can be written as follows: $C_i = A_i + B_i N_i$. Then,

$\partial C_i/\partial N_i = B_i$ = average additional cost incurred for processing at stage 12 per additional individual charged with crime i inserted at stage 6.[6]

$(\partial C_i/\partial N_i)/(C_i/N_i) = B_i N_i/(A_i + B_i N_i)$ = average fractional increase in cost incurred at stage 12 for processing individuals charged with crime i per unit fractional increase in individuals charged with crime i inserted at stage 6.

More succinctly, the first partial derivative in this case is an incremental *cost per person* and the elasticity is the *fractional increase in cost per unit fractional increase in the number of persons.*

As an example, we may be interested in the incremental change in total system direct operating cost (C_t) caused by the addition of one robbery defendant in the flow N_{ad_1}, the number of adults who are charged with a felony in magistrate's court. For this case,

---

6. This cost could be calculated directly as the product of the unit cost of processing at stage 12 and the probability that an individual inserted at stage 6 will reach stage 12; this latter probability is not explicitly calculated.

the incremental cost per additional robbery defendant (i.e. $\partial C_t/\partial N_{ad_1}$ for robbery) is calculated to be $4,800. This means that an average robbery defendant charged by a magistrate's court costs the system $4,800 (for the current offense) in addition to costs already incurred in previous stages. The value of $4,800 is the expected value of the total subsequent costs (i.e. the sum of each of the unit costs at the magistrate's court and later stages weighted by the probability that the defendant passes through each particular processing stage).

If C_i is a flow, then $\partial C_i/\partial N_i$ is an incremental flow per additional person inserted. For instance, if we let C_i be the number of jury trials for robbery defendants (the robbery component of N_{t_1}) and N_i be the robbery component of N_{ad_1} (the number of adults charged with a felony in magistrate's court), then the incremental number of robbery jury trials per additional robbery defendant from magistrate's court is calculated to be 0.10. This figure can also be interpreted as the probability that a randomly selected robbery defendant from magistrate's court will proceed to and have a jury trial.

Now let us consider an example involving elasticity. Suppose that C_i is the number of burglary defendants placed on straight probation, the burglary component of N_{s_1}, and that N_i is the number of defendants found guilty of burglary in jury trials, the burglary component of N_{tg_1}. We calculate that $(\partial C_i/\partial N_i)/(C_i/N_i) = 0.07$. This means that a 1 percent increase in the number of burglary defendants found guilty in jury trials would cause a 0.07 percent increase in the number of burglary defendants placed on straight probation.

TABLE 24-III

INCREMENTAL COSTS PER REPORTED CRIME

	Robbery	Assault	Burglary	Auto Theft	Rape
C_t	$1,083	$437	$169	$170	$904
C_{co}	760	197	87	58	534
C_{ct}	59	34	9	8	108
C_p	82	52	37	25	124
C_{pd}	71	44	25	16	108

C_t = total system cost. C_{co} = cost of the correction system. C_{ct} = cost of the prosecution and courts system. C_p = cost of police. C_{pd} = cost of police detectives.

TABLE 24-IV

INCREMENTAL FLOWS PER ARREST

(Including Juvenile Arrests)

	Robbery	Assault	Burglary	Auto Theft	Rape
N_I	0.41	0.09	0.09	0.04	0.16
N_P	0.10	0.02	0.03	0.02	0.03
N_{t2}	0.02	0.04	0.02	0.02	0.06
N_{tg}	0.12	0.07	0.09	0.08	0.16
N_f	0.19	0.14	0.14	0.11	0.28

N_I = number of adult-years served in prison. N_P = number of adults sentenced to prison directly from Superior Court. N_{t2} = number of adults having bench trials. N_{tg} = number of adults who plead guilty. N_f = number of adults who receive a Superior Court felony disposition.

Other illustrative calculations made for the 1965 California CJS system are shown in Tables 24-III and 24-IV. Table 24-III shows various incremental costs per additional reported crime. Of the crimes presented,[7] robbery costs are highest ($1,083), primarily because of the high increment in correction costs; the incremental costs for auto theft are lowest. These calculated costs combine many factors, including the probability of apprehending a suspect, the dismissal probabilities along the way, and the costing procedure.[8]

Table 24-IV presents incremental flows resulting from one additional arrest. The first-row entry (additional number of adult-years in prison) is the average man-years served in prison per additional arrest. This can also be interpreted to be the incre-

7. No entries are given in Table 24-III for homicide or larceny because of the lack of uniformity of definition of these two crimes in the various processing stages. For instance, police report the incidence of "grand theft, except auto" whereas most (but not all) other processing stages report the number of defendants associated with "theft except auto," a large category which includes petty theft with prior and receiving-stolen-property offenses (see State of California, 1965, pp. 207-209). Even for the five crime types considered here there are minor deviations of definitions in various parts of the system.

8. The procedure for calculating police costs was a product of time components and time pay rates. For detectives, the time components were preliminary investigation, arrest, and case development. Cost assignment for the police patrol force is somewhat more troublesome. The force spends a large fraction of its time on "preventive patrol," and it is difficult to apportion this time to individual crimes. In the current model, a lower bound on patrol costs was used. The time allocated to crimes was taken as twice the average time to service a call.

mental prison population per additional arrest. All other entries have a probabilistic interpretation; for instance entries in the second row indicate that 10 percent of those arrested for robbery are sentenced to prison from Superior Court and only 2 percent of those arrested for assault.

ESTIMATION OF FUTURE REQUIREMENTS

Administrators of the CJS at all levels, from state attorneys general, crime commissions, and budget directors to planners in the various local agencies, require projections of future workloads, costs, and manpower requirements. These projections are needed for earlier decisions that must be made in anticipation of future changes in workload. For instance, new buildings (e.g. courts or correctional institutions) can be designed and constructed or additional personnel can be hired and trained.

In this section we report two applications of the model, using data from the State of California. First, we investigate the degree to which the branching probabilities are constant. Following that, we project for California workloads, costs, and manpower requirements into the year 1970, on the basis of data collected through 1965. Since the number of reported crimes is a basic input to the model, we must independently project the number of crimes that will be reported; a linear extrapolation is used for that projection. Then we develop estimates of the number of arrests per year, and use the model to obtain projections of CJS workloads, costs, and manpower requirements.

Trend in the Number of Arrests per Reported Crime

A comparison of system branching ratios over a five-year period indicated that system workload is most sensitive to changes in the average number of arrests per reported crime.

The branching probabilities P_{Ac} (the number of arrests per reported crime[9] for California in the years 1961 to 1965 are shown

---

9. Numerical values for P_{Ac} are computed simply by dividing the total number of arrests (adults and juveniles) by the total number of crimes reported. Strictly speaking, it is an estimate of the average number of arrests per reported crime. We often refer to it as the "arrest probability," knowing that some crimes generate more than one arrest and that the suspect arrested may not be the perpetrator of that particular reported crime.

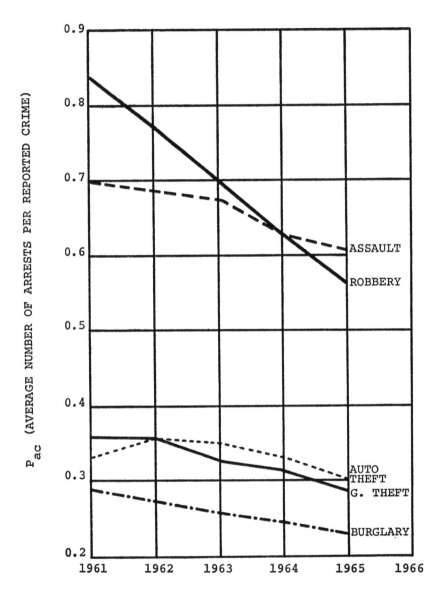

Values of P_{AC} as a function of time.

Figure 24-4

in Figure 24-4 for aggravated assault, robbery, auto theft, grand theft (in California, larceny of $200 or more), and burglary. (The crimes of homicide and rape are not included because the definition of these crimes changes from the crime report to the arrest stages.) Each rate exhibits a negative slope, with robbery showing the greatest rate of decrease. Indeed, arrests for robbery have shown a marked decline of about 32 percent from 0.83 per reported crime in 1961 to 0.57 per reported crime in 1965. The burglary arrest probability has decreased by approximately 20 percent.[10] The general downward trends could be caused by a combination of several factors:

1. More frequent reporting of crimes to or by police.
2. More accurate police classification of reported crimes.
3. Fewer arrests of individuals not associated with the crimes.
4. Saturation of limited police manpower resources.
5. Greater difficulty in solving crimes, caused by such problems as mobility of criminals, lowered citizen cooperation, etc.

Many other possible reasons could be advanced. Without having to attribute cause, however, it is possible to project P_{AC} somewhat into the future. This parameter describes the system's first processing stage of arrest, and its value linearly affects workloads and costs in all other system stages.

Trends in Final Disposition Pecentages

To test the constancy of the branching ratios further, a linear extrapolation was performed to estimate trends in the other branching ratios for California. Specifically, for each of the years 1960 to 1965, the ratios of final disposition of adult felony arrests to total arrests were investigated. The final dispositions were:

1. Released.
2. Assigned to other jurisdiction.
3. Dismissed.
4. Acquitted.

---

10. More recent data that have since become available indicate a continuation in these trends. For the year 1966, the number of arrests per reported robbery dropped to 0.52, per burglary to 0.21, and per assault to 0.59. Auto-theft and grand-theft probabilities remained about constant.

5. Misdemeanor prosecution.
6. Superior court conviction.
   a. Civil commitment.
   b. Prison.
   c. Youth Authority.
   d. Probation.
   e. Jail and fine.

The most significant trend ($t = 5.3$) was found in the fraction receiving probation. (Significance was tested with a Student's t-test of the difference from zero of the linear time term; the value $t = 5.3$ causes us to reject, even at the $a = 0.001$ level of significance, the hypothesis that there is no linear time trend in the fraction receiving probation.) During 1960 to 1965, a fraction of approximately 0.13 of felony arrests received probation at the sentencing stage, and this value is increasing 0.00631 per year. No other trends were significant (at the 0.05 level), and none was as important as the trend in P_{AC}.

Although not all of the individual branching ratios were examined in detail, the steady-state assumption appeared justified for all important branching ratios except P_{AC} and those relating to the probation decision.

In making projections with the model, it was especially important to consider the downward trend in P_{AC}, since changes in this fraction propagate throughout the entire system. It was felt that for short-range projections, it would not be necessary to adjust the probation or other branching ratios.

For short-range projections, it was decided to compute output in two ways:

1. Linearly extrapolate the trends in P_{AC} and use the resulting projection of P_{AC}.
2. Use the 1965 value of P_{AC}.

These two projections can be expected to bound the actual future values. In our calculations we use the average of the two projections.

Crime Projection

The future numbers of crimes reported to police were projected using a linear time extrapolation of the reported crimes for the

TABLE 24-V

LINEAR PROJECTION OF INDEX CRIMES REPORTED TO POLICE
IN CALIFORNIA

Offense	Mean No. of Reported Crimes 1958-1966 (N = 9)	Standard Deviation of Reported Crimes 1958-1966	Standard Error of Linear Estimate	Correlation Coefficient of Estimating Equation	Constant Term in Equation	Linear Coefficient in Equation (Yearly Increment)	T-Value of Linear Term
Criminal homicide	677	128	42	0.956	440	47	9
Forcible rape	3,309	528	302	0.863	2,427	177	5
Robbery	16,501	3,402	1,144	0.955	10,209	1,259	9
Aggravated assault	21,724	4,402	1,046	0.978	13,388	1,667	12
Burglary	168,022	43,408	8,910	0.983	85,351	16,534	14
Grand larceny	97,146	27,795	7,948	0.968	45,060	10,417	10
Auto theft	62,059	14,957	4,565	0.963	34,163	5,579	9

Data Source: Uniform Crime Reports for 1958 through 1966.

years 1958 to 1966;[11] the results of this analysis are shown in Table 24-V. All the correlation coefficients (except for the crime of forcible rape)[12] exceed 0.95, indicating that the linear fit is a good one. Particularly important to criminal justice system administrators in this table are the yearly growth coefficients in the next-to-last column. Note that the number of reported burglaries is increasing by the largest magnitude at 16,534 per year (with 95% confidence, the yearly growth coefficient is between 13,000 and 20,000 burglaries per year).

Arrest Projection

Using the projections of reported crimes from the linear extrapolation, we obtained the approximate upper and lower estimates (keeping P_{AC} constant and projecting its trend, respectively) for the number of arrests in 1970 given in Table 24-VI. The results are expressed as percentages of the numbers of arrests in 1965. The upper estimate indicates about a 30 percent increase in system workload during this five-year interval while the lower estimate indicates that the increasing trend in reported crimes is almost compensated by the decreasing trend in arrest probability, and so system workloads will remain about constant (with some fluctuations by crime type, of course). If the declining trend in robbery arrest probability were to continue, the robbery-arrest workload in 1970 would be about half that of 1965. On the other hand, it appears that the arrest probability for auto theft has almost kept pace with the increasing number of reported auto thefts; auto theft exhibits the largest lower estimate in Table 24-VI.

To project a numerical value for arrests in 1970, we arbitrarily average the upper and lower bounds in Table 24-VI; these results are shown in Table 24-VIa.

---

11. UCR figures for California were used. The definitions of some of the seven crimes are different from the "seven major offenses" of California. Most notably, larceny of $50 and over is counted by the FBI as an index offense whereas "grand larceny" in California requires theft of property valued at $200 and over.

12. In contrast to a simple linear relation, the number of reported rapes was found to remain approximately constant (about 3,000 per year) until 1964, when it jumped to 3,621, and then to 4,432 in 1966.

TABLE 24-VI

PROJECTED NUMBER OF ARRESTS BY CRIME TYPE IN 1970
(Expressed as a percentage of the number of arrests in 1965)

	Homicide	Forcible Rape	Robbery	Aggravated Assault	Burglary	Grand Larceny	Auto Theft
Upper estimate ...	129.6	124.2	129.8	132.0	138.0	140.4	134.2
Lower estimate ...	—	—	55.7	109.0	100.0	93.5	121.0

TABLE 24-VIa

PROJECTED NUMBER OF ARRESTS IN 1970
(Obtained by averaging the upper and lower estimates)

Crime Type	Percentage of 1965 Arrests
Homicide	130
Forcible rape	124
Robbery	93
Aggravated assault	120
Burglary	119
Grand larceny	117
Auto theft	128

Projections of System Variables

Using these arrest projections we can compute, using the steady-state model, projected values of system variables in 1970; several of these calculations are shown in Table 24-VII. We see that a projected total of 119 additional detectives and 73.9 additional patrolmen will be required to handle increases in the seven major crimes. A projected total of 1,393 additional defendants will be placed on probation in 1970. The additional yearly cost to California's criminal justice agencies for increases in the seven major crimes is computed to be $17.3 million. About 41.6 percent of this additional cost is due to additional burglary workloads, about 22.5 percent to additional auto-theft workloads. In the 1965 calculations, burglary costs accounted for 31 percent of the total and auto theft costs 10 percent. Grouping auto theft, bur-

TABLE 24-VII

PROJECTED INCREASES IN VALUES OF CJS VARIABLES IN CALIFORNIA FROM 1965 TO 1970

	Homicide	Rape	Robbery	Assault	Burglary	Theft	Auto Theft	Total
N_{ad1}	900*	1,700	4,200	4,600	13,700	4,400	4,400	33,900
	+270	+400	−300	+920	+2,600	+750	+1,200	+5,840
M_a	24	22	85	65	310	115	75	696
	+7	+5	−6	+13	+60	+19	+21	+119
U_p	3,600	9,100	35,000	31,000	415,000	45,000	115,000	654,000
	+1,000	+2,200	−2,600	+6,200	+78,000	+7,400	+32,000	+124,000
N_{t1}	180	100	420	260	500	195	77	1,730
	+54	+25	−30	+53	+94	+33	+22	+251
M_p	2.1	5.3	21	18	240	26	67	379
	+0.6	+1.3	−1.5	+4	+46	+4.5	+19	+73.9
N_{t2}	130	190	290	570	1,200	700	410	3,490
	+40	+50	−20	+110	+220	+120	+115	+635
N_s	590	700	1,950	1,800	5,900	3,000	2,300	16,200
	+180	+170	−140	+360	+1,200	+520	+640	+2,930
N_{s1}	90	280	95	600	1,200	1,000	500	3,770
	+30	+70	−7	+120	+230	+170	+140	+753
N_{s2}	140	150	290	420	1,400	660	440	3,500
	+40	+40	−20	+75	+270	+110	+125	+640
N_4	320	110	1,200	340	1,450	420	400	4,240
	+100	+30	−85	+70	+280	+70	+110	+575
C_t	8.1	3.3	23	11	38	15	14	112.4
($ million)	+2.4	+0.8	−1.7	+2.2	+7.2	+2.5	+3.9	+17.3

* For each pair of entries, the projected increase is given below the 1965 value.

N_{ad1} = number of adult felony arrests which result in a felony charge.

M_a = total number of detectives required.

U_p = total number of patrolman manhours allocated (to these crimes).

M_p = total number of patrolmen required (for these crimes).

N_{t1} = number of jury trial defendants.

N_{t2} = number of bench or transcript trial defendants.

N_s = number of convicted defendants.

N_{s1} = number of convicted defendants granted straight probation.

N_{s2} = number of convicted defendants granted probation with jail as a condition.

N_{s4} = number of convicted defendants sentenced to state prison.

C_t = total system direct operating costs.

glary, and larceny as the "property crimes," we see that they accounted for 54 percent of the cost in 1965, but are projected to account for 57 percent in 1970.

Extensions and Further Analyses With the Linear Model

These projections can be expected to deviate from the future observations. The differences will result from inadequacies of the current model, errors and incompleteness in the reported data, and basic changes in the operation of the California CJS. As actual results are compared with past projections, calibration of the model and the data sources will result, leading to an improved projection methodology.

As the model is improved, other useful analyses can be performed. The effects on CJS operations of significant changes in system branching ratios can be explored. For instance, introduction of new police hardware (e.g. an electronic automobile-license-plate scanner or automated fingerprint files) might dramatically change one or more branching ratios (e.g. the probability of arrest for auto theft or burglary) and thus affect the workloads at subsequent stages. More widespread provision of free defense counsel, especially for juveniles as a result of recent court decisions, might provide additional strain on prosecution and court workloads. Greater use of nonadjudicative treatment (e.g. use of social service agencies as an alternative to prosecution) will require the introduction of additional flow routes in the model and can be expected to reduce court workloads. A change in sentencing policies (e.g. more use of community treatment or longer sentences) might affect decisions on construction of new correctional facilities or hiring and training of additional parole and probation personnel.

Crime projections can be improved by taking into account changes in such demographic characteristics as age, income, education, and urbanization. Similarly, since many of the branching ratios also depend on these characteristics, they can be used for more accurate estimation throughout the system.

In our model, the branching ratios were assumed to be mutually independent. In a number of cases, interaction can be expected. For instance, if the number of convictions increases, and if prisons operate near capacity, one might expect a reduction in probability of prison sentence or the time served. Such interaction must be explored to improve the model.

FEEDBACK MODEL

This section summarizes a feedback model that describes the recycling through the CJS during the course of an individual's criminal career. The model has several important applications. First, given the age of an offender at first arrest and the crime for which he is arrested, the model computes his expected criminal career profile (i.e. the expected crimes for which he will be arrested at each age). Second, using the cost results of the linear model, the model computes the average costs incurred by the CJS over a criminal career. Third, recidivism parameters (e.g. rearrest probabilities) can be varied to assess how each parameter affects criminal careers and cost. For instance, we can study the effect of an intensive rehabilitative program that reduces rearrest probability by a specified amount. Fourth, and most fundamental, the model provides a unified framework in which to study the process of recidivism and in which to test the effects of proposed alternative CJS policies on recidivism.

Over-All Structure of the Model

As in the linear model, flows are distinguished by crime type. In addition, each flow variable is broken down by the offender's age. The input to the model, rather than crimes reported to police, is the numbers of arrests during a year, by crime type and by age, of individuals who have never previously been arrested for one of the crimes being considered. In the model, these "virgin" arrests are added to recidivist arrest (i.e. arrests of individuals who have previously been arrested) to obtain the total arrests during the year.[13] The total arrests then proceed through the CJS just as they do in the linear model.

---

13. Although reported *crimes* are a more adequate variable upon which to compute police workloads and the over-all magnitude of the crime problem, *arrest* is the first event linking crime to a specific individual. Statistics describing recidivism often use arrest as the index of recidivism, even though the arrest may not necessarily indicate that one or more crimes have been committed by the individual arrested. In this model, recidivism is consistently measured by rearrest. Using arrest as the basis for measuring recidivism introduces two types of error:

Since the offender flows comprise individuals who cycle back into the system after dismissal or release from the CJS, it is necessary to compute the number that do recycle, when they are rearrested, and for what crime. At each possible dismissal point, the offender is characterized by a probability of rearrest that is, in general, a function of his age and his prior criminal record. The expected number who will be rearrested at some later time is computed by multiplying the number in the flow by the appropriate rearrest probability. Then, the age at rearrest is computed by using the distribution of delay between release and the next arrest. Finally, the crime type of the next arrest is computed from a rearrest crime-switch matrix, where the matrix element p_{ij} is the conditional probability that the next arrest is for crime type j, given that rearrest occurs and the previous arrest was for crime type i ($1 \leq i, j \leq I$). A flow diagram of the model is given in Figure 24-5.

There are two different interpretations of the computed flows: as a cohort-tracing model or as a population-simulation model. In the first, a cohort of virgin arrests can be inserted at some age and the aggregate criminal career of that cohort can be traced. For a fifteen-year-old cohort, for instance, the model will compute the expected number of arrests by crime type incurred at ages sixteen, seventeen, etc. Alternatively, in the second case, we can input as virgin arrests the total present distribution of such arrests, by age and by crime type; in this case, invoking a steady-state assumption, the computed flows represent the current distribution of all individuals (including recidivists) processed by

---

crimes for which no offender is arrested are not counted, and offenders who are erroneously arrested are counted. Using a later stage for counting (e.g. conviction) would introduce the additional, more serious error of omitting the many crimes for which evidence is insufficient to warrant conviction. In much of the criminological literature, where the concern is principally on the correction process (e.g. Glaser, 1964), recidivism is often defined in terms of the imprisonment-to-imprisonment cycle. It should be clear that, for the same amount of crime repetition, the measured probability of recidivism decreases as one measures it at stages of successively deeper penetration into the CJS. Thus, FBI estimates (UCR, 1966) of rearrest recidivism of about three-quarters are consistent with Glaser's (1964) estimate of reimprisonment recidivism of about one-third due to the arrests that do not result in imprisonment. A simple Markov model, using a reasonable value of 0.75 for arrest-to-imprisonment attrition probability, shows this compatibility.

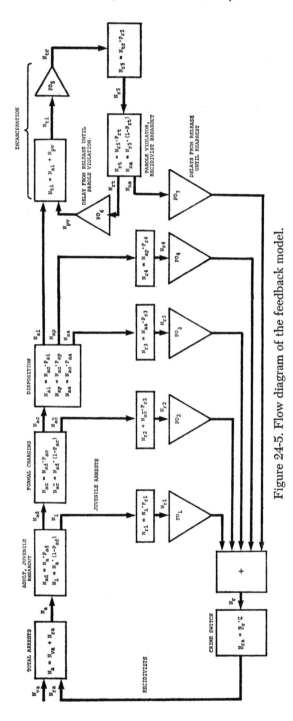

Figure 24-5. Flow diagram of the feedback model.

Variable or Parameter Name	Definition
N_{va}	Number of virgin arrests
N_{ra}	Number of recidivist arrest
N_a	Total number of arrests
N_{ad}, P_{ad}	Number (proportion) of arrests which are adult arrests
N_j	Number of arrests which are juvenile arrests
N_{ac}, P_{ac}	Number (proportion) of adult arrests formally charged
$N_{a\bar{c}}$	Number of adult arrests not formally charged
N_{ai}, P_{ai}	Number (proportion) of charged adults incarcerated
N_{ap}, P_{ap}	Number (proportion) of charged adults granted probation
N_{aa}, P_{aa}	Number (proportion) of charged adults released or acquitted
N_{tl}	Total number of adults who are incarcerated
N_{tr}	Number of adults released from incarceration
N_{ri}, P_{ri}	Number (proportion) of arrested juveniles who are rearrested
N_{r2}, P_{r2}	Number (proportion) of adults arrested but not formally charged who are rearrested
N_{r3}, P_{r3}	Number (proportion) of adults released or acquitted who are rearrested
N_{r4}, P_{r4}	Number (proportion) of adults granted probation who are rearrested

Variable or Parameter Name	Definition
N_{r5}, P_{r5}	Number (proportion) of adults released from incarceration who recidivate*
N_{rt}, P_{rt}	Number (proportion) of adults released who violate parole and are reincarcerated
N_{pv}	Number of adult parole violators who reenter prison
N_{na}	Number of adult releases who are rearrested
N_r	Total number of those who will be rearrested
C	Rearrest crime-switch matrix
PD_1	Distribution of time until rearrest of juvenile recidivists
PD_2	Distribution of time until rearrest of adults not formally charged and who are rearrested
PD_3	Distribution of time until rearrest of adults acquitted or released and who are rearrested
PD_4	Distribution of time until rearrest of adults granted probation and who are rearrested
PD_5	Distribution of time from entrance until release from prison
PD_6	Distribution of time from prison release until parole violation, for those adults who violate parole
PD_7	Distribution of time until rearrest of adults released from prison and who are rearrested

* Adults released from incarceration who recidivate either violate parole or are rearrested.

the CJS. With this interpretation, the computed number of arrested twenty-year-olds, for instance, represents arrests of both virgins and recidivists. If the virgin-arrest distribution were known for the U.S., this use of the model would be a good check on the validity of the model.

Feedback Branching Ratios

Many details treated explicitly in the linear model are aggregated in the feedback model. Only four branching probabilities are required to determine flows through the trial stage:

1. P_c = probability that an arrested adult is formally charged with a felony.
2. P_i = probability that an adult who is charged will be incarcerated in a state correctional institution.
3. P_p = probability that an adult who is charged will be placed on probation or in a local jail.
4. P_a = probability that an adult who is charged is dismissed before or during trial or is acquitted.

The values of these probabilities that were used in the current model are given in Table 24-VIII, based on California statistics (State of California, Department of Justice).

One of the facts noted from these data is that assault charges, most of which result from attacks on relatives or acquaintances, frequently result in dismissal and only rarely in incarceration. A similar situation exists for rape charges. Larceny charges, probably many of which are against first offenders, most often lead to probation.

TABLE 24-VIII

BRANCHING RATIOS FOR THE FEEDBACK MODEL

	Homicide	Robbery	Assault	Burglary	Larceny	Auto Theft	Rape
P_c	0.68	0.41	0.34	0.50	0.53	0.42	0.59
P_i	0.43	0.35	0.09	0.15	0.12	0.17	0.10
P_p	0.29	0.22	0.31	0.27	0.55	0.35	0.30
P_a	0.28	0.43	0.60	0.58	0.33	0.48	0.60

Reference: Approximated from 1965 California data (State of California, Department of Justice).

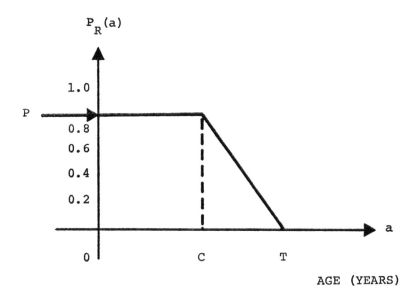

Figure 24-6

Rearrest Probabilities

Rearrest probabilities are specified at each point of dismissal and are functions of age and crime of last arrest.[14] The variation with age of the offender is typically a gradual decrease after about thirty years of age. To approximate this decrease, we allowed the rearrest probability to be the following function of age:

$P_R(a)$ = probability that an offender dismissed at age a would be rearrested for an index crime

$= P\min\{1,[1/(T - C)]\max(T - a, 0)\}$.

This function is plotted in Figure 24-6. The three parameters of this function have intuitive definitions:

P = probability of rearrest of individuals released who are less than C years of age at time of release.

---

14. Rearrest probability data (e.g. the data on criminal careers in UCR, 1966) exhibit a marked variation by type of crime of the last arrest and the type of disposition.

TABLE 24-IX

PARAMETER VALUES FOR THE REARREST PROBABILITY FUNCTION

	Homicide	Robbery	Assault	Burglary	Larceny	Auto Theft	Rape
Disposition 1							
P ...	0.65	0.80	0.785	0.833	0.770	0.833	0.65
C ...	40	35	40	35	40	60	25
T ...	100	80	65	80	75	100	55
Disposition 2							
P ...	0.25	0.573	0.375	0.572	0.539	0.675	0.33
C ...	35	30	30	30	35	40	25
T ...	100	80	64	75	75	100	55

Disposition 1: Adults who are formally charged but not found guilty.
Disposition 2: Adults who are found guilty and who are placed on probation or in a local jail.

C = age at which the rearrest probability starts declining linearly to zero.

T = age beyond which rearrest does not occur.

Table 24-IX shows values of these parameters for two types of dispositions:

1. Adults who are formally charged but not found guilty.
2. Adults who are found guilty and who are placed on probation or in a local jail.

These values were estimated from data presented in UCR/ 1966, pp. 32-42. There is a marked decrease in likelihood of recidivism for those placed on probation, even though they were found guilty.[15]

Time Between Release and Rearrest

Data describing times between release and rearrest are sketchy, at best, and the distributions which were used were chosen to have a mean of about two years.[16] An illustrative delay distribution function of this time interval is given in Figure 24-7.

---

15. It may be that supervision during the probationary period provided a relatively successful rehabilitative environment. Part of the effect noted, however, must be attributed to the selection of probationers, since those granted probation were judged good risks during the pre-sentence investigation.

16. A mean of two years was chosen to match the UCR/1966 statistics which showed that about 0.5 index arrests per year occurred from the start of an individual's criminal career. Delay-distribution data for time from release on parole

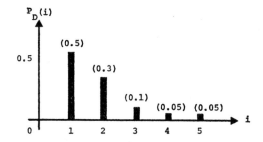

$P_D(i)$ = PROBABILITY THAT THE DELAY FROM DISMISSAL UNTIL
REARREST IS i.YEARS, GIVEN THAT REARREST OCCURS
(i IS A POSITIVE INTEGER)

Illustrative distribution of delay from dismissal until rearrest.

Figure 24-7

Rearrest Crime-Switch Matrix

In the present model, the same crime-switch matrix is used for all recidivists, regardless of age and number of prior arrests. Even with this simplification, forty-two independent probability estimates are required to specify the matrix for seven types of crime. Thus, a relatively large sample of recidivists is required for accurate estimation. Those few studies that have reported data from which a crime-switch matrix can be developed have either had an inadequate sample size or their sample was biased in some important sense. Table 24-X presents the rearrest crime-switch matrix that was used in most of our studies. This matrix was based primarily on a sample of about 500 recidivists who were studied by the Minnesota Board of Corrections.[17] In this matrix, none of the on-diagonal terms is greater than 0.50, indicating a strong tendency to commit (or at least to be arrested for) different types of crimes.

---

until parole suspension for parole violation are published for California (Department of Correction, 1963). These data, because of many unique characteristics about the parole process, are inadequate for the model.

17. The data were obtained from *Crime Revisited* (Mundel, 1963), Minnesota Board of Corrections. The estimates for murder and nonnegligent manslaughter, forcible rape, and aggravated assault were best estimates based on inadequate data. The Federal Bureau of Prisons statistical tables for fiscal year 1965 were also used in estimating the matrix where the Minnesota sample was too small.

TABLE 24-X

REARREST CRIME-SWITCH MATRIX 1[a]

If arrested again for an index crime, the probability it will be for—

Last index arrest for:	Murder and Nonnegligent Manslaughter	Forcible Rape	Robbery	Aggravated Assault	Burglary	Larceny ($50 and over)	Auto Theft
Murder and nonnegligent manslaughter[b]	0.025	0.025	0.150	0.400	0.200	0.100	0.100
Forcible rape[b]	0.020	0.150	0.110	0.260	0.200	0.140	0.120
Robbery	0.015	0.010	0.350	0.060	0.350	0.115	0.100
Aggravated assault[b]	0.025	0.040	0.150	0.300	0.085	0.200	0.200
Burglary	0.010	0.020	0.135	0.063	0.459	0.282	0.031
Larceny ($50 and over)	0.010	0.020	0.140	0.025	0.400	0.275	0.130
Auto theft	0.010	0.027	0.045	0.028	0.390	0.222	0.278

[a] Based on data from *Crime Revisited: Minnesota Board of Corrections;* 1965 "Uniform Crime Reports," pp. 29-31; and Federal Bureau of Prisons, statistical tables, fiscal year, 1965.

[b] Best estimates based on inadequate data.

Table 24-XI presents a rearrest crime-switch matrix based on a sample of several thousand recidivists; it was computed primarily from the Federal Bureau of Prisons statistical tables for the years 1961 to 1965.[18] The sample was biased in the sense that a disproportionate number of offenders had been arrested for federal offenses, the definitions of which often differ from those of local jurisdictions (an example is inter-state auto theft, the perpetrator of which is prosecuted under the Federal Dyer Act). In this matrix, the on-diagonal terms for both burglary and auto theft are greater than 0.50, the burglary probability being higher at 0.63. We will compare results computed from the model using each of these matrices to see how the matrix affects the criminal careers depicted.

---

18. The entries for robbery, burglary, grand larceny, and auto theft were calculated from the Federal Bureau of Prisons statistical tables for the years 1961-65. The entries for forcible rape and aggravated assault were estimated from Report of the President's Commission (1966). The row for murder and nonnegligent manslaughter was set equal to the row for aggravated assault.

TABLE 24-XI

REARREST CRIME-SWITCH MATRIX 2

If arrested again for an index crime, the probability it will be for—

Last index arrest for:	Murder and Nonnegligent Manslaughter	Forcible Rape	Robbery	Aggravated Assault	Burglary	Larceny ($50 and over)	Auto Theft
Murder and nonnegligent manslaughter[a]	0.03	0.03	0.12	0.31	0.26	0.14	0.11
Forcible rape[b]	0.03	0.10	0.08	0.30	0.21	0.20	0.08
Robbery[c]	0.03	0.00	0.42	0.06	0.34	0.04	0.11
Aggravated assault[b]	0.03	0.03	0.12	0.31	0.26	0.14	0.11
Burglary[c]	0.02	0.00	0.15	0.04	0.63	0.04	0.12
Larceny ($50 and over)[c]	0.01	0.01	0.12	0.06	0.40	0.15	0.25
Auto theft[c]	0.01	0.00	0.10	0.03	0.29	0.06	0.51

[a] Set equal to the row for aggravated assault.

[b] Forcible rape and aggravated assault based on District of Columbia data, reference 4, appendix, p. 605.

[c] Robbery, burglary, grand larceny and auto theft based on Bureau of Prisons statistical tables for the years 1961, 1962, 1963, 1964, 1965.

Simplifying the Assumptions of the Current Model

Before this feedback model can be used confidently to make decisions regarding rehabilitative programs and over-all allocation of resources, appropriate data must be collected and analyzed. Limitations of existing data have required that we make a number of simplifying assumptions in our model such as the following:

1. Future criminal behavior is determined solely by the age of the offender, the crime for which he was last arrested, and the disposition of his last arrest.

2. The crime-switch matrix depends only on the crime type of the last arrest, not upon age, disposition, or otherwise upon prior criminal career.

3. CJS branching ratios are not a function of age or prior criminal career.

4. Delay until rearrest is a function only of disposition.

Because of these assumptions, the numerical results must still be treated with caution. The model, however, has identified the required data and provides the framework in which to use them once they become available.

SOME RESULTS FROM THE FEEDBACK MODEL

Recognizing these limitations, we computed some illustrative results by using the feedback model. In the first set of runs, 1,000 twenty-year-olds are first arrested for crime $i(i = 1, 2, \ldots, 7)$ and their criminal careers are traced. Table 24-XII presents the mean number of subsequent career arrests for crime type j (the columns) among the population of 1,000 people first arrested at age twenty for crime type i (the rows). This matrix was computed using the rearrest crime-switch matrix of Table 24-X.

Those who are initially arrested for auto theft have the greatest average number of career arrests (3.76) and represent the only type of initial arrests that has an off-diagonal term greater than one (i.e. those initially arrested for auto theft will commit an average of 1.084 burglaries). Table 24-XII also presents the total average number of career arrests for the seven crimes, the career costs using results from the linear model.

For comparative purposes, we show in Table 24-XIII the career arrest matrix for the same cohort, but using the rearrest crime-

TABLE 24-XII

CAREER MATRIX FOR 1,000 20-YEAR-OLD NEW ARRESTEES
(Using rearrest crime-switch matrix 1)

Crime of Original Arrest	Total number of career arrests							Total Career Arrests per Person	CJS Direct Operating Costs
	Homicide	Robbery	Assault	Burglary	Theft	Auto Theft	Rape		
Homicide	1,038	330	426	645	412	262	57	3.17	$8,100
Robbery	28	1,486	154	816	427	230	41	3.18	4,500
Assault	43	379	1,402	687	561	395	78	3.55	3,600
Burglary	28	371	176	2,021	634	200	56	3.49	3,500
Theft	26	336	128	900	1,574	261	51	3.28	4,000
Auto theft ...	31	309	157	1,084	657	1,455	70	3.76	3,500
Rape	34	296	326	656	437	269	1,144	3.16	3,400

TABLE 24-XIII

CAREER MATRIX OF 1,000 20-YEAR-OLD NEW ARRESTEES
(Using rearrest crime-switch matrix 2)

| Crime of Original Arrest | Total number of career arrests | | | | | | | Total Career Arrests per Person | CJS Direct Operating Costs |
	Homicide	*Robbery*	*Assault*	*Burglary*	*Theft*	*Auto Theft*	*Rape*		
Homicide	1,052	338	353	860	209	404	32	3.25	$8,100
Robbery	52	1,569	145	909	117	384	5	3.18	4,400
Assault	61	395	1,413	1,005	245	472	37	3.63	3,500
Burglary	52	435	148	2,385	138	475	5	3.64	3,400
Theft	39	365	151	1,060	1,211	576	13	3.42	3,900
Auto theft ...	46	416	146	1,162	177	1,993	5	3.95	3,400
Rape	52	302	355	810	256	377	1,081	3.23	3,400

switch matrix of Table 24-XI. Over-all, the total number of career arrests appears to be only slightly greater; the number of career grand theft and rape arrests appears to be significantly less. As we would expect, the total numbers of arrests (which depend principally on the rearrest probability) are much less sensitive to the crime-switch matrix than are the crime-type distributions.

In another run, 1,000 fifteen-year-old virgin arrestees were taken as the cohort. The distribution of initial arests, by crime type, was made to approximate the actual distribution of total fifteen-year-old arrests reported in UCR/1965. Because of low age, this distribution is probably based largely on virgin arrests. The output distributions are shown in Table 24-XIV for ages sixteen and twenty. Also shown in Table 24-XIV is the arrest distribution of all arrests of twenty-year-olds as reported in the UCR/1965 (this distribution is made up of virgin arrestees as well as recidivists with various lengths of prior criminal careers). Even though the model-derived distribution is only for those with five-year-old criminal careers, and the UCR distribution includes all arrestees, we would expect a similarity in the two distributions to be a modest validation check. We see that the distributions are roughly similar, with only the fraction that are assaults deviating significantly from the UCR value.

TABLE 24-XIV

ARREST DISTRIBUTIONS OVER CRIME TYPE FOR A
15-YEAR-OLD COHORT

	Age 15 Input Distribution from UCR/1965	Model-Derived Distribution for Ages		Arrest Distribution for All 20-Year-Old Arrests
		16	20	
Homicide	0.002	0.011	0.01	0.01
Robbery	0.047	0.115	0.15	0.11
Assault	0.045	0.054	0.07	0.14
Burglary	0.335	0.398	0.39	0.35
Grand theft	0.246	0.248	0.24	0.19
Auto theft	0.317	0.149	0.11	0.17
Rape	0.008	0.024	0.02	0.03

The recidivism model also permits examination of a crucial question confronting CJS administrators: How does reduction of recidivism probability affect a criminal career? Many experimental programs have been run to try to discover how various rehabilitative programs affect recidivism probability. For instance, one study of youthful offenders, which was part of the California Community Treatment Project, included randomly separate treatment and control groups. During a twenty-four-month period, the institutionalized control group had a failure probability of 0.61

TABLE 24-XV

CAREER MATRIX FOR 1,000 20-YEAR-OLD NEW ARRESTEES
(Assuming a one-third reduction in rearrest probabilities)

Crime of Original Arrest	Total number of career arrests							Total Career Arrests per Person	CJS Direct Operating Costs
	Homicide	Robbery	Assault	Burglary	Larceny	Auto Theft	Rape		
Homicide	1,017	124	223	205	128	96	22	1.81	$6,600
Robbery	11	1,223	55	301	130	85	13	1.82	2,900
Assault	19	142	1,202	188	200	168	33	1.95	1,800
Burglary	10	136	63	1,400	248	57	20	1.93	1,800
Larceny	9	123	38	340	1,222	102	18	1.85	2,400
Auto theft	11	88	46	402	239	1,209	27	2.02	1,600
Rape	14	103	159	209	145	103	1,079	1.81	1,900

and the Community Treatment Group had a rate of 0.38, or about a ⅓ reduction in recidivism probability (Warren *et al.*, 1968). To investigate what a factor of a ⅓ reduction of recidivism probability implies in terms of criminal careers, the model was run with twenty-year-olds first arrested for crime type *i*, with the rearrest crime-switch matrix of Table 24-X and with all of the rearrest probabilities reduced by one-third. The results are given in Table 24-XV. The total career arrests are reduced by about a factor of 2 by reducing recidivism probability by one-third.

SUMMARY

This paper has described means of modeling the CJS—both in a detailed way with the linear model and in a more aggregated way using feedback to account for recidivism. Clearly, the focus here was on the CJS itself, and so we did not address the many public and private means outside the CJS by which criminal behavior is controlled, nor did we address the deterrent effects of the CJS. Our goal has been to describe in a quantitative way the operation of the system that tries to apprehend, adjudicate, and rehabilitate offenders, and to assess some of the effects of this system on their future criminal behavior. Within the constraints of the available data, these models allow us to study questions regarding the CJS, its costs, workloads, and resource requirements, and the effects of alternative rehabilitative procedures on criminal careers.

Future studies can include more realistic assumptions within the framework of these models, and more complete and accurate data for performing the calculations. The end goal of such studies should be to improve the management of the system, including appropriate allocation of public resources to minimize the total social and dollar costs of crime and its control. The models also provide a research tool for examining the behavior of the CJS in order to understand its impact on the problem of crime.

REFERENCES

Blumstein, A., Christensen, R., Johnson, S., and Larson, R.: Analysis of crime and the overall criminal justice system. In *Task Force Report: Science and Technology*. President's Commission on Crime and Administration of Justice, Washington, U. S. Government Printing Office, June 1967, Ch. 5.

Crime in the United States: Uniform Crime Reports, published annually by the Federal Bureau of Investigation, U. S. Department of Justice, Washington, U. S. Government Printing Office. Referred to as UCR or UCR/j, where j is the year of publication.

Department of Correction, Research Division, Administrative Statistics Section: *California Prisoners 1961, 1962, 1963* (summary of statistics of felon prisoners and parolees). Sacramento, 1963, p. 128.

Federal Bureau of Prisons, statistical tables, published each fiscal year.

Glaser, Daniel: *The Effectiveness of a Prison and Parole System.* New York, Bobbs-Merrill, 1964.

Hazard, Geoffrey C.: The sequence of criminal prosecution. *Proc National Symposium on Science and Criminal Justice,* June 22-23, 1966, Washington, Government Printing Office.

McIntyre, Donald M.: *Law Enforcement in the Metropolis.* Chicago, American Bar Foundation, 1967.

Mundel, M. G., *et al.: Crime Revisited.* Minnesota Department of Corrections, 1963.

Omnibus Safe Streets and Crime Control Act of 1968, Public Law 90-351, enacted on June 19, 1968.

President's Commission on Law Enforcement and Administration of Justice: *The Challenge of Crime in a Free Society.* U. S. Government Printing Office, 1967a.

President's Commission on Law Enforcement and Administration of Justice: *Task Force Report: Crime and Its Assessment.* U. S. Government Printing Office, June 1967b.

Report of the President's Commission on Crime in the District of Columbia, Washington, Government Printing Office, Appendix, 1966, p. 605.

Space-General Corporation: Prevention and Control of Crime and Delinquency in California. El Monte, July 29, 1965.

Roy, Robert H.: An outline for research in penology. *Opns Res, 12:*1-12, 1964.

State of California, Department of Justice, Division of Criminal Law and Enforcement: *Crime and Delinquency in California,* Bureau of Criminal Statistics, published annually.

Warren, M., *et al.:* Community Treatment Project, An Evaluation of Community Treatment for Delinquents, Fifth Progress Report, State of California, Youth and Adult Corrections Agency, Department of the Youth Authority, Division of Parole and Division of Research, August 1968, p. 59.

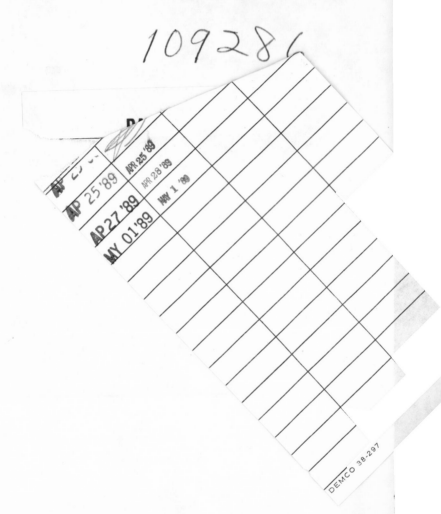